EDWARD PAICE was a History Scholar at Magdalene College, Cambridge and winner of the Leman Prize. After ten years working as an investment analyst in the City he spent the best part of four years in Kenya and newly independent Eritrea, writing travel and natural history guides. He regularly lectures and contributes articles on a variety of African topics, is a Fellow of the Royal Geographical Society, and a member of the Royal Institute of International Affairs.

Edward Paice currently divides his time between Africa and London, where he also runs his own corporate strategy consultancy.

Lost Lion of Empire

The Life of 'Cape-to-Cairo' Grogan

EDWARD PAICE

HarperCollins*Publishers*

HarperCollins*Publishers*
77–85 Fulham Palace Road,
Hammersmith, London w6 8jb

www.**fire**and**water**.com

This paperback edition 2002
1 3 5 7 9 8 6 4 2

First published in Great Britain by
HarperCollins*Publishers* 2001

isbn 0 00 653073 7

Maps by Leslie Robinson

Set in Postscript Linotype Janson by
Rowland Phototypesetting Limited,
Bury St Edmunds, Suffolk

Printed and bound in Great Britain by
Clays Ltd, St Ives plc

To my parents,
for their love and valour

CONTENTS

ACKNOWLEDGMENTS

The journey in search of Grogan would never even have got underway were it not for the wholehearted support of the following members of the Grogan *sept*, and of related families: Carolyn Bateman; Kimbo Beakbane; Ruth Brunton; Adrian Coleman; Gertrude Chapman; Bill Crawford; Jean Crawford; John Elliot; Arthur and Helen Grogan; Richard and Penelope Grogan; Nigel Hunter; Di Hunter; Ian and Anne Kyle-Milward; David and Jeni Slater; June Sutherland; and Diana Wasbrough. I thank them all for their patience, kindness and hospitality and hope that the Grogan who emerges from this tome is one whom they will readily recognize.

Of equal import was the assistance received from a host of individuals – the few surviving friends of Grogan's, academics from all corners of the globe, and friends of mine who provided help and advice 'above and beyond the call of duty': Petal Allen; Dr David Anderson; Veronica Bellers; Neil Collingwood; Peter Colmore; Sister M. Dominic Craufurd; Basil Criticos; Juanita Carberry; Archie and Emily Cotterell; Susie Dowdall; David and Suki Darnborough; Sarah Elder; John Farrant; James Foster; Jonathan and Debo Gage; Terence Gavaghan; Donald and Kathini Graham; James Gill; Joan and Deborah Goodhart; James Hamilton; Sir Wilfrid Havelock; Eddie Hollister; Husseinbhai A. Hebatullah; the late Arthur Horner; Leslie James; John Tomno Kiplangat, Administrator of Maji Mazuri; Tom and Valerie-Letham; Dr Alan Linsell; Heini Lustman; Sir Charles Markham; Philip and Charlotte Mason; R. R. Meinertzhagen; Mickey Migdoll; Professor Bill Nasson; Maggie Noach; Tom Ofcansky; Alex Papadopoulis; Liza Ravenshill; Alison Pedder-Davies; Edward Rodwell; Michelle Rodwell; Sol and Ruth Rabb; Sister Jean Sinclair; Dr Frank Solomon; the late Kit Taylor; Tom Tomlinson; Harry Underhill; Sheila Vickers; Dr Robert G. Weisbord; Gladys Wright; Stefan and Ruth Willheim and Joy Williams.

I would also like to thank all those institutions and other corporates who made the execution, and in particular research, of the book possible: African Studies Library, University of Cape Town (Sue Ogterop); Alpine Club (Livia Gollancz and Margaret Ecclestone); Bodleian Library, University of Oxford; Brenthurst Library of the late Mr H. F. Oppenheimer (Heather Sander and Rae Simkins); British Empire & Commonwealth Museum; British Library; the Syndics of Cambridge University Library; Carlile Dowling (Anthony Wilson, senior partner); Churchill Archives Centre (Stephen Plant); Church of England Record Centre (Dr B. L. Hough); Dalgety plc (Catherine Coulson); Department of Zoology, Cambridge University (Adrian Friday); Gertrude's Garden Children's Hospital (Andy Bacon and Diana Barwa); HarperCollins (Michael Fishwick, Kate Morris et al.); Honourable Society of the Middle Temple (Janet Edgell); Jesus College, Cambridge (Dr Frances Willmoth and Muriel Brittain); Kenya National Archives; London Metropolitan Archives (Geoff Pick); Magdalene College, Cambridge; Ministry of Natural Resources, Kenya (Mines and Geological Department); Museum of Archaeology and Anthropology, Cambridge University (Dr David Phillipson); National Archives of South Africa, Pretoria; National Army Museum (Marion Harding); Natural History Museum (P. D. Jenkins); National Library of New Zealand (Tracy Jacobs); Newcastle-under-Lyme Borough Council (Delyth Enticott); New College, Oxford; Tatton Park (Maggie McKean); Public Record Office; Rhodes House Library (John Pinfold and Allan Lodge); Royal Geographical Society Library (Rachel Rowe and Yvonne Sarrington); Saffery Champness (David S. Watson); South African Library, Cape Town; The Standard Limited, Kenya (Yayha Mohammed); The Star, South Africa (Michelle Bowes and Theresa de Haan); Winchester College (Dr R. D. H. Custance) and Ziwani Camp (George Kariuki, Prestige Hotels Ltd); The Zoological Society of London (Michael Palmer).

I blame my dear grandmother, long since departed, for first telling me about the dashing young man she had known in the 1920s – the man with the iridescent eyes who had trekked from Cape to Cairo in the last years of Queen Victoria's reign. I also blame Dave Anderson for bringing Grogan the irascible politician alive during tutorials, and for pointing me in the right direction two decades later. And I blame David

Darnborough, hotelier and host extraordinaire, for taking me to see Grogan's Castle in the lea of majestic Mount Kilimanjaro – the safari during which I decided to embark on telling Grogan's uncommon tale.

Richard Ambani at the Kenya National Archives was outstanding: he not only steered me swiftly through the vast quantity of hitherto untouched material relating to Grogan, but he volunteered to help me 'process' (i.e. wade through) fifty years of Kenyan newspapers. Without him I can honestly say that this book would have been another year in the making. Terry Barringer, the indefatigable Librarian of the Royal Commonwealth Society Collection in the Cambridge University Library, did an equally marvellous steering job and always knew someone somewhere who would be able to help with thorny problems of research. Kathleen Dobson, Grogan's one time secretary and now – I hope – a firm friend, backed me to the hilt (and kept me chuckling with tales of the old man's wicked sense of humour). David Slater, Grogan's eldest grandson, gave generously not only of his hospitality but of his time – meticulously (and valiantly) working his way through the manuscript *twice* and correcting me on a number of key points. Tim Weaver also kindly studied a second Paice tome. Jeremy and Cathryn Withers-Green I cannot thank enough for the many, many ways in which they have helped this project along and kept me afloat – including incisive editorial advice. And last, but certainly not least, I thank my family for maintaining their, and my, enthusiasm for fully three and a half years. In particular my mother, who has read, commented on and corrected more drafts of *Lost Lion* than I should reasonably have expected of her.

To anyone I have forgotten: I apologize unreservedly . . .

LIST OF ILLUSTRATIONS

Images 8, 9, 10 are sourced from vol. 1, *The Story of the Cape to Cairo Railway and River Route*. Images 28 and 31 are sourced from *African World Annual 1903*. Images 33, 34 and 35 are sourced from vol. 3, *The Story of the Cape to Cairo Railway and River Route*. All the above are reproduced by kind permission of the Syndics of Cambridge University Library.

All other images (except where indicated) are reproduced by kind permission of members of the Grogan family from Grogan's published works or private collections currently in the possession of Kimbo Beakbane, Ruth Brunton, Jean Crawford, Richard Grogan, Anne Kyle-Milward, June Sutherland and Diana Wasbrough.

LIST OF MAPS

Grogan's Principal Assets
in Kenya

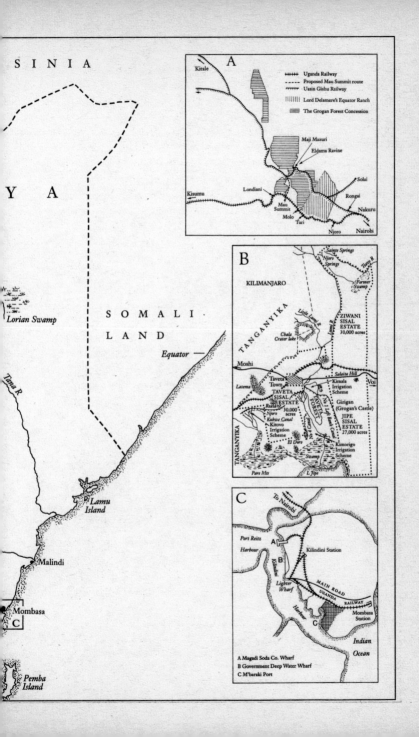

ONE

A Most Singular Child

CAPTAIN DUNN shook his head in disbelief. As Medical Officer of the Peake Expedition, which was trying to cut a navigable waterway through the weed-clogged Upper Nile, he was certainly used to treating his men for delirium. Every day the savage heat, dysentery or fever robbed some of them of their sanity. But the tale of his seemingly healthy Sudanese sergeant was more preposterous than anything he had heard jabbered by a dying man. Grinning from ear to ear and in a state of high excitement, his hitherto trusted NCO was asking him to believe that a *white* man was approaching camp. On foot.

It was impossible, of course. It was days since Dunn had temporarily parted company with Peake in order to indulge his love of hunting and, apart from his colleagues in the main camp, he knew that there were no white men for hundreds of miles in any direction. Besides, any European would have to stick to the river to survive; only locals, or the insane, would travel on foot through such inhospitable terrain.

It was the sergeant's grin that alerted Dunn to the fact that the whole story must be a practical joke. Not wishing to spoil it, he determined to play the part expected of him. The first priority was to look his best for the phantom visitor. So Dunn straightened his jacket, dusted down his trousers, ran a sweaty hand through his hair, and set off after his chuckling henchman. The sight that greeted him as they emerged from the tall reeds on the riverbank was enough to make him doubt his own sanity for several minutes. An unshaven young man of medium height, with jet black hair and an easy smile, detached himself from a group of bedraggled porters, and strode forward to shake him by the hand. As he did so, Dunn was immediately struck by the newcomer's extraordinary eyes, easily discernible below the rim of his slouch hat. A startling yellowy-green, like those of a leopard caught at night in a beam of light, they seemed to look straight into his soul. Indeed they were the only feature, apart from movement, that convinced Dunn that he was not staring at a ghost but at a fever-ridden, half-starved, living man. A *white* man.

Dunn pulled himself together, and regained his powers of speech. Observing the strict rules of encounters with strangers in the bush, he steered clear of any questions that might be deemed too personal. The ensuing, quintessentially British, conversation went as follows:

> Dunn: 'How do you do?'
> Stranger: 'Oh, very fit thanks; how are you? Had any sport?'
> Dunn: 'Oh pretty fair, but there is nothing much here. Have a drink? You must be hungry; I'll hurry on lunch. Had any shooting? See any elephant?'[1]

It was not until the two men had almost finished the meal that Dunn thought it excusable to enquire about the identity and provenance of his guest. He was far from ready for the astonishing answer. The man's name, soon to be lauded throughout the Empire, was Ewart Grogan. More significantly, Dunn learnt that he was just completing the first ever south–north traverse of the African continent – one of the most hazardous and daring journeys in the history of Victorian exploration.

The year was 1900; and once met, as Captain Dunn had discovered, Grogan was never forgotten.

Ewart Grogan was born in 1874 and of necessity mastered the art of attracting attention at a very tender age. His father, William, had the greatest difficulty even remembering the names of most of his twenty-one offspring. An affectionate man, he would often greet a passing child with a pat on the head and a friendly 'How's Margaret today?', only to find that he was unknowingly addressing Dorothy. Most of the time his confusion mattered little, but it did prove rather embarrassing when a suitor presented himself to request the hand in marriage of one of his daughters, and a baffled William had to confess that he wasn't at all sure which of ten possibles was the prized bride-to-be.

Ewart brooked no such quandary over his identity. A combination of elfin good looks, a rapier-like gaze, and precocious self-assurance and intellect distinguished him at the outset from his siblings – leaving his delighted father in no doubt that he had sired a 'thruster' who would leave his mark on the world. Just how great a mark William could not possibly have imagined: the multi-talented Ewart's prodigious achievements appear to have been completely without precedent in his family's poorly documented history.

The Grogans were fiercely proud of their Irish lineage. Their *sept*, or clan, could be traced back to John Grogan of Antrim, who was born in about 1570 and whose great-grandson of the same name gained possession through marriage of Johnstown Castle in County Wexford. Ardcandrisk Estate was later added to the family's holdings and by the last quarter of the eighteenth century Cornelius Grogan derived an income of £8–10,000 from his estates. His comfortable life was, however, brought to a premature and grizzly end when he was hanged and then, for good measure, beheaded for his rather reluctant part in the 1798 Rebellion against the Crown.

It was characteristic of the complexity of Irish politics that two of Cornelius's brothers actually fought on the opposite side during the Rebellion. Thomas was killed at the Battle of Arklow, but John Knox survived and regained the family's title to Johnstown Castle after a lengthy legal battle which cost over £10,000. By this time the relationship between Ewart's direct forebears and the prosperous clan leaders of the same name was almost certainly a distant one.[2] Ewart's great-grandfather, Nathaniel, presented no claim to Cornelius's property. His only legacy to his great-grandson seems to have been an anomalous cocktail of the rebelliousness of some of his clansmen, the passionate loyalty to the Crown of others, and the fighting spirit of all of them.

Nathaniel himself was a rebel, not a loyalist, who is known to have 'suffered at the hands of the Government of the day'.[3] Like many of his countrymen he left Ireland in search of a better life and settled in

London; but of his profession, the extent to which he succeeded in his quest, or even his parentage, there is no record. The implication is that the origins of his branch of the Grogan *sept* were humble. But with Nathaniel's son, Nicholas, its fortunes started to improve. He established a solid position for himself in 'trade', as a wine merchant with premises in Princes Street, and bought a house in St James's. Furthermore, his marriage on 13 May 1810, to the illiterate Sarah Beal, took place at fashionable St George's, Hanover Square.

The couple had eight children, of whom William was the second youngest. It was he who inherited Nicholas's entrepreneurial skills (as, in time, would Ewart). In 1849, the year after Nicholas's death, William started out by establishing an estate agency and auctioneering business at 66 Park Street, Mayfair. Five years later its success was assured when he received instructions from Gladstone, then Chancellor of the Exchequer, to sell his house in Carlton Gardens;[4] and with the benefit of this lucky break William was set to enjoy increasing renown among the aristocracy and other leading figures of Victorian society. With staunch Liberalism (and Gladstone's support for Home Rule in Ireland) as the galvanizing factor William and Gladstone became friends for life. At the opposite end of the political spectrum, Disraeli was also a client: William's political beliefs never stood in the way of good business.

By the mid 1860s not only was William's business flourishing but he was also set fair on his Olympian course of paternity. Having married Mercy Mary Adams in June 1847 at St Giles-in-the-Fields he had sired his first thirteen children although one, James, died in infancy. It is perhaps no surprise that having borne him all these offspring Mercy Mary also died on Christmas Eve 1868, aged forty-two. Gladstone sent William his condolences on hearing the news as well as a copy of Thomas à Kempis. William wrote back, thanking the newly elected Prime Minister 'most sincerely for this and many other acts of kindness received at your hands'.[5]

In the early 1870s William, despite being solely responsible for a large family, expanded his business by merging with the older practice of the Boyd family to create Grogan & Boyd.[6] The tie between the two families was further strengthened when Jermyn Boyd married William's fifth daughter, Alice. In the light of William's confusion with suitors one must hope that it was indeed Alice's hand that Boyd requested.

The new partnership was not the only change in William's affairs at this time. In March 1871 he received confirmation of his status as one of the foremost estate agents in the land when Queen Victoria appointed him Surveyor General of Houses and Buildings for the Duchy of Lancaster. This prestigious position gave him the charge of all matters relating to buildings in the Duchy – their upkeep, purchases and sales, and dealings with tenants. With his reputation thus greatly enhanced, William soon started to cast around for a new wife. His search did not last long.

In the summer of 1873 Jane Sams was spotted by William as he gazed out of the window of Grogan & Boyd's new premises at 125 Piccadilly. He was a great admirer of women – another trait which would be inherited by Ewart – and was especially taken by Jane's shapely ankles. Without a second thought he scooped up his hat and gloves and strode out of the office to make her acquaintance. Within days William was proposing marriage, which presented Jane with a dilemma. Aged twenty-seven, she was fully twenty-two years William's junior and was being asked to take on twelve children. Furthermore, she had already suffered an unhappy marriage to an alcoholic who had recently died. On the other hand, the senior partner of Grogan and Boyd was obviously a well-to-do suitor and, with his great mutton-chop whiskers, thick head of dark hair and twinkling eye, not an unattractive one. He proved to be as persuasive a romantic as he was an estate agent: one month after their first meeting William and Jane were married.

After a five-year respite William returned eagerly to the business of procreation. Sixteen months after their wedding Jane duly presented him with the son who, not unlike a fledgling cuckoo, would demand pride of place in the family. The boy was christened Ewart in the Chapel of the Savoy, courtesy of William's royal appointment. His name was also the middle name of his godfather, Gladstone, who despite his recent resignation as Prime Minister and defeat at the hands of Disraeli in the general election was on hand to perform his duties and present the infant with a silver christening mug. A name, the mug, and a sympathy with the cause of Home Rule for the Irish were all Ewart took from his godfather: his own filibustering political career would be characterized by a fierce disdain for liberalism in any shape or form.[7]

Ewart's birth prompted considerable logistical rearrangement in the Grogan household. In 1870, four years earlier, William had moved his tribe from Eaton Square to an even grander house at 97 Queens Gate. Now, safe in the knowledge that Jane was 'functioning properly' and in anticipation of further additions to the family, William decided to buy the building next door and the two properties were knocked together to create a home with forty-two rooms and quarters for the twelve servants. His position as Surveyor General was clearly not only prestigious but profitable. For the independent-minded William Grogan it was also not without its drawbacks.

The cracks in William's relationship with his patron, Queen Victoria, started to appear soon after his marriage. While on holiday in Scotland one summer he received a summons to appear before her at Osborne House on the Isle of Wight. This was inconvenient to say the least, and as William considered the matter that she wished to discuss to be trivial he suggested delaying their meeting until they were both back in London. This rebuttal was not appreciated by his monarch; the summons was curtly repeated and William reluctantly obeyed her command. His appointment as Surveyor General was duly renewed in August 1875, the year after Ewart's birth – but for the last time. After an exchange of rather barbed letters with the Clerk of the Duchy in the latter half of 1876, William was relieved of his position and given a consolatory silver canteen for five years' service. Such was the well of paternal behaviour – stubborn, impetuous and with a deep-seated antipathy to taking orders from anyone – at which the infant Ewart drank.

Grogan & Boyd did not suffer from William's setback in the slightest. His attention returned to his non-regal clients, and to the serious business of filling all the rooms in the Queens Gate house. Philip, Norman, Dorothy, Margaret and Archibald followed Ewart within a five-year span (although Norman died of scarlet fever in 1880, aged three). After a brief pause to catch her breath, Jane then produced Quentin in 1883 and Hilda in 1888, by which time the size of the family had assumed comic proportions. Quentin wryly observed of his

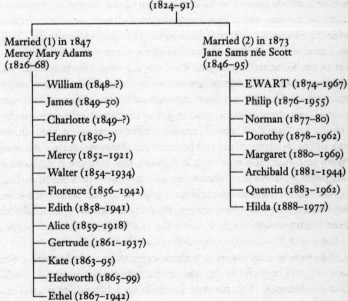

WILLIAM GROGAN'S
Twenty-one Offspring

?

NATHANIEL
(b. *circa* 1760)

NICHOLAS
(1784–1848)
Married Sarah Beal in 1810
and had eight children:
Harriet, Edmund, Emma, Henry, Charles, Alfred, Caroline and

WILLIAM
(1824–91)

Married (1) in 1847
Mercy Mary Adams
(1826–68)

— William (1848–?)
— James (1849–50)
— Charlotte (1849–?)
— Henry (1850–?)
— Mercy (1852–1921)
— Walter (1854–1934)
— Florence (1856–1942)
— Edith (1858–1941)
— Alice (1859–1918)
— Gertrude (1861–1937)
— Kate (1863–95)
— Hedworth (1865–99)
— Ethel (1867–1942)

Married (2) in 1873
Jane Sams née Scott
(1846–95)

— EWART (1874–1967)
— Philip (1876–1955)
— Norman (1877–80)
— Dorothy (1878–1962)
— Margaret (1880–1969)
— Archibald (1881–1944)
— Quentin (1883–1962)
— Hilda (1888–1977)

own arrival that 'as far as I am aware there was no comet to mark this auspicious event, and as I was the twentieth child in the family, the elder members were not particularly impressed either'. In later life he would add that he never knew his eldest brother as he had died before he, Quentin, was born.[8] It is impossible to verify this quip as William had by then fallen out with his eldest son by his first marriage, also called William, who had hot-footed it to Canada never to be heard of again. Its inference is clear enough: fully forty years separated the eldest Grogan child from the youngest.

Whatever the cause of William's rift with his eldest son it was not strictness. He doted on his children, and was anything but the stereotypically austere and distant Victorian father closeted behind a green baize door. Quentin fondly recalled that his father liked to give the children 'a piece of a stick of chocolate wrapped in very pretty pink and green paper when he came to say Good Night'[9] – an unusual gesture at a time when children were more commonly required to present themselves to their fathers to say goodnight. But despite William's progressive attitude to child-rearing, there was no lack of discipline in the Grogan household. This was dispensed by Jane, who was both strict (she was 'Mrs Grogan' to her stepchildren) and rather highly strung. She showed little patience with occurrences of common children's ailments, possibly due to a fear that she might lose another child as she had lost little Norman, and she expected the highest standards of behaviour from all her charges. Deportment classes were held for an hour each morning, and music lessons were conducted in an atmosphere of tension because the children were nervous of making mistakes. This emphasis on excellence appears to have had little lasting influence on most of them except Ewart – in whom it unleashed a fiercely competitive streak, a thirst for challenges, and a love of the limelight.

The irony is that Ewart was the exception to all Jane's rules. She doted only on her first-born, who in turn knew instinctively how to please his mother. To this end he dedicated his full armoury: the charm, the good looks, the hypnotic gaze and the sense of mischief of a loveable little rogue. Against such formidable opposition the other children were non-runners in the contest for their mother's affections. When Jane was disturbed one day by the sound of a child falling down the stairs she nervously called out 'Is that you darling?' to which a little voice answered: 'No mother, it's only me – Philip.' There was never any doubt in the mind of 'poor Philip', as he was often referred to in later life, and Ewart's other siblings as to which one of them was 'darling'. By the same token, any child late for meals went hungry – except Ewart. If *he*, the apple of his mother's eye, arrived late at the breakfast table he would greet her with a winning smile and cheeky 'Sorry you're early, Mother,' after which he would sit down to enjoy his meal without rebuke.

As a result of his favoured status Ewart developed boundless self-confidence, and seems to have enjoyed a blissful childhood. His earliest memories were of watching the aerobatics of swallows from his pram, and wondering how they did it; keeping a mynah in the conservatory, and loving it even when all its feathers had fallen out; being kissed by a dairy maid, and never forgetting the delicious thrill of it; and, most portentous of all, booting a visitor in the shins with his father's steel-shod shooting boots after the man had tried to pick him up by his neck. He was only four or five at the time, the boots enormous on his child's feet, but later cited this incident as 'proof of the Mendelian theory; for is not the blood of every Irishman richly suffused with distaste of self-assertive authority or indeed any damned authority at all?'[10] The consequence of this early tilt at authority was a sound thrashing in the drawing-room – from which Ewart emerged grinning and wholly unrepentant.

The profits of William's business acumen ensured that private education, from which he had not himself benefited, was a *sine qua non* for all his children. When the time came for Ewart to go away to prep school he uncharacteristically 'shook with irrepressible tears' at the thought of forcible separation from his mother. She, it seems, was 'in a similar but disguised state of distress'.[11] Their fears were groundless. Grove House, near Guildford, proved to be an unqualified success due to the relaxed regime of the school's owners, Mr and Mrs Priddow, and their second-in-command, a bachelor named Prouen.

Ewart responded quickly and positively to Prouen's enlightened teaching philosophy, which sought to provoke curiosity in his young pupils rather than stuff them full of useless facts and figures. This was an unusual approach at a time when learning was more commonly acquired by rote, and one which Ewart never forgot. Furthermore, the Priddows and Prouen were not the only good things about Grove House: perhaps because of Jane's specific instructions about how her eldest was to be treated, Ewart was considered 'delicate' and given a glass of thick cream every morning. He was also not forced to attend any classes that he didn't want to, and consequently spent a lot of time roaming – and hopping – over the Merrow Downs to the east of Guildford. This propensity to hop everywhere while indulging his passion for the outdoor life earned Ewart the nickname 'Frog' or 'Froggy', which in later years underwent an alliterative transformation to 'Grog', and ultimately to 'Grogs'. All in all Grove House presented few hardships and was, in the opinion of his pampered and increasingly independent son, an inspired choice on William's part.

When term ended the Grogan family holidays were mostly spent in fashionable and genteel Hove, where William had bought 6 First Avenue to replace an equally large but less accessible holiday house at Bonchurch on the Isle of Wight. First Avenue was on the 'right' side of the border between Hove and Brighton. The distinction was an important one: Hove was for 'gentlefolk', whereas Brighton was for 'gents' (specifically, as Ewart put it, 'wealthier gents secretive about the details of their weekends'[12]). He and Philip were given a free rein by their parents to amuse themselves much as they wanted, and Brighton's promenade offered entertainment ranging from the exotic (minstrels from faraway Africa singing their set piece 'I've got a pair of lips like a pound of liver split/ And a nose like an India rubber shoe') to the alluring (furtive glimpses of ladies in bathing machines hired for sixpence an hour). Equally enticingly, it also offered ginger beer, bullseyes, fishing trips at half a crown a time, and boundless opportunities for mischief-making among the crowds.

Some years, in order to broaden the children's education, William led holiday trips to France. Ewart's first such foray was in 1880 or 1881, when it was decided that he and Philip should 'take the waters' in Clermont-Ferrand. Ewart was by no means convinced by claims of the therapeutic powers of the water, but he was profoundly influenced by meeting the elderly Dr Samuel Smiles. Smiles was the bestselling author of *Self-help*, and a household name in Victorian Britain. He was an immediate hit with Ewart and Philip because he treated them like adults and took them on numerous walks through the French countryside. For two weeks the boys listened avidly as their new mentor extolled the virtues of being self-reliant and independent of others at all costs. The logic of this simple but apparently revolutionary philosophy, in part inspired by Thomas Carlyle, impressed Ewart no end. Like the Priddow–Prouen trio the genial Smiles was accorded a special place in his memories alongside the waiter who sneaked him an extra croissant at breakfast, in strict contravention of the rules of the hotel.

By the time Ewart was thirteen his intellectual abilities were obvious to all, despite having spent so much of his time at Grove House on the Merrow Downs rather than in the classroom. It was therefore decided that he should be sent to that breeding ground of conspicuous intellects, Winchester, to which he won an Exhibition in September 1888. In just three years he reached the Junior Division of the Sixth Book, the highest class. All the while Prouen's philosophy continued to exert a powerful influence on his attitude to learning, and Ewart concentrated on absorbing that which interested him rather than that which was compulsory. His main academic interest was in words, and he increasingly 'developed a profound love of my mother tongue with its infinite range and means of expressing the succulent nuances of human thought'.[13] To further his semantic education, and to give him a better than fighting chance against his examiners, he spent hour after hour reading the *Oxford English Dictionary*. This obsession may initially have been pursued quite innocently, but in later life his colossal vocabulary would be deployed with devastating effect as an instrument of power: it was at Winchester that Ewart learned that it is hard to contradict a speaker – whether at the dinner table or on the hustings – whose vocabulary is so extensive that he can only be partially understood.

Outside the classroom his still diminutive stature limited Ewart's success on the games field. He participated, playing a bit of rugby (he was in the Commoners XV) and cricket (for Mr T. Kensington's 'D' house), but without any great distinction. It was only in rifle shooting that he excelled. His keen interest in this sport was first aroused by reading Frederic Courtenay Selous's *A Hunter's Wanderings In Africa*, which recounted the adventures and hardships of the greatest of the white hunters. Then, when Ewart was eleven, *King Solomon's Mines* was published and from the moment he opened Rider Haggard's thrilling tome he was determined to try and emulate its hero, Allan Quatermain.[14] By the time he was selected to represent Winchester in the schools rifle championship at Bisley his ambitions were fixed: he was determined to bag a lion, a rhinoceros and an elephant – and to see Lake Tanganyika.

Ewart was popular among his classmates. His closest friend was the easy-going Vyner Brooke, son of the second White Rajah of Sarawak. As Rajah Muda, his father's heir, Vyner's address was simply 'The Palace, Kuching' which impressed Ewart no end. More importantly, the example set by the Brooke family's paternalistic regime deeply influenced his own views on the role of the British Empire and its avowed mission to bring 'civilization' to all corners of the globe. Other good friends included Claud Tritton, of the great banking family, who was to become a fellow pioneer in British East Africa; Henry Yorke, with whom Ewart would serve in the Royal Munster Fusiliers; and Hon. Frederick Guest, who later participated in the Nile Expedition of 1899–1900, became ADC to Field Marshal Lord French during World War I, and then private secretary to his cousin Winston Churchill.[15] But gregarious and popular though he was, it became increasingly obvious during his teens that there was something about Ewart that simultaneously rendered him an outsider, a maverick, a young man who stood out and stood apart. That something was not his impressive intellect, his unwavering self-confidence, his sense of purpose, or his love for a challenge; these were characteristics which were, after all, common to many of his contemporaries at Winchester. Rather it was his supreme individualism and self-containment. His upbringing and schooling, Smiles's teachings and a good dose of independent Irish blood had seemingly created someone who was very much the master of his own destiny and who rejected being pigeon-holed. Ewart could, quite simply, survive and thrive on his own. He had no deep-seated need for the support and intimacy of others.

It was this self-sufficiency which enabled him, as a sixteen-year-old, to cope with the first setback in a hitherto untroubled life: on 19 June 1891, his father died in his bed in the family's house in Hove at the ripe old age of sixty-six. This left Jane in sole charge of their seven children, the youngest of whom was only three. Her only consolation was that Grogan & Boyd had continued to flourish, leaving the family well provided for through a family trust. This included the houses in Queens Gate and Hove, two further investment properties in Belgravia and a not insubstantial sum of cash. All William's children were, like their mother, entitled to draw an income from the trust on reaching the age of majority; housing was to be provided for any unmarried daughters; and his sons were to receive an additional £2,000 each, the equivalent of almost twenty years pay for an army subaltern, to help them start their careers. For Ewart, his parents' golden boy, there was a further bequest: as the eldest son of William's second marriage he was to share his father's stake in Grogan & Boyd with his half-brother Hedworth Herbert, the twelfth child of William's first marriage.[16] This left Ewart comfortably off, but within a few years his ambitions were to become so gigantic that even William's entire estate would not have proved sufficient for their fulfilment.

By the end of the year Jane had moved the family out of the Queens Gate house, which was let and subsequently became a hotel. As the children of William's first marriage had flown the nest it had become quite excessive for her requirements, and home became a smaller house near Sevenoaks, called Kirkella. No sooner had she completed this move than she faced the second disaster of the year: her beloved Ewart succumbed to measles. Within days of contracting the illness he also developed severe complications – a collapsed eardrum and disturbingly irregular heartbeat – and the doctor told her that any form of strenuous exercise was liable to prove fatal. To carry on in the rough and tumble of school was considered out of the question and an extended period of rest was prescribed. The Short Half (Michaelmas term) of 1891 was therefore Ewart's last at Winchester.

Whatever the state of his health, Ewart did not relish the prospect of indefinite incarceration in the Kentish countryside. His mind was full of Africa, about which he now read every tome he could lay his hands on, and he nurtured a dogged determination to get there as soon as possible. As an invalid, he was able to draw some consolation from the fact that no less a figure than Cecil Rhodes had arrived in Africa in a similarly debilitated state, and yet was now that continent's

'Colossus'. Ewart, by contrast, was set on disproving his doctor's doom-laden prognosis *before* setting out for the 'Dark Continent' to fulfil his ambitions.

As soon as his health had stabilized Ewart informed his mother of an audacious strategy for cheating death high in the mountains of Switzerland, and as he now regarded himself as the head of the family she and his siblings were required to fall into line with his plans.

TWO

From Mountains to Matabeleland

G ROGAN STARTED TO RECOVER as soon as he set foot in Zermatt, thanks to the invigorating air and the majesty of his surroundings. He revelled in being free from the shackles of Winchester, free to enjoy the outdoor life, and in being able to be as independent and self-reliant as Dr Smiles had counselled. The mountains towered above him like 'veritable cathedrals of the Almighty', and the silence was 'broken only by the tinkling of cow bells and folk chatting to one another across its yawning valleys'. He was also greatly impressed by the Swiss, whom he considered to be 'kindly and unpretentious', and who 'resisted and repelled every attempt to embroil [them] in the strife, massacres and vulgarities of [their] surrounding peoples'.

As his strength returned he began to prepare for the challenge he had set himself, which was 'to see what the world looked like from the sky'. It was his good fortune that what at first sight appeared to him to be a 'grumpy old recluse'[1] sitting in front of the fire in his hotel turned out to be Edward Whymper, who that very summer of 1892 was awarded the Royal Geographical Society's Royal Medal in recognition of his mountaineering feats. Whymper was not only a regular in Zermatt, but also the sole surviving member of the team which had first scaled the Matterhorn in July 1865.[2] There could be no better tutor for Grogan, who quickly made friends with the old man and was given lessons on the moods of high altitude ice. The equally famous Alfred Mummery, who was destined to perish in the Himalayas three years later, simultaneously became his instructor in the finer points of rock climbing.

Jane was immensely proud of Grogan's climbing exploits, but the zeal with which he took to the sport terrified her. She had only just lost her husband; now her eldest son was daily risking life and limb. She knew she could not stand in his way, but decided that that did not mean she had to put herself through the agony of witnessing *all* his ascents. Besides, there were her six other children to look after and educate. The family therefore shuttled to and from the Alps according to the school terms, except for three-year-old Hilda who never left Kirkella and the watchful eye of Nanny Redwood. This arrangement left Grogan to his own devices, which was exactly what he wanted.

His mother's concern was partly mitigated by the fact that it was soon obvious that Grogan had, as he had set out to do, disproved his doctor's worst fears. By his second summer in Switzerland he had put on four stone in weight and grown to almost six feet in height. With a short trunk, and unusually long legs and reach, he had completed a thorough metamorphosis from a diminutive and sick teenager into something altogether more dashing. He was also utterly fearless, and the stronger he became the greater was the improvement in his mountaineering skills. With his guides, Peter Perren and Johan Summermatter, he started to range all over the Alps in search of new challenges: from Zermatt to the north side of the Rhône valley to the Dents du Midi, east of Champéry. Soon he was making ascents unassisted, the Petite Dent de Morcles being the first of these, and by the end of the 1893 season was adjudged ready for his first ascent of the mighty Matterhorn.[3] It proved an elusive prize; twice he, Perren and Summermatter made the shoulder, only to be beaten back by bad weather; and as the season drew to a close Grogan realized that it would have to wait for another year. The Matterhorn was not all that had to wait: his African ambitions also had to be put on hold when Jane insisted that he finish his education.

Grogan arrived at Jesus College, Cambridge as a Freshman in the Michaelmas term of 1893 and moved into rooms in Chapel Court. At the time the College was under the sway of two formidable Fellows – 'Black' and 'Red' Morgan – who derived their nicknames from their respective hair colours. Henry Arthur 'Black' Morgan was the popular and worldly Master who had arrived at the College as an undergraduate in 1849 and never left, dying in harness sixty-three years later. No academic of note, he considered the sole yardstick for judging the

College's fortunes to be the success of the College boat on the river. But while 'Black' Morgan was the titular Master neither Grogan, nor his fellow undergraduates, nor the Fellows were under any illusion about who really ran the college: that distinction belonged to Edmund Henry 'Red' Morgan, the Dean and Senior Tutor. Everyone was in awe of him, and that included the Master. Foakes-Jackson, the college chaplain, summed him up in the following extract from a play of his own composition set to the music of Gilbert and Sullivan:

RED MORGAN: I am the tutor, bursar, butler, dean:
I rule the College with imperial sway.
The very Master owneth me supreme,
The Fellows tremble and my rule obey.

CHORUS: The Czar of Russia and our gracious Queen
Are not so potent as our noble Dean.[4]

Fearsome though 'Red' Morgan's reputation was, Grogan took an instant liking to the man. It was he who presided over Grogan's interview and sitting of the entry exam to read law, thoughtfully shutting his prospective student in a room filled with all the reference books necessary to secure a pass. The Dean, Grogan concluded, had apparently 'recognized at once that the state of my mind had been washed clean of every vestige of previous education'[5] during a year in the Alps. His entry thus assured, Grogan cast around to see what Cambridge had to offer.

Undergraduates were divided into two categories: 'Smugs' (the intellectuals) and 'Pugs' (the sportsmen). Grogan, whose individualism had become even more pronounced during his year in the Alps, refused to be slotted neatly into either. As far as 'Smugdom' was concerned he remained wedded to Prouen's philosophy of learning only what he considered it useful to learn rather than acquiring knowledge of no practical value for its own sake. Consequently he never visited his law tutor, and never attended any of his lectures. He did, however, put in appearances at classes in medicine (for which he displayed some aptitude) and mathematics (at which he excelled), and continued to read voraciously about any subject which interested him. The extent of his knowledge, general or otherwise, was seldom put to the test. Exams were not compulsory for undergraduates, and if anything they were the exception rather than the rule. In his Previous exams (the equivalent of today's Prelims) he was awarded a First in a French exam, thereby repaying his father's faith in the usefulness of the childhood trips across the Channel, and he passed a general paper in the Lent term of 1895. As far as formal measurements of his academic prowess go, that appears to have been that.

Grogan's dabblings with 'Pugdom' were equally diverse. He rowed in the Freshman's Trial Eights in the number four position, the 'engine room', and his boat was victorious in spite of the fact that he had adopted the habit of smoking a pipe while rowing. He was again in the number four position in the 'getting-on boat' in the Easter 1894 Bumps, but then abandoned aquatic sports in favour of rugger, for which he won his college cap. The Lent 1895 *The Chanticlere*, the college magazine, judged that 'his collaring is really good. But he has not yet learnt how to shove. He ought to be good when he knows the game better.' His real talent, however, was for hammer-throwing, although his enquiring (and arguably pedantic) mind questioned why the heavy metal ball was called a 'hammer', and why spinning around in faster and faster circles until suddenly releasing this dangerous weapon was called 'throwing'. On sports day in his first term he won the hammer contest with a throw of 66 foot 7 inches; his long legs also secured him second place in the high jump. The greatest hammer throw of his career he saved until his last term, Lent 1896: representing Jesus against New College, Oxford, he recorded a throw of 73 foot 8 inches.

The main purpose of all this sporting endeavour, however, was to keep him fit for his mountaineering. Grogan returned to the Alps in 1894 and in this, his third season, he excelled. By the middle of the summer he had successfully conquered all the principal peaks around Zermatt and set out, once again, to get the better of the Matterhorn.[6] This time, with Pierre Cabotz as his guide, he triumphed at the unusually young age of nineteen. Of equal, if not greater, distinction were his rock climbs in the Chamonix area, which included the first unaided traverse of the twin peaks of Aiguille de Dru and a traverse of the formidable Grépon. A less remarkable traverse of the Weisshorn nearly proved his undoing. Back with the old 'firm' of Perren and

Summermatter, Grogan suddenly disappeared down a crevasse pulling Summermatter down after him. The rope connecting the three men arrested Grogan's fall after fifty feet but then Summermatter hit the back of Grogan's neck on his way down, knocking him unconscious. When he came to after a half hour during which Perren had had to brace himself with his ice axe on the lip of the crevasse to prevent all three of them plunging into the abyss, it was to the sound of Summermatter muttering guttural profanities fifty feet below him. By an extraordinary stroke of luck two other climbing parties were not far away and, with their assistance, Grogan and Summermatter were hauled inch by inch out of the icy grave. For a second time Grogan had cheated death, and he delighted in recounting the story of his escape to his horrified mother after returning home for the new term.

Although Grogan relished the solitude of his Alpine adventures, and was becoming more and more of a maverick, he was as gregarious at Cambridge as he had been at Winchester. He was humorous, a brilliant conversationalist, supremely self-confident and with an easy charm that drew people to him like a magnet. This resulted in any number of invitations to join societies, many of which were organized by his good friend Eddie Watt, a New Zealander. Indeed, Watt, in his capacity as secretary of the Cranmer Debating Society, was responsible for Grogan's first recorded display of public speaking. In opposing the motion that 'Popular Demonstrations Are Both Dangerous And Useless', which he successfully defeated by a large majority, Grogan appears to have spoken from the heart: thirteen years later his leadership of a 'popular demonstration' that proved dangerous and largely useless almost proved to be his undoing.

Debating was not the only pastime which saw Grogan take centre stage. His talent on the mandoline and banjo, learnt during his mother's music lessons, and a penchant for theatricality also stood him in good stead at the soirées of Eddie Watt's Halliwell Shakespeare Society. Just about the only society which did not at one time or another occupy Grogan's interest was the Fabian. When some of its members tried to enlist his support he made it quite clear that he regarded them, and all socialists, as 'a very unwholesome gang of chinless men and bosomless women'.[7]

Ultimately, it was neither Grogan's musical talent nor his sporting abilities that ensured his undergraduate career was never forgotten: it was his penchant for practical jokes. On one particularly infamous occasion he was lying on his sofa practising 'The Dead March' from *Saul* after an eccentric lunch of half a dozen boiled eggs when the door suddenly flew open. A freckled youth then stuck his head around the door, shouted 'Are you saved?', and promptly disappeared.

Grogan considered this extraordinary performance for a few minutes, and then decided that something had to be done about this impudent Freshman who occupied the rooms next to his own. So he went to call on his friend 'Lux' Luxmoore,[8] and with Lux's help Grogan put his mountaineering skills to work. Armed with a bucket of water, he climbed out onto the roof of Chapel Court and emptied its contents down his neighbour's chimney. Safely back on terra firma, Grogan and Lux peered expectantly into the neighbour's room. But what they saw alarmed them considerably: the freckled one was peacefully enjoying tea and toast with his elderly mother. There was no evidence whatsoever of the eagerly anticipated explosion of soot across the hearth.

Grogan's first thought was to rush in and rescue the elderly lady in case the explosion had somehow been delayed. It was only as he turned on his heels that he noticed the swirl of soot spiralling from his own open window. Although the college servants were 'like their reigning sovereign, "not amused"'[9] at the indescribable state of Grogan's rooms, the incident was deemed worthy of a place in the College's official history.

In March 1895 the relaxed tempo of Grogan's university life was shattered by the worst news imaginable: his beloved mother had died while washing her hands before lunch. Jane was just forty-nine and had been suffering from heart disease. Grogan's twelve-year-old brother Quentin was home from Grove House for the Easter holidays at the time, and articulated the sentiments of all the children when he wrote: 'this was the first great shock of my life, as I had never realized that anyone whom I had loved so much as my mother could just pass away suddenly for ever. The last I saw of her she was lying on her bed looking so calm and peaceful with a bruise on her forehead where she had fallen.'[10] For Grogan, the sudden loss of the most important person in his life also left him responsible for six siblings of whom the youngest, Hilda, was only seven.

As Grogan had not quite come of age he was not left to shoulder the burden alone. A half-brother Walter had been nominated in William's will as legal guardian to any minors in the family in the event of Jane's death, but Grogan left Walter and his siblings in no doubt that whatever his age it was *he* who was in charge. Kindly Walter's services were only required when it suited Grogan, as was made abundantly clear to him during several well-intentioned visits to Kirkella. Despite his uneasy relationship with his headstrong half-brother, who was twenty years his junior, Walter stuck faithfully to his duties. After all, Grogan still had to graduate and until then Walter resolved to keep a fatherly eye on the younger children, in partnership with Nanny Redwood.

A second death the same year, that of 'Red' Morgan in August, also had important consequences for Grogan. With the departure of this most formidable and respected brake on his high spirits, his pranks started to become increasingly ambitious. Before long, in early 1896, Grogan finally overstepped the mark. One afternoon, he spotted a small flock of sheep that had meandered their way from Jesus Common to feed on the geraniums in the college gardens and, having had a particular 'Smug' tutor in his sights for weeks, saw an opportunity not to be missed. Believing that the man would be dining late, and 'having nothing better to do', Grogan and a 'New Zealand pastoral friend' proceeded to herd the sheep into the hapless tutor's rooms. Unfortunately for both Grogan and the don the latter was not out for dinner but had gone to London for the night. When he returned the sheep had eaten most of his carpet, his tablecloth and his prized aspidistra. Worse still, his rooms 'stank like a shearing shed'[11] and were uninhabitable for weeks.

Grogan immediately confessed to his crime, leaving 'Black' Morgan no option but to impose a suitable punishment. He correctly judged that for all Grogan's great charm and talent his interest in academia was on the wane, so his Cambridge career was prematurely terminated by mutual agreement. Seventy-four years later the College's obituary of one of its most swashbuckling and famous sons diplomatically recalled that Grogan had 'read a certain amount of Law but was more interested in other activities'.[12]

Grogan did not regard being sent down as a setback. No sooner had he left than he was accorded an honour which in his mind was of considerably greater worth than any degree. The previous summer he had deposited his siblings on Walter and returned to the Alps for his fourth season, wholly undeterred by his brush with death on the Weisshorn. Once again he reached the summit of the Matterhorn, and made a number of other testing ascents.[13] By any standards his record by then was an impressive one and led to his name being put forward in February 1896 for membership of the Alpine Club. His proposer was A. G. Topham and his seconder E. L. Strutt, the second-in-command of the 1922 Everest expedition. A month later Grogan was notified of his successful election to the Club as its youngest member. It was a signal achievement, as was his simultaneous election to the Swiss Alpine Club on the recommendation of Perren and Summermatter. Grogan's reaction to this dual honour was both surprising to fellow mountaineers and revealing to his friends. It was the challenge that had meant everything to him, and the challenge, once met, was no longer a lodestar. His mountaineering ambitions fulfilled, Grogan never climbed in the Alps, or anywhere else, again.

After his departure from Cambridge Grogan's mind turned once more to the possibility of pursuing his African ambitions, but he knew that big game hunting was about the most expensive sport of all, and that the sort of expedition he envisaged was certainly beyond his means. He was forced, reluctantly, to consider a career. This posed a dilemma: for Grogan, city life and the prospect of being placed in a straitjacket of any description were anathema. He had the option of joining Grogan & Boyd, in which he still owned the share that his father had left him, but the family business did not interest him in the slightest. As a stop-gap he fell back on the law, having secured membership of the Middle Temple prior to being sent down.[14] Being a barrister was at least a solo occupation, and Grogan had long since decided that he preferred to travel through life as his own master.

His legal career did not last long. There is no doubt that he did attend some lectures at the Middle Temple during the Spring of 1896, because in later life he was fond of recounting that the only piece of information he retained from them was that in Roman times patricides were wrapped up in a bag with vipers and tossed into the Tiber. Next he surfaced in other, most unexpected, surroundings. Grogan's attendance at classes at the Slade School of Art was informal – he turned up when he wanted to – and he surprised everyone by showing a considerable aptitude for drawing. But the art lasted about as long as the law. Grogan knew he was drifting and hankering after some new adventure – and though he was impressed by those of his fellow students who 'were seriously studying art as a means for future liveli-hood', he disliked the fact that the prevailing atmosphere at the Slade was one 'of long tousled-haired males and scrubby-headed females with flaming ties and what-nots'. It all seemed to him to be a 'pathetic imitation' of life on Paris's *rive gauche*.

The antidote to his restlessness came sooner than he expected. In late March the first gruesome reports of an uprising by the Ndebele of Southern Rhodesia appeared in the newspapers – and Cecil Rhodes was calling for volunteers for the fight. The prospect of adventure in the name of the Empire immediately intoxicated Grogan. So when the Slade's Principal, Frederick Brown, next inspected Grogan's dood-lings of cherubs during a class in which he was supposed to be crafting a likeness of a 'sad-faced, saggy-breasted' model, and told him that with ten years of hard work he might get somewhere, Grogan decided enough was enough. He took a halfpenny from his pocket, and declared that if it came down heads he would put his back into his artistic career; tails and he would become a policeman. The mystified Brown asked what exactly he meant by a 'policeman'. Grogan expanded: he would answer the call to arms in Matabeleland. After all, it was to Africa that he had to venture in order to fulfil his hunting ambitions and desire to see Lake Tanganyika – and reaching Matabele-land would be a start. With that thought he tossed the coin and it came down a 'bobby'.

Within a week his siblings were once again in the care of the ever-patient Walter at his house in Wonersh and Grogan, the gentle-man adventurer, was on a boat bound for Cape Town.

THREE

Rhodes's 'Bloody Trooper'

GROGAN HAD NOT BEEN on a sea voyage before. The sense of freedom that it engendered was as intoxicating as being in the Alps, and he was thrilled at the prospect of playing a part in the defence of one of the Empire's outposts. Never far from his mind were the 'tales of atrocities, women raped and hacked to pieces, little children thrown into heaps of dry grass and set on fire'[1] that he had read in the newspapers. These tales placed what he had left behind in stark relief: others may have been content with the humdrum banalities of a cosseted life at home, but for Grogan they held no appeal whatsoever. He needed a sense of purpose and now he had one; Rhodes, he reflected, was right in saying that 'to be born an Englishman is to have won first prize in life'.

The two and a half weeks at sea passed quickly. Grogan took full advantage of the usual sports, dances and deck games on board ship, but as Cape Town drew steadily nearer he began to worry. His vision of Africa was defined by the books of Rider Haggard and Selous, and from them he knew that one needed a plethora of talents to survive in the bush. He was of course supremely confident that he could rise to any challenges that the so-called 'Dark Continent' might throw at him: he was a conspicuously good shot, had a mountaineer's stamina and a physique more imposing than that of any other volunteer on board, but he was concerned that as an amateur, a gentleman adventurer rather than a trained soldier, his services might be rejected. He need not have worried: one morning, when he was having an altercation with a 'vocal anglophobe of indeterminate racial origin',[2] a cavalry officer with a stupendous moustache intervened. The man took Grogan aside and told him that if he reported to him in Cape Town he would find a more constructive outlet for his patriotic fervour. As the ship steamed into port, and Grogan caught his first glimpse of Africa – majestic Table Mountain, the low castle under repair, the turreted and verandahed buildings of Adderley Street, Malays selling their *snoek* fish on the docks – he was assured of a role in the relief of Matabeleland.

Until the 1890s the British public largely ignored goings-on in most of Africa, unless they involved feats of exploration. There was similarly no great governmental enthusiasm for splashing the continent red and little conscious design behind the fact that by the time of the Ndebele uprising almost two million square miles of Africa had already been brought within the British 'sphere of influence'. Developments like the first, almost reluctant, steps towards controlling the Nile (and Gordon's last stand at Khartoum in 1885) had of course caused a stir, but they were largely caused by a strategic imperative that had little to do with an interest in Africa per se: the need to protect the Suez Canal and the vital trade route between Britain and India. Other than in Egypt and the Sudan there were few signs of a cohesive imperial mission, and policy – such as it was – was more reactive than proactive. For the most part those who were busy furthering 'British' interests – explorers, missionaries and entrepreneurs – were acting either in their own interests or those of non-governmental bodies.

In southern Africa, however, Cecil Rhodes forced successive British governments to pay closer attention. By the end of the 1880s, this initially frail and liberal son of a rector from Bishop's Stortford had charmed, bullied, bribed and schemed his way into a position of extraordinary power. Born in 1853, by the age of just thirty-five Rhodes controlled the supply of ninety per cent of the world's diamonds, had a substantial stake in the newly discovered goldfields of the Witwatersrand, and was soon to become Prime Minister of Cape Colony. He also made no secret of his desire to bring all of southern Africa under the British flag, an ambition which well and truly captured the public imagination.

Rhodes's methods may have varied from the inspirational to the downright criminal but in the consciousness of the twenty-two-year-old Grogan, and a generation of other young imperialists, it was the *mission* that mattered. Of the minutiae of the *means* employed by Rhodes considerably less was widely known until more than half a century after his death. In March 1888, the year Grogan went to Winchester, Rhodes succeeded in securing a vital endorsement of his ambitions. At the inaugural annual general meeting of his De Beers Consolidated Mines company he was authorized to 'raise armies, form secret services . . . and acquire any tracts in Africa or elsewhere, and expend such sums of money as may be deemed advisable in the development and government thereof'. In short, Rhodes was legally empowered to do whatever he wanted and with imperial expansion in Africa still largely carried out by proxy, it mattered little to most observers that there was a blurred distinction between the pursuit of his own ends and those of the Empire.

Soon Rhodes was casting covetous glances across the Limpopo river, and his first objective was to annex Mashonaland, today's eastern Zimbabwe. The fact that the territory was nominally under the sway of Lobengula did not deter him. As far as he was concerned Lobengula's 'people of the long shields', the Ndebele, were interlopers, having been led north across the Limpopo by Lobengula's father, Mzilikazi, to escape the attentions of Shaka Zulu. Furthermore, they had settled to the west of Mashonaland and their authority over the weaker and politically fragmented Shona was only maintained by sporadic displays of force. The Ndebele were far from being the only target in Rhodes's sights. In order to succeed in establishing hegemony over land north of the Limpopo, Rhodes knew that he would have to outmanoeuvre President Kruger and the Boers of Transvaal and the Orange Free State, not to mention sundry European powers also seeking to extend their influence in southern Africa.

Lobengula was an impressive and shrewd opponent. Over six feet tall and weighing twenty stone, he insisted that all visitors – black and white – had to crawl on their hands and knees before him. Rhodes chose his tactics carefully and opted to try to bring his opponent down through skulduggery, veiling his real intentions as a desire simply to secure mineral rights in Lobengula's territory. The plan succeeded. In agreeing to sign the so-called 'Rudd Concession'

Lobengula effectively (but unknowingly) relinquished both his supremacy over Matabeleland and his authority in Mashonaland in return for a promise of weapons.

It did not take Logengula long to realize that Rhodes's interpretation of the concession differed radically from his own, and that he had been tricked, but by then he had little chance of reneging on it. He took care not to accept the rifles (an act which would have de jure sealed the agreement); and he despatched two of his most trusted *indunas* (chiefs) to London to appeal directly to Queen Victoria for support.

Rhodes was always one step ahead of the Ndebele chief. In the summer of 1889 he either bought off or won over all those who stood in his way, from ministers in the British government to missionaries to rival concession-seekers. This was his forte: no one was better than he at convincing people of completely disparate persuasions that their aims, be they religious or political, would be best served by backing him, and Rhodes's handling of this particular challenge was executed with characteristic guile. As a result Lobengula failed to secure any support from Britain and Rhodes gained the ultimate sanction of his game plan when his newly formed British South Africa Company was granted a Royal Charter in October 1889. From then on his actions were implicitly authorized not only by his shareholders but also by his monarch.

The Royal Charter was an even more significant boost for Rhodes's vast ambitions than the De Beers Trust Deed. Many years later Grogan would cynically – but not without a hint of admiration – describe the powers it conferred as follows:

> it was authority ... to appropriate the landed property of any potentate incapable of prolonged resistance, to draw an imaginative boundary around the said property and to paint the enclosed area red on the world's maps as indication that the areas had passed under the indefinite suzerainty of Her Majesty ... Sometimes this transaction, to give the humorist Mr Labouchère of *Truth* something to write about, was *pro forma* endorsed in a formal document. The Chartered transferred some flintlock guns and a large number of

bottles of gin specially distilled in London, probably from town waste, available in any quantity at a wholesale price of one shilling a bottle to promote trade and the spread of the Gospel. The Chartered in a moment of alcoholic exhilaration then applied a greasy thumb to the document supported by two greasy thumb prints of sub-chiefs as witnesses, believing that this document was the white man's incantation guaranteed to produce rain at will. Thus our Empire was built.[3]

With the Charter safely in his clutches Rhodes was free to deal with Lobengula much as he liked, and the Ndebele chief was powerless to prevent the consequences of having been outmanoeuvred. In 1890, a heavily armed Pioneer Column of some 200 men led by twenty-three-year-old Frank Johnson marched clean through south-eastern Matabeleland and into Mashonaland. Johnson was paid the enormous sum of £87,000 for his efforts and, with the legendary Selous as their guide, the pioneers were able to hoist the Union Jack over Salisbury on 13 September. Their feat was lauded in the pages of *The Times* and throughout the Empire.

The arrival of the pioneers in neighbouring Mashonaland positioned Lobengula between a rock and a hard place. The 'small prospecting expedition' that he had agreed to in the Rudd Concession had turned into conquest pure and simple, but he knew that to unleash his *impis*, who were baying for blood, would play straight into Rhodes's hands and could also result in the loss of Matabeleland to the clatter of the Maxim gun. For the time being he resolved to sit and watch what happened next.

By the end of 1890 Rhodes's brinkmanship had seemingly proved that the entrepreneur could do more to extend the Empire than the British government. With the conquest of Mashonaland a further 400,000 square miles of Africa had been added to the Chartered Company's balance sheet, and to the British 'sphere of influence', and Rhodes was elected Prime Minister of Cape Colony. But not all his expansionist plans succeeded. At home the 'Exeter Hall' liberals,[4] stirred up by missionary bodies, prevented him from seizing control of the African Lakes Corporation in Nyasaland and persuaded a reluctant

British government to declare the territory a protectorate. In copper-rich Katanga he was stymied by Leopold II of Belgium, a man he considered 'Satanic'. His interest in Portuguese East Africa was also thwarted. Most disturbing of all was the discovery that Mashonaland was not, after all, the El Dorado that Johnson's pioneers had been promised. There was precious little sign of gold in the territory, and a shortage of supplies, exorbitant prices, torrential rains and disease rapidly shattered the first settlers' hopes.

In the three years following the conquest of Mashonaland, which cost the Chartered Company over £400,000, Rhodes became increasingly troubled by the catastrophic prospect of producing a nil return for his shareholders' money. Many of the poorer settlers drifted away and Dr Jameson, the territory's administrator, slashed the police force and dispensed with most of the administrative staff in an effort to cut costs. As a last resort he also began to sell off Mashonaland's most viable commodity – the land itself. One concessionaire alone, Sir John Willoughby, amassed 600,000 acres of land and thousands of mining claims by the turn of the century. None of the crisis measures were capable of promising short-term solutions of the magnitude demanded by Rhodes. Indeed, the land grants had an almost instantaneous deleterious effect: coupled with brutal treatment of the Shona by Jameson's police and vigilante groups, they swiftly caused increasing unrest among the local populace.

As the failure of Rhodes's gamble in Mashonaland became apparent the remaining settlers, and the canny Jameson in particular, started to take a covetous look over the garden fence. Across the Umniati river in Lobengula's Matabeleland not only were there some 300,000 head of prime cattle, but there were rumours of gold. Smashing the Ndebele therefore seemed the obvious solution to the dwindling fortunes of the Chartered Company and it did not take Jameson long to conjure up a pretext for war that would satisfy both Rhodes and the Colonial Office back in London. Lobengula's persistent attempts to maintain the peace, including a further direct appeal to Queen Victoria that went unheeded, were not enough to save him from what happened next. Jameson marched on Matabeleland.

When Jameson's well-armed force of 700 recruits entered his territory, Lobengula was forced to stand and fight for the very survival of his people. It was not an even contest, and there was no repetition of the humiliation of the British military by the Zulu chief Cetshwayo at Isandlwana just fourteen years earlier. In the first major engagement, by the Shangani river, the volunteers' Maxim guns forced the Ndebele to abandon a daring night attack. One week later Lobengula's main force was annihilated at Bembesi. Again the Maxim gun, firing eleven bullets per second, proved itself to be 'the symbol of the age':[5] estimates of the losses among the courageous Ndebele *impis* vary between one and three thousand men, whereas Jameson's casualties numbered just four. In disarray Lobengula torched his *kraal* at Bulawayo and retreated northwards with the remainder of his men. His kingdom lost, this once mighty ruler then proceeded to take his own life. On 4 November 1893 Jameson entered the smouldering remains of Bulawayo.

Rhodes, with the assistance of the Cape Parliament which he now controlled, once again succeeded in stifling the few expressions of distaste at the actions taken in the name of the Chartered Company. Its right to jurisdiction over Matabeleland was confirmed by the British Government in July 1894, and the company's share price soared. Rhodesia, as Mashonaland had been renamed after its conquest, officially doubled in size; and Jameson's volunteers grabbed their booty of 6,000 acres each, accounting for a total of 10,000 square miles of Matabeleland.

By the time the Ndebele drifted back to their grazing grounds from the north they found themselves dispossessed not only of their land but of their cattle. Over 230,000 head out of a total of approximately 300,000 were confiscated. This was to have devastating social ramifications. It undermined the Ndebele system of marriage, as cattle played an important part in the system of dowry, and it forced them to sell their labour as the only means of survival – which robbed them of their pride as a warrior people. A hut tax of ten shillings per annum was also imposed in order to ensure the settlers had an adequate supply of labour.

To make matters worse a series of natural disasters coincidentally followed the signing of the Rudd Concession and the arrival of the pioneers in Rhodesia. Successive swarms of locusts ravaged the land; drought took hold in 1894; and by early 1896 a deadly new viral cattle disease swept into the country from the north – rinderpest. In the course of the next two years most of southern Africa's two and a half million cattle died or were culled in an attempt to stop the spread of the disease. Most of the few cattle that the Ndebele had managed to retain perished. Such was the backdrop to what has been described as 'the first African war of independence precipitated by the Scramble',[6] the 'Scramble' being the term coined in the 1880s to describe the European powers' competition for hegemony in Africa.

Having provided the Ndebele and Shona with ample motive for an uprising Rhodes proceeded to hand them the opportunity on a plate. By the end of 1895 his attention was firmly fixed on the next item on his agenda. On 29 December Jameson, at Rhodes's behest, invaded Kruger's Transvaal. The aim was to gain political control of the vast auriferous wealth of the Rand and to unify the Boer and British colonies of South Africa under the Union Jack once and for all. But Rhodes and Jameson had miscalculated. The Raid was doomed from the moment Jameson crossed the Bechuanaland border and realized that a simultaneous uprising planned in Johannesburg by the 'Uitlanders', the non-Boers of the Transvaal, had failed to materialize. Within days Kruger's Boers rounded up the invaders and carted them off to face judgement in Pretoria, and Rhodes once again faced ruin. This time the political ramifications of his aggression were much wider: Rhodes may have been the instigator of the Raid but 'Pushful Joe' Chamberlain, the Colonial Secretary, was equally implicated in this act of international piracy that brought Britain to the brink of war with Kruger's ally, Germany. By now political rivalries and personal ambitions were increasingly transforming British governmental perceptions of the Transvaal – and Chamberlain, in particular, considered it strategically vital to gain unrestricted access to the gold which backed the British currency.

With Jameson's troopers incarcerated in Pretoria it soon became obvious to the Ndebele that were was only a skeleton force of policemen left behind in Rhodesia, and that the 5,000-strong white community was virtually undefended. With the backing of their spirit mediums an uprising was planned for 29 March, the night of the full moon. But the chiefs could not hold their men in check that long. On 23 March the first white farms were attacked, and within a week almost 200 European men, women and children had been butchered and mutilated. The survivors fled to the towns of Bulawayo and Gwelo.

For Rhodes, the uprising was an answer to his prayers. It diverted attention away from the Jameson Raid, and gave him the perfect excuse not to attend an official inquiry into his transgressions that was due to convene in Cape Town. Instead he set out from Beira, in Portuguese East Africa, at the head of a column of volunteers and struck west to 'save' Matabeleland for the Empire. By the end of the first week in April it was apparent that he was the recipient of another stroke of luck: the Ndebele had not pressed home their advantage. This was fortunate for Grogan too, considering he was already on the high seas and eagerly anticipating an adventure.

In Cape Town the moustachioed cavalry officer was as good as his word to Grogan and immediately deputed him to run a wagon-load of ammunition up to Bulawayo. Grogan teamed up with a shipmate by the name of Wilson Fox, a teller at the Bank of England, and set about the necessary preparations with gusto. This was by no means easy: the rinderpest epidemic had caused severe logistical problems in Cape Town, not to mention starvation, and oxen were nowhere to be found. But Grogan's luck was in: a shipload of mules from the Argentine arrived just as he did and soon he, Wilson Fox and their truculent new charges were bundled onto a train for the four-day journey across the Karoo to Mafeking.

The railway terminus at Mafeking had turned into a bustling supply depot since the start of the uprising. Beyond its small corrugated iron house and goods shed lay hundreds of 'Gladstone bags on wheels, labelled coach', as well as great mounds of supplies under tarpaulins. While waiting for his mules to be off-loaded, Grogan wandered off to recruit a driver for his 'Gladstone bag' and chose a Cape 'boy' who won his immediate admiration with his ability to 'flick a fly off a mule's back'[7] with a double-handed whip. Without further delay he set out on the 335-mile journey to Palapye, the driver perched in relative comfort on the single front seat while Grogan and Wilson Fox bounced around on top of their cargo of ammunition.

The Great North Road of Africa, along which Frank Johnson and his pioneers had travelled on their way to hoist the flag in Salisbury less than six years earlier, failed to live up to Grogan's romantic expectations. There were no wayside inns or shady trees to rest under, only miles of 'damn all'[8] – waterless veld and rock-strewn river beds. The putrefying remains of cattle which had succumbed to rinderpest littered the track on either side, each carcass hosting its own swarm of flies which rose to engulf them as they passed. It was with considerable relief that after six days in the 'Gladstone bag' Grogan reached Palapye, the *kraal* of the Bechuana chief Khama.

Khama, and Palapye, greatly impressed him. Although the chief had himself lost 95,000 head of cattle, the carcasses had been burned, the town was well kept and watered, and the sale of liquor was banned. Such orderliness Grogan assumed to be the result of British influence – influence which he intended to play his part in reimposing on the 'renegade' Ndebele.

Grogan's wagon lumbered into Bulawayo in the first week in May, having perilously run the gauntlet of the *impis* still very much at large in the surrounding area. The town had become, in the opinion of Selous who was holed up in it, 'probably the strongest [*laager*] ever constructed in Africa'.[9] The defensive square, in which all the townsfolk took refuge when they heard a bugle call, consisted of two rows of wagons chained together and packed with sandbags. From the corners of this square the muzzles of Maxim guns and field guns protruded. Beyond it three barbed-wire fences had been planted, and beyond them there was an outer perimeter of thirty yards of broken glass. Once safely inside this formidable barricade Grogan delivered the ammunition to the Exchange Buildings and bade a fond farewell to his driver, whom he entrusted to the care of a party leaving for Cape Town. He was well aware that he probably owed his life to the man, and acknowledged that 'few people . . . realize what a part these Cape boys played in the early development of Africa; their patience, endurance of hardship, varied skills and good humour under adverse circumstances was an abiding marvel to me'.[10]

To Grogan's great surprise new arrivals in the town were not required to report for duty, and when he attempted to do so he met with an unambiguous rebuff. The town's administrator told him to 'get the hell out of here' as he had seen 'enough bloody bums today'.[11] Everywhere nerves were on edge – twenty men had been lost in April and a further fifty wounded – but Grogan considered that even more reason to have an ordered chain of command. Instead Bulawayo resembled a 'Wild West' town with armed townsfolk, the disciplined Matabele Mounted Police, volunteers, a few regular army officers and African scouts all doing their own thing. After wandering aimlessly for hours around the streets surrounding the *laager* Grogan and Wilson Fox settled down for the night under a tree.

The two men woke at dawn and the first thing that permeated their senses was the dreadful stench. In the dark they had been unaware that the tree that they had chosen to sleep under had been used to string up the previous day's Ndebele captives. Now, warmed by the rising sun, bits of human detritus were dropping to the ground around them, though even this grisly awakening failed to take the edge off their hunger and they repaired to 'the Silver Grill' for breakfast. This insalubrious eatery, a long shed built of corrugated iron, offered Welsh rarebit at four shillings, or very small slivers of meat for the exorbitant price of ten shillings – more than a day's pay for a volunteer. Grogan was desperate, whatever the cost, and as a result experienced his next lesson in the harsh realities of life under siege. When his meat arrived his attention was momentarily distracted by his neighbour and the next time he looked at his plate it had gone. The neighbour's dog wore an expression of sublime contentment.

Heading off in search of better luck elsewhere Grogan struck up a conversation with a man with a sergeant's stripes who was busy skinning a hyaena. By now he was ready to eat anything, hyaena included, but was told that this was inadvisable and that the sergeant's friend was on his way with a tin of bully beef. When the friend arrived he introduced himself to Grogan as John Norton-Griffiths, and the sergeant gave his name as Bobby Coryndon.[12] Over 'breakfast' the two men, who were to reappear at crucial junctures in Grogan's life, signed him up on the spot as a member of the Matabele Mounted Police.

Grogan's morale soared when he was issued with a horse, Martini-Henry rifle, gun bucket and curry comb. He felt like a 'somebody' again, even if only a 'bloody trooper who for five bob a day, a cupful of mouldy rice, and a blown tin of bully beef swore and sweated in the ... task of painting the map red'.[13] His friend Wilson Fox, on the other hand, did not sign up. Even though he was extremely myopic he had seen enough of Bulawayo to make him head straight back to Cape Town just as Grogan prepared to ride out of the *laager* on his first foray to confront the enemy on the veld.

With each passing day the atmosphere in Bulawayo became less tense, buoyed by the knowledge that Major Plumer and some 700 regular soldiers were expected from Mafeking imminently and that Rhodes's relief column was approaching from Salisbury. It was with the aim of linking up with the latter that Grogan and 300 other troopers were ordered out of the town on 11 May. Eight days later the two forces met for a decisive engagement with the Ndebele by the Umguza river. There, Grogan witnessed first hand that the prophecies of the Ndebele's spirit mediums were not always reliable:

> at dawn we reached the river; one of our spies had informed us that the *impi* had been told by their medicine man that when we crossed the river our horses would fall dead and our bullets would turn to water, that they should wait till we crossed and then dash in with their spears and slaughter us in the resulting confusion. Our instructions, therefore, were not to fire a shot, but having crossed the river charge the line of warriors at full gallop, expecting that in their astonishment they would turn and run, which they did. As we were mounted we could easily overtake them. The carnage was terrible till we could find no more. On our return to the river we finished off any oddments we could find in pig-holes or other hiding cover.

Thinking only of the deaths of the white families two months earlier, Grogan had few qualms about the fact that 'the unwritten but well recognised law was "no prisoners, no quarter"'.[14] Five days later Plumer finally relieved Bulawayo and Rhodes rode triumphantly into the town on 1 June.

The Ndebele realized that with their opponents becoming stronger by the day guile would stand them in better stead than attempts at engaging the enemy in open warfare, and they retreated to the Mambo and Matopo Hills. But Rhodes's problems were far from over. No sooner had he left Salisbury for Bulawayo than the Shona had started to plan their own uprising. When it happened its ferocity matched that of their Ndebele overlords three months earlier: in the middle of June every outlying European farm within eighty miles of Salisbury was attacked and their hundred or so occupants murdered. Suddenly it was Salisbury's turn to transform itself into a *laager*, and Rhodes was faced with war on two fronts. Grogan was assigned to the hastily formed Salisbury relief column and embarked in the opposite direction on the gruelling journey that Rhodes had just completed.

The principal privation was the desperate shortage of rations. Grogan and his fellow troopers were forced to subsist on their 'cup of mouldy rice a day'; very occasionally this was supplemented by *biltong* broth or a tin of bully beef which more often than not was 'blown' and would explode on opening. All food was shared with swarms of flies. On one occasion an increasingly resourceful Grogan was reduced to grilling a vulture despite his doubts that 'trussed vultures . . . would find a ready export market in the better class of restaurants in Paris'.[15] Lack of food was not the only hardship: torrential – and unseasonal – rain fell, forcing the drenched troopers to take shelter under the wagons at night rather than huddle round a fire. In a futile attempt to keep part of him dry Grogan resorted to sleeping with his saddle over his stomach.

The column's progress towards Salisbury was painfully slow, held up by the hit-and-run tactics of the Shona and the search for civilian survivors of the initial massacre. One wretched soul it encountered – delirious, filthy, and barely recognizable as a human being – had somehow survived being dumped down a mine shaft by a Shona war party and then bombardment with dynamite cartridges. Soon after this rescue Grogan succumbed to 'the fever'[16] and dysentery, and was forced to travel most of the rest of the journey in a singularly uncomfortable and overcrowded hospital wagon staffed by nuns. 'My God, what heaven must have in store for those nuns;' he reflected, 'night especially was a weary time listening to the obscene ravings of one's close companions and the hideous cachinnations of the hyenas disinterring the day's dead.'[17]

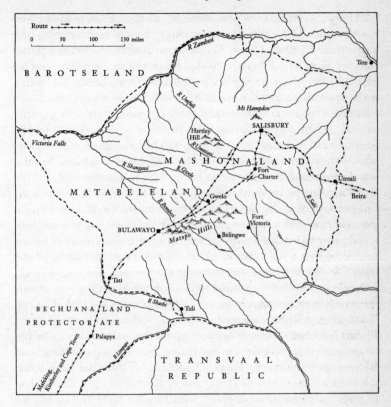

Grogan's Route: Matabele War, 1896

When the column finally rolled into Salisbury Grogan had escaped
the hospital wagon but, still very weak, was asleep in the saddle. He
found it hard to fathom what was worth saving in the town, or worth
savouring except for food and a bed, but even those were denied him
for long. Within days he was informed that he had been promoted to
the position of a 'number four' on a muzzle-loading seven-pound gun,
under the command of Lt. Tyndale-Biscoe (RN), and was leaving
immediately to relieve Hartley Hill, seventy-five miles south-west of
Salisbury.

Hunger remained the overriding preoccupation on the march to Hartley Hill. The column even ate two of its mules, the victims of a successfully repelled ambush. When the settlement was within striking distance Grogan volunteered to slip ahead and see what comestibles he could ferret out for his fellow gunners. Once inside the town's main store all he found were tins labelled 'Digby chicks', which he assumed were some sort of tasty fowl. He was in for a shock: that evening, when eagerly opening the first tin, he discovered that the 'chicks' were withered and heavily salted herring, quite useless in an area without drinking water. The journey had also proved to be a waste of time: there was no one left to save in Hartley Hill and the following day the column turned about and headed back to Salisbury. Grogan arrived in the capital nursing a squashed toe, run over by the gun, but was told to prepare to leave for Bulawayo. Reclassified as a scout, a proven veteran, his orders were to join Rhodes's personal escort.

There was a stalemate in Matabeleland. From the safety of the jumbled mass of granite *kopjes* of the Mambo and Matopo Hills the Ndebele had launched sporadic raids on the surrounding countryside during Grogan's absence, but to no great effect. On 5 July General Carrington, who had assumed command of the regular troops from Plumer, ordered a surprise dawn attack on the Mambos in an attempt to dislodge the Ndebele. He succeeded, but the action almost cost Rhodes his life when he found himself cut off from the main force. Throughout the campaign those around him noticed that Rhodes had displayed a conspicuous courage bordering on recklessness, but his own lucky escape and the sight of the blood-soaked bodies of eighteen of his men who were not so fortunate appeared to have a deep effect on him. He returned to his camp in pensive, rather than jubilant mood.

There were compelling financial reasons for Rhodes's subsequent course of action: the costs of the campaign were threatening to bring the Chartered Company down around his ears. But it is equally the case that those, like Grogan, who were with him at this time were treated to a display of the 'Colossus of Africa' at his most magnetic best. Rhodes decided to reject Carrington's request for 10,000 additional men to surround the 1,750 square miles of the Matopos and starve the Ndebele out, and to sue for peace. In pursuit of that end he established contact with the Ndebele, at great personal risk, by walking unarmed into the hills. There followed a succession of peace *indabas* during which Rhodes listened to the many grievances of the people and responded with great tact and patience. It was a very difficult task; at any moment the atmosphere could have changed and Rhodes could have lost his life. His conduct, as one recent biographer conceded, 'revealed his great gifts of imagination and perception, as well as his extraordinary qualities as a leader . . . This single episode in his life stands apart, perhaps because it is one of the few occasions when his own interests coincided with the best interests of others.'[18]

As a member of Rhodes's small retinue during the *indabas* Grogan never forgot the evenings in his Sugar Bush Camp. He later recalled that:

> It was his wont to brood in solitude dreaming the destinies of men. There was no moon or shadows other than that cast by the dancing flames of the camp fire. The inky sky in the rarefied atmosphere of the highlands was all a-twinkle with myriad stars winking as if amused by the absurdity of puny man. All around lay old Africa, thorn and rock stretching as far as the mind could reach. A virtually unpopulated, immeasurable immensity of nothing waiting to be tamed. The great silence of the African night emphasised by the occasional cry of a jackal enveloped us. It was cold – the piercing cold of the starlit nights on the high plateau of Africa.

Rhodes did not always sit 'in solitude'. Often he joined Grogan and the other scouts by the fire and would relate his vision for Africa. He spoke of his dream of a railway and telegraph running the length of the continent, with arterial lines to all the ports, thereby opening up even the remotest areas of the interior to the 'civilizing influence' of the colonial powers; of the need to forestall Germany's expansionist ambitions; of his dream of a million happy English homes in the highlands of Africa; and of 'teaching the African trades and the skills of government'. *This* was the Rhodes that Grogan would remember, the Rhodes for whom there was 'no ceremony'; for whom 'all men black or white, Kaiser or scullion, be they men, were one'; and whose scorn was directed only at 'unctuous rectitude, hypocrites, and the 'little ones' who, in Kipling's words, 'feared to be great'.[19] Indeed, it was during one of these fireside soliloquies, when 'the spell of greatness was in the air', that Grogan suddenly experienced in himself 'the crystallisation of a set purpose to which self, family, everything had to be subservient' when Rhodes pointed directly at him and declared 'you younger men must devote your lives to the great task'.[20]

When peace terms were finally agreed between Rhodes and the Ndebele, the 'bloody troopers' were out of a job. The uprising in Mashonaland stuttered on for another year (or five in the case of one rebel chief), but it was not on the scale that had at first been feared. Grogan's part in the conflict was over and he joined the escort of Lord Grey, Jameson's successor as Administrator of Rhodesia, and headed east towards Portuguese East Africa. At the border he was formally released from the employ of the Chartered Company and given his campaign medal. He had survived what was his first, but would certainly not be his last, involvement in the Scramble for Africa.

Grogan drifted into Portuguese East Africa in the company of three Dutchmen and a South African professional hunter named Penney, who suggested some sport. Grogan jumped at the opportunity. He was in no great hurry to return home to consider the specifics of how to play his part in the great task of painting the map of Africa red, and the chance to fulfil one or possibly more of his childhood ambitions sounded too good to miss. The expedition nearly cost him his life, so unhealthy was the territory into which Penney led him.

Grogan was exhilarated by the sight of vast herds of buffalo and by bagging his first African trophy. But there was no sign of lion, rhino or elephant. Much of Portuguese East Africa had been shot out years earlier, and before Penney was able to take his party elsewhere the three Dutchmen fell ill. One died, and had to be left to the wild animals as it proved impossible to bury him in the rock-hard ground; the other two were carried by Grogan and Penney as far as a surveyor's camp nearby. There, the hunting trip ended. For the second time in a matter of months Grogan found himself racked by fever and only just managed to stagger into the railway settlement of Fontesvilla on the Pungwe river before collapsing. During a brief remission he forced himself to hunt again, alone, to pay for his board and keep, but within days his fever was so bad that he lost consciousness.

When he came to he was in a stinking corrugated iron room with an empty water bucket by the bed. Lacking the strength to rise from his bed he fired two pistol shots through the ceiling and a dishevelled man duly appeared with water. Grogan stayed conscious just long enough to enquire about the source of the foul smell. The answer was not encouraging. It emanated from the corpse of a man in the adjoining cell who had died three days earlier, and could not be interred; the rains were expected, and buried corpses had a nasty habit of reappearing in the streets when it rained. As Grogan's own condition worsened the owner of the shack, fearing that he too was about to die, wrapped him in a blanket and loaded him onto an open truck on the Beira train. Within twenty-four hours he lay, still unconscious, in a railway siding in the port city. It was his great good fortune that on that day Alfred Lawley was doing his rounds of the terminus.

The thirty-four-year-old Lawley was chief engineer of Pauling & Co., who built most of southern Africa's railways, and as the son of a Sussex farm hand had been 'nourished on beer from the age of six months'.[21] Recently released from jail in Pretoria for his prominent part in organizing the aborted Uitlander uprising that had been planned to coincide with Jameson's Raid on the Transvaal, Lawley was also no stranger to fever. One attack in 1893 had caused this great bear of a man's weight to plummet from fifteen stone to ten. Furthermore, that year and the next he had lost sixty per cent of his workers on the Beira railway, which he only completed on time due to his unique brand of leadership skills. 'Mile a day, boys, mile a day' was Lawley's catchphrase, and his men would work flat out for six days before being released for the seventh to drink themselves unconscious.

Recognizing that despite no visible signs of life the thing in the blanket must still be alive or his sense of smell would have told him otherwise, Lawley ordered his men to carry Grogan to his house. For days he looked after his patient 'like a mother'[22] as Grogan fought not only the blackwater fever but also a burst liver abscess, a complication arising from his attack of amoebic dysentery on the way from Bulawayo to Salisbury. For one who but three years earlier had been told to live out his days in the Kentish countryside, so poor was his health, Grogan again displayed a dogged defiance of the medical profession. Finally he regained consciousness and found himself on a wide breezy verandah overlooking the Mozambique Channel. The worst was over.

To begin with Grogan was too weak to leave Lawley's house, so he whiled away the hours counting the passing funeral cortèges of fellow troopers who had died of the fever before being able to secure a passage home. The highest number in a single day was twenty-seven. As soon as he could muster the strength he also began to take evening strolls to supplement his macabre daytime recreation, but found Beira to be singularly devoid of attractions. Trooper Robert Foran, whose path he would again cross a decade later, described the port as 'a spot from which escape could not come too soon to preserve sanity of mind and peace of soul. There was absolutely nothing to do; nothing to see and nowhere to go. Every known and unknown evil was Beira's birthright.' In short it was 'Satan's own summer palace'.[23]

Lawley, Grogan soon observed, had developed his own way of coping with living in 'Hell': the man who was universally held in awe for having once told an over-excited Rhodes to stop squeaking like a rabbit derived his comfort from 'liquids and solids'.[24] On one forty-eight-hour tour of inspection on the Beira railway Pauling, Lawley and one other were known to have demolished 300 bottles of German beer, to which they were (evidently) extremely partial, and at a famous breakfast at Delagoa Bay the same trio had forged an unwavering path through eight bottles of champagne and a thousand oysters. Such gargantuan indulgence was not for Grogan, whose drinking and eating habits tended towards the ascetic. In fact, though he greatly enjoyed Lawley's company, the only thing he really craved was to return home and convalesce.

The opportunity came sooner than Grogan had expected. One evening he and a few friends were out dancing when a Portuguese officer caught him casting admiring glances at a shapely cousin. In a town where tensions between the Portuguese and Rhodes's demobbed troopers had been rising daily this gesture was not appreciated by the officer. He lunged at Grogan with a knife, received a sharp punch in the face for his efforts, and fell to the ground. There he remained, quite motionless: hitting his head on the floor had killed him.

In no time the British consul had an international incident on his hands. When he arrived at the dance hall he was met by a crowd of Portuguese baying for Grogan's blood, and was thrown in the gutter. He hurried off to his office and, fearing an escalation in hostilities, telegraphed for immediate naval assistance. The following morning a British cruiser was standing by offshore, and Lawley succeeded in spiriting Grogan to safety on board a German ship preparing to leave port for Zanzibar.

Grogan's first African adventure was at an end.

FOUR

Grand Tour

O N BOARD SHIP Grogan had few opportunities to walk into
the same sort of trouble as he had encountered in the dance
hall in Beira. The only female passenger had 'passed the age
when not even Eve with a barrel-load of Ribston pippin apples could
have tempted anybody', although this did not prevent her from trying
to make the most of being surrounded by handsome young troopers.
When the men could bear her attentions no longer they called on the
help of her cabin steward, who obliged by hiding the lady's dentures
under her mattress. Thus deprived she confined herself to her cabin,
which became known as 'the hermitage',[1] for the remainder of the
journey to Zanzibar.

Grogan's arrival on the island towards the end of 1896 was certainly
stylish. The British Consul, Basil Cave, was a friend of the family and
on seeing Grogan's name on the passenger list he sent the Sultan's
launch to bring him ashore and install him in the Club – a welcome
change from the cramped, stuffy conditions on board ship. Once
settled in his new quarters it soon became apparent that Zanzibar was
an even thirstier spot than Beira; it was common knowledge that the
local padre had to be forcibly put in 'cold store' on Saturday evenings
to ensure his sobriety at matins the following day. Grogan's only
interest, however, was in hearing from Cave and the Sultan's First
Minister, General Sir Lloyd Mathews, about the dramatic recent hap-
penings on the island.

It was six years since the British government had declared a protectorate over the Sultan's domains in November 1890, thereby providing
further evidence of the rapidly rising tide of official, as opposed to
unofficial, interest in Africa. Foremost among the Foreign Office's
objectives were the desire to put an end to Zanzibar's substantial slave

trade (which would appease the liberals at home) and the need to counter German territorial ambitions in East Africa (which would appease the hawks). The following year British ambitions took a step closer to fulfilling these aims when their Agent, Gerald Portal, orchestrated a bloodless coup d'état and nominated Sayyid Hamid ibn Thuwain as Sultan.

While Grogan had been fighting in Matabeleland, however, the sultan had died and his cousin, Sayyid Khalid ibn Barghash, had seized the palace and proclaimed himself the rightful successor. In so doing he provided the Foreign Office with a pretext to consolidate its control of Zanzibar: no one had the right to succession without its stamp of approval. On 26 August, with five ships of the Royal Navy under Rear-Admiral Harry Rawson lying offshore, Khalid had been ordered to lower his flag. When he refused a single shell sank his sole 'battleship', the *Glasgow*, formerly a steamer on the Clyde. With the naval confrontation lost, Khalid hastily removed the harem from the palace which, after the expiry of another ultimatum, was heavily shelled by the British. Some 500 of Khalid's troops were killed.

The whole 'war' lasted just thirty-eight minutes, making it the shortest in history. It was akin to using a sledgehammer to crack a nut, but the British intended their message to be a clear one: the aim was to show both Khalid and the Germans on the mainland, who were suspected of siding with him, who wielded power in Zanzibar. The new sultan that they appointed, Hamoud ibn Muhammed, was promptly forced to declare the abolition of legal slavery.

In a bizarre incident indicative of the way that the Scramble, like the Great Game in Central Asia, was at times played out according to codes of conduct more redolent of a gentleman's club than a field of conflict Grogan was taken by Cave to meet the deposed Sultan in Dar-es-Salaam two days after his arrival. The German authorities, who greeted the British party politely, seemed uncertain what to do with their new guest, the more so now that the Navy had made it so abundantly clear that his return to Zanzibar as a German puppet was not an option. Grogan found the unfortunate Khalid to be 'depressed, as well he might be'. However unwavering his loyalty to the Empire he still regarded it as 'a sad day for Africa when these great Arab personalities lost their power', but added that 'no gentry hating usury and traditionally committed to unlimited hospitality could survive under modern circumstances'.[2] Those 'modern circumstances', as Grogan well knew, were that Britain and Germany were intend on carving up East Africa like a birthday cake as the Scramble for Africa intensified. And as far as he was concerned that was a competition that the Empire had to win at all costs; it was, as Rhodes was wont to say, 'the essential must of things'.

By the time Grogan set sail for London his health had again taken a turn for the worse and he only just reached Kirkella, the family home near Sevenoaks, before the worst hit him. Another excruciatingly painful liver abscess burst while he was lighting one of his favourite black cigars, and he also suffered recurrent bouts of the fever. Both afflictions – the price of his African adventure – were now with him for life. Grogan always bore them stoically and in silence, but there can be little doubt that such continual intimations of his own mortality prompted an ever-increasing, at times manic, desire for 'action'. This soon returned, and it was his Cambridge friend, Eddie Watt, who came to the rescue.

Watt had seen out his full term at Jesus, graduating with a BA in law just at the time that Grogan should have been doing the same (but was confronting the Matabele *impi* at the Umguza river instead). Now he was planning to return home to attend his sister Helen's marriage, but, unbeknownst to Grogan, Watt also had a hidden agenda. As undergraduates the two of them had often been invited by Watt's aunt, Caroline Eyres, to stay with her at Dumbleton Hall, and after the death of Grogan's mother it was 'Aunt Carrie' who had taken it upon herself to polish him and ensure that he learnt how to behave on a large estate. In a brief period of good health since his return from Africa Grogan had also been to stay with Mrs Eyres and her brother 'Harry' Sharp at Sligahan, a beautiful estate they had rented on the Isle of Skye with what he described as a 'treeless expanse of mountainous moorland, curiously termed a deer "forest"'. There he was placed under close observation while being taught to stalk deer, cast for salmon and play a decent game of whist.

Despite his headstrong rejection of the finer points of the rules of both whist and stalking, Grogan's good looks, easy charm and spark-ling conversation persuaded Mrs Eyres that she should pursue the next stage of a plan she had been hatching. To this end she had a quiet word with Eddie, who suggested that Grogan join him on the voyage to New Zealand. Grogan jumped at the invitation, anxious to do anything rather than remain in Kent, and again entrusted the care of his siblings to 'uncle' Walter. He was not aware that what lay behind the invitation was Mrs Eyres's specific intention that he should be introduced to Gertrude, the second of Eddie's three sisters.

The long sea voyage was uneventful, and gave Grogan the opportunity to recover his strength and good spirits. In Colombo he noted that it was difficult to tell the difference between the male and female Singhalese, while in Melbourne he counted the barmaids among the most beautiful he had ever seen. In other words, his attentions were never far from the fairer sex – which was exactly what the Watt family wanted. Finally, after more than two months at sea, Grogan was treated to the sight of the 'staggering grandeur'[3] of Milford Sound as the ship anchored off South Island. There he disembarked and took a smaller steamer round to Invercargill, whose dreariness was mitigated only by the fact that its oysters, 'nurtured in the clean waters of the South Pacific as opposed to being fattened on London sewage', cost ten shillings for a sack of a hundred dozen as against a shilling a dozen at Scott's in London. This was Grogan's first introduction to the 'endless commercial possibilities of New Zealand' after which, having feasted 'to the Plimsoll line',[4] he and Watt set out to do the rounds of their former contemporaries at Jesus.

The tour was to have as marked an effect on Grogan's ambitions as Rhodes's fireside soliloquies, and it defined his view of both the opportunities and the rewards that seemed to be there for the taking in the colonies. He was immensely impressed that wherever he went the land seemed to be being converted into 'a new edition of England', complete with English cattle, pigs, sheep and even bumble bees to pollinate the clover (developing, in the process, a big export trade in clover seed with Britain). It also made people wealthy: although Grogan was hardly a pauper, the affluence of his young farming friends was far greater than he had ever imagined when they were simply fellow undergraduates.

At the Teschmakers' substantial estate at Otago Grogan learned to crack a stock whip with the same aplomb as the Cape 'boy' who had driven his wagon from Cape Town to Bulawayo, and how to break in a horse; and at Teddy Grigg's 12,000-acre Longbeach ranch he observed how what had once been a swamp had been converted into prime pastureland through an extensive drainage programme. But nowhere was it more evident that the New Zealand pioneers, and their offspring, had done extremely well for themselves than at the Watts' house, Waititirau, perched atop the hill in Napier. This Mediterranean-style forty-roomed villa with its huge gardens, double tennis court protected by a windbreak of fir trees and fleet of servants had been built by Eddie Watt's father, James, at a cost of £7,000 – three times what Grogan's father had spent on his grand houses in London's Queens Gate.

What enthused Grogan most about this obvious prosperity of the Watts and other grandees of Hawke's Bay was that it had been won through hard graft and ingenuity. Furthermore, the fact that the New Zealand colonists were mostly of humble origin – and not 'Johnnies'[5] – appealed to a fiercely meritocratic streak in his nature. James Watt, the son of a Dundee merchant, was a prime example: when he had died in 1879, aged just forty-five, he was widely believed to have been one of the wealthiest men in New Zealand.[6]

Watt's seven-year marriage to Carrie Eyres's and Harry Sharp's sister, Hannah, left the latter with four small children – Eddie, Helen, Gertrude and Florence – as well as a very large inheritance. No clue remains as to how Hannah, the daughter of a wealthy landowner from Gilstead Hall in Yorkshire, came to be wooed by the self-made Watt, but having made Napier her home she was set on staying in New Zealand. Before long she was being courted by James Coleman, another pillar of Hawke's Bay society, and on 13 March 1880 the two were married.

Coleman was, like James Watt, a very successful entrepreneur.[7] An irrepressible, thick-set man with an enormous white walrus moustache, he had been forced to retire due to ill health some fifteen years before Grogan first met him, but Coleman showed about as much respect for the advice of doctors as Grogan, and was destined to live to the ripe old age of ninety-five. In his fifty-year 'retirement' he was a private investment banker. Each day he would descend the Napier hill to harass his solicitor, Mr Humphries of Cotterill & Humphries, and then proceed to dish out the same treatment to his banker; thereafter, this ebullient character would retire for the afternoon (and sometimes most of the night) to the Hawke's Bay Club. A cartoon of the period depicts Hannah patiently waiting well into the night by the fireside at Waititirau with his slippers.

Grogan relished the generous hospitality extended to him in the Coleman-Watt household. He was also, just as Carrie Eyres had hoped, instantly smitten by Gertrude. She was a tall girl – almost as tall as Grogan – with soft blue eyes and thick, lustrous brown hair, but what attracted Grogan most was her booming laugh, which was infectious, her serenity and the exceptionally warm heart that she had inherited from her mother.

Grogan's feelings were reciprocated. Gertrude had never met such a handsome and swashbuckling young man, nor had she ever been gazed upon by such an extraordinary pair of eyes. She also quickly noticed that whenever her brother's friend entered the room at Waititirau, no matter how many people were gathered there, he seemed to draw everyone to him like a magnet. He had the easy charm of a man supremely confident of his own abilities, a dry and sometimes wicked sense of humour, and a fund of thrilling stories from his time in the Alps and fighting with Cecil Rhodes. What's more, he was more articulate than anyone she'd ever met, and quite fearless. Of one thing she was certain: a life with Grogan would never be dull.

Grogan's mind turned as swiftly to marriage as his own father's had when he spied Jane from the window of his office in Piccadilly: within days the young couple were discussing the possibility of nuptials. But Grogan realized – indeed he had seen the evidence all about him since his arrival in New Zealand – that there was a glaring obstacle in his path. Everyone he had come across was a 'somebody'; all the local young men – the Teschmakers, the Griggs, Eddie Watt and the Lowrys of Okawa station (which dwarfed even Watt's Longlands station and into whose family Gertrude's sister Helen was marrying) – had their futures mapped out for them. Grogan, on the other hand, was aware that he had only 'enough to live on and move about the world but nothing to offer to family life except a skinful of amoeba, malaria germs and similar parasitic mementoes of the least healthy part of Africa plus a head full of vagrant ideas'.[8] Despite this he was not to be deterred, and decided to broach the subject of marriage with James Coleman.

As trustee of the sizeable inheritances left to the Watt children by their father, and being their stepfather, Coleman was keen to question Grogan about his prospects. He was far from ready for Grogan's breathtakingly audacious answer. Inspired by Rhodes's dream of a Cape to Cairo railway and telegraph – an imperial highway through Africa – and the fact that no man had ever surveyed the whole route, Grogan declared his intention to make his name by undertaking the first south to north traverse of Africa. According to Grogan's nephew, the following exchange then ensued:

> Coleman shuffled. 'I can only presume that you are try-ing to be funny. If so, I do not appreciate it.'
>
> 'Oh no, sir. Certainly not. I am quite serious – never more so.'
>
> 'Then you must be a fool! You mean to say that you really contemplate crossing the entire continent of Africa? My good man, do you realise what that would mean?'
>
> 'Perfectly.'
>
> 'Then tell me: how would you propose to cross the jungles of Central Africa? They are impenetrable. Stanley managed to traverse certain districts by water, but he took an armed guard of several hundred to beat off the native tribes. There are no rivers, not even ox-wagon transport, in many of the areas you would cross. *You* would have to travel largely on foot. What chance would you stand? Surely you don't place yourself above Stanley! You would need a small army to see you through; that would be your only hope!'
>
> 'I don't agree, sir,' Grogan argued. 'On the contrary a large expedition might arouse suspicion and antagonism, and would probably fail on that account alone. I believe that, if I were to make the attempt with just a small party of *askaris* and porters, I might get through. Anyhow I mean to try. After all, if I fail nothing is lost. On the other hand, if I succeed – well, I shall hope to have proved worthy of your stepdaughter.'[9]

Sceptical though Coleman was about Grogan's chances of success in his extraordinary undertaking, he could not help but admire his pluck. Besides, he had rather taken to his stepdaughter's suitor. The two men shared many interests, foremost among them a love of rifle shooting,[10] and as a self-made man Coleman was not minded to dismiss Grogan's scheme for proving himself 'something of a somebody'[11] out of hand. A few days later Grogan said his farewells to Gertrude and her family in Napier, and set out for home.

He chose the longest route. Not only was he keen to cross the Pacific, but he also needed time to think about the challenge that he had set himself. In fact, by the time his steamer put into the Bay of Apia, in the Samoan Islands, he appears to have been in no hurry whatsoever: rather than continue on board the steamer he eagerly accepted the invitation of a wild Irish-American to join him on board his copra trading schooner. 'Captain Pat' was, according to Grogan, 'a somebody, and a rather peculiar one'[12] and was making his last trip to Honolulu to sell the schooner and hang up his seaboots.

Captain Pat knew *everyone* along their route. When the schooner eventually reached Honolulu, Grogan was introduced to no less a personage than Prince David, heir to the throne of the Hawaiian Islands, who entertained his guests lavishly. This 'charming fellow' even tried to persuade Grogan to stay for good, and offered him a piece of land adjacent to what later became Pearl Harbor. Grogan declined the offer, but not without regret: he had greatly enjoyed meeting the Pacific islanders and envied them the apparent simplicity of their lives. They had, he remarked, 'learnt the soothing art of doing nothing, and *never* doing it in a hurry'[13] – something he was far from good at. But he knew he had to press on and after a short stay he and Captain Pat left 'the lotus land'[14] on a steamer bound for San Francisco – and more 'further education'.

The tempo of life in the brash west coast city was very different from anything that Grogan had encountered before, and a particularly marked contrast to what he had left behind him in the Pacific. Everybody was in a hurry, and nobody seemed to have time to do anything *because* they were in such a hurry. The bars never closed, and newspaper boys were out on the street at 4 a.m. hollering about the latest murder. There were compensations for the frenetic pace: Californian hospitality matched Prince David's – although it was of a rather different kind. As soon as Grogan had booked in to the best hotel he could find he was taken out on the town by Captain Pat to meet some of his 'boys'. The introductions effected, the Irish skipper inexplicably disappeared, but before abandoning Grogan he offered an ominous-sounding piece of advice: that on a night out with the 'boys' it was advisable to jot down the names of the last three cocktails consumed on one's cuff and then recite them in order to the next barman encountered, who would duly prescribe what should come next. That way, Pat assured him, 'you should reach your hotel under your own steam and intact'.[15] When Grogan duly returned to his hotel at 5 a.m. the following morning he had to admit that the Captain Pat technique was sound. The list of 'Bosom Caresses', 'Helps To Heaven' and 'Coffin Busters' which had begun on his cuff reached almost to his elbow – but he was still upright.

A few nights later Grogan was also treated to a tour of the seamier side of the city by the Chief of Police, a fellow Irishman and one of Captain Pat's 'boys'. It began in the red light district, which did not impress Grogan. He found the long line of dimly lit windows displaying bored ladies of every race on the globe 'the living negative of the glory of mating love', and rated it well below what he had admiringly observed in Paris as a schoolboy (but well above the 'furtive Piccadilly bobby-and-tart game of hide-and-seek'[16] of the streets of London). After the red light district he was taken to Chinatown for a one dollar dinner at the suspiciously nicknamed 'Puppy Dog' restaurant, and from there to the opium dens – an 'indescribable scene of human degradation'.[17]

The last experience of Grogan's unorthodox journey home ended with an incident with which he was only too familiar. He decided on his last day in San Francisco to revisit the 'Puppy Dog', in defiance of a warning from the Chief of Police that white people walking alone in Chinatown had a nasty habit of disappearing. Arriving in the late afternoon, he noticed that he was the only person in the restaurant except for the waitresses and a minatory character who took up a position between him and the stairs down to the street. Grogan immediately scented trouble of the Beira dance-hall variety, rose slowly from his table and sauntered over towards this man. As soon as he was close enough he launched a pre-emptive attack, giving him 'the best of my right and left and a hard kick where it hurts'.[18] The man fell to the ground, and Grogan bounded down the stairs. As he reached the door a pair of knives thudded into the woodwork by his shoulder. He dashed out into the street, and made straight for the steamer home.

Back in London, Grogan wasn't the only maverick adventurer pondering his future: Winston Churchill, twelve days his senior, had just delivered his maiden political speech near Bath, and his words featured in most of the newspapers. Churchill had declared:

> There are not wanting those who say that in this Jubilee
> year our Empire has reached the height of its glory and
> power, and that we now should begin to decline, as Babylon,
> Carthage, and Rome declined. Do not believe these croak-
> ers, but give the lie to their dismal croaking by showing
> by our actions that the vigour and vitality of our race is
> unimpaired and our determination is to uphold the Empire
> . . . and carry out our mission of bearing peace, civilization,
> and good government to the uttermost ends of the earth.

This paean to Empire could well have issued from Grogan's own mouth, but the two men were, more often than not, to find themselves in opposition over the coming decades of their eventful lives.

There were considerable similarities between Grogan and Churchill. Both were ambitious thrusters who were easily bored; both were well-connected, anti-authoritarian when authority didn't suit their personal agenda and bumptious. They shared a love of words, drawn from reading voluminously, and a growing skill for deploying their vocabularies to great effect. Churchill's schoolboy prowess at fencing was matched by Grogan's skill with a rifle; and just as Grogan had already proved his courage with his exploits in the Alps and Matabele-land, so Churchill had fought with distinction on the North-West

Frontier before embarking on a literary career based on despatches from the war in Cuba and India. Both men were bent on seeking the pecuniary wherewithal to pursue their grandiose ambitions.

Much was happening in the rapidly expanding Empire to foster their ambitions. Even the perceptive and highly intellectual Lord Salisbury, three times Britain's Prime Minister during the most hectic years of the Scramble, declared himself unsure of the cause of this 'sudden revolution'. Everywhere there was action, and action spelt opportunity. For Grogan the most important news gleaned on his return from his Grand Tour of the Pacific concerned Rhodes, the man who had exhorted him to give himself to Africa. In his absence it seemed that the criticism Rhodes had attracted after Jameson's attempt to invade the Transvaal had all but evaporated. British pride had been badly damaged by what was now perceived as the humiliation of Jameson's troopers at the hands of President Kruger, and patriotic passions were further aroused by French and German expressions of sympathy for the Boers. As tensions between the Great Powers escalated, the Raid soon came to be regarded throughout the British Empire as a decidedly heroic episode.

Grogan approved of this development wholeheartedly, and was far from alone in not seeing what all the original fuss in London had been about. He had only ever seen Rhodes at his magnetic best, seemingly fighting his way out of a corner in the name of Empire, and regarded Rhodes as the key to unlocking Britain's 'destiny' in Africa. He wasn't even convinced that Rhodes had ordered the Raid in the first place, for one simple reason: it failed, and as far as he was concerned Rhodes never failed. Even if he *had* ordered it, Grogan thought Rhodes had had ample justification for planning 'a desperate stroke to force the British government to act [to protect the Empire's interests in South Africa against Kruger and his German allies] before it was too late'.[19] Such was the faith of Grogan, and a generation of young imperialists, in Cecil Rhodes.

Grogan, and indeed the British public, were unaware of the extent to which Rhodes had stage-managed his political rehabilitation, supported by jingoistic exhortations from *The Times*. By the time Rhodes faced the House of Commons inquiry charged with investigating his part in ordering the Raid – a few months prior to Grogan's return from New Zealand – he had squared almost everyone of influence who could possibly have brought him to account. Even the twelve-man committee, with the exception of Liberals Sir William Harcourt and Henry Labouchère, comprised Rhodes sympathizers, thereby guaranteeing him an easy ride and earning the inquiry the nickname of 'the lying-in-state at Westminster'.

Rhodes did admit to supporting the cause of the Uitlanders in Johannesburg; he also did not attempt to deny all foreknowledge of the Raid (but asserted that Jameson had in the end acted without his authority). On the other hand, he withheld, and was not pressed to divulge, certain key facts about both his role and that of the Colonial Secretary, Chamberlain, who was himself a member of the select committee. Chamberlain had tacitly supported Rhodes's plans, a fact which – if it had become known – might well have forced his resignation from the government. Instead Rhodes sold his silence on this delicate matter in exchange for assurances that he would retain his all-important Royal Charter.

The lack of rigour displayed by the inquiry into what amounted to a criminal attempt to hijack the independent Boer Republic of the Transvaal was indicative of the changing political climate in Europe, Britain and South Africa. In the year of Queen Victoria's Diamond Jubilee, with the Marquess of Salisbury's Conservative–Liberal Unionist government in power, the imperialist Chamberlain at the Colonial Office and the Scramble for Africa intensifying by the month, Rhodes had become – quite simply – what the British government and public wanted. At the end of April he returned to Cape Town, with Grogan's friend and former 'bloody trooper' Bobby Coryndon among his entourage, without even waiting to hear the inquiry's conclusions. When delivered, they amounted to a qualified censure: Rhodes had to resign as Prime Minister of Cape Colony and stand down from the chairmanship of the Chartered Company. Neither 'loss' mattered a jot to him: he had kept his Royal Charter, and that was all that mattered for the fulfilment of his immediate ambitions.

Rhodes's virtual exoneration was extremely significant for Grogan. What had been fanciful (or, in James Coleman's opinion, ludicrous) talk about a Cape to Cairo 'imperial highway' became a distinct possibility. The appointment of arch-imperialist Sir Alfred Milner as

Governor of Cape Colony in May 1897 was a further signal that Rhodes's and the British government's ambitions had become largely synonymous. That Rhodes knew as much was confirmed by the flurry of activity following his return to Cape Town. At his behest Lawley, Grogan's saviour in Beira, drove the railway at his customary rate of a mile a day from Mafeking to Bulawayo by the end of October 1897; Bobby Coryndon was installed as Governor of Northern Rhodesia with the brief of preparing the way for the next northward stage of construction; and Dr Jameson, with his reputation largely untarnished, returned to southern Africa and was charged by Rhodes with supervising the work on the telegraph line.

In North Africa there were also developments which played into Grogan's hands. In 1897 General Kitchener had been despatched from the British Protectorate of Egypt with the intention of retaking the Sudan, lost to the Dervishes eleven years earlier, and forestalling French and Belgian ambitions in the Bahr-al-Ghazal region of the Upper Nile (which threatened British control of Egypt and therefore the trade route to India). So just as Milner and Rhodes were bent on extending the Empire's reach northwards, Kitchener was driving the railway south from Wadi Halfa. Grogan summed up the situation by observing that 'the stew pan of Africa was evidently simmering and liable to froth and boil at any moment'; it was, he added, all 'very intoxicating stuff'.[20] Suddenly it seemed as though his dream of traversing the continent and, most importantly, being the first man comprehensively to survey the area of central Africa through which the railway and telegraph would have to pass, was now a matter of imperial necessity as well as the means of proving himself worthy of Gertrude's hand.

Two things concerned Grogan. The first was that he could not be sure that he would get to central Africa before anyone else, and he was absolutely determined to be the first to traverse the region. To try and allay his fears on this score he consulted friends at the Foreign Office. From them he learnt that there were any number of expeditions underway in north-east Africa. A 'secret' one led by Major James Macdonald had set out from Mombasa for the headwaters of the Nile in an attempt, like Kitchener's, to head off a French thrust at the Upper Nile being led by Captain Jean-Baptiste Marchand. Colonel

Matyr was also planning to carry a portable steam launch from the East African coast to Lake Albert, whence he intended to descend the Nile to intercept Marchand. But no one, it seemed, was planning to strike due north from Lake Tanganyika to the Nile. Such an expedition, Grogan's Foreign Office friends were sure, was tantamount to committing suicide. The warning only served to harden Grogan's resolve.

Grogan's second problem was money: his expedition would require lots of it. Unsure how he might muster the necessary wherewithal, he decided to pay a visit to Carrie Eyres to seek advice. The trip to Dumbleton Hall proved more successful than he could have dared hope. After listening to Grogan's plans Mrs Eyres pronounced herself willing to give him every assistance in proving to James Coleman that he had a future, and was worthy of Gertrude's hand. It was, after all, she who had sought to bring the two of them together in the first place. There was an additional reason for her enthusiasm: she was worried about her brother. The very laid-back Harry Sharp was, as Grogan put it, 'bored with the dismal day to day life of the ultra-rich'. He had been called to the Bar after graduating from Jesus in the early 1880s, but had never practised and never married. In short, he needed something to imbue him with a sense of purpose in life, and accompanying Grogan on his expedition sounded like just the ticket to his sister.

Armed with his new patron's promise of generous financial support and the companionship of Sharp, Grogan hastily set to work on plotting the finer details of his 'short cut to fame'.[21]

FIVE

Towards the Great Unknown

Amongst the few trusted friends in whom they confided, Grogan and Sharp's plans were greeted with amazement. The difficulties confronting them were immense, but Grogan believed implicitly, with 'the arrogance of youth', that 'difficulties are a figment of the imagination and tend to dissolve when squarely faced or can be toddled round'.[1] He was convinced that he had the courage and requisite qualities of leadership to succeed, not to mention the luck of his Irish cousins. That is not to say that he was cavalier about the challenge that lay ahead: he set about the meticulous planning vital to the success of any expedition with a thoroughness that would have greatly impressed, and surprised, the Fellows of Jesus College.

This lengthy process began as soon as he returned to London from Dumbleton Hall and took months to complete. Mountains of supplies and equipment had to be ordered, and their shipment to Africa arranged; there were rifles and ammunition to be bought; and many a new skill to be learnt. Grogan and Sharp both underwent a crash course in map-making from Mr Coles, the Map Curator at the Royal Geographical Society, and Grogan immersed himself in every book about African travel that he could lay his hands on. He also called on as many 'old hands' as would see him. The most helpful of these was Frederick Lugard,[2] a veteran of expeditions in east and west Africa, who had been instrumental in persuading the British government to declare Uganda a protectorate in 1894.

At the end of January 1898 the two men were finally ready to depart, intoxicated by the peculiarly – although not exclusively – British desire to conquer 'the unknown' without regard for any considerations of personal safety. One month later, 'in the company of sundry German officers and beer enthusiasts, [they] took part in the usual D.O.A. Liner's manoeuvre of violently charging a sandbank in the bay of Beira on a flood-tide, to the ear-smashing accompaniment of the German National Anthem'.[3]

As far as Grogan was concerned he had already completed the Cape Town to Beira leg of his expedition in 1896, so it was from Beira that he was restarting his quest for the Empire, Rhodes and Gertrude. His over-riding impression of 'Satan's summer palace' was that, although it had grown beyond recognition, little else had changed in his absence. He was greeted by the same old Lawley, and on a tour of the city observed that Portuguese 'ruffians' still fired volleys down the main streets at night; that the death rate from malaria and other afflictions was still appalling; that the administration was still corrupt; and the townsfolk still thirsty.

Grogan's first objective was to organize a lengthy hunting trip. He was not only keen to pursue his childhood hunting ambitions which had been thwarted by ill health on his previous visit to Portuguese East Africa, but also to establish a feint in order to keep his aim of achieving the first south–north traverse of Africa secret. Time was not of the essence. Even though Marchand had long since set out from the west coast of Africa for Fashoda, and Grogan still entertained a fanciful hope of beating the Frenchman to the Upper Nile, no one – least of all the French government – had any clue where Marchand actually was. Grogan was fully justified in believing that he had years, rather than months, in hand. Moreover, all the advice that had been drummed into him by the likes of Lugard was predicated on the need to allow a period of acclimatization before setting off on the journey proper. Grogan took this advice seriously, however impetuous his nature: he had already learnt enough about Africa to realize the good sense of the Swahili proverb *'mwenda mbio hujikwaa dole'* – 'he who hurries stubs his toe'.

The first hunting foray was not a great success. Grogan and Sharp took the train to Umtali, on the border between Rhodesia and Portuguese East Africa, and then hired a wagon to transport them to the Sabi river where they had heard there were plenty of lion. After a number of days they arrived on foot at chief Mtambara's *kraal*, on the Umvumvumvu stream, and from there struck out for the Udzi into which it flowed, accompanied by 'Jim', Mtambara's son. It was then a two-day walk until they reached the edge of the high veld, below which lay 'the bush-clad plain of the Udzi, a carpet of green picked out with the occasional silver of the river itself, and in the hazy distance stretched an unbroken range of purple hills, backed by the silvery green and dull smoke-red of sunset'.[4] Striking though the scenery was, there were few signs of lion. Sharp missed the only one they saw, and the two men decided that it would be better to try Grogan's former hunting grounds on the fever-ridden Pungwe flats.

While Sharp went back to Mtambara's to collect the bulk of their loads, Grogan struck out cross country for Umtali, where he hoped to find a wagon to collect Sharp and some of their porters who were ill. It was, he knew, of the utmost importance that he put his own health to the test as soon as possible, and after an initial hike of twenty miles up the Udzi he managed to cover, with his trademark loping swagger, a further sixty-mile stretch in just nineteen hours to reach the town and gulp down a memorable brandy and soda. But no sooner had he seemingly proved himself 'fully operational' and sent a wagon for Sharp than he was struck by the fever. This confirmed Grogan's worst fears: fever was going to be a constant companion.

Two days later Grogan was a little stronger and he was well enough to attend a concert for the opening of Umtali's newest hotel. Grogan dismissively described the event as 'a typical South African orgie'. As he had learnt during the Matabele campaign, Africa attracted a mixed bunch, all of whom seemed to be represented in Umtali. He observed 'faces yellow with fever, faces coppered by the sun, faces roseate with drink, and faces scarred, keen, money-lustful, and stamped with every vice and some of the virtues'; and concluded that a 'pat-on-the-back-kick-you-when-you're-not-looking air permeated everything'.[5] This was truly frontier territory, where the booze flowed freely and stories of shooting lions even more freely. Grogan did not think much of it, and departed at the first opportunity to rendezvous with Sharp at Fontesvilla.

Fontesvilla was another place in which Grogan had no wish to linger. It was there, eighteen months earlier, that he had been dumped half-dead in the railway truck bound for Beira. He and Sharp, accompanied by Portuguese East Africa's leading 'Nimrod', Dan Mahony, left the town as soon as they could and headed north-west along the

Urema river. This second hunting trip proved rather more eventful than the first, thanks to Mahony's intimate knowledge of the area. Sharp, much to his companion's chagrin, shot his first lion soon after the party had set up camp and Grogan, 'in a frenzy of desire',[6] was determined to even the score as soon as possible. He did not have to wait long: by the end of the following day he and Sharp were even, and the first of Grogan's childhood ambitions was fulfilled.

The two men spent three weeks with Mahony on the Pungwe flats. They shot a prodigious quantity of game, even though the vast herds of buffalo which Grogan had encountered on his previous trip had disappeared – the victims of rinderpest and hunters. Each day their bush-craft skills improved, they learnt more about managing their small team of porters, and they confronted new challenges. On one occasion Grogan narrowly missed stepping on the head of a fourteen-foot python which, once shot, took eight men to straighten out. On another Mahony led him across a crocodile-infested river in pursuit of waterbuck. Other less life-threatening trials arose from their porters' understandable lack of familiarity with the idiosyncrasies of Victorian gentlemen. A request for soap produced, in slow succession, a bottle of Worcestershire sauce ('without which life,' Grogan declared, 'or rather native cookery, is intolerable')[7]; a pair of pyjamas; and some boot-trees. A call for cocoa saw the cook place cups of water in the fire and the kettle on the breakfast-table. 'Thus', Grogan wrote, 'passed many delightful days.'[8] On 22 May the party struck camp and marched away from the flats via a bridge of tangled vegetation over a deep stream through which, at one point, the portly Sharp vanished. Fortunately, he was rescued before the hippos and crocodiles lurking below had time to respond to the arrival in their midst of an unexpected tasty morsel, and the men reached Fontesvilla without further mishap.

Grogan could not resist one final attempt to find buffalo before continuing north. This time Mahony, Grogan and Sharp followed the Pungwe river, rather than the Urema, north-west to the extremities of Gorongoza's plain, and the sight which greeted them on arrival fulfilled Grogan's wildest dreams. There were enormous quantities of game. Where the plain was at its widest, back in the direction of the Urema, the estimated headcount was between forty and fifty thousand, mostly of blue wildebeest, which parted as the group advanced and

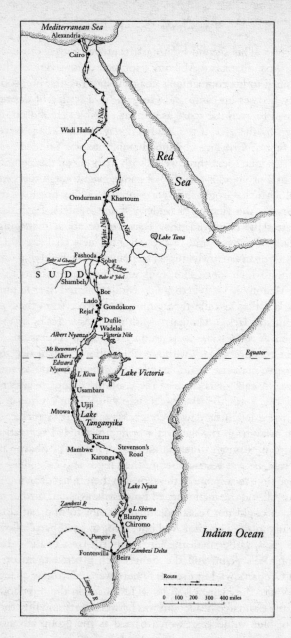

Grogan's Route from Beira to Cairo

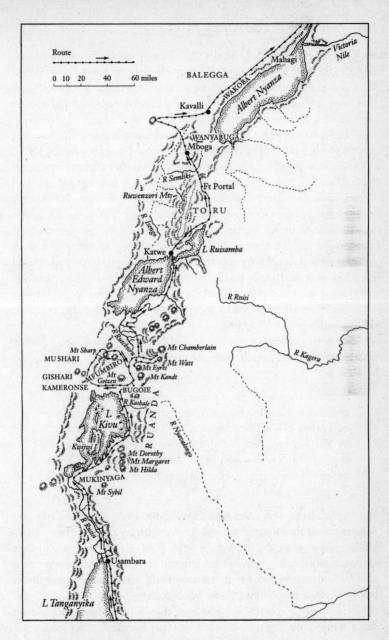

Grogan's Route through the Central Lakes Region

then closed ranks again behind them. The opportunities were countless. On the first day Grogan and Sharp chased three eland, unsuccessfully, for eight miles before pitching camp in the late afternoon; and that same evening Sharp brought down four buffalo with his double .303 as they emerged from a *donga*.

The buffalo, most dangerous of all African mammals, were not always so obliging. A few days later Sharp and Grogan went on ahead of their caravan and between them dropped another from a large herd. As they approached it the 'dead' buffalo suddenly rose up and charged from a distance of thirty yards. Grogan fired both barrels into its chest to no effect before turning on his heels, but Sharp, in Grogan's opinion, 'had not yet learned his buffalo' and stood his ground as if receiving a cavalry charge. He fired a single shot, and the buffalo rolled to a stop just three yards short of him. Grogan was struck dumb. He knew that Sharp only had soft-nosed .303 bullets and had put odds of 'ninety-nine to one on the buffalo'. 'Now,' he mused, 'Sharp knows his buffalo, and is prepared to back himself, when one turns nasty, to do his hundred in $9\frac{4}{5}$ seconds.'[9]

The men returned, triumphant and relieved, with Sharp's trophy to a riverside camp which Mahony had pitched in

> the most perfect spot imaginable ... in all directions we could see herds of game grazing; flocks of fowl flighted up and down the watercourse, huge crocodiles leered evilly at us as they floated like logs on the oily water, broken only by the plomp-plomp of the numerous fish, and now and then the head of a mud-turtle rose like a ghost from below, without even a ripple, drew a long hissing breath, then as silently vanished.

But by night the new camp was a less idyllic spot: the whine of ever-present mosquitoes lasted till dawn, and curious and vociferous lions circled just beyond the light cast by the fires. To his great annoyance Grogan also lost his collapsible bath and best waterbuck trophy to a raid by hyaenas, but was compensated within days by bringing down two lion measuring 9 foot 10½ inches and 10 foot 4 inches respectively.

New hazards continued to present themselves. Sharp was laid up for a while with jiggers[10] in his foot, and during his convalescence vowed never to eat local 'duck' eggs again after one of them hatched prior to cooking to reveal a baby crocodile (which hissed its disapproval at being so rudely disturbed). Grogan was charged by a herd of zebras being rounded up by lions, and he learnt not to taunt a porcupine when he was skewered through the big toe and leg. One of the porters suffered the same misfortune, and died two days later from blood-poisoning. It was the safari's first fatality, and one which Grogan was powerless to prevent. Soon afterwards his rudimentary medical skills were again put to the test.

Stumbling one day across the camp of two men collecting trophies for the British Museum, Grogan was taken to inspect a porter who had been bitten on the finger by a puff-adder. The man was delirious and close to death, so Grogan opted for extreme measures: he arrested the circulation in the bitten finger with the use of some string, slit it open, and exploded some gunpowder in it. Repeated injections of permanganate of potash were also administered, but to no avail: the whole of the patient's left side continued to swell until it assumed elephantine proportions. An even more desperate remedy was obviously called for; this involved plunging the man's hand in boiling water and permanganate until the skin peeled off. Then, and only then, did the swelling start to subside, and by the next morning the man was starting to recover. Such were the horrors of bush medicine.

Grogan and Sharp were loath to end their hunting, but decided that three months of acclimatization was sufficient and that it was time to return to Beira. They were satisfied that they had not only successfully established a feint to anyone curious about what they were doing in Africa, but also that they had completed an important rite of passage. Big game hunters were idolized in Europe and America, and there was a widespread belief that stalking large prey was the surest way of teaching a man to shoot straight, as well as being good exercise and an outlet for emotions which, if suppressed, could prove 'dangerous'. The trophies and specimens Grogan and Sharp collected for the curious curators of various museums were also a 'banker', helping to defray the substantial costs of the expedition. That said, Grogan was not completely blind to the disastrous consequences for Africa's wildlife of over-zealous hunting, as would become clear in the aftermath of his great trek.

After paying off the porters in Beira Grogan and Sharp had to make a 750-mile detour by steamer to Durban to stock up on supplies, purchase more .303s, and obtain the time and rate for their all-important chronometer (which Grogan had inadvertently allowed to run down during a bout of fever) before continuing north. A few weeks later they were back in Portuguese East Africa and boarded the paddle steamer *Peters* for the short journey up the coast to Chinde, at the mouth of the Zambezi. Disastrous news awaited them there: all their heavy luggage had been loaded on the wrong vessel and was on its way goodness knew where. It was eventually discovered in Delagoa Bay (today's Maputo) and sent after them, minus their full-plate camera and sundry other prized possessions.

The delay was to cost six weeks. In the meantime Chinde hardly seemed the place to wait as 'there was nowhere to go and nothing to shoot'.[11] So Grogan decided they should head off up the Zambezi to Chiromo, at the junction of the Ruo and Shiré rivers.

It was fortunate for Grogan and Sharp that they had shared their passage on the *Peters* with Mr Mohun of the Congo Telegraph Company, who was leading a large survey party westwards. Hearing of the plight of his fellow passengers Mohun lent them a tent and other essential items so that they could proceed to Chiromo while waiting for their own luggage to catch up with them.

The journey up the Zambezi was slow and the scenery monotonous. After passing the coconut plantations of the delta there weren't even any trees to be seen above the high banks of the crocodile-infested river. As far as the sanguinary Grogan could tell there seemed to be no game either, and the tedium was broken only by being regularly stranded on sandbanks. When the *Peters* reached the junction with the Shiré Grogan and Sharp bade farewell to Mohun, and transferred onto an 'animated tea-tray, by courtesy called a steamer'[12] for the rest of the journey to Chiromo. Among the discomforts that his vessel presented was a marked dearth of food: three skinny chickens and a few tins of sardines were the entire ration for the five European passengers for two and a half days.

Chiromo ('the joining of the streams') was the gateway to Nyasaland, the British Protectorate of Central Africa. Scottish missionaries and businessmen had been responsible for bringing the territory within the British 'sphere of influence' following Livingstone's exploration of the territory, but it had not been formally declared a protectorate until seven years before Grogan's arrival when famed Africa hand Harry Johnston was appointed its first commissioner, charged with crushing the activities of Arab slavers. Rhodes had had a hand in this theatre of the Scramble too: although his Chartered Company was denied outright control of Nyasaland by the stentorian protestations of missionary bodies, he financed Johnston's expedition and took a substantial stake in the African Lakes Corporation, the country's foremost commercial organization. Thus, not for the first time, Rhodes had secured a position of great influence via the back door.

The return to British territory was welcomed by Grogan, for whom Nyasaland would prove as influential as New Zealand in shaping his views about what constituted 'constructive colonization'. Chiromo was not without its perils: fever was endemic due to its proximity to the huge Elephant Marsh, as was a rare form of beri-beri. Lions also roamed the streets at night; notwithstanding all this, Grogan found a degree of order about the place which he considered to be a benchmark against which all other colonies should be measured.

His host was Mr MacDonald, the vice-consul, whose house appeared to be the only cool place in all Chiromo – temperatures in the shade regularly reached 120°F. MacDonald had been born in Nyasaland and was in Grogan's opinion a 'proper' administrator, 'the true type of one of the mighty nations that are now forming in serried ranks round the old mother-country preparatory to striding forth together – a combination such as the world has never dreamt of; a combination that will rapidly carry the principles of justice and progress into the uttermost ends of the earth'.[13] His good humour and hospitality were to go a long way towards easing the annoyance caused by the enforced delay at Chiromo; furthermore, after the privations of the journey from the coast, MacDonald proved himself able to provide a magnificent piscatory dinner simply by firing a .303 round into the river.

Grogan spent much of his time observing and making notes about the economic potential of Nyasaland, which Harry Johnston had described as 'the Cinderella among the African protectorates'. His meticulous attention to detail attests to his increasing interest in business (as well as a streak of pedantry). Thus, when describing a company extracting fibre from *sensebrea* he noted the type of machinery used (a Foulke's patent fibre-cleaning machine); the type of *sensebrea* (*S. cylindrica* and *S. guiniensis*); the average length and diameter of the leaves; how they were treated; and the exact costs of production. Of equal interest to him were the sugar plantations; the brickworks of the African Flotilla Company; and the fast-growing coffee industry which was fuelling the growth of Chiromo as the river port for the protectorate. 'The fact is', he concluded with an eye to the future, 'that Africa is supinely neglected where it cannot flaunt the magic war-cry, Gold.'[14]

While conducting his survey of the local economy Grogan heard that there were rhino in the vicinity of Mount Chiperoni, some forty miles south-east of Chiromo, and immediately set aside his notebook. MacDonald provided him with porters for an expedition, but told him that permits could only be obtained from the Portuguese administration across the river. Grogan was momentarily concerned about this: in the absence of his luggage he had very few clothes and had learnt that with the Portuguese, as with African dignitaries, appearance meant everything. With that in mind he collected whatever appropriate items he could find in Chiromo and eventually was rowed across the Shiré to the Portuguese side resplendent in spurs, a red and white medal ribbon torn from a pin-cushion and a Number 6 helmet. The necessary permits were easily secured over a whisky and soda.

After an initial (fruitless) sally in the direction of Zoa, Sharp left Grogan in order to go on ahead and start the laborious process of hiring porters for the crossing of the Tanganyika plateau, so missing the excitement of Grogan's first encounter with a bull rhino, near Chiperoni. Grogan successfully brought down his quarry – but only after a two-and-a-half-hour chase. His first shot with a four bore had penetrated two feet, shattering the rhino's shoulder in the process, yet it still required two further shots with the four bore and three solid .303 bullets to finish the hapless beast. The second of his coveted

African prizes was Grogan's, and soon afterwards, to his equal satisfaction, a messenger arrived to tell him that the baggage had finally arrived at Chiromo. He hurried back to begin the journey north to meet Sharp.

On 28 November 1898, exactly eight months after arriving in Beira, Grogan boarded the *Scott* for the passage up the Shiré towards Lake Nyasa (today's Lake Malawi). The disappearance of the baggage had cost six weeks, but he took the delay in his stride: 'such', he wrote, 'is African travel'.[15] He was equally unperturbed by the fact that the passengers had to take charge of the steamer as the skipper was down with the fever. The responsibility did not fall to Grogan alone: Mac-Donald was also on board, as was Alfred Sharpe, the vice-consul of Nyasaland. Another fellow passenger, whom Grogan held in utter contempt as the sort of 'Bible-flaunting, prayer-moaning ... evangelical madman who should be caged, or at least prevented from running loose amongst the natives',[16] was apparently not asked to help.

The first stop on the Shiré was at Makwira's *kraal*. Makwira was an 'old rogue ... of no little acumen',[17] of whom Grogan approved as thoroughly as he did of 'rollicking Zulus'.[18] At the *kraal* Grogan bade a fond farewell to MacDonald and Sharpe and disembarked a few hours later at the point where the Shiré ceased to be navigable because of rapids. While his men were ferrying their loads to the top of the rapids, Grogan headed off alone up the track towards Blantyre, the commercial centre of Nyasaland's highlands. The sun was just setting and the view back down the Shiré valley was as striking as anything he had yet seen. All around him were lush woodlands, green grass carpeted with millions of crocus-like purple flowers, and well-ordered coffee plantations in blossom. It was cooler on the plateau, and for a fleeting moment he thought he might be back in Kent.

After three days in Blantyre, Grogan started out for Zomba, the administrative capital. The town further convinced him that Nyasaland offered 'an unrivalled opening for British capital':[19] rubber, coffee and cocoa plantations were all thriving. What's more, Zomba boasted magnificent views west over forests to Lake Shirwa (Lake Chilwa), and a Government House set amid a tropical garden in which Grogan was invited to tea and tennis parties by the administration's Mr Bowring. It was only with the utmost reluctance that after recovering from another bout of fever he continued the journey towards Liwonde and thereafter to Lake Nyasa.

At Liwonde he boarded the *Monteith* for Fort Johnston and crossed Lake Pamalomba, on which – he was warned – marsh gas was likely to ignite if anyone absent-mindedly lit a match. From Fort Johnston he then took the *Domira* for passage up Lake Nyasa. On the first day out he was intrigued to see that Monkey Bay resembled his old haunts in the Pacific: there was white sand along the shore, the water was crystal clear, and he observed 'picturesque groups of natives . . . scattered about the beach, and the little piccaninnies playing on the skeleton of a wrecked Arab dhow, little dreaming what that dhow had meant to their fathers a few years before'.[20]

On arrival at Florence Bay Grogan was invited by a Miss MacCallum to visit the Livingstone Mission at Mount Waller. Grogan accepted, despite the fact that his views on missionary activity in Africa were (like his opinions on most things) forthright; they were also, by this point in his trek, set in stone. He was, 'given the appalling state of misery at home', adamant that it was 'a dastardly impertinence' for anyone – be they missionary or administrator – to presume they had the right to 'upset the, in many cases, admirable state of society in Africa';[21] and he was particularly scathing about those who sought to tamper with traditional customs and rituals. This non-interventionist approach may have conveniently overlooked the fact that the very presence of the white man was bound to 'upset' African societies – but it was nevertheless, by the standards of the time, quite an enlightened viewpoint.

Despite his misgivings Grogan was impressed by the Livingstone Mission, for the simple reason that it seemed to concentrate less on evangelical activity and more on teaching practical skills such as printing, carpentry, farming and quarrying to anyone interested in learning them. One student presented him with a folding chair for the long journey ahead, and Miss MacCallum loaded him to the gunwales with fresh butter and huge watermelons produced on the mission's farm.

Grogan returned to the *Domira* in high spirits and the next day reached Karonga's *kraal*, within striking distance of the start of the 'Stevenson Road', the track through the dense bush of the Tanganyika plateau to Lake Tanganyika itself. Of Sharp, with whom he was meant to rendezvous at Karonga's, there was no sign.

It did not take Grogan long to discover that Sharp had decided to go on to Lake Tanganyika in order to arrange their transport north. He had taken as many loads as he could manage, but owing to the simultaneous presence in the region of Mr Mohun's telegraph expedition porters were hard to come by. It was also the sowing season, which meant that Grogan's men, having fulfilled their contracts, left him for their homes further south. Stranded with most of the loads and no porters, Grogan was forced to stay put for six weeks.

Ever the doer, he immediately set about repacking all the baggage to kill time. He had not fully inspected the loads since Beira and now found that his London agent had done a shocking job. Bars of chocolate (as indispensable to Grogan as tobacco) had been wrapped in paper and laid in hay in leaky boxes, which 'as a venture in fungiculture . . . was a complete success';[22] crate after crate of foodstuffs was riddled with worms, and tins of sausages were now of such explosive potential that they all had to be thrown out. Even the hyaenas would not touch what he discarded. When the task was complete Grogan succumbed again to fever, and spent Christmas day of 1898 in bed with nothing more festive than a cup of tea. He was looked after by Dr Castellote, the Mohun expedition doctor, and when he recovered the two men decided to go hunting (Grogan's favoured form of convalescence) on the river Songwe.

Before they left Grogan had his first recruiting success at a nearby Watonga village, courtesy of some good old Irish blarney. It was to prove a particularly important one in the months ahead. Addressing a group of villagers in quasi-Biblical parlance he related how his journey to the Mediterranean would take

> many moons; that we should go to Tanganyika, that north of Tanganyika we should find another lake, then mighty mountains that made fire, then another lake, then still mightier mountains so high that the water became as stones;

then a fourth lake, out of which flowed a great river which, after several moons, took one to the dwelling places of the white man – large even as hills.

He also promised that anyone who joined him would be sent home in 'steamers as large as villages'[23] when the journey was complete. Grogan was as amused by the villagers' sceptical reaction as they were by his eyewash, but four men and a small boy did volunteer, including a minor chief by the name of Makanjira who immediately assumed the role of Grogan's gun-bearer, lieutenant and principal adviser. Five followers, however, scarcely made a caravan, and Grogan knew that before making for Lake Tanganyika he would have to wait until enough willing hands could be recruited by the local administrator.

After the first hunting foray on the Songwe with the affable Dr Castellote, Grogan moved his camp twelve miles to a village called N'kana in one of a series of little glades. From this new base he collected large numbers of butterflies which were despatched to the Natural History Museum. In all, sixty-six specimens reached their destination intact, two of which were found to be 'new' species. To Grogan's great satisfaction they were named after him: *Amauris Grogani* and *Gnophodes Grogani*. In the Songwe valley he also found a hitherto 'unknown' species of antelope. It was the size of a reedbuck with a beautiful silver-grey coat, white undersides and dark brown legs. This, too, Grogan was subsequently given the right to name *Cervicapra thomasinae*[24] ('Thomasina' being his nickname for Gertrude, whom by now he had not seen for over eighteen months). For these and other discoveries, Grogan was made a Fellow of the Royal Zoological Society.

The enforced delay also enabled Grogan to explore the locality extensively and make copious notes about the people he encountered. The Wankonde, whose metalwork was the finest he had yet come across, made zithers and other musical instruments which fascinated him. He also took a great liking to the Awemba, whose chiefs were smoked for a year when they died. These chiefs also kept personal bands for welcoming visitors, and Grogan was invited to attend a performance. Good musicians, he was informed, had their eyes removed in order to stop them leaving the village.

At last Grogan received a note on his perambulations which told him that enough porters had been recruited on his behalf to start the 210-mile journey north to Lake Tanganyika. After waiting for another attack of fever to pass he started up the Stevenson Road on 24 January 1899. Behind him stretched the caravan, led by Makanjira and the four other Watonga. The first days could hardly have been worse. After passing the Nyasaland frontier at Fort Hill the men were attacked by large blood-sucking flies whose proboscises penetrated half an inch under the skin of the face or neck. The rains had also arrived, and for several days it was impossible to light a fire. At night everyone slept in the wet, as Sharp had most of the tents in his loads, and Grogan found that even his sou'wester and oilskins provided little protection against the deluge.

Two weeks later the caravan struggled into Mambwe, and Grogan suffered yet another very severe attack of fever which remained with him for the next two months. He was so ill that he had to be carried to Abercorn in a *machila* (a hammock) and collapsed on arrival in the town; for a week his only sustenance was derived from an unconventional diet of limes and Worcestershire sauce. It was not until a month after setting out across the Tanganyika plateau that the caravan finally made it to Kituta, having averaged just seven miles a day. At last Grogan was able to feast his eyes on the sight of Lake Tanganyika, but his jubilation at reaching what he regarded as 'the real starting-point of our Odyssey'[25] was short-lived: Sharp had again despaired of waiting for him and had continued north.

Grogan stayed in Kituta no longer than was necessary to regain some strength and revictual. On 2 April he and his rather disconsolate band boarded the African Lakes Corporation's *Good News* and set off up Lake Tanganyika after Sharp. Once again he found himself in the company of Mohun's survey party, which made for very cramped conditions on board. To make matters worse, the steamer was infested with cockroaches, some as large as mice, and on the first day out it ran into the lake's infamous heavy seas. For several hours Grogan's men were all horrendously ill and he fully expected the boat to turn turtle. Eventually the storm abated, the temperature soared to over 100°F, and the settlement of M'bala was safely reached although all the loads were soaked through, and Grogan ordered everyone off the boat to recover from their ordeal.

Grogan spent the few hours on shore having dinner with the Catholic Pères Blancs at their mission. The Algerian wine flowed freely and he was greatly impressed by the fact that the worldly fathers did not, in contrast to what he believed to be generally true of most of their Protestant counterparts, 'ply one with fantastic accounts of the work that they are doing'. When the *Good News*'s whistle blew, and Grogan was forced to leave, he was presented with great baskets of potatoes, tomatoes, pomegranates and various other fruits and vegetables for the next leg of the journey – a further kindness which endeared the White Fathers to him for life.

The *Good News* slowly zigzagged its way up the lakeside settlements, Belgian Congo on the port side and German Tanganyika on the starboard, and at M'towa, the principal station on the Congolese side of the lake, Grogan finally caught up with Sharp. Their reunion was a muted affair. It transpired that the reason Sharp had continued north was in an attempt to escape the fever, from which he had been suffering even worse than Grogan. Sharp's once portly frame had been ravaged and he told Grogan that he had been on the brink of death in Ujiji; he had only been saved by the timely arrival of the itinerant Dr Castellote, who had hastily transferred him across the lake to the higher, and therefore healthier, ground at M'towa. There, Castellote had nursed Sharp back to some semblance of health, but then succumbed to the fever himself. He had died within days and was buried overlooking the lake, very far from home. It was an ominous reminder to Grogan and Sharp of the risks of pressing on when neither of them was in good health.

Disease was not the only thing that forced Grogan to consider the sagacity of continuing the trek. At M'towa he soon learnt that he was on the fringes of a very troubled region, and that the security situation to the north might be even worse. M'towa itself resembled a fortress, and all Congolese officials from the surrounding district had retreated to it. For years the so-called 'Arab Zone', between the lake and Leopold II's commercial interests in the Congo Free State, had been in more or less open revolt. Few outside the country had known why, but now, word of the extraordinary brutality of Leopold's regime during the previous decade was just starting to filter out. Within a few years the last vestiges of his philanthropic posturing would be destroyed when it became known that the Belgian monarch was responsible for the deaths of a staggering five to eight *million* Africans. Grogan was unaware of the scale of the atrocities, but in the months ahead his suspicions grew that something very sinister was going on not so far to the west.[26]

In the meantime Grogan's main objective was to cross the lake to Ujiji as soon as Sharp could be moved, in order to gather further intelligence from the German administration there. As the steamer neared their historic destination Grogan wrote: 'It was with a feeling of curiosity that I looked for the first time on the one historic spot in Central Africa ... such was Ujiji, the meeting-place of Stanley and Livingstone, the heart of the great slave-raiding ulcer'.[27] With considerable difficulty all their loads were conveyed to the beach by canoe, and Grogan and Sharp headed off on donkeys to find lodgings. The beach, they noticed, was littered with grinning skulls, a legacy of the days of Arab paramountcy.

Hauptmann Bethe, whom Grogan pronounced 'a most delightful specimen of a German officer' with his round face, large moustache and sticky-out ears, was the town's administrator and he greeted his two British visitors as if they were royalty. The day after their arrival they were invited to lunch with Bethe and his German officials and were treated to a 'bewildering succession of drinks, starting with port, then through successive courses of champagne, brandy, beer, Vermouth, and claret'.[28] This bacchanalian feast was hardly a tonic considering both men were almost prostrate with fever and the temperature outside was 110°F in the shade, but their hosts steadfastly maintained that copious quantities of hard liquor were the best antidote to fever, and that no teetotaller who came to Ujiji had ever left alive.

Grogan gleaned plenty of useful information from Bethe in between successive bouts of fever, one of which temporarily robbed him of the use of his hands. The most intriguing thing he learnt was that the Congolese rebels had sent Bethe a deputation saying that they were planning another attack on the Belgians and requested that, if this failed, they be allowed to surrender to him and settle in German territory. This was much more of a clue to what was happening in the Congo than anything Grogan had learnt at M'towa, but he still had no way of knowing that it was anything more than 'an indication of the natives' feeling towards the Congo Free State Administration: a mixture of contempt and distrust'.

Bethe, echoing the words of James Coleman almost two years earlier, also advised Grogan that it was folly to head north without at least a hundred armed men. But Grogan was determined to continue, and equally set on only arming ten Asiska men he had recruited in Nyasaland and the five Watonga. Any greater display of weaponry was, he insisted, only courting disaster. Bethe was not convinced, but agreed to give Grogan every assistance. His generosity and organizational skills prompted Grogan to declare himself a great admirer of the colonial methods of the 'wily Teuton';[29] indeed Grogan could see no sign that Bethe was hampered in his work either by 'the penurious stinginess' which he considered prevalent in the British Colonial Office, or by the 'ignorant babblings of the professional philanthropist, who now appears to be an accepted British institution'.[30]

Within days Bethe had recruited enough porters to make up a full strength caravan. Most of the men, Grogan noted, were from the Manyema tribe whom he knew to be famed for their strength and stamina (but also for their ill-discipline and cannibalistic tendencies). At dawn on 12 April Grogan, Sharp, the Watonga contingent (bearing the Union Jack), the ten armed Asiskas and 150 porters marched out of Ujiji accompanied by an escort of German soldiers to deter any early desertions. Loads averaged about sixty pounds per man; carefully packed in boxes was everything required for the journey north – food, tents, beds, collapsible baths, tables and chairs, medicine (including vast quantities of quinine, permanganate of potassium and Elliman's Embrocation), Grogan's substantial library, tobacco, two spare Union Jacks, ammunition, surveying equipment and (most important of all) gifts for the chiefs through whose territories the caravan would pass. It was not until four in the afternoon that the last porters left Ujiji, and camp was pitched not far from town. The 'real Odyssey' had begun.

In the morning the caravan followed a track through the fertile country abutting the lake; progress was slow as high grass overhung the track, and the damp did little to help Grogan's fever. Sharp was also suffering: during the night his hands had been almost sucked dry by mosquitoes and had turned septic. The terrain was hilly, and every valley had a stream which needed to be forded. On the fourth day out of Ujiji the caravan struggled up an almost sheer incline until Grogan gave the order to pitch camp at 6,000 foot. In late afternoon the mist closed in, shutting off the view over the forested hills to the lake and the 'forbidding-looking hills on the Congo side'.[31] The men retreated to their tents as darkness descended and the temperature plummeted.

After a week on the high ground, during which the first grumbles were heard in the ranks, the trail descended a slope so steep the men had to slide down it. At the bottom they were once again on the shores of Lake Tanganyika, and there the trail ended. The only way forward was along the soft shingle; Grogan described negotiating this obstacle as 'one long penance' akin to wading through treacle. It was further complicated by the fact that every few yards the bush would close in on the lake and force the caravan out into the water, which was 'rather exciting'[32] as the lake was swarming with crocodiles.

During the ordeal of negotiating a way up the shoreline Grogan noted with great relief that the Watonga contingent, whom he nick-named 'the Guinea-fowls' on account of their uniforms of dark blue cotton wraps and blue-green fezzes, began to come into their own as invaluable guides and trustworthy headmen. Not all the men were proving so enthusiastic and one afternoon the ten Asiska men who formed the armed guard suddenly downed their rifles and deserted. This was an acute setback: the Asiska had been drilled in Nyasaland by a Zanzibari sergeant in the Mohun expedition, and Grogan had hoped they would stay with him all the way to the Mediterranean. Soon, however, he was preoccupied with a more immediate concern: his fever returned with a vengeance.

By the time the caravan struggled into Usambara (today's Bujum-bura) Grogan's temperature had risen to 106.9°F, and Sharp was semi-comatose. They had made it to the top of Lake Tanganyika, but a realistic appraisal of the prospects of going any further was far from encouraging.

SIX

Cannibals and Kings

FOR DAYS Grogan lay prostrate in Usambara. He knew he was very close to death, but during more lucid moments he was able to sit upright in his bed and gaze up the vast, wide valley formed by the Rusisi river. This was 'the path that led to the unknown', which 'with its eddying mists and fading hills, [was] redolent of mystery'. He knew that beyond those hills lay the 'mysterious waters of Kivu and the giant volcanoes (the pulse of Africa)',[1] and it was there that he still hoped to graduate from traveller to fully fledged explorer. The beauty of the scene before his eyes was real enough; what was doubtful was whether he would live to enjoy it.

On 7 May a decision was reached by von Gravert, Usambara's German administrator, and Sharp. Grogan was adamant about continuing the trek, despite being unable to walk. So von Gravert suggested that if he could be carried to the higher ground around Kivu, his fever might abate. It was a risk to move him at all, but a risk that the irrepressible Grogan was prepared to take. Von Gravert produced a team of twelve of his own porters with a *machila* and instructed them to lead the caravan to the headquarters of Dr Kandt, a German who had spent three years on Lake Kivu 'making an exhaustive study of all the "ologies"'.[2] If Grogan survived that far then he would almost certainly, von Gravert encouraged him, be strong enough to continue further north.

In the cool of the evening camp was struck and the long train of men and beasts moved out of Usambara, keeping close to the lake shore. There was almost no moon, but in his delirious state Grogan caught glimpses of scores of fishermen flitting hither and thither in the half light as they pushed their dugouts into the shallow lake for the night's fishing. Each canoe had a flaming torch in the bows which cast a dancing phosphorescent light across its wash, and for a fleeting instant Grogan imagined that he was being conveyed to Valhalla.

With Sharp in an equally weak state, though able to walk, discipline in the caravan immediately became a problem. A new cook and three other men recruited at Usambara disappeared during the first night, taking with them their pay for a month and two months' rations. The men looking after the cows and goats produced almost nothing from their charges and what they handed over was sour, while the Manyema porters started to lag behind in an attempt to avoid fatigue duties on arrival at each new camp. Grogan, issuing commands from his *machila* like some eastern potentate, decided that the solution to this last problem was to allow the porters a half-hour margin within which to arrive in camp each evening. Anyone who missed the deadline, he told the men, would have to stand with his load on his head in the middle of camp until sunset – or for as long as he deemed fit. Grogan found this threat of 'detention' far more effective than resorting to fines or flogging, a punishment he meted out considerably less frequently than most explorers, as it prevented the men from taking their cherished afternoon nap or from strolling off with their friends to visit the local villages (and local beauties).

Progress up the valley of the Rusisi, which flowed from Lake Kivu 100 miles to the north before disgorging itself into Lake Tanganyika through five distinct mouths, was painfully slow. Although at a glance the terrain in between the two lakes appeared flat and straight, obstacles were encountered at every turn. The ground was often broken, forests had to be struggled through, and whenever the caravan was forced off the valley floor it met the seemingly continuous wall of mountains which enclosed the valley on both sides. Grogan and Sharp soon found themselves negotiating a succession of high passes and fast-flowing streams. Goats were washed downstream and had to be rescued by the 'brilliant swimming'[3] of the Watonga contingent or by the Manyema porters, who were adept at shooting the rapids 'like arrows'.[4] The cattle mostly had to be manhandled across these streams using ropes. At the end of each exhausting day the mosquitoes – 'colossal of stature'[5] – made sleep well-nigh impossible, hyaenas raided the camps, and Grogan's little toe was invaded by an enormous jigger, which Makanjira extracted along with a bag of eggs 'the size of a marrowfat pea'.[6] As this left only the skin and protruding bone he feared he might lose the toe, but it healed eventually with the help of copious applications of permanganate of potash.

There were few people about to watch their painstaking advance. The only settlements of note were two German forts manned by Sudanese officers and Wanyamwesi troops from the Congo, the first by the Nyakagunda river and the second just north of the Kasilo. Both, Grogan noted, were in fact well inside Congo Free State territory (as defined by the German–Congo treaty of 1885) thereby not only taking advantage of the natural defence against forays by Congo rebels afforded them by the river below, but also laying claim to ownership through effective occupation of the land right up to the river. Despite this obvious transgression on the part of the Germans, the caravan was received courteously at both forts and Grogan kept his shrewd observations to himself.

After leaving the second fort the climb out of the Rusisi valley commenced, and Grogan plotted a course east of a range of conical hills and then due west on to the high plateau. By now he was insisting on walking, and even on chasing the occasional unfortunate elephant. Once atop the plateau, camp was pitched in a position which gave a commanding view of the Rusisi snaking its way down to Lake Tanganyika in the far distance. That was what lay behind: ahead was the country of the 'mighty Ruanda' – and the prospect of an uncertain reception.

Grogan was greatly impressed by the fertility of the plateau to the north-east of the Rusisi valley, which supported vast banana plantations and countless fields of peas and beans. The area was heavily populated and after passing through a number of villages the chief, Ngenzi, came to welcome the caravan, accompanied by a hundred followers and an ever-present attendant bearing a 'gourd of *pombe* and the regal sucking-straw'.[7] Any concerns about the friendliness of the Waruanda, about which Hauptmann Bethe had been very sceptical, were for the time being allayed. After a six-hour march through the hills, accompanied by the apparently genial Ngenzi, the caravan climbed a ridge and Grogan and Sharp caught their first glimpse of Lake Kivu. It was a great moment. 'The mighty sheet of water, dotted with a hundred isles and hemmed in by a thousand imposing hills,

was of surpassing beauty; it was the only one of the vast lakes of
Central Africa that had not been first gazed upon by British eyes,'
Grogan remarked with admiration – and not a little justifiable satisfaction. Speke and Grant had heard tell of Kivu during their expedition
to Lake Victoria in 1860–63, the expedition which confirmed Lake
Victoria as one of the sources of the Nile. The German Count von
Götzen had also visited it briefly in 1894. But Grogan and Sharp were
the first Britons to set eyes on Kivu,[8] a fact which went a long way
towards making all their travails worthwhile.

When the caravan had descended the escarpment and reached the
German fort on the lake's south-western tip, close to the modern
town of Bukavu, it was given a great welcome by the ten-man Sudanese
garrison. Only later did Grogan discover that the ceaseless stream of
cattle, sheep and goats brought in for him by neighbouring chiefs had
in fact been requisitioned on derisory terms by the Sudanese officer
in charge of the fort and his 'brother ruffians', after which they were
sold on to the caravan at vastly inflated prices. Grogan, who always
insisted on paying a fair price for supplies to their *rightful* owners,
was livid when he uncovered this deception but by then it was too
late to rectify the matter. After the strain of the journey from Usambara
his mood, as was usually the case when he was ill, was fractious – and
prompted him to call the sergeant's behaviour 'the invariable result
of placing natives in a post of responsibility without constant super-
vision'.[9]

The caravan rested at the fort for just a day before heading off
north-east around the lake shore to find Dr Kandt. Grogan and Sharp
knew that, notwithstanding Kandt's presence, Kivu offered them one
of the most important opportunities of the entire trek to break new
geographical ground. Although strictly amateurs they set about noting
everything they saw in meticulous detail, and Grogan's health
improved still further on the higher ground. Before long, utilizing the
knowledge they had gained from Mr Coles's crash course in mapping
at the Royal Geographical Society, the two men realized that such
maps of the area as existed were hopelessly inaccurate, and they set
about amending them as best they could.

The hills surrounding the lake descended rapidly from an altitude
of 5,500–6,000 foot to the shore, where Grogan's mean aneroid

reading was 5,000 foot. They then plunged into the deep lake via a multitude of promontories which cut the shoreline into a series of bays and led Grogan to hazard a guess that the total length of the coastline must rival that of any body of water in the world of the same dimensions. There were no beaches, unlike at Lake Tanganyika, and no marshes except for the odd papyrus swamp where feeder streams joined the main body of water. In the middle of the lake was a network of islands, the largest of which was the black-cliffed, foreboding mass of Kwijwi. Grogan attributed the surprising absence of crocodiles and hippos to the abruptness of the meeting of land and water. There were instead huge numbers of otters and demoiselle cranes, which Grogan delighted in watching for hours on end. His verdict on the lakeside scenery was that it resembled 'a happy blend of Scotland, Japan, and the South Sea islands'.[10]

Away from the lake the surrounding country was packed with small hills which appeared 'to have been sprinkled on with a pepper-pot till not a single one more could find room'.[11] This made for slow progress: there were no connecting ridges between the hills so the caravan was continually either descending or ascending through mile upon mile of banana plantations, more fields of peas and verdant pastureland. The population was enormous by comparison with the hinterland of the Rusisi, and the land exuded an air of prosperity which prompted Grogan – now in a considerably better frame of mind – to judge the kingdom of the Ruanda 'a striking indication of the possibilities of native races left to work out their own destiny'.[12]

Dr Kandt, whom Grogan found in his camp at Ishangi, was surprised by the unexpected arrival of a large caravan, but was helpful. His survey of the lake, which he agreed to share, interested – and impressed – Grogan no end. On a recent expedition around the lake Kandt, 'with characteristic German thoroughness',[13] had counted his every step and taken three bearings a minute, finding that after the 560-mile round trip his positional estimate was only a quarter of a mile out. Although Grogan and Sharp made full use of what they learnt from Kandt when planning the best route north, they were subsequently – to their credit – at pains not to 'forestall his work'.[14] In the absence of permanent names for the major geographical features they did, however, choose their own: the inlet at the lake's south-western corner Grogan named Gertrude Bight, and four peaks on the south-eastern corner they named Mounts Sybil (after Mrs Eyres's daughter), Hilda, Margaret and Dorothy (after Grogan's sisters).

As they progressed deeper into the kingdom of the Ruanda the people interested them as much as the geography. Although collectively known as the Waruanda, famed far and wide for their unity (which had apparently done much to deter incursions by Arab slave raiders), Grogan soon learnt that there were in fact two very distinct tribes. The Watusi overlords were, he was told, the descendants of a wave of Hamitic invaders centuries earlier. They were a cattle-centric society, breeding long-horned cattle. He was struck by their distinctive appearance and described them as 'tall, slightly-built men of graceful, nonchalant carriage, [whose] features are delicate and refined. I noticed many faces that, bleached and set in a white collar, would have been conspicuous for character in a London drawing-room. The legal type was especially pronounced.'

The Watusi appeared to do little manual work, except milking and making butter. Everything else seemed to be done for them by the 'abjectly servile' Wahutu who, although vastly outnumbering the Watusi, were the 'hewers of wood and drawers of water'.[15] Indeed there were only a couple of Watusi in each village Grogan came across, and their main function was to oversee a kind of feudal system at the head of which was their *kigera* (the king) who owned all the cattle in the kingdom. Under the rigid authority of the *kigera*'s satraps it seemed to Grogan that the Wahutu had had 'any pristine originality or character ... stamped out of them'.

However much Grogan admired the Watusi and the unity that they imposed on their kingdom, he had been warned by Kandt that the Waruanda were renowned for their 'light-fingered ability'.[16] Despite taking the precaution after leaving Ishangi of closing all the tents in camp and posting extra guards, one night he was woken by Makanjira with the news that a tin box weighing sixty pounds and two canvas kit-bags had disappeared. This was a catastrophic loss. Among the missing items were the sextant, thermometers, artificial horizon, a bag of 100 sovereigns, most of Grogan's clothes and notebooks, and many photographs of the early months of the trek.

The chief suspect was Ngenzi, who had continued to follow the caravan at a distance. He was immediately summoned for questioning, but pleaded complete ignorance. Grogan was not convinced and incarcerated Ngenzi in the guard tent, denied him his cup-bearer and tobacco, and told him that he would not be released until the missing items reappeared. Grogan's suspicions were soon proved correct: a few shirts and caps were returned by Ngenzi's followers – but that was all. Grogan was in no mood to let the matter rest, and he decided that the chief and his men needed sterner treatment.

The camp was swiftly prepared for defence, and Sharp issued Snider rounds to the caravan's ten amateur riflemen who had been nominated to replace the Asiska deserters. Meanwhile Grogan grabbed his revolver and an old French cutlass, and strode out to the nearest village accompanied by Makanjira and Zowanji, the Watonga headmen. He explained to the villagers, who showed signs of preparing to attack him, the wrong that had been committed and proceeded to round up 190 head of cattle as retribution for their chief's misdemeanour. When anyone attempted to rush him with their spears he waved his cutlass theatrically about his head, which halted their advances. 'Such', he wrote tetchily, 'were the terrible Ruanda people, whose reputation has spread far and wide, and whose country has been left alone for fear of their military organization. At least five thousand men sat on the hill-tops and watched three men with a revolver, cutlass and two rifles drive off one hundred and ninety head of cattle.'[17]

The following morning, after a tense night in camp with the cattle bellowing and Sharp and Grogan on guard against possible attack, Sharp drove the herd to Kandt's camp at Ishangi where he was met by the Sudanese officer from the German fort, who took charge of the cattle. A full report was sent back to von Gravert and Grogan released Ngenzi, who had become 'most respectful'.[18] Nevertheless, searches by the Sudanese troops in the surrounding countryside unearthed no more of the missing belongings. Grogan, still seething, knew that there was now nothing else to be done except move on.

News of Grogan's punitive action spread quickly. He learnt by messenger that one chief near Ishangi had asked Kandt whether he should flee the 'invaders' but was reassured that the explorers meant no harm. 'Terrible accounts' of what they had done also preceded them up the lakeshore, with the result that 'the entire population bolted to the hills',[19] making the purchase of supplies well-nigh imposs-ible. Fearing retaliation Grogan kept the caravan in close formation and in a state of constant alert. At night 'no one stirred from camp without two spears, a sword-knife, and if possible a gun with fixed bayonet'.[20]

There were other, less predictable, consequences to the cattle raid. A large number of Wahutu, when satisfied that they would not be attacked, came into camp to thank Grogan and Sharp for punishing Ngenzi; and a thief, caught by Grogan at night and turned over to his chief, was promptly beheaded by the latter and the head placed as a warning to others. That, Grogan wrote, 'settled the thieving question'.[21]

As the threat of attack waned the now familiar problems of camp life soon resurfaced. The Manyema porters began to use their fearsome reputation to swindle any Waruanda they came across. They also took to sub-contracting their duties by coercing local boys to carry their loads for them, which meant that the caravan – and the number of mouths to be fed – started to swell to alarming proportions. Grogan decided the time had come to reorganize before chaos ensued, and ordered all hangers-on out of the camp (except those who could prove that they had come with a Manyema master from Ujiji or Usambara). He also instituted a system whereby every transaction between a Manyema and a local had to be witnessed by him. Finally, as a last resort, he inflicted 'condign punishment' on two Manyema caught stealing. Even this failed to restore complete control, and before long the caravan experienced its first large-scale desertion.

The first sign that all was not well was an 'unusual stir'[22] in the ranks one lunch time, and Grogan went on a tour of investigation. He found, to his alarm, that most of the porters were packing up to leave, and a headcount revealed that thirty had already gone. Without the porters Grogan knew that he, Sharp and the loyal Watonga would get no further and that a speedy reaction was called for. He grabbed his rifle and, accompanied by Makanjira and Zowanji, rushed off in pursuit of the deserters while Sharp stood guard in camp and threat-ened to shoot the first man who moved. It didn't take long to catch up with the thirty deserters led by Sulimani, one of the caravan's most persistent trouble-makers. Grogan fired at him, 'fully intending to kill him'[23] in his rage, but succeeded only in knocking off his fez at 200 yards. All the deserters then dropped to the ground, terrified, and Grogan sent Makanjira to tell them that the affair was now over and that if they returned to camp he would not know which of them had ever left. All were present at roll-call half an hour after dark.

That evening Grogan addressed the men at length. He explained that good relations with the local population were vital, and that stealing from them jeopardized the safety of all in the caravan. He added that if the Waruanda were too scared to come to camp to sell food how would all of them have enough of the things 'that rejoiced the stomachs of men?' This lecture was treated as a great joke by the Manyema, who returned to their fires 'to howl with laughter into the night'. The mutiny looked to have been averted, and Grogan was relieved to note – not for the first time on the trek – that 'from discontent to merry laughter is but a momentary transition with the African'.[24]

Grogan and Sharp continued their survey work assiduously on the way north. They kept detailed notes of all that they observed of local customs – encompassing a plethora of subjects from the smoking habits of the Waruanda to their superstitions to their skill at cattle husbandry – and as they had done throughout the trek they purchased numerous artefacts such as bracelets from the Nyema region of the Congo, Pygmy bows and black clay pipes. When they had almost made it to the top of Lake Kivu, however, they began to hear unsettling rumours from further north. In the kingdom of Bugoie, they heard, there were unspecified goings-on that disturbed the local populace considerably more than the antics of the caravan's Manyema porters.

As the expedition crossed the Kashale river and entered the district of Bugoie on the lake's north-eastern corner, it left the kingdom of the Waruanda. The wall of hills abruptly ceased and a steep descent led down to a small bay on the lake's northernmost tip. To the north-west lay the mighty volcanoes that Grogan had been eagerly hoping to see, and in the evening he scaled an isolated hill to get a better look. After the trials of the trek up Lake Kivu this was the moment that made everything worthwhile:

> I think that the view is the finest I have ever seen. Far to the south stretched the mighty expanse of water, dark promontories of every shape and size jutted far out into the lake; Kwijwi stood out in bold outline; and the mighty wall of mountains on the west was dimly visible on the far horizon. Below me stretched a great plain ... To the west, the plain was covered with young forest. To the north towered the terrific mass of Mount Götzen, vomiting forth a great volume of black smoke. The old volcanoes towered aloft above the clouds, which swirled in constant eddies about their base. Entranced with the view, I waited till the sun declined and dropped like a molten ball behind the bold outline of the hills; and then the moon came up, bathing waters of the lake in silvery light.[25]

Grogan's vantage point was close to modern Gisenyi, and within his field of vision lay not just the active Mount Götzen but five other major volcanoes. It would be another two years before a German-led commission arrived to survey the area comprehensively and in the meantime, although von Götzen had preceded him, Grogan was able to map what lay before him in the knowledge that every step he took in the volcanic region was most probably on ground hitherto untrod by Europeans.

His efforts to ascertain the local names for the volcanoes proved confusing. While the great, smoking crater of Mount Götzen seemed to be commonly referred to as Karissimbi or Kirunga, the others had a bewildering array of names: one peak alone had thirty-six. During the next two weeks Grogan set about naming everything himself, a favourite pastime for European explorers. The enormous flat-topped volcano to the north-west of Götzen, which the locals insisted had formed since von Götzen's visit, he called Mount Sharp. The mighty peak to the east, whose height he estimated at 13,000 feet above sea level, he called Mount Eyres after his benefactor. Like the forest-clad Götzen its highest reaches were snow-covered in the mornings, and from one angle it reminded him of the view of the Matterhorn from the Riffelalp. The smaller volcanoes further east he called Mount Kandt, Mount Watt and Mount Chamberlain. He did not, unlike many of his illustrious predecessors, indulge in naming anything after himself.

Although no geologist, Grogan knew that he was now traversing the 'engine room' of Africa, an area whose volcanic activity had shaped the geography – and history – of the entire eastern side of the continent. 'Even to unscientific observers like ourselves,' he remarked, 'it was evident that the country between Kivu and the Albert Edward is the key to the whole modern geographical and geological problem of Africa, as probably Ruwenzori is the key to the problem of the past.'[26]

However impressive the sight of these peaks, the main question which began to tax Grogan concerned the route he should take towards Lake Albert Edward. His dilemma was further complicated by the intelligence he gathered from the hundreds of locals who came to visit their camp, bearing presents and offering supplies for sale. From them Grogan learnt that there was no water in the pass between Mount Götzen and Mount Eyres – the most direct route – but he decided to procure gourds for all members of the caravan and try it anyway. After camping at the last spot where there was fresh water, just four miles from the lake, he struck out 'with many misgivings'[27] for the pass over a chain of small extinct volcanoes and onto a flat swampy plain with the lava-stream disgorged by Mount Götzen to the west. Although the caravan's herd of cattle was attacked along the way, and one of the herders killed, it managed to reach the summit of the pass in a single day and pitched camp at an altitude of 7,000 feet.

From this eyrie Grogan could see that to the north the trail, such as it was, descended into forested ravines filled with clouds of butterflies, giant moths and blazing orchids. This, he knew, was elephant country, an extension of the great Aruwimi forest, and as both he and Sharp were now fit they decided to split up and go hunting before they moved on. This was by no means easy, as the forest proved to be almost impenetrable. Paths had to be cut with axes and often, for hundreds of yards at a time, tracks led over – rather than round – a jumble of fallen tree-trunks. In these challenging surroundings any elephant whose spoor Grogan detected had a distinct advantage.

On one occasion he only spotted his quarry through the gloom when its head was directly above him. He fired both barrels of his .500 magnum, but – drenched in the fleeing elephant's blood – was hurled yards backwards into a thorn bush whence he was retrieved by Zowanji. Sharp was no more fortunate and 'lost two stone'[28] from his efforts to cut a way through the bush. At night both men camped wherever they ended up after the day's pursuit, huddled naked around fires at high altitude and with the rain pouring down about them.

Elephant weren't the only inhabitants of the forest that Grogan startled. There were also Pygmies, whom he described as the 'all-knowing children of the Dawn of Man'.[29] These sturdy men, who survived by hunting elephant and collecting honey which they traded with the Waruanda, fascinated Grogan. He was particularly impressed by their bush-craft skills. The more shy ones, never having seen a white man before, would bolt on hearing him approach and 'the pace at which they ran was extraordinary . . . the combination of immense strength necessary for the precarious hunting life they lead, and of compactness, indispensable to rapid movement in dense forest, where the pig-runs are the only means of passage, is a wonderful example of nature's adaptability'.[30] Grogan, by contrast, was less well adapted: when he had eventually had enough of hunting and returned to the main camp, he slept for fifteen hours without stirring and his men 'were almost dead with fatigue'.[31]

Abandoning any thoughts of more 'sport' in the forest, Grogan decided to make an attempt to cross the lava slopes of Mount Götzen in order to investigate Mushari, on the west side of the towering volcano. There were two reasons for his interest: his natural curiosity, and stories Dr Kandt had told him about massive elephants that wandered the region. Having set out in a state of eager anticipation he was forced to return when his local guide mysteriously disappeared as they picked their way through the scrub on the edge of the lava flow. His next attempt to reach Mushari, this time accompanied by Sharp, was also thwarted: a new guide tried to escape as they were leaving camp and Grogan was forced to attach himself to the man with a rope. The guide remained distinctly unenthusiastic, even after being promised a hefty reward, and warned Grogan that the path would cut their feet to ribbons and that there was no food or water for two days.

Once again he was forced to turn back. A third attempt, this time with six porters, was curtailed when the latter started to disappear en route. Grogan fired round after round into the air to let his men know his whereabouts, but to no avail. Three never reappeared, and as Grogan and his remaining companions settled down for a freezing night in pouring rain he began to give greater credence to the rumours that something sinister was going on in the region.

The next day Grogan returned to join Sharp at the main camp and took a few days' rest to consider what to do next. Not having managed to survey the route towards Mushari it was out of the question to attempt to lead the whole caravan over difficult terrain which seemed to swallow porters, so it was agreed that Sharp should lead the main body of the caravan across easier terrain to the south of Mount Götzen, and meet up with Grogan on the west side of the volcano. This plan suited everyone. Sharp was in the early stages of another bout of the fever; the porters were not keen to retrace the steps of their disappearing comrades; and so the irrepressible Grogan was able to set out for a final attempt to round the volcano on its north side and reach Mushari.

This time he opted to take the most direct route across the lava streams with Makanjira, Zowanji and a handful of porters. All efforts to secure local guides proved useless, but Grogan was prepared to follow his nose and ordered the men to equip themselves with sandals, and food and water for two days. When they reached the edge of the lava, he found that only the Watonga had followed his instructions, and most of the Manyema porters were claiming to be sick. They only 'recovered' when it became clear that there was a path of sorts across the flow, and that further protests were useless. 'There is one thing to be said for the Manyema,' Grogan conceded, 'they play their game right to the end.'[32]

The party progressed across the razor-sharp lava at the sedate pace of half a mile an hour. Grogan estimated that the flow extended for some twenty or thirty miles and at its narrowest point was two miles wide. Judging by the fossilized bones all around them he also reckoned that large numbers of elephants had been buried by lava in the most recent eruption. Despite making such slow progress the flow was eventually crossed, and on the far side Grogan was met by a number of Wachenzi people coming the other way. Now, at last, he discovered for sure that all was not well in the lee of the brooding volcano. The Wachenzi explained that they were being forced to flee Mushari by Baleka raiders from the Congo and most had been reduced to eking out a living in the forest. Furthermore, Grogan learnt that the Baleka were cannibals, and as his party moved on in a westerly direction with Mount Götzen to their left it began to come across an increasing number of dead bodies.

Grogan briefly considered turning back. The atmosphere had grown 'most undesirably warm',[33] and he knew his small party was virtually defenceless if confronted by a concerted attack by hostile Baleka. But his curiosity and stubbornness got the better of him, and he decided to push on. On the second evening after leaving Sharp he reached a stream and did his best to feed a group of refugees he found there, and the following morning he began to climb a steep slope leading to the uplands of Mushari. This trail was lined not only with bodies but with grinning skulls, skeletons and dried pools of blood.

On the plateau, amid beautiful rolling countryside, stood a village. Grogan looked about him, and decided that the scene seemed innocuous enough. But then he heard distant shouts: he had been spotted, and 'black figures brandishing spears and howling at the expected feast' started to appear in the distance. Grogan quickly conferred with one of the Manyema, and the reply – 'they are coming to eat us'[34] – confirmed his suspicions. He chose his targets, loaded his .303, and started to fire; he continued to fire even when the attackers had turned tail and fled, bowling over six of them and wounding another two.

When the attack was over Grogan took stock of his position, and decided to move his men to the now deserted village as it would offer some protection. It was only then that he noticed the vultures circling overhead, giving him an 'inkling of what we were about to see'. The scene in the village 'defied description'. 'It haunts me in my dreams;' Grogan wrote, 'at dinner it sits on my leg-of-mutton, it bubbles in my soup, *in fine* [my] Watonga would not eat the potatoes that grew in the same country and went without food for forty-eight hours rather than do so.'[35] There were human entrails drying on sticks, pots of soup with 'bright *yellow* fat', gnawed thigh-bones and forearms, a head with a spoon left sticking in the brains, a hand toasting on a stick, and above all 'a stench that passeth all understanding'.

The next two days Grogan considered to be the worst of his brief life. He decided to move at speed as 'rapid movements alone could save us from annihilation',[36] and allowed no rests between sunrise and sunset. Each corpse-strewn valley through which he and his men passed seemed to have suffered at the hands of the Baleka, and when he heard reports from a number of fugitives that the regions of Kishari and Kameronse to the south-west of Mushari had also been ravaged he hazarded a guess that a total area of some 3,000 square miles had been laid waste.

Grogan was so amazed by what he came across that, on reaching the village of Kameronse, he took a woman and three children prisoner. His intention was to convey them all the way back to London in order to demonstrate not only what a Baleka cannibal looked like but also as living verification of his experiences. The kidnapping nearly proved unwise in more ways than one: when rounding up his prisoners Grogan was suddenly 'confronted by half-a-dozen gentlemen of anthropophagic proclivities on supper intent'.[37] One hurled a spear at him, but before the attack gained momentum he shot the man through the heart, whereupon the others fled. This was to be Grogan's last sight of the dreaded Baleka. Eventually he, his Watonga headmen (who were as horrified by the experience as he), his Manyema porters (who were not) and their four Baleka captives rounded the south side of Mount Götzen and returned to the relative safety of Bugoie.

As soon as he was sure that he had escaped the cannibals' pot, Grogan's concern turned swiftly to Sharp. He had no way of knowing that his friend, laid low by fever, had opted to pitch camp by Lake Kivu rather than circling the south side of Mount Götzen to meet him. As a result Grogan feared that Sharp might be on his way to Kameronse, and would miss him. While cutting a way through the forest on Götzen's southern flanks, however, a fortunate thing happened: an elderly Pygmy appeared from nowhere and told Grogan that Sharp had passed that same way a few days earlier and was safely on the lake shore. A greatly relieved Grogan sent two men ahead with a note for Sharp, and then continued east to get food for his now ravenous Watonga and Manyema in the vicinity of their former camp near Mount Eyres. Sharp struck camp on receiving the note and led the main caravan to join Grogan. Both men were keen to leave the district as fast as possible.

On 26 June 1899 – three months after leaving Ujiji – the caravan started the hundred-mile march up the Rutchuru valley to Lake Albert Edward, first discovered by Stanley in the 1870s. Grogan kept well to the east of the main river but was forced to cross stream after stream, the largest of which was the thundering Kako. As he was now 4,000 feet lower than the camp by Mount Eyres, the view back to the volcanoes was even more majestic than from the Kivu side. Eventually the going became easier and the track altered direction to cut through rolling grasslands. Grogan waxed lyrical about a herd of fifty elephant that crossed ahead of him, reminding him of an

> old print of the Spanish Armada, as they sailed past through
> the long grass; their huge ears flapping to and fro' gave the
> impression of sails; and their gliding action over the uneven
> ground was exactly similar to the motion of a ship. The
> grass covered their legs, and the peculiar swinging action
> of the elephant, who moves both the legs on one side at
> the same time, gives the appearance of a beast on wheels.[38]

His response was predictable, and at last he fulfilled the final one of his childhood ambitions by bagging a magnificent bull elephant. He declared himself to be a 'proud man'.[39]

Now that a safe distance had been put between them and the marauding Baleka the Manyema porters again became restless. Grogan threatened to shoot anyone he caught stealing, but to no avail. The source of the discontent was that food was scarce in the Rutchuru valley, but the porters were not the only ones to suffer: Grogan and Sharp were themselves reduced to attempting to eat the trunk of the bull elephant. Even boiled for twelve hours it was far from appetizing and only of any interest to their perpetually ravenous Baleka captives

– two of whom mysteriously disappeared on the way up the valley. Given the paucity of food and the fact that he ensured the four Baleka were better fed than anyone else, Grogan immediately suspected his own Manyema sentries of effecting the disappearance.

By the time the caravan reached the point where the Rutchuru flowed through a reedy swamp packed with hippos into Lake Albert Edward, Grogan was again suffering from fever. To make matters worse lions visited the camp every night, 'keeping up a terrific concert'[40] which rendered sleep impossible. Grogan took to a *machila* and as the caravan progressed up the lake, with the Wakondjo mountains forming the backdrop to its west shore, he derived little satisfaction from the knowledge that he and Sharp were the first Europeans to attempt to map the east side of Albert Edward. The prevailing atmosphere was one of loneliness and gloom, and by the time they reached the top of the lake Grogan's thermometer told him that his temperature had reached an improbable 108.4°F despite Sharp's 'motherly attentions'.[41] It was with considerable relief that the two men finally crossed the channel connecting Lake Albert Edward with Lake Ruisamba (Lake George)[42] and found themselves back on British soil.

Uganda had been declared a British protectorate in 1894, largely due to the efforts of its forceful administrator, Lugard, in persuading a reluctant Liberal government at home that if it did not act the territory would immediately be snapped up by the Germans. It was therefore Lugard, one of Grogan's mentors, whom he and Sharp toasted when they marched into the British fort on the border with the Congo. There, for the first time since leaving Ujiji, they were able to enjoy sleeping with a roof over their heads (albeit one shared with 'thousands of mosquitoes and armies of rats').[43]

After two days' rest, during which Grogan's fever abated somewhat, he led the caravan out of the fort. Ahead lay an eighty-mile march to Fort Portal, nicknamed Fort 'Gerry', the administration post for the Toro region of Uganda. To the east of the trail lay the snow-capped Ruwenzori mountains, discovered in 1888 by Jephson and Parke, members of Stanley's expedition to rescue Emin Pasha from the Dervishes.[44] The legendary Mountains of the Moon, which had first featured on a Ptolemaic map of Africa in the second century, were an awesome sight even though their peaks were shielded from view by dense mist. Grogan soon learnt that spiritual control of the terrain through which he passed was being violently contested by the supporters of rival missions, the Protestant Church Missionary Society and the Pères Blancs, but the caravan reached Fort Portal at the end of July without incident and was welcomed there by Bagge, the British administrator.

Fort Portal provided a welcome first opportunity in over six months to despatch letters and read English newspapers. In addition, Bagge was a considerably more up-to-date source of information than the latter and was able to tell Grogan about recent developments on the continent. The news from the north was of particular interest to him. At Ujiji, von Bethe had told him about Kitchener's defeat of the Mahdists at Omdurman; but it was from Bagge that he now learnt that the Khalifa, the Mahdists' leader, had been killed during his last stand at Kordofan in January, and that the Sudan – through which he would be traipsing next – was once again entirely in British hands. Grogan also learnt that Marchand had pulled off a remarkable coup by reaching Fashoda the previous July – while Grogan was still hunting in Portuguese East Africa. This had triggered a serious diplomatic incident between England and France, and in December Kitchener had dislodged Marchand from his base on the Upper Nile. Meanwhile, to the south, the storm clouds were gathering over the Transvaal and a war between Britain and the Boers looked increasingly likely. This final piece of news did not surprise Grogan and hardened his resolve to complete his traverse of the continent as soon as possible: if there was to be war in South Africa he wanted to be there.

It was not long before the Manyema porters, having little to do in the British fort except avail themselves of an unlimited supply of *pombe*, became troublesome. One night they raided the fort's milk supply and beat up some of its staff, and the following day, after the ringleaders had been flogged by Bagge's sergeant, the Manyema all declared that they were going to head home to Ujiji. This was a huge setback as Grogan had hoped that the Manyema would stay with him all the way to the Nile, but he could tell that this time they really had had enough, and that to take them further would be more trouble than it was worth. Grogan paid the men off and thanked them individually for sticking with him. Whatever trouble they had caused

Grogan would always remember them as 'a likeable lot of rogues' who, in his opinion, 'had thoroughly enjoyed themselves'.[45] Little did he know that sixteen years later he would be reunited with Manyema porters, and would once again have good reason to be thankful for their phenomenal powers of endurance.

Altogether more disappointing for Grogan was Harry Sharp's decision to return home. At Fort Portal an urgent telegraph message had caught up with him saying that there were pressing family affairs at home that needed his attention. Sharp had, like Grogan, suffered almost continually from fever for six months; he was also ten years older than Grogan and not nearly as athletic. In short, he was more than willing to go home by this time, although he and Grogan had forged a deep friendship during eighteen months in the bush and he was loath to leave Grogan to go on alone. After a final two-week hunting trip in Toro, the two men – to Grogan's 'great regret'[46] – said their farewells and Harry Sharp marched out of Fort Portal at the head of 100 Toro porters carrying the possessions that Grogan no longer needed: crate after crate of artefacts from the trek; tusks (the largest of which weighed 138 lbs); skins and other trophies; most of the armoury; and the hapless, sole surviving Baleka cannibal, who did not last the journey to suffer the indignity of being put on display before a curious British public.

Sharp's destination, the East African coast, was some 800 miles away but could mostly be travelled by steamer or train. Grogan, on the other hand, was still over 2,000 miles from Cairo and all that was left of the caravan were the persistent Watonga contingent, two Waruanda, a cook-boy from Ujiji and a dozen Manyema porters who had been confined to the brig when their comrades had left for home. The latter were hardly enthusiastic about the prospect of marching still further north, but rapidly changed their minds when grisly news filtered back to the fort. It transpired that the main group of Manyema had been attacked south of Lake Albert Edward, in the Rutchuru valley, after availing themselves of the possessions of some of the locals. Twenty of them including Sulimani, their headman, were dead. This was nothing if not a reminder to Grogan of how lucky the caravan had been on the way north, and a warning of what dangers still lay ahead. With that in mind, rather than recruit extra porters he resolved to travel fast and light as far as Wadelai, a British station on the Albert Nile to which Sharp had promised to despatch supplies for the journey north to Khartoum. He knew that moving on without plentiful supplies of food and no reliable armed men (save Makanjira and Zowanji) was not the stuff of the explorer's handbook, but hoped instead to gain something every bit as valuable – speed.

On 28 August Grogan and his small band left Fort Portal and struck north-east past the northern spur of the Ruwenzoris. Only once in two months in the region did he catch a glimpse of the magnificent snow-capped peaks of Mount Mackinnon and Mount Gordon Bennett; the rest of the time they were shrouded in mist 'as though jealous of the future, a future of Cook's tours, funicular railways, [and] personally conducted ascents (with a sermon and ginger beer thrown in)'.[47] After a hike of some thirty miles he reached a crocodile-infested river, which he crossed in an 'appallingly leaky piece of firewood (called by courtesy a canoe)',[48] and then turned west and climbed onto the Congo plateau. Before making for Lake Albert he could not resist this quick detour in search of elephant, whatever his hurry and however great his suspicions about what was happening over the border.

Once in Congolese territory, Grogan found that he was again a curiosity – a welcome one when the news spread that he was hunting. The first elephant he brought down lured a mass of people to descend from the hills to the north to feast on the carcass, and a

> weird sight it was; stark naked savages with long greased hair . . . were perched on every inch of the carcase, hacking away with knives and spears, yelling, snarling, whooping . . . covered with blood and entrails; the new arrivals tearing off lumps of meat and swallowing them raw . . . others were crawling in and out of the intestines like so many prairie marmots.

In two hours all that remained of the elephant were the 'gaunt ribs like the skeleton of a shipwreck'.[49]

Satisfied with having gained possession of tusks of 98 lbs and 86 lbs, Grogan cut north-west for thirty miles to the volcanic lakes at Vijongo before descending from the plateau back to the Semliki valley, whose marshes he described as a 'sea of misery'.[50] In many places the grass was between eight and ten feet high, and its roots, a tangle of 'matted whipcord' reached almost to his knees. The mosquitoes once again 'defied description', even in the middle of the day; and at night Grogan took every precaution possible to barricade himself in under his mosquito net – deploying his boots, cartridge bags and anything weighty to keep down its edges – but to no avail. Within an hour he was always aware that he shared his bed with hundreds of unwelcome intruders, and concluded dismally that the mosquito must be 'possessed of the properties of the Röntgen ray'.[51]

Rounding the southern tip of Lake Albert Grogan entered the kingdom of the Wanyabuga. He was struck by their 'delicate features, gazelle-like eyes, light colour, lithe limbs and genteel nonchalance',[52] and also by the prevailing atmosphere of mystery by the lake. At times it seemed as if he were wandering through a perpetual mirage in which 'groups of huts [would] suddenly appear where all was shimmering light, and as suddenly vanish; a canoe with its two upright punters glides past apparently in the sky, a goose suddenly assumes the proportions of an elephant, and an elephant evolves out of what one took to be a goose . . . And thus,' he noted, 'the scene is ever changing, till the grey of evening and the crisp light of the rising sun bring out in strong relief the placid sheets of water.'[53]

Grogan found it to his great advantage that he was now in country in which Lugard was well known. People who had met 'Kapelli', as Lugard was affectionately remembered, arrived from far and wide to greet the man from 'Kapelli's tribe'. All wanted to see Grogan's copy of Lugard's *The Rise Of Our East African Empire* and a photograph of one of his deputies, William Grant, and to recount their memories of these two great explorers. The stories they had to tell about their Belgian overlords were rather less complimentary. The old chief, Katonzi, described a catalogue of atrocities committed against his people by the 'Billygee'. The more Grogan heard about Leopold's regime, the more he was wont to castigate him as 'a vampire, [who] intended to suck the country dry, and to provide a happy hunting-ground for a pack of unprincipled outcasts and untutored scoundrels'.[54]

Katonzi begged Grogan not to continue on his journey north, saying that everything ahead was wilderness, and that there were no paths, no food and no one left alive. The population had apparently been decimated by sleeping sickness and by Congolese soldiers, whom Grogan called 'blue-uniformed cannibals [who] practise the goose-step to the accompaniment of interminable bugle blasts',[55] seeking out rebels and mutineers from their ranks. But Grogan ignored Katonzi's advice and, having stocked up with several days' provisions, started confidently up Lake Albert towards Wadelai.

SEVEN

Dinka and Dunn

A s Grogan progressed into the 'valley of death' on the eastern side of Lake Albert he swiftly realized that Katonzi's warning had indeed been true. The population was in a state of 'utter destitution' and those who did not flee immediately at the sight of a white man confirmed the stories of 'rapine and murder' at the hands of King Leopold's Congolese soldiers. One formerly prominent village marked on his map had been reduced to about five 'dirty little muck-heaps'. Grogan's disgust at what he saw was not, however, shared by his local guide whom he suspected of wanting to burn and loot everything they came across. The man also made continual attempts to desert until Grogan, who was wholly reliant on him to pick the quickest route past the villages, offered him 'a race with a .303 bullet'.

Lake Albert appeared to Grogan to be a 'weird, uncanny world of its own, with its endless bands of yellow weed, its pearl-tinted waters and its islands of papyrus'.[1] On reaching Kahoma, a Wakoba village whose inhabitants had fled after soldiers carried off four of their women and children, Grogan sent the guide off to try and lure some of the villagers back. He succeeded, and Grogan learnt from a 'tremendous swell . . . with anything from 15 to 20 lbs. of red clay on his head, an enormous ivory bracelet and multitudes of iron rings' that trying to proceed on foot would be a waste of time: numerous rocky headlands to the north would prevent any further progress along the shore. The caravan was forced to take to canoes.

The most hazardous of the canoes were leaky 10-foot craft whose cross-section resembled that of an egg with the top lopped off. Grogan could get into his 'egg' easily enough, 'like a pickle into a pickle-jar', but then realized that, 'as with the pickle, extrication is a matter of time and patience'. Steering a direct course soon proved impossible, so Grogan was forced to paddle an erratic route back to the beach. Clutching his guns and a tin box containing his most precious possessions, he then put himself in the hands of a more skilful pilot.

Although the surroundings were magnificent in their wildness, with innumerable little streams and waterfalls running down to the lake through gorges clad with 'luxuriant tangles of vegetation',[2] progress was slow and wet. Grogan had had no way of replenishing his wardrobe since Ngenzi had relieved him of most of it, and his best remaining shirt now shrunk to the 'insignificant dimensions of a chest preserver'. This was all he wore for two or three days, exposing his legs and midriff to the relentless rays of the sun. The result was that he became a 'sort of perambulating three-tiered Neapolitan ice', a phenomenon that gave one of his porters a huge surprise when he caught sight of Grogan trying to relax one afternoon in his collapsible bath. Later, he tried to make something respectable out of his remaining items of tattered clothing, but found it no easy task. This prompted him to carp that

> of the various arts and crafts that one is called upon to undertake in Africa, such as cooking, shoe-mending, washer-womaning, doctoring, butchering, taxiderming, armoury work, carpentering, etc., *ad infinitum*, I think perhaps tailoring is the most trying; the cotton *will* not go into the eye of the needle, and the needle *will* go into one's fingers, and then when you think it is all over, you find you have sewn the back of your shirt to the front . . .[3]

Grogan's lack of clothing caused him further consternation when the caravan reached the village of Viboko. There, he was told that a '*muzungu*' (white man) was coming to meet him with ten canoes, an event for which he wanted to be suitably attired. By now his men were badly in need of a rest, and Grogan was again suffering from fever, so he called a halt. Having made enquiries about the identity of the *muzungu*, he decided from the answers that it must be a Belgian official. In keeping with explorers' etiquette he set about preparing to welcome the man, however trenchant his views on Belgians had now become.

This was quite a rigmarole. Although the *Frontiersman's Pocket-Book*, to which Grogan subsequently contributed, was still a tome of the future its section on 'Manners' reflected what was already required practice in the bush:

> if in camp, should a white man arrive, ask him to dismount, offer a drink. *South African Practice*: tell him to off-saddle, and ask him if he has fed. *Australian, New Zealand practice*: a man NOT asked to stay may take the hint and go. *American practice*: a man is not asked to stay, but expected to give some reason if he does not. *All countries*: it is insulting to ask personal questions, but the visitor may, at his leisure, volunteer information as to who he is, what doing, where from, whither going. Except in South Africa, it is rude to interfere with a man's horses, which he handles himself while able to stand.[4]

Even thousands of miles from the drawing-rooms of Victorian London, things had to be done *properly*.

First, Grogan slaughtered a sheep and some birds which resembled dorkings; then he settled down with a copy of Zola's *Rome* to brush up on his French, in anxious anticipation of a little 'talkee-talkee'; and finally he managed to dig a tie out of one of the loads and make himself as respectable as possible. There was a stiff southerly breeze on the lake which delayed the arrival of the flotilla until dark. When it finally appeared Grogan gave a 'last twirl to my heavy cavalry moustache . . . and composing my features to the ironclad smirk indispensable to such occasions, I advanced to do the honours'. After the hours of waiting he was, however, monumentally disappointed to find that the *muzungu* ('my gallant Belgian staggering under the gold braid of a hat of that peculiarly unbecoming shape affected by French guards and German tourists, and majestically trailing the orthodox 30-franc sword')[5] was in fact a local chief who apparently passed for a *muzungu* by dint of his possession of a very old piece of clothing manufactured in Manchester. The man's canoes, however, were sturdier than the 'eggs'; Grogan hired them on the spot and was ferried to Mswa's *kraal*.

Grogan initially judged Mswa to be 'an intelligent old native' who remembered meeting the famous Major Vandeleur years earlier, and recognized him from his photograph on the cover of Grogan's copy of his book *Campaigns on the Nile and Niger*. But when Mswa failed to find crews for Grogan's new canoes, he swiftly changed his mind and accused the chief of being 'either incompetent or trying to make a fool of me'.[6] In desperation, he decided to crew the unfamiliar canoes with his own men – who were becoming increasingly skilled at turning their hands to anything their indefatigable leader required.

When the small flotilla finally reached Mahagi, at the north-western tip of Lake Albert, it was after dark. In the half-light Grogan could see that the hills which had lined the shore had receded, giving way to an alluvial plain a couple of miles wide – and the start of the Albert Nile. Chief Tukenda welcomed the aquatic caravan to his *kraal*, and in the morning Grogan noticed that the locals seemed to be in a much ruder state of health than anyone he had come across at the foot of the lake. As the whole region was experiencing the worst drought in years, he was puzzled by this – until he shot five elephants, whose carcasses were consumed by Tukenda's people at a single sitting. They must, he concluded, have to live like boa constrictors – gorging themselves when they could and living on nothing in between times. At Tukenda's, Grogan also found that he was as great a curiosity to the villagers as they were to him, 'especially to the ladies of these communities, who came in large numbers to inspect me (front seats at bath time being in great request').[7]

On 1 October, five weeks after leaving Fort Portal, Grogan arrived at Wadelai, the British station on the Albert Nile where he hoped to find the supplies sent by Sharp. Sharp had indeed kept his promise, but the baggage failed to arrive. This was a considerable blow to morale and while Grogan considered what to do next he carried out an inspection of his surroundings. The fort was built on a hillock overlooking a small lake, and here he was received by Lieutenant Cape, RA, one of the officers who had been on the *Matyr* expedition which had attempted – as unsuccessfully as he – to beat Marchand to Fashoda. After the trying journey to Lake Albert without Sharp he was glad of company, his prolonged isolation having caused him to find out 'what a terribly uninteresting fellow one is'.[8]

A hunting trip with Cape in the hills surrounding Wadelai failed to raise Grogan's spirits, although they spotted large numbers of rhino.

Great storms broke every night, depositing water as would 'an inverted bath'; Grogan's tent was washed away; and the conditions put both men increasingly on edge. They were awake for three nights in a row, hammering at tent pegs and trying to hold up poles, and finally decided to return to Wadelai as 'life had become rather a burden'.[9] By now Grogan's sense of desperation was mounting. He continued to record details of everyone he met, and of local customs that he witnessed; but he was constantly ill and increasingly anxious to reach home.

The enforced delay in Wadelai added to his frustrations, and three weeks after arriving there he finally gave up waiting for Sharp's supplies. He paid off the ten Manyema porters who had accompanied him from Fort Portal, and gave them strict instructions to return home via Kampala. It was not the most direct route, but one which he hoped would enable them to avoid meeting the same fate as their comrades in the Rutchuru valley. That done, he cast off down the Albert Nile, heading for Khartoum, with his five loyal Watonga; the cook-boy who had been with him since Ujiji; and two men recruited in Ruanda. He was now determined to travel even faster and lighter than before.

Grogan's greatly diminished band made swift progress downriver, despite the alarming interest shown in them by countless hippos. At night mosquitoes rendered sleep impossible, and his 'wretched' men lay awake talking 'of the happy lands flowing with milk and honey now left far behind'.[10] Three days after setting out, having narrowly avoided shooting the rapids at Dufilé, they took to the shore once again and headed several miles east to the British station. There, they collected thirty Madi porters to help with the heavier loads and marched north-west for four days across dry, stony country to Fort Berkeley (Gondokoro) – the southernmost British post on the Upper Nile.

Swamps to the south and west of the station added to the 'general salubrity' of this hell-hole, but it was an important landmark as Grogan was now 'anxious to obtain the latest news';[11] whether this was news of Gertrude, of Sharp's safety, or of the war in South Africa he did not specify, but the mere mention of this desire indicates that he was now most definitely a man in a hurry. Thus, when Captain Dugmore broke the news to Grogan that the fort's steam launch was missing it 'nearly broke [his] heart':[12] when he had left Uganda he had been fully intending to be home for Christmas. Instead he seemed to 'have come to a full-stop'.[13]

Help suddenly came from an unexpected direction – the Belgian settlement at Rejaf, the steamer port located across the river from Fort Berkeley. Its commandant introduced Grogan to Inspector Chaltin, the Belgian administrator of the Welle district of the Congo Free State, and during an 'amazing sequence of various wines and spirituous liquors'[14] Chaltin offered Grogan a passage north to Kero on a Belgian steamer. He also promised that when Grogan reached Kero, he would be given every assistance in his search for transport to Khartoum. Chaltin may have been a Belgian, and one who had led a thrust attempting to dispossess Britain of the Sudan in 1897, but Grogan was singularly loath to languish in Fort Berkeley for months until its steamer reappeared. So he swallowed his pride, accepted the offer, and left the mushroom rock of Rejaf a few days later.

The Belgian boat arrived at Lado, 'a howling waste in a wilderness of swamps',[15] after a few hours' paddling and then proceeded to Kero, a 'paradise of malaria, misery and mosquitoes'.[16] The town was the temporarily agreed border station between the Congo Free State and territory to which the French were still laying claim in the wake of the Fashoda incident. Grogan was forced to admit that whatever the health risks its solid buildings, fleet of well-kept whale-boats, and prodigious supply of fish skilfully caught by the local Anzande people were a 'marvellous example of energy'[17] – and a 'very agreeable contrast to the . . . chaos'[18] he had witnessed elsewhere in the Belgian Congo. What was even more heartening was that at Kero Chaltin proved as good as his word.

Anxiety was mounting on both sides of the Nile about the missing British steam launch, the *Kenia*, which was carrying Dr Milne and Captain Gage of the 7th Dragoon Guards (who, like Cape, were former members of the Matyr expedition). There was also increasing concern that no word had been received from a Belgian paddle-steamer, commanded by Commandant Henry and Lieutenant Bertrand which was accompanying it. Chaltin decided to send a relief party under Commandant Renier as far as Shambeh to see if there was any news of the boats there, and he agreed that Grogan could accompany Renier. As Grogan was now suffering excruciating agonies from a 'congestion of the liver' – an abscess which made it hard for him to stand up straight – this was another offer for which he was grateful. He was now concerned that reaching the Mediterranean, and medical assistance, had become a matter of life or death.

From Bohr or Shambeh, eighty miles further north, Grogan knew he would have the choice of continuing up the Bahr-el-Jebel[19] (the White Nile) if it was passable, or proceeding overland. He sincerely hoped that the former would be a viable option, and with that hope in mind he set out with Renier on 20 December, with no desire ever to 'set eyes on Kero or any other spot on the Upper Nile again'.[20] In addition to a dozen soldiers under Renier's command, a call by Grogan for volunteers to help with his loads had been answered by a motley crew consisting of a small boy, a Dinka, a criminal lunatic in chains, and a Dervish prisoner with what looked like a broken leg. His once formidable caravan was increasingly starting to resemble a travelling circus, complete with freak show.

For three days Renier's whaler forged a course past the weed, innumerable hippos and sand spits of the Upper Nile. Landing places were few and far between, and the ever-present squadrons of 'minia-ture vampires' arrived on cue at sunset, but on Christmas Eve the boat made it to Bohr. Its Dervish fort, abandoned towards the end of 1898, was now a relic of a fast-receding episode of the Scramble for Africa and Britain's reconquest of the Sudan. As Grogan wan-dered among scattered skulls and bones he reflected that 'the past fades fast in Africa; yet another year, and the cotton-bush will have hid the mouldering relics of the earthworks, and the white ant will have seen the last grin of those gruesome jaws'. It was not where he would have chosen to spend Christmas, and the festive meal consisted of fish 'lured' from the river with the assistance of a few dynamite cartridges.

At Bohr Grogan met his first large gathering of Dinka, who were not at all as he had expected. These proud and formidable tribesmen had seemingly been reduced to living as 'miserable, amphibious objects, eking out a precarious existence on semi-submerged islands'[21] by the attentions of the Dervishes, who had robbed them of most of their cattle. Being a cattle-centric people, with over a thousand words in their vocabulary to describe matters bovine, this had in effect pulled

the rug from beneath Dinka society. Their forlorn appearance, Grogan
noticed as he tried without success to buy supplies, was compounded
by their habit of daubing their bodies with ash as protection against
the mosquitoes. But the state of the Dinka and the lack of food were
far from being Grogan's main concern as he and his retinue set off
for Shambeh.

Chaltin had warned him that at Shambeh there were Senegalese
troops under a French officer, de Tonquédoc, insurgents from French
Equatorial Africa to the west, and that they were believed to be marching on Abu Kuka and possibly south as far as Bohr. They might,
Chaltin had suggested, even be responsible for the disappearance of
the Belgian and British steamers. Grogan, more suspicious of the
French (with whom Britain had come close to war over the Fashoda
Incident) than any other Europeans, was doubtful whether a surprise
meeting with a French officer would be as pleasurable as his recent
experience of their Belgian counterparts. He pushed on up the Nile
regardless, and for three days was fully occupied in keeping the Biblical
swarms of mosquitoes at bay. At times they were so invasive that he
resorted to torching the reeds in an attempt to create a mosquito-
brake; the fire, a 'picture of indescribable grandeur . . . thundered away
like a mighty sea of molten iron, licking up the country as it sped
eastwards', gave him the satisfaction of knowing that 'billions'[22] of his
tormentors were perishing. But whatever action he took there always
seemed to be billions more.

As the boat approached Abu Kuka there was no sign of any hostile
French force,[23] but Grogan was surprised to spot what looked like a
swaying tree trunk in the distance. As he had only seen one tree since
leaving Chaltin he was baffled, and not at all sure that he wasn't
hallucinating. All of a sudden, Makanjira shouted 'Steamer!', and as
they rounded a bend in the river there before them was the *Kenia*,
the 'missing' British steam launch. Mulders, its American skipper, had
a remarkable story to tell.

For three months the *Kenia* and Commandant Henry's Belgian
steamer, the *Vankerchoven*, had desperately tried to hack a way through
the *sudd*[24] towards Khartoum. After living all that time stranded in the
strangling weed, besieged by mosquitoes and never able to find a
landing place, Captain Gage had eventually ordered Mulders to turn

back in order to ferry the sick to Kero and to revictual. Meanwhile Gage, Milne and Henry had decided to strike out on foot across the *sudd*, dragging three steel lifeboats with them, in the hope of breaking through to the free river beyond it or at least of finding a settlement with enough food to keep them alive until Mulders returned. They had agreed that if he could not find them again by mid-March, Mulders was to abandon his search and leave them to their fate. As Grogan listened to the American skipper's account of events, his thoughts swiftly turned to the fate of the main party, which he assumed was still trying to find a way out of 'that vast expanse of weed of a hopelessness beyond civilized conception ... not knowing where they were, nor, in characteristic British fashion, caring, yet ever keeping their face forward, strong in the knowledge that perseverance must succeed'.[25] Henry and Lieutenant Bertrand, it seems, had become honorary Britons by dint of their courageous conduct.

Mulders had other news which was equally perplexing for Grogan. Downstream the Nile was at its lowest level for some hundred and fifty years, the result of the drought that Grogan had witnessed at every stage of his journey up the river. This was what had caused the two steamers so much difficulty, and Grogan was told that there was no chance of him being able to land on terra firma anywhere north of Bohr. Renier gallantly offered to accompany him if he wanted to try to find a way through the weed, but Grogan knew that to attempt such a feat would most probably land him in the same trouble as had befallen the British steamer. There was nothing for it but to return to Bohr and to try to strike north overland. That meant a forced march more hazardous than any he had yet undertaken.

Back at Bohr Grogan prepared as best he could for the 300-mile march due north to the British station at Sobat, but gathering supplies was as difficult as finding sufficient men to carry them. One of the two Waruanda died of fever and the Dinka guide and the Dervish disappeared, so he was left with the five Watonga, the cook-boy from Ujiji, the criminal lunatic, a small boy from Kero, and the surviving man from Ruanda. Renier helped as best he could by providing an additional five Congolese *askaris*. Thus, with a total complement of fourteen, Grogan marched out of Bohr on 30 December and covered the first six miles across the 'Titan sponge'[26] of the *sudd*. His few remaining luxuries, such as his bed and collapsible bath, were all left behind at Bohr.

For the first days of the new year the diminutive caravan pushed on through southern Dinkaland, the men wading up to their necks through lagoon after crocodile- and hippo-infested lagoon which flowed into the Nile to the west of them. The cook-boy from Ujiji, who was carrying Grogan's revolver and prismatic compass, disappeared completely on one occasion, but was rescued just as the crocodiles closed in on him. Between the lagoons, Grogan was surprised to find that the bush supported huge numbers of Dinka, despite the drought and resultant famine.[27] But their herds had been so decimated by Dervish incursions that bartering for supplies at villages was a time-consuming and usually fruitless process, accompanied by great suspicion on both sides.

Whenever possible, Grogan sought to win the confidence of the Dinka by shooting elephant for them to eat. Indeed elephant were so numerous that at times Grogan had to fling stones in order to clear a way through their ranks, and he rued the time he and Sharp had wasted hunting in the impossible terrain by the volcanoes north of Lake Kivu. The valuable tusks were all left behind as Grogan had no men to carry them, but he did entrust a dozen particularly fine ones to a group of three Dinka, with instructions that if they conveyed them to the nearest administration post and handed them in he would reward them. He was sure he would hear nothing more about it. But two years later, to his considerable surprise, he received notification that the tusks were on their way to London, whereupon he hurried to Hill's of Haymarket and had three *kukris* made with Dinka figures on the handles. Each bore the inscription 'to an honest man'. These he sent to the local British district officer in the Sudan with instructions to hand them over to the three men with his thanks.

To begin with the 'well-bred'[28] Dinka, who were in slightly better shape than those Grogan had encountered in Bohr, displayed nothing more threatening than boisterous curiosity towards the caravan. Grogan was the main object of interest: 'beautifully built'[29] men as tall as seven feet continually appeared to inspect the white man in their midst and would treat him to the traditional greeting – spitting at him. Each carried a long-bladed spear, a pointed fish-spear and a club made from a heavy purple wood, and their leaders were distinguished by ivory bracelets on their upper arms. These, and marabou feathers worn in the hair, were the only items of apparel that any Dinka sported, and Grogan was immediately struck by their similarity to water-birds: they walked like herons, and stood like storks (with one foot resting on the knee of the other leg). Above all, he found them to be utterly fearless. But soon his fascination with the Dinka started to wane. The more they became used to his presence, the less the elephants shot for them, and gifts of Diamond Jubilee medals and beads, seemed to count for anything.

The daily attentions of hundreds of abnormally tall followers soon started to prey on the nerves of Grogan's men, but escape was impossible as the caravan was seldom able to cover more than ten miles in a day's march across the stultifyingly monotonous landscape. By night the situation was even worse, with the silence broken only by the occasional splash of a fish. Grogan would stand guard in shifts with Makanjira, smoking local tobacco and 'praying for morning',[30] when he would wake 'perfectly dazed from the amount of poison injected by the mosquitoes during the night'.[31] The Waruanda porter went the way of his comrade, 'literally sucked dry'[32] by the insects, and one night the 'criminal lunatic' disappeared into the ether. What little food the men managed to obtain did not always make it to their stomachs: at one camp a kite swooped in to seize Grogan's meagre dinner out of the frying pan.

Six days out of Bohr the bush receded some forty miles from the watercourse they were following, which Grogan had named the Gertrude Nile as if in some desperate attempt to keep his incentive for tramping through this 'uttermost end of the earth'[33] in the forefront of his mind. The bush was replaced by a vast swamp of matted reed scored by small channels of water. Pythons lurked everywhere, as numerous as 'cowpats in a meadow',[34] but for a while the caravan was at least spared the attentions of the Dinka. Eighty miles north of Bohr, however, the men re-entered Dinka territory and things started to go badly wrong.

The first serious altercation began when a piece of cloth was stolen from one of the Watonga. Grogan punched the offender as he tried to escape, and cut his hand badly on the man's teeth; for the rest of the day he kept one hand on his revolver and the other on his whip. This incident proved to be only a minor test of his mettle. Others followed, but it was not until two days later that a hundred Dinka closed in on the caravan with real intent. As they approached, a porter panicked, and that was the signal for the real hostilities to commence. One of the Congolese *askaris* fell, skewered through the heart by a Dinka spear, and two others had their skulls cracked open with clubs.

Grogan reacted by shooting the Dinka chief and his 'prime minister', but as he turned to look for the boy from Kero who was carrying his revolver he found he had fled, leaving him to fend off a crashing club blow with his forearm. He shoved his empty rifle hard into his assailant's stomach, forcing him to retreat a few steps, and after reloading felled him with a dum-dum bullet. The exit wound was so horrifying that the Dinka hastily turned tail, leaving Grogan to survey the bloody scene about him. 'It was all over in a shorter time than it takes to tell the tale,' he wrote, 'but while it lasted it was fairly warm. I never expected to see my happy home again.'[35] At his feet lay one Congolese soldier in his death throes; a little further away three more lay unconscious with gaping wounds to the head. The others had mostly fled to the reeds and it was some time before Grogan managed to coax them back.

As soon as his men's wounds were dressed Grogan gave the command to jettison further loads and move on as fast as possible. Groups of sullen Dinka watched them from a distance but were not minded to risk a further attack – although a Congolese *askari* who kept lagging behind disappeared without a trace. Soon, news of the skirmish outstripped the caravan's progress and Grogan had to resort to making occasional 'pacific demonstrations'[36] with his rifle before finding a suitable place to camp. The night passed without further incident, but sleep was impossible due to the delirious moaning of the wounded men.

In the morning Grogan led his band east – away from the swamps

– in an attempt to speed their progress and avoid any Dinka. Once on firmer ground he struck due north again for fifteen miles, searching all the while for desperately needed fresh water, before meeting more marshland which stretched as far east as he could see. The sight alarmed Grogan considerably: he had no idea how far he might have to march to get around this seemingly impenetrable barrier, and turning back was not an option. After a short deliberation he decided to force his disconsolate men straight through the middle.

The first night in this marsh was spent camped on a layer of burnt vegetation no more than a few feet above the waterline. Grogan spent all the hours of darkness vomiting up the muddy water they had all been reduced to drinking; to make matters worse, his battered arm had stiffened up and he discovered that his last two tins of tobacco had gone mouldy. As he stuffed it into his pipe regardless of its taste, clouds of mosquitoes descended on its rim 'waiting their turn for a space on [his] epidermis'.[37] Among his men, the cook-boy now had severe dysentery and one of the wounded Congolese *askaris* was half-dead. All in all, Grogan wrote sardonically, 'we were a jovial party, our joviality being materially increased by the impossibility of making a fire, owing to lack of fuel'.[38]

The 'jovial party' emerged from the marsh sooner than Grogan had dared hope, then trudged for three days across a featureless plain, and eventually reached a major *khor* (stream) which Grogan guessed was the boundary between Dinkaland and Nuer country. He was in no mood for celebration. He and his men were now starving and constantly sick from drinking dirty water; at times the wounded had to be forced onwards at the point of a spear. Once across the *khor*, which flowed west into the Bahr-el-Zaraf[39] (a continuation of the Bahr-el-Jebel), the Congolese *askari* with the worst wounds disappeared after falling behind. Grogan searched for hours but had to give up in the end, amazed that the Nuer had managed to 'spirit away'[40] an armed man in open countryside. Having reached the bank of Bahr-el-Zaraf approximately thirty miles north of its junction with the Bahr-el-Jebel, Grogan turned north-east and struck out for the Bahr-el-Abiad – some hundred and twenty miles distant.

Although the men started to make faster progress over easier terrain, this did nothing for morale. For several days their only food was what Grogan could shoot, which was mostly pelican or marabou. 'Ye Gods, what a land,' he wrote, 'there was no sign of hope.'[41] Only when they were within thirty miles of the Bahr-el-Abiad did they re-enter game country – but now it was the game that was after them, not the other way round. Soon after pitching camp at sunset, Grogan heard two lions roaring to each other across the plain. They met about a mile from the camp, after which all went silent. He knew then that they were being stalked, and ordered the men to make large fires. By the time the fires were blazing the lions were already in camp, and had to be beaten off with burning torches. As they fled, they treated Grogan to 'a farewell roar that will long linger in my ears as Savage Africa's farewell!'[42]

On the approach to the Bahr-el-Abiad Grogan calculated that it was another four days' march to Sobat, and doubted whether anyone in the caravan would survive it even if his maps were correct. But while contemplating their likely fate, he suddenly noticed a curved pole swaying in the distance. As he was in a state of total nervous exhaustion he was not ready to trust his eyes, but the harder he squinted at the pole the more he became convinced that it was not the trunk of some distant palm tree. Figures then started to move on the horizon, figures that appeared to have spotted him. He blinked hard, and the next thing he knew a Sudanese soldier had walked right up to him, inserting a cartridge in his rifle as he approached. Grogan shouldered his own rifle, smiled and extended a hand. The soldier, 'with a 3ft 6in grin', drew his cartridge out of the breech and shook Grogan's hand, now blackened by the lack of fruit and vegetables in his diet. 'I could scarcely believe it was all over,' he wrote of being escorted to his famous meeting with Captain Dunn, 'that all my troubles were ended!'

After Dunn had taken Grogan in hand and fed him and his starving men, all of them collapsed on Dunn's boat. Grogan woke the next day to find it moored off the base camp of Major Peake's expedition, which was trying to cut a way through the *sudd* to clear the waterway between Khartoum and Rejaf. He revelled in the scene before his eyes, half expecting that this too would prove to be a dream, but it was real enough. In his notebook he recorded his feelings thus:

the transition from ceaseless anxiety and hungry misery to full-bellied content and tobacco-soothed repose had been so sudden; I was as a man who, after a long time staggering in the dark, is suddenly thrust into the full glare of sunlight... Nothing to do but sit and be carried along towards clean shirts, collars, friends, all that makes life a joy. How many people realize what all these things mean? How many people have ever caught the exquisite flavour of bread-and-butter? The restful luxury of clean linen? The hiss of Schweppe's? One must munch hippo-meat alone, save one's sole shirt from contact with water as from a pestilence lest it fall to pieces, and drink brackish mud for days, to realise all this.[43]

His achievement, and that of his men, in negotiating the Upper Nile, 'a desolation of desolations, an infernal region, a howling waste of weed, mosquitoes, flies, and fever, backed by a groaning waste of thorn and stones – waterless and waterlogged' started to sink in. After what he had been through since leaving Wadelai he was convinced that he need have 'no fear for the hereafter'.[44]

Things suddenly started to happen at a pace almost beyond Grogan's comprehension after his two years in the bush. All he had to do was sit 'on gunboats and in trains being made a fuss of by innumerable kindly people'.[45] Captain William Hayes Sadler, the Governor of Fashoda district, offered to take him and the Watonga to Khartoum in his gunboat and Grogan was more than happy to accept the offer after bidding farewell to his other men. A few hours later he arrived at Sobat, the British station he had thought he would never reach, and from there he despatched what he proudly called 'the first ever transcontinental post-bag'. Inside were letters and postcards to friends and family that he had written since leaving Fort Portal. Each was stamped – with great ceremony – with the bright red seal of Fashoda.

After the Sobat junction the Nile turned north-east and then due north. Hayes Sadler's steamer stopped briefly at Fashoda itself, some 500 miles south of Khartoum, where Grogan was able to survey the remains of Marchand's small French encampment which had brought Britain and France so close to war. What struck him most forcibly was the folly of fighting over such a 'God-forsaken, dry-sucked, fly-blown wilderness'.[46] At Djebel Ain the gunboat stopped again, as this was the most southerly point on the telegraph line, Grogan was finally able to send cables to Gertrude and his family to let them know he was alive and on his way home. Hayes Sadler's orderly, who looked after him, thought him a very strange *effendi*. For one thing he now had no moustache like the other *effendis*; and for another he was not a soldier. So why, the man asked, had he travelled the length of Africa? It was a good question, to which Grogan could only answer that he was from a different tribe to the other *effendis*.

Above the ford at Djebel Ain, Grogan left Hayes Sadler to join another steamer bound for Khartoum, for the simple reason that it was carrying two passengers who were exciting every bit as much talk as he was. Captain Gage and Doctor Milne had eventually managed to drag their canoes hundreds of miles across the *sudd* to within ten miles of the open water of Lake No. There, on 19 January 1900, they too had reached safety by stumbling across members of the Peake expedition. In Grogan's opinion, Gage and Milne had pulled off what he considered to be 'one of the most daring feats ever accomplished in the history of African travel'.[47] The three men filled every minute of their journey to Omdurman swapping tales of their exploits and when they arrived there, on 8 February, they found that their fame had preceded them. Sir Reginald Wingate, the Sirdar, welcomed them in person and insisted on holding an 'explorers' dinner' at the Omdurman Club. In addition to Grogan, Gage and Milne, de Tonquédoc, Henry and Bertrand were present and all British and Egyptian officers in town were summoned.

Omdurman was in festive mood: a visit by Prince Arthur, the Duke of Connaught, was looming, and the Sirdar had turned a number of Greek prisoners out of jail on the proviso that if they didn't decorate Omdurman to his satisfaction they would be hanged. The result, Grogan noted, was 'a quite startling example of patriotism and loyalty to the Royal Family'.[48] The explorers' dinner itself was equally memorable. The menu consisted of ten courses, including such delicacies as *caviare au Dervishe*, *dinde rôti avec pomme de terre au Congo*, *mayonnaise de poisson au Rejaf* and plum pudding *à l'Anglaise*; and when the feast was over the national anthems of Egypt, Britain, France and Belgium were played. The evening was concluded with a magnificent torchlight tattoo, featuring participants from each of the thirteen major tribes of the Sudan. The following day the newspapers all told of the 'Remarkable Gathering at Khartoum'.

After allowing himself a few days to recover from the revelry and look around Omdurman, Grogan took a succession of steamers and trains to Cairo. There, after an audience with Lord Cromer in which the Proconsul of Egypt quizzed the young explorer on his opinions about how the *sudd* could be tamed, his journey was almost over. But before he boarded the boat for home he had one very important promise to fulfil. The five Watonga were still with him, and they had to be safely conveyed home to Nyasaland. As he had jokingly promised he would in their little village thousands of miles to the south, he had shown them the great palace in Omdurman – the 'house as big as the hills' – but they were unimpressed. At the railhead at Wadi Halfa he had also shown them a train – and Makanjira had reacted by reaching for Grogan's four bore. Now they all stood by the 'water without end',[49] the Mediterranean, and Grogan was sure that the Watonga believed this too was nothing but an illusion.

Grogan made 'indestructible labels' bearing the Watongas' names and the location of their village, and then saw them safely onto a steamer bound for the south. Makanjira was entrusted with a letter to Charles Bowring, Nyasaland's treasurer, in which Grogan asked Bowring to ensure that his loyal companions arrived home safely. All did so except one, Chacachabo, who died on board ship. Over sixty years later Grogan would write that words could not describe 'the affinity which still persists in memory between me and these great souls'.[50]

His promise fulfilled, in the third week of February 1900 Grogan himself boarded the first ship bound for Genoa. His great trek, the first ever south–north traverse of the African continent, was at an end.[51]

EIGHT

A Veritable 'Somebody'

A s GROGAN STEPPED OFF the ship in Dover towards the end
of March 1900 he was met by a barrage of correspondents
from the national newspapers led by Ralph Blumenfeld,[1] the
news editor of the *Daily Mail*. Blumenfeld, like every one of his competitors, was eager to land a good story emanating from Africa –
especially one with a British hero who might have stepped straight
from the pages of a John Buchan novel – because the news from the
South African war was far from encouraging and a flu epidemic at
home was killing more than fifty a day.

When Chamberlain, Milner and Rhodes had finally succeeded in
pushing Kruger and the Boer republics of the Transvaal and Orange
Free State into war the previous autumn no one in London had
thought that the conflict would last much beyond Christmas.[2] But the
heavily outnumbered Boers had proved to be ruthlessly determined
and inflicted comprehensive defeats on General Buller at Colenso and
Spion Kop either side of the New Year. Suddenly, the myth of the
invincibility of the Empire's war machine lay in tatters, and successive
defeats at the hands of a rabble of 'ignorant farmers' was humiliation
indeed for the British public.

By the spring of 1900 British fortunes had improved a little and
the *Pall Mall Gazette* was once again proclaiming the empire to be
'the greatest show on earth',[3] but the tide of the war had still not
turned. In the middle of February Lord Roberts's great army relieved
Kimberley where Rhodes had been trapped since October; by the end
of the month the 118-day siege of the British forces in Ladysmith was
finally broken; and by the end of March the Orange Free State had
been annexed (and renamed the Orange River Colony). It was to be
another three months before Baden-Powell's forces, encircled by the

Boers at Mafeking, were freed. In the meantime, Grogan was just what the newspapers wanted to lift their readers' spirits. The morning after his arrival they were full of his exploits; he was now famous and, just as he had set out to be, a veritable somebody.

Gertrude was waiting for Grogan at 74 Lancaster Gate, her Aunt Carrie's town house overlooking Hyde Park, having been sent to London to attend finishing school. She must have been nervous about the reunion after almost three years apart, but when Grogan crossed the threshold she was as certain as ever of her affections. Within days the two were engaged, and were soon given the blessing of James Coleman – who was more than satisfied that Grogan's prospects now looked bright. More than that, Coleman admired the fact that his future son-in-law had displayed a level of tenacity, courage and resourcefulness that was far from normal.

'The status of being engaged,' observed Grogan, 'is not without its perils,' one of which was the rigmarole of being inspected by Gertrude's many relations. Two of her Scots maiden aunts were the most challenging inspectors, believing as they did that anyone who had been mixed up with cannibals and wild beasts was quite beyond the human pale. Nevertheless they came to London, at Gertrude's insistence, to cast their beady eye over the 'monster pretender to incorporation in the clan of Watts'.[4] Grogan took them for dinner at the Savoy, showed them that he could in fact dress properly and had acceptable table manners, and was duly passed fit for 'incorporation'.

A potential complication soon arose. As the war in South Africa dragged on Grogan found himself being 'torn between Mars and Venus'.[5] He certainly wanted to marry as soon as was possible, but he also felt it was his duty 'as a ribbon wearer'[6] to join up, and started making enquiries about where his knowledge of Africa could be best utilized. In the middle of April he received a message from Field Marshal Lord Wolseley, a fellow Anglo-Irishman, leader of the Gordon relief expedition in 1885, and former commander-in-chief of the British Army,[7] offering him a command under Carrington (who had led the column which relieved Bulawayo during the Matabele War). Grogan was on the point of accepting when Gertrude intervened. She was already exercising a much-needed grounding influence on her impulsive husband-to-be and pointed out that he was, quite simply, in no fit state to depart for Africa again so soon. His liver troubled him almost incessantly and he was still suffering recurrent and severe bouts of malaria. To march straight off to war would most likely have been the end of him and, as if to prove the point, he only needed to look at the fate of his brother, 'poor' Philip, who had signed up with the South Wales Borderers. No sooner had Philip arrived in South Africa than he was invalided home with enteric fever, as typhoid and a host of other ailments were commonly labelled.[8]

The thought of simply swanning around London while men were dying in South Africa was, however, deeply unappealing to Grogan. So he chose to compromise, an unusual occurrence in itself. On 27 April he was commissioned with the rank of captain into the 4th Royal Munster Fusiliers[9] (the 'Kerries'), a militia battalion based at Grangefield Camp in Gosport. By his own admission his appointment was 'not on account of any deep knowledge of military procedure, but [due to the] acclaim I had gathered from my African venture'.[10] As a reservist, Grogan was at least able to feel he was doing *something* to support the war effort. It also gave him the satisfaction of following in his father's footsteps by joining an Irish regiment – William Grogan had briefly served in the Wicklow Regiment – and of being able to come and go much as he pleased.

The importance of retaining a considerable degree of independence became clear just three days after Grogan received his commission. On Monday 30 April Sir Clements Markham, President of the Royal Geographical Society, rose to his feet after dinner in the Society's premises in Savile Row,[11] and introduced Grogan as the evening's guest of honour. In a packed audience were Harry Sharp, offering moral support but taking his preferred back seat in the proceedings, the King of Sweden and Norway, and two of the Society's foreign gold medallists – Captain Louis-Gustave Binger (the Frenchman who had made his name exploring the interior of the Ivory Coast and Niger) and Hermann von Wissman (the enterprising former Commissioner of German East Africa, whom Grogan had met in Dar-es-Salaam while making his way back from the Matabele War). The evening's proceedings were exceptional: at twenty-five years of age, Grogan was the youngest man ever to be accorded the honour of addressing the Society.

Grogan began by declaring that 'there is a saying in Africa that every one who has drunk *dop* (a brandy made in the Cape) and smoked Transvaal tobacco will, in spite of all inducements to the contrary, in spite of all the abominable discomforts inseparable from life in Africa, continually return to the old untrammelled freedom of the veldt'.[12] These words proved to be prescient in his case, but what struck the audience most, as Grogan delivered his lecture, was his exceptional ability as an orator. In the most eloquent terms, he concentrated specifically on those aspects of the trek which he knew were of most interest to the Society's Fellows: geography, ethnology and natural history. His delivery was measured, sprinkled with his own brand of very dry humour, and confident. Towards the end of his allotted hour he finally turned to general observations about another topic on which all explorers were required by the Society to give their views: the treatment of the 'natives'.

Grogan left no one in any doubt as to where he stood on this contentious issue. *His* experience had taught him that more could be achieved with 'tact and firmness than by a display of force, which makes them believe their country is threatened'. He expressed his pride in only once being forced to take food without paying for it, and only twice having to act 'in self-defence when actually attacked'.[13] His final words contained a precocious and thinly veiled swipe at Henry Morton Stanley, who had acquired a reputation for brutality during his expeditions – a reputation of which the Society was well aware. Grogan pointed out that on his march from Fort Portal to Wadelai, a journey through terrain whose perils Stanley had described as being so great as to be a 'waste of ammunition', he had not once had to resort to firing a shot in anger.

When Grogan had finished, Markham rose to his feet to deliver a few closing words. He said that he had been asked by Grogan to record 'the immense importance it was to [him] to have had such a travelling companion as Mr Sharp, and he felt it a great loss when Mr Sharp had to leave him to return by way of Uganda'. He added that the Society knew how important 'a good, well-tried companion' was on such expeditions, and invited Sharp – a Fellow of the Society – to speak. Sharp modestly declined, not wishing to steal Grogan's thunder. Binger also declined to comment on the lecture, as he spoke little English; but von Wissman insisted that the minutes should record that 'the only fault ... with the lecture we have just heard is that it was too short' and that Grogan should be congratulated on his 'great ability in dealing with the natives'.

Less than a month later Markham's minutes, and his considered verdict on Grogan's achievement, were read to the Society:

> One of the most striking journeys of the past year has been that accomplished by Mr Grogan, who has, for the first time, actually traversed the centre of Africa from Cape to Cairo ... the journey was a remarkable feat, but it was a great deal more. For [he] has brought back much valuable information respecting the remarkable region round Lake Kivu and on the eastern shore of Lake Albert Edward, as well as concerning the Dinka country to the east of the upper Nile.[14]

To this glowing commendation Markham added that he was sure that Grogan could 'look forward to a long career as a geographical explorer'.[15]

By now, Grogan had become a household name. At his *alma mater*, Jesus College, the editor of *The Chanticlere* wrote: 'how Mr Ewart S Grogan has been covering himself with glory is known to every reader of the newspapers which, towards the end of last term were full of his experiences, always interesting, often amusing and sometimes thrilling ... We congratulate him heartily on his exploits and on his safe return.'[16] Indeed the *Spectator*, complimenting Grogan on his 'vivid powers of description', forecast 'a fortune' for him 'if his book is one half as good as his paper' and added that 'he has seen places and tribes never seen before, and he can write about it with a literary skill which was not given to Livingstone'.

'His book' was the next task on Grogan's agenda. Mrs Eyres kindly offered him the use of Dumbleton Hall as a retreat, so he set off for the country in his latest acquisition – a fashionable Pennington three-wheeler – leaving Gertrude in London to complete her stint at finishing school. 'Terms were agreed with a daring publisher,' wrote Grogan, 'and all that remained was to wait for the glorious day when [the book] would appear on the bookstalls and I could give the first copy to Gertrude.'[17] 'All that remained' was an understatement. One complication that had to be dealt with was the dearth of photos. Most of those taken before the plate camera had disappeared in Beira had either perished in Africa or been lost in transit. An artist, A. D. McCormick, was hastily summoned to Dumbleton Hall to fill in the gaps with the help of Grogan's numerous notebooks and illustrations, of which his tutors at the Slade would have been proud. McCormick also took some photographs in the safety of the billiard room where Grogan quipped that he 'could pose as a Dinka in the nude without risk of intrusion by attentive footmen or more easily startled butlers'.[18] If such a photograph was indeed taken it has not survived.

McCormick could be of no help with the writing, and Grogan soon discovered that 'condensing a day to day diary into a book with some semblance of sequence is not easy for one who has never in his life written anything – even an essay of any dimension'.[19] Harry Sharp, who liked to keep his life as uncomplicated as possible and did not share Grogan's brazen ambition, was of little assistance. He explained to Grogan that he was happy to let his fellow explorer tell their story, just as he had been at the Royal Geographical Society. When pressed he did at least contribute one rather turgid chapter on his solo journey from Toro to the east African coast, but it did not survive into the book's second printing.

That Grogan finished the 377-page tome in less than four months was a feat almost as remarkable as the trek itself, especially as his attention was frequently diverted. During the summer months he was also producing detailed reports of his experiences for the Foreign Office and the Colonial Office,[20] and his presence remained in great demand. London's society hostesses wanted him to address dinners held in his honour; acquaintances sought his friendship; *The Times* commissioned a series of articles by him on big game hunting; and he was 'required' to deliver numerous lectures. Some of these were more straightforward than others. The boys at Grogan's old prep school, Grove House, were easily enthralled by his jaunty description of the trials and tribulations of African travel, but altogether more harrowing was addressing a fund-raising event for 'loyal colonials who have suffered by the war' at Grosvenor House. The audience consisted of over a hundred well-heeled ladies 'who', Grogan wrote, 'sat like stone images on Easter Island devoid of all expression and peering at me through long-handled lorgnettes. They reminded me of a grim experience with crabs in the mangrove swamps near Beira.'[21] One of the 'crabs' invited him for dinner afterwards, to which his quick-witted – and cheeky – reply was that his mother did not like him being out after dark.

Grogan was also summoned by Stanley, in spite of his comments to the Royal Geographical Society. He had lunch with the Grand Old Man of African exploration at his house in Woking, but the experience only made Grogan's opinion about the man even more irreverent. Stanley was not yet sixty, but was aged by his exploits beyond his years, and Grogan described him as a 'pathetic-looking little figure like a wizened parrot'. He also showed little sympathy when Stanley told him, with 'a tear [trickling] down his cheek . . . how he had failed to persuade Britain to take over the Congo'.[22] It was this failure that had supposedly 'forced' Stanley to join the payroll – and advance the ambitions in the Congo – of Leopold, King of the Belgians, a defection which Grogan found impossible to forgive. Four years after their meeting Stanley was dead.

An altogether more satisfying meeting occurred at Balmoral. There, Grogan was given the opportunity to present his father's former employer, Queen Victoria, with one of the three Union Jacks he had carried the length of Africa. A letter to Grogan penned by Ponsonby, her private secretary, after the presentation read as follows:

> The Queen desires me to thank you for your kind thought in presenting to Her the Union Jack which you carried on your remarkable journey from the Cape to Cairo. Her Majesty is glad to possess so interesting a memento of your famous journey; a journey which, the Queen understands, no other traveller has hitherto succeeded in accomplishing. I am desired to forward for your acceptance the accompanying signed photograph of the Queen as a present from Her Majesty.[23]

Grogan is reputed to have reciprocated the gesture by sending his monarch a signed likeness of himself.

A royal audience was certainly a feather in Grogan's cap, but there was no one he was keener to see than Rhodes, the man whose fireside exhortations and dream of a Cape to Cairo railroad and telegraph route had inspired Grogan to undertake his trek. He was delighted when Lord Grey informed him that 'the Old Man', having been sprung from Kimberley, would also like to have one of his Union Jacks. A lunch hosted by the Duke of Abercorn, the Chartered Company's chairman, was fixed for the presentation and Grogan was instructed to come early in order to have a private chat with Rhodes. But when he arrived he found that Rhodes, never one to stand on ceremony, had already started lunch. Undeterred, Grogan handed over the flag,[24] wrapped in a brown paper parcel. Rhodes thanked him, stuffed the parcel in a pocket of his gamekeeper's coat and then left with Grogan before any of the other guests for the official lunch had even appeared.

The two men subsequently had a number of meetings between April and June, during which Rhodes bombarded Grogan with questions about his travels and his opinions on the best route for the railway and telegraph route. He even asked Grogan if he was interested in becoming Bobby Coryndon's deputy in Barotseland, an offer Grogan was disappointed to have to decline on account of his still unpredictable state of health. Despite this rebuff, Rhodes paid him a further – quite exceptional – compliment by promising to write the introduction to his forthcoming book. Rhodes was traditionally no letter writer, but in late September Grogan duly received a note from Philip Jourdan, Rhodes's personal secretary, explaining that 'Mr. Rhodes has dictated the accompanying letter to me which he has signed. He says if you care to use it as an introduction to your book you are at liberty to do so. It is the only one he can give you as he never writes anything formal.'[25]

When he wasn't lecturing, dining or writing the book Grogan managed to put in an occasional appearance at Grangefield Camp and found that he was in distinguished company in the Kerries. The Earl of Kenmare was colonel of the regiment, his second-in-command was Mr McGillycuddy of the Reeks and Viscount Castlerosse was one of Grogan's fellow officers. Nonetheless, the formality of regimental life was a far cry from the realities of the bush war in Matabeleland, and with his inbred distrust of authority Grogan soon decided he was far from cut out for the British army. He did take part in one or two 'grand manoeuvres', which generally involved his men bayoneting sheep 'in the first flush of excitement';[26] but for the most part his duties, such as they were, entailed keeping apart the British and Irish battalions in Portsmouth (and keeping the Royal Navy from joining the fray).

One sailor who was allowed to visit his barracks was Grogan's youngest brother, Quentin, who had chosen Dartmouth and a naval career as 'the most straightforward way of avoiding Latin and Greek'. His most vivid memory of Grangefield was of being treated to a spin in the Pennington three-wheeler, an experience he did not quickly forget: 'he (Grogan) took me around the parade ground at what seemed to be a fantastic speed, in fact about 15 or 16 miles per hour, when he shouted 'duck', which I did, as we whizzed under a wire set up to take the neighbour's washing'.[27] Thus, wrote Grogan, 'passed many happy days'.[28]

As the summer of 1900 drew to a close it seemed less and less likely that the Kerries would ever be posted to South Africa. General Roberts had captured Johannesburg and Pretoria by the end of the first week in June, and won what appeared to be a decisive battle against the Boers at Bergendal on 27 August. In October, Kruger fled South Africa. Grogan was sure the action was over, so he resigned his commission and left the Kerries with Castlerosse's blessing.[29] On 11 October he and Gertrude were married at Christchurch, Lancaster Gate. Eddie Watt led his sister up the aisle; William Hayes-Sadler, the Governor of Fashoda, was Grogan's best man; and Caroline Eyres and her daughter Sybil were among the witnesses.

The service, a little surprisingly, was conducted by none other than 'Black' Morgan, Master of Jesus College, who clearly bore no grudge against Grogan for his erstwhile terror campaign against the college's Fellows. Indeed in one of the few letters that have survived from this period of Grogan's life, Morgan wrote him a glowing reference asserting that he possessed

> remarkably robust and vigorous mental powers, unflinching energy and perseverance, a calm and sound judgement and that perfect nerve and readiness of resource so necessary where difficulties have to be faced and successfully met. He

should prove especially valuable in any position – more particularly one connected with the colonies.

Grogan was, Morgan concluded, 'a highly capable and cultivated gentleman'.[30] Following the service a reception for hundreds of guests was held at Mrs Eyres's town house. 'It's a long way to Tipperary,' Grogan remarked, 'but it's a damn sight longer way from New Zealand via the Cape and Cairo to my *ultima thule* – Gertrude. At last she was mine.'[31]

Grogan and Gertrude spent ten days in Paris after the wedding, and returned home on the day that General Roberts proclaimed the annexation of the Transvaal. The honeymoon was deliberately kept short because on 26 October *From The Cape To Cairo* went on sale across the country. Gertrude received the first copy and another was immediately despatched to James Coleman. The latter was signed by Grogan, rather eccentrically, 'with love'.

The book was dedicated to Rhodes, whose rare introductory letter read as follows:

My dear Grogan,

You ask me to write you a short introduction for your book, but I am sorry to say that literary composition is not one of my gifts, my correspondence and replies being conducted by telegrams.

I must say I envy you, for you have done that which has been for centuries the ambition of every explorer, namely, to walk through Africa from South to North. The amusement of the whole thing is that a youth from Cambridge during his vacation should have succeeded in doing that which the ponderous explorers of the world have failed to accomplish. There is a distinct humour in the whole thing. It makes me the more certain that we shall complete the telegraph and railway, for surely I am not going to be beaten by the legs of a Cambridge undergraduate.

Your success the more confirms one's belief. The schemes described by Sir William Harcourt[32] as 'wild cat' you have proved are capable of being completed, even in that excellent gentleman's lifetime.

ABOVE LEFT William Grogan: Ewart's father, Queen Victoria's Surveyor General to the Duchy of Lancaster and legendary procreator.

ABOVE RIGHT Jane Grogan with her beloved Ewart and his younger brother Philip.

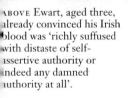

ABOVE Ewart, aged three, already convinced his Irish blood was 'richly suffused with distaste of self-assertive authority or indeed any damned authority at all'.

ABOVE The elfin Ewart leaving for Grove House aged seven.

LEFT Ewart and Philip take to the boards.

Grogan, second from left, and fellow 'bloody troopers' in Matabeleland, 1896.

'Gladstone bag on wheels labelled coach' negotiates the 'Great North Road', Matabeleland 1896.

c

b

a 'It was his wont to brood in solitude dreaming the destinies of men': Cecil Rhodes in Matabeleland, 1896.

b Rhodes (third from right) under the tree where most of his famous *indabas* with the Matabele chiefs took place.

c Rhodes with the Matabele chiefs at 'World's View' in the Matopo Hills in 1897, the year after the famous peace *indabas*.

Rhodes and Milner were hell-bent on extending the Empire's reach northwards, while Kitchener was driving the railway south from Wadi Halfa: 'the stew pan of Africa was evidently simmering'.

'Loathsome Hags Danced A Wild Fandango'.

Grogan and Makanjira under attack from Baleka cannibals: 'The Diabolical Noise Made By The Onrushing Natives Showed The Matter Was Serious'.

TOP Grogan's illustration of his camp to the east of Mount Götzen.

ABOVE 'I Met An Elderly Pigmy'.

RIGHT 'I Advanced With Outstretched Hand': the lives of Grogan's greatly diminished band are saved by stumbling across Captain Dunn's shooting party by the Upper Nile, February 1900.

Grogan settling down to lunch with Captain Dunn moments after their fortuitous meeting.

'The Tourists' team photograph at the Palace, Khartoum, February 1900. Grogan is second from the right in the back row, smoking his customary cigar. He is joined by fellow European adventurers Lt Bertrand, Commandant Henry, Capt Gage, Dr 'Daddy' Milne, Lt de Tonquédoc, Sous Officier Salpin and a number of their African guides.

The face that launched a man from Cape to Cairo: Gertrude Grogan, née Watt.

Grogan's Palace in Nairobi: Chiromo, 1905.

Yet another children's party at Chiromo.

As to the commercial aspect, every one supposes that the railway is being built with the only object that a human being may be able to get in at Cairo and get out at Cape Town.

This is, of course, ridiculous. The object is to cut Africa through the centre, and the railway will pick up trade all along the route. The junctions to the East and West coasts, which will occur in the future, will be outlets for the traffic obtained along the route of the line as it passes through the centre of Africa. At any rate, up to Bulawayo, where I am now, it has been a payable undertaking, and I still think it will continue to be so as we advance into the far interior. We propose now to go on and cross the Zambesi just below the Victoria Falls. I should like to have the spray of the water over the carriages.[33]

I can but finish by again congratulating you, and by saying that your success has given me great encouragement in the work I have still to accomplish.[34]

The advertisements placed in all the newspapers by the 'daring' publishers, Hurst & Blackett, proudly announced the arrival of 'The Greatest Book on African Travel and Sport ever published, being an Account of the First Traverse of the Dark Continent from South to North'. With its maps, McCormick's 115 full-page illustrations, numerous sketches of Grogan's and photographs it was very much a coffee-table book, which was reflected in its price – one guinea. To those who could afford it, part of its appeal was that Grogan was simply a young maverick: he was not a soldier-explorer like Lugard, a missionary-explorer like Livingstone, or a journalist-explorer like Stanley. In other words, though Grogan was clearly a believer in the Empire's 'mission' in Africa and an admirer of Rhodes, his observations were regarded as being relatively unbiased. The *Morning Post*'s reviewer called the book 'a notable and attractive addition to the great library of African travel'. The *Pall Mall Gazette* remarked that 'optimism has long been wanting on Africa, and Mr Grogan's high spirits are most refreshing'. The *Scotsman* hailed the newcomer's 'way of getting through regardless of consequences to himself . . . his pluck is splendid – he is "clear grit" as the Americans say'. Even the *Daily News*, usually lukewarm on matters imperial, commended Grogan on 'captivating his readers from the very beginning of his story', and added that 'the volume abounds in good practical sense and shrewd observation'. Only the Alpine Club, unappeased by Grogan's apology for not having climbed more peaks during the trek, received the publication sniffily: 'we mention this book not for what it contains, but for what is omitted . . . the interesting record-breaking which the book describes we have not to do with here'.[35] The club's vanity would have surprised few; even the achievements of Whymper – one of its most illustrious members and Grogan's mountaineering tutor – were not always accorded the recognition they deserved for the simple reason that Whymper, as the son of a wood engraver, was regarded as *trade*.

The sole contribution of Grogan's siblings to all the adulation was one he might have preferred to do without. His sister Maggie, who was rapidly earning herself a reputation as being rather wayward, was going through a literary phrase and decided to add the following poem to her growing output of 'great' works:

> ### THE LAY OF THE MAN WHO WENT
> ### FROM CAPE TO CAIRO,
> ### ON HIS ARRIVAL AT THE LATTER
>
> Air – ('The Man Who,' etc)
>
> I've just got here from Cape Town,
> After months of weary toil;
> I from Cape to Cairo went,
> On exploring business bent,
> Dame Fortune smiles upon me as she's smiled on none before,
> Now my object I've obtained and I'm content.
>
> They think me a swell at the Grand Hotel,
> I have taken my lodgings there,
> You should see the people stare,
> I might be a polar bear.
> You should see them watch with a wondering eye,

A Veritable 'Somebody'

> You should hear them say with a whispered sigh,
> It's the man who crossed the land from Cape to Cairo.[36]

Maggie's *Parodies And Other Poems* did not meet with the same critical success as her brother's great oeuvre.

NINE

———◦✦◦———

Back to Kindergarten

WHEN THE GROGANS RETURNED from their short honey-moon in Paris there was still nothing in the news to lead Ewart to believe that the decision to resign his commission in the Kerries had been precipitate. The 'Khaki' General Election called that same autumn by Lord Salisbury secured public endorse-ment of the Conservative government's optimistic and bellicose stance on the South African war: their overall majority over a divided Liberal/Irish Nationalist opposition increased to 134 seats. Since General Roberts's confirmation of the annexation of the Transvaal on 25 October it was widely believed that the Boers were defeated. Grogan turned his mind to more pacific pursuits: he had been invited to make a short lecture tour of New York and Washington, and Gertrude wanted to parade her dashing husband in New Zealand. The newly weds were in no great hurry; with Grogan's name made, and Gert-rude's considerable dowry[1] behind them, they were able to treat the forthcoming year as an extension of their honeymoon and set sail on the *Lucania*, bound for New York, at the beginning of November.

Grogan found on arrival that his fame had spread expeditiously: the *New York Times* carried an article welcoming him as a man who 'although only twenty-six years old, has placed himself in the front rank of African explorers'.[2] To his and Gertrude's delight the hospital-ity they were shown on America's east coast matched that experienced by Grogan in San Francisco three years earlier, and he was again impressed by 'the easy manner of the Americans compared with the stodgy mannerisms of the still class-conscious English'.[3] Over thirty clubs invited him to become an honorary member, and at a stag dinner given in his honour Grogan was introduced to some of the leading members of America's 'generation of fortune-builders',[4] including

John D. Rockefeller. It did not escape him that American tycoons commanded fortunes which dwarfed those of Rhodes and the Randlords, and he concluded that – however powerful the British Empire – New York was unlikely ever to be dislodged from its position as the world's financial capital.

While making his mark in New York Grogan also lunched with William Randolph Hearst, the newspaper magnate, who secreted one of his reporters under their table to record an unauthorized 'Interview With The Great Explorer'; with Mark Twain, who teased him 'with his usual sense of humour';[5] and with society hostess Mrs Strong, whom he had met in Cairo at the end of the trek. The latter took her young friend to a dinner with Woodrow Wilson, at which the President of Princeton University treated Grogan to a stern lecture on his duty to the world. This did not enamour Wilson to Grogan, who thought he had just met the reincarnation of Dickens's Mr Pecksniff – a mean, treacherous arch-hypocrite. When the shrewd Mrs Strong intimated that 'Pecksniff' would be a future president of America, Grogan's swift rejoinder was 'God help the USA'.[6] Some two decades later, when Grogan again met Mrs Strong in London she embraced him and declared, to Grogan's great satisfaction, 'Sonny, God did not help the USA.' By then his own opinion of the American president had plumbed new depths: he derided him as 'the Valkyr of The Wind-Feast of History'[7] and instigator of 'that bag of Kilkenny cats',[8] the League of Nations.

Before the end of the month Grogan moved on to Washington to deliver his main lecture at the National Geographic Society, whose President was Alexander Graham Bell, the Scottish-American inventor of the telephone. He had some justification in being wary about relating his African experiences, not least because America had greeted the first reports of his trek with all the incredulity that had been accorded to missionary-explorers Krapf and Rebmann in Europe when they claimed to have spotted snow-covered mountains in Africa half a century earlier. The April edition of *National Geographic* magazine had entitled a report of Grogan's adventures 'Where Exploration Is Needed', and recorded 'without comment . . . a number of [his] startling statements'.[9] The focus of its scepticism was his scrap with the Baleka cannibals, and his discovery that herds of elephant had been buried by lava from the recent eruption of Mount Götzen. In the event Grogan's fears proved unfounded and he dazzled the geographical world's most prestigious audience with his lecture.

One man who was particularly impressed by Grogan's performance was Walter Page, a partner in the great publishing firm of Doubleday Page Inc. and future Ambassador to the Court of St James. The two soon struck up a friendship, and as a result Grogan agreed to write an article about Rhodes for Page's journal the *World's Work*. This five-page paean is a significant, if rather alarming, document which provides an all-encompassing picture of the twenty-six-year-old Grogan's vision of Empire. For him, Rhodes could quite simply do (almost) no wrong, and Grogan was certain that his mentor's 'full influence on the world' would 'receive its true valuation centuries hence'. Indeed, after defending Rhodes against every allegation levelled at him by his enemies, Grogan finally concluded that he 'stood forth like a rugged mountain rising from a plain; the same calm, unbending dignity, the same incomprehensible pre-eminence characterize them both'.[10] Sixty years later he remained unrepentant (and, it must be said, as substantially unaware of the murkier details of Rhodes's transgressions as the rest of the British public), but he did acknowledge that the forcefulness of his opinions had been precocious. 'I was', wrote Grogan, 'an impetuous young man, self-confident and self-opinionated to the verge of impudence; a dedicated apostle of Rhodes's theme of British destiny, individualistic to the core . . . [and] honestly attempting to portray Africa and its peoples as he saw it, without any attempt to fabricate or exaggerate passing events'.[11]

With the one exception of this article Grogan wisely confined himself to talking about exploration, rather than politics, during his American tour. The same could not be said of that other cigar-toting young maverick for whom Africa and writing had proved the gateway to fame – the equally opinionated Winston Churchill. Both men, it transpired, were tramping the American lecture circuit at the same time, having assumed the South African war to be over. Where Grogan had achieved fame through his trek, Churchill had by now made his name through his famous escape from a Boer prisoner of war camp, and the publication of *London to Ladysmith: Via Pretoria* and *Ian Hamilton's March*. Furthermore, the money earned from the books had enabled him to throw himself wholeheartedly into a political career, and he had secured election as the Tory MP for Oldham in the 'Khaki' Election that autumn.

Churchill's particular difficulties with his American audiences were caused by two political beliefs which he might have been well advised not to air. Firstly, he attracted overt criticism from the Irish-American lobby who objected to Tory opposition to Home Rule for Ireland; and secondly, he misjudged the strength of pro-Boer feeling in America. At the Waldorf-Astoria on 12 December Churchill's views were publicly denounced by Mark Twain, who had also teased Grogan about his strident imperialism just a few weeks earlier. This was just one of a number of public relations setbacks which limited the success of Churchill's tour, and by the time it was over he may have wished that he had taken up a very different offer instead of visiting America.

In July, Churchill had been approached by Abe Bailey, one of Rhodes's foremost allies among the Randlords, and asked for his help. Rhodes and Bailey wanted to undertake a survey of the potential for European settlement along parts of the route that Grogan had forged from Cape to Cairo; and they wanted Churchill to deploy his literary skills to help publicize their findings. Churchill had initially expressed a great interest in the scheme, but insisted that he achieve his goal of securing a seat in Parliament first. That done, his interest waned – but for a few months in the summer of 1900 there existed the intriguing possibility of Churchill following directly in Grogan's African footsteps.[12] This would have delighted Grogan in more ways than one: for much of the next decade the two men's divergent views on how best to extend the Empire's influence in Africa were to place them in open conflict – and Grogan was convinced that the cause of this conflict was Churchill's ignorance of the continent.

After Grogan had completed his lectures he and Gertrude headed south to visit Walter Page's aunt in Virginia. Hospitable though she was, her matronly attentions were not sufficient to induce in Grogan a desire to linger in America's southern states. The endemic racial intolerance affronted his own, albeit paternalistic, outlook on life. Indeed the evidence before him convinced him that America's oft-heard call for 'equal rights for all men' was as selectively applied as in the Boer republic or Leopold's Congo. He was not sorry when the time came to set out for the west coast by train.

Grogan was particularly eager to show Gertrude round San Francisco, and when they finally arrived she was thrilled by 'the splendour of the city and its surroundings'. As Grogan's bachelor days were over he resisted the temptation to go and seek out Captain Pat's 'boys', and was also careful not to be caught admiring the city's Hispano-American beauties – even though now and again when Gertrude was looking into a shop window 'some smutty-eyed dream would drift past and flutter her eyelids'[13] at him.

From San Francisco the couple sailed for the Hawaiian islands. Grogan was unable to find the hospitable Prince David, whose disappearance he attributed to the recent annexation of the islands by the United States; but ever alert to a potential commercial opening he sent Rhodes a cable suggesting that the timber of the indigenous algebra tree might be useful in South Africa. He received a reply by return which read 'send me a ton'. It was here in the mid-Pacific that Grogan also heard of the death of Queen Victoria, and he and Gertrude were invited by the American authorities to be the guests of honour at a moving ceremony on the beach. They then boarded a Dutch steamer for the long, dreary voyage across the Pacific.

'New Zealand', Grogan remarked, 'was still the quiet, contented, rather humdrum, hospitable, ultra-British New Zealand,'[14] but news of his exploits ensured that the first few days after arrival were far from dull. He and Gertrude were asked to attend a reception for the Duke and Duchess of York, and Grogan was also summoned to a meeting with Prime Minister Seddon, during which the two men discussed the possibility of introducing moose and chamois into the country's alpine areas. But other than these two official functions the months in New Zealand were devoted to visiting friends, fishing trips, helping out on dagging days, attending *hakas*, and intermittent returns to Napier to spend time with Gertrude's family.

Eddie Watt was by this time managing Longlands station and displaying acumen worthy of his father. Although increasingly known as a turf man as opposed to a rancher he had, by April 1900, built up Longlands' flock to over 25,000 head and had also established a Shorthorn stud herd in addition to the stud flock of 2,000 Lincoln ewes. As his homestead at Pukalu had burnt down that summer it was to a new one at Ngatara ura that he welcomed his sister and his old sparring partner from Cambridge. There is no record of how James Coleman greeted the man who had so ambitiously asked for his step-daughter's hand some four years earlier, but it was obvious to all that Gertrude was blissfully happy with her jaunty, keen-eyed husband and that was most probably good enough for Coleman. Besides, his attentions were now concentrated on the credentials of another (relatively) impoverished suitor for one of his stepdaughters: Francis Baden-Powell was assiduously courting Gertrude's younger sister, Florence. Once again Coleman, despite some reservations, did not ultimately stand in the way of the match, and like Grogan and Gertrude the couple visited New Zealand on their honeymoon the following year.[15]

While the Grogans were staying at Napier they received a surprise visit from Quentin, who took some leave to meet his new sister-in-law when his ship – HMS *Juno* – put in to Wellington. Although nine years younger than Grogan, Quentin was already just as independent minded as his eldest brother, and he and his sister Dorothy were the only ones in the family who ever seemed to poke fun at 'the bees' in their famous brother's 'bonnet'. The particular 'bees' which amused Quentin during his stay were his brother's insistence on using soda water for brushing his teeth, and that it was essential 'not to wear shorts in the tropics, as the Sun would get you'.[16] In spite of, or perhaps because of, this sort of ribbing it was Quentin and Dorothy who among their siblings were destined to remain in closest contact with Grogan over the ensuing decades.

By midsummer Quentin had returned to his ship, and Grogan became increasingly restless. He was keen to embark on his quest to establish himself as successfully as Eddie Watt and other New Zealand friends had done, and that meant returning home. So he and Gertrude said their farewells and boarded a steamer which took them round Cape Horn to Montevideo and the Argentine, where Grogan made a comprehensive study of local farming methods to add to what he had learnt during his time in New Zealand. They arrived in London in November 1901, and it was then that Grogan was told that all the plans he had cooked up during the long sea voyage would have to be put on the back-burner: Gertrude was pregnant.

Grogan was ecstatic at the 'awe-inspiring, enchanting prospect of soon becoming a father', even though he harboured suspicions that fatherhood entailed becoming 'anybody's anybody' at the mercy of Gertrude, Nanny Redwood and the soon-to-arrive 'curly-headed little bundle of tantrums'.[17] In preparation for the birth he leased 6 Embankment Gardens and there, on 3 May, Gertrude gave birth to a baby girl who was christened Dorothy. Grogan had assumed that his first-born would be a boy, but accepted the gender of the new arrival philosophically. He anticipated that Dorothy was, after all, to be the first of many – though he had no intention of challenging his father's extraordinary record.

When Grogan was called upon to sign Dorothy's birth certificate he found it frustrating that the only occupation he could declare was still that of 'Captain, 4th Royal Munster Fusiliers'. In January 1902 he had again met up with Rhodes and the 'Old Man' had again exhorted Grogan to 'give himself to Africa'. But before any specific role could be found for him Rhodes died from an aneurysm of the aorta at the age of just forty-eight. The newspapers declared 'that the whole of the British Empire [was] in mourning',[18] and South Africa came to a standstill. Tens of thousands of mourners, black and white, filed past his coffin and turned out along the railway line as it was conveyed for burial in the Matopo Hills – the scene of Grogan's first meeting with the man whom he regarded as 'the incarnation of Cape to Cairo'.[19]

Rhodes's death served to harden still further Grogan's resolve to return to Africa. The months spent waiting for Dorothy's birth had convinced him that London held few attractions for him. The demise of Rhodes and Queen Victoria within the space of a single year also imbued him with an uneasy feeling that 'the staid splendour of the Victorian era was on the wane'.[20] In Africa, on the other hand, there was action and opportunity – and it was on troubled South Africa that Grogan increasingly focused his attention.

Far from ending in 1900, as Grogan had once thought it would, the Boer War had dragged on into 1902 due to the Boers' stubborn and brilliant use of guerrilla tactics. A large part of their success was, ironically, attributable to two generals who had been at Cambridge with Grogan: the die-hard De Wet and Jan Smuts. Neither had been close friends, but Grogan remembered Smuts as a 'remote, studious, self-contained man' who in the opinion of 'us less responsible undergraduates [cut] a somewhat dismal figure'. Little had Grogan realized at the time that just a decade later Smuts would be 'defying and holding at bay the massed might of the British Empire', nor that the two men's paths would again cross after Smuts had emerged as 'a dominant world figure'.[21]

What preoccupied Grogan most about the Boer War was the damage it had done to British prestige. The British response to the Boers' resistance, orchestrated by Kitchener, had been to order troops to 'sweep the veld clean'[22] and starve the enemy into submission. As a result, as many as 28,000 Boer men, women and children had died in British concentration camps to add to the 6,000 Boer combatants who had been killed in action. The death toll among the Africans – combatant and non-combatant – who suffered the most in the white man's war was much, much higher. The war had also cost Britain a staggering £200 million and some 20,000 casualties (of whom a substantial number were accounted for by enteric fever which had invalided Grogan's brother Philip). The peace that was hammered out by June 1902, soon after Dorothy's birth, was largely unsatisfactory for all involved. South Africa was devastated, but to Grogan this parlous state of affairs seemed on reflection to promise just the sort of opportunity to 'give himself to Africa' that he was after.

His optimism was based on two facts. The first was that, whatever the cost, the Empire had at last gained control of Africa's richest country, thereby bringing the total number of African territories under British control to fifteen. The second was that arch-imperialist Lord Milner was in the driving seat as High Commissioner of the new South Africa, and Grogan knew that Milner was determined to win the peace by anglicizing South Africa to such an extent that the Boers would be marginalized even in what had been their own republics. Thus, Grogan zealously concluded, Rhodes's hopes of winning Africa's 'Great Game' were still very much alive.

By the end of the summer of 1902 any lingering uncertainty on Grogan's part about his career prospects was dispelled when Milner personally summoned him to South Africa. Milner was in the process of enlarging his 'Kindergarten' – a retinue of like-minded young imperialists whom he had charged with rebuilding the war-torn country – and had heard through his private secretary, John Buchan, that Grogan was both a doer and one of Rhodes's more capable and reliable protégés. As soon as baby Dorothy was old enough to travel the Grogans set out for Durban, accompanied by Nanny Redwood, Edith the parlour maid and Martin the gentleman's gentleman. This was just the vanguard of the clan that eventually descended on Johannesburg: in his capacity as head of the family (and authoritarian keeper of its purse) Grogan decreed that South Africa should become his siblings' home as well. As a result Philip sailed for Natal on the Carisbrook Castle on 20 December 1902, and by midsummer of the following year Archie and Margaret had also sailed south. Quentin followed later, having charmed the Admiralty into cancelling a warrant for his arrest issued after he had absconded from the Navy because he felt that it no longer had 'a very thrilling outlook' and that 'peace would reign indefinitely'.[23] The only two who did not join Grogan in South Africa were sister Dorothy, now married, and little Hilda who was still at school in Eastbourne.

Grogan took a house in the upmarket district of Belgravia close to that of Julius Jeppe, the mining magnate, and settled the family in. As the latter stages of the Boer War had mostly been fought out on the veld, Johannesburg (like Pretoria) had suffered little physical damage. But the brazen 'auriferous' town, which had sprung up in less than twenty years still had the feel of the Wild West about it: it was untidy – 'full of corrugated iron buildings of all sorts and sizes with a few modern shops and offices scattered in between' – and gave the impression of being only half-finished. Horse-drawn trams plied the streets, and everyone seemed to Grogan to be in as great a hurry as in that other precocious settlement of his acquaintance, San Francisco. In Johannesburg the hurry was to make money, whether from the seams of gold that lay beneath it or from the business of reconstruction.

Milner was renowned as a brilliant scholar, a skilled diplomat who had served as financial secretary to Lord Cromer in Egypt, and a man whom Whitehall considered to be a lot 'safer' than Rhodes. His long face, patrician bearing and steely grey eyes added to his aura of gravity but he took an instant liking to Grogan, in whom he recognized all the characteristics he was looking for in his young lieutenants: intellect, courage and energy. Both men were critics of British parliamentary politics, or 'Bumbledom' as Grogan called it, and both shared a common vision of Britain's imperial goals and responsibilities. Many years later Grogan would write that Milner, 'an outstanding character', suffered from only one failing: 'he believed that everyone he met was inspired with the same selfless, sincere devotion to life's purpose as himself'.[24]

Grogan had no hesitation in accepting an appointment to Milner's 'cabinet', which he remarked was 'a collection of remarkably intelligent young men'[25] even by his standards, and joined his new friends Buchan and Jeppe on the Johannesburg Town Council. He was also instructed to rent a farm near Middelburg as part of Milner's strategy to break the Boer dominance of the agricultural sector, and became a director of Jeppe's African Farms Company Limited, which bought up more than a million acres of prime Transvaal farmland during 1903. Grogan's 'Good Hope' farm did not live up to its name despite the best efforts of Quentin and a former cavalry officer called Knapman. There was no market for its crop of black wattle, and a plague of puff-adders put paid to attempts to rear chickens. What's more, relations between Boer and British farmers were far from good, and after an attack of dysentery Quentin decided to move on to another farm near Germiston before sailing home at the end of 1903. Grogan's interest in the farm also waned, and he soon decided that his time was best spent on Town Council work alone. His particular duties were to carry out an investigation into retail pricing, and to inspect the new factories springing up everywhere for the Public Health Committee on which he sat.

In Johannesburg Grogan and Gertrude swiftly got to know many of the movers and shakers involved in the reconstruction. He greatly enjoyed the company of Buchan, Jeppe, Kipling and the financier C. S. Goldmann, and he paid regular visits to his old friend Lawley, who was running Barberton's Victoria Gold Mining Company during a lull in railway-building. Rhodes's assorted old hands – whom Grogan described as members of 'that strange medley of Jews, aristocrats, roughnecks and statesmen'[26] were also much in evidence. Among those he regularly came across were Alfred Beit, whom Grogan described as the 'genius who kept Rhodes's finance on the rails'; the 'piratical gambler' Abe Bailey, who 'choked with laughter' when he recounted to Grogan how 'he had outwitted his father in some financial deal'; and Hans Sauer, another 'pirate' who had been intimately involved in the murkier aspects of Rhodes's fight for dominance in Kimberley. All in all, Grogan's lasting impression of the town was that it was one of 'violent contrasts between the quiet living of the professional and civil servant elements', with whom he preferred to identify, 'and the competitive ostentation of the get-rich-quicks'.[27]

The biggest and most controversial issue confronting Milner, Grogan and all members of the Council during 1903 was the dearth of labour. With that in mind Milner established the Transvaal Labour Commission in July and charged it with investigating how to meet the needs of the mine owners. Its conclusion was that there was a shortage of 300,000 labourers and that the only way to solve the problem was to import large numbers of Chinese 'coolies' on short-term contracts. There was widespread opposition to this scheme, but Milner pointed out that labour had to come from somewhere if the economy was to improve and that, in the absence of sufficient numbers of Africans (or a willingness on the part of most Europeans) to work in the mines, there were few alternatives. Milner's arguments prevailed, and towards the end of the year he deputed Grogan, among others, to draft the terms of the Chinese labour initiative. But in early December Grogan's name suddenly disappeared from the list of those seeking re-election to the Town Council. He was once again suffering from a liver abscess, and by Christmas he was at death's door.

Grogan was rushed to hospital and operated on immediately. As anaesthesia was rudimentary he did not remain fully unconscious throughout, and later remembered hearing the doctors saying 'he will never be happy until we open him up and have a look'. They were amazed at what they found – an abscess as large as a coconut had to be drained. That was not the end of his troubles: he was 'put out to grass' in a nursing home on the outskirts of Johannesburg from which it became impossible to escape when it was isolated due to an outbreak of pneumonic plague. As supplies started to run low the surviving patients turned to Grogan for a lead and, despite his debilitated state, he organized a system whereby provisions were passed through a window in exchange for corpses. Eventually the epidemic exhausted itself, and a fortunate Grogan attributed his survival to being 'so over-populated with bugs that this alien [plague] could find no port of entry'.[28]

By the time Grogan was able to return home to Gertrude in Belgravia the South African economy had started to boom. Over 300 new companies floated in 1904 alone and even before the first Chinese labourers arrived in June most gold mines were functioning again. But an election was looming at home, and Milner and his 'Kindergarten' started to attract accusations of condoning slavery for their decision to import the Chinese labourers. Grogan paid close attention to the ruckus which would lead to Milner's downfall and the election of a Liberal government the following year, and he started to reconsider his future. Above all, he was convinced that South Africa would be the worse off if Milner's opponents succeeded in ousting him, and that the country might well end up in the hands of the Boers if Milner's plans for reconstruction were abandoned. His interest in South Africa was diminishing fast, but he was far from sure where to go next.

The answer to Grogan's predicament was not long in coming, and was provided by an enterprising Canadian to whom Lawley introduced him. Frederick R. Lingham was renowned as the 'Lumber King' of the Transvaal[29] and had recently been shown some samples of yellow wood and cedar from 'a mysterious land north of German Tanganyika ... with an ancient dhow port – Mombasa'.[30] These had greatly impressed him, and he had secured an option on a substantial concession in the 'mysterious land' from which to extract such timber. Now he needed a partner, and asked Grogan if he would be interested in going into business with him.

It did not take Grogan long to make up his mind. His fascination with terra incognita was as strong as ever, and he knew that there was a vast demand in South Africa for timber for pit props. He had also learnt plenty about British East Africa's putative prospects the previous year when its Collector of Customs, Mr A. Marsden, had toured South Africa appealing for settlers. Without further ado, he sent Dorothy, Nanny Redwood and the rest of the staff home to England via the cooler Atlantic route, and boarded a steamer bound for the Red Sea with Gertrude. On 14 May 1904 they arrived in Mombasa on what was described by the *African Standard* as 'the busiest day Mombasa has ever seen': *two* ships were in port carrying a total of thirty passengers. The paper singled out Grogan's arrival as worthy of mention, although it was a little wide of the mark when citing the details of how he had become famous. 'Capt. Grogan', it advised its readers, 'distinguished himself by his famous bicycle ride from the Cape to Cairo'.[31] In a very short space of time, however, Grogan would see to it that everyone knew exactly who he was and what he was doing in the East African Protectorate.

TEN

'A Great Man who will be Even Greater'

T HE CORAL ISLAND of Mombasa was a striking sight for the Grogans. Across the clear blue water of the Indian Ocean, on which bobbed myriad native dugouts and other craft on their way to greet the DOA's *Feldmarschall*, could be discerned the more prominent features of what amounted to a tableau of the ancient port's history. The approach to the harbour was dominated by Fort Jesus, built centuries earlier by the Portuguese; then there were the numerous, almost equally old, Arab buildings; and finally the symbol of the newcomers – the headquarters of the British Administration.

Here and there along the shore were dotted the whitewashed and red-roofed houses of the small European community, peeking out from the lush tropical bush. Mango, baobab and palm trees fringed the shore, and everywhere the senses were assaulted by vivid greens and by the sweet smell of hibiscus and frangipani. The atmosphere was one of contentment, a delicious lethargy. Most who saw this sight for the first time agreed that they could not hope for a more visually pleasing welcome to their new home. The fact that the port was insanitary, always experienced a shortage of fresh water and a scarcity of decent food (tinned salmon or corned beef were the standard fare), and that after dark the streets were the domain of hyaenas, jackals and leopards did not apparently detract from the romance. Grogan was used to much worse, and the ever-game Gertrude took everything in her stride.

There was, in addition to the scenery, another good reason for passengers always to be pleased about arriving in Mombasa: it put an end to the journey on a DOA liner. German passengers, as Grogan's fellow East African pioneer Lord Cranworth noted with disdain, were seldom interested in the traditional British shipboard pursuits of playing games or taking exercise and tended to show a 'complete disregard for the convenience, or indeed feelings of their fellow passengers'. Their only recreation, it seemed, was beer drinking on a prodigious scale which impressed the youthful Cranworth considerably more than his fellow passengers' manners. Regular contests were held on deck in which competitors would be primed with a glass of beer every two minutes and instructed to do their worst. 'Gradually', Cranworth observed of one such contest, 'the rabbits, including a few ambitious and over-optimistic Britons, were eliminated and at sixty glasses the competitors were reduced to two.' The winner then put paid to his opponent after another ten glasses and celebrated with a gratuitous three more, after which 'bowing right and left, he strode purposefully to the side and gracefully inserted a finger in his throat, and behold it was just as if one had removed a bung from a barrel!' To his amazement Cranworth learnt, on enquiring if the winner was a national champion, that the man was 'not more than half-way up the second class' in this German 'national sport'.[1]

In 1904 there were still no piers or proper wharves in the harbour, nor would there be for many years to come, so passengers and their luggage were transported to terra firma by lighter, and then carried through the shallows by obliging 'natives'. After clearing customs, a mere formality, the Grogans headed for the Grand Hotel by covered trolley, pushed by two Africans in sailor suits of white or khaki along rails that had once formed part of the never completed (indeed scarcely begun) Central African Railway. There was a double track from Ras Serani to Treasury Square, and branch lines to the British Residence, the residential districts and the Mombasa Sports Club. On the single-track branch lines a strict order of precedence was observed when meeting another trolley: 'junior' personages had to supervise the man-handling of their trolleys off the line to allow 'superiors' to pass.

The choice of where to stay was a reasonably straightforward one for Grogan: accommodation in Mombasa was limited to the Grand, the Africa and the Cecil and he chose the first because its proprietors also, conveniently, owned the neighbouring Colonial Stores, where they were able to purchase necessities for their journey up-country. Provisioning for any trip in the tropics was a complicated business for a European, as Grogan knew better than most. Although he had the basics with him, such as his enormous pith helmet and red felt spine pad inserted in a pocket at the back of his shirt as protection against the sun (without such attire the tropical sun was believed to engender any number of dangerous 'nervous dispositions'), there were still other things that needed to be bought for his journey to the interior.

At this, as it would turn out, historic moment of Grogan's arrival no observer of the tall, long-legged man with the dazzling yellowy-green eyes and unmistakable aura making his way to the Grand could have guessed what an impact he was to have on the new protectorate; none, indeed, would have known why exactly Grogan was even there – and that suited him fine. For the time being his business needed to remain his, and his alone.

Once installed in the Grand it did not take Grogan long to discover that the 'non-Muslim Mecca' in town was the Mombasa Club, whose 'hours of devotion were 11 a.m., 12.30 p.m., and 6.30 p.m.'.[2] Here he set about gleaning as much useful intelligence about British East Africa as possible, and was helped considerably in this task by the fact that his charming and astute old acquaintance from Nyasaland, Charles Bowring, had taken up the post of Treasurer in the Protectorate three years earlier. Bowring was two years older than Grogan and a product of Clifton, that prolific breeding ground of servants of Empire. With his closely cropped hair, steel-rimmed glasses and purposeful jaw he had something of the look of a Prussian military officer – and conducted his business with the thoroughness of the type. Grogan could not have wished for a more capable man to introduce him to the workings of the country, and Bowring's presence reinforced his fast-growing impression that East Africa might prove to be a jewel in the Empire's crown.

As Grogan took stock of his new surroundings he was well aware that just twenty years earlier no European had had much clue about what lay inland from Mombasa. The hinterland boasted the twin perils of the Taru desert and the legendarily ferocious Masai, so it was rarely traversed even by Swahili slave caravans. When Uganda and what was to become British East Africa were deemed by an 1890 Anglo-German agreement to fall within the British sphere of influence, there had still been no great upsurge of official interest in the territory between the Indian Ocean and Lake Albert. Its administration was delegated to the Imperial British East Africa Company, formed by wealthy Glaswegian ship-owner and philanthropist Sir William Mackinnon, with a vague hope that he might make something of it.

By the mid-1890s the IBEA was bankrupt and only a brilliant campaign orchestrated by Grogan's mentor, soldier-explorer Frederick Lugard, stopped the British government from abandoning Uganda altogether. For three years a fierce debate pitted imperialists on both sides of the Houses of Parliament against opponents whom they labelled 'Little Englanders', and eventually Gladstone – Grogan's godfather and leader of the 'doves' – was outmanoeuvred by Lord Rosebery, his own Foreign Secretary. By 1895 Uganda and British East Africa had officially been declared British protectorates, and Rosebery succeeded Gladstone as Prime Minister. Although he lost the election the following year to Lord Salisbury's Conservative/Liberal Unionist[3] coalition, by then his plans to 'save' Uganda were already well underway and Salisbury, with a firm belief in what he referred to as 'responsible imperialism', saw no reason to meddle with them.

Rosebery's victory was symptomatic of the way in which decisions regarding 'the Scramble for Africa' were usually taken in London: as a 'disorderly business that defies orderly description'[4] it was far more complex than a simple battle between the expansionist lobby and 'Little Englanders'. Indeed it was particularly striking that Rosebery's adherents on the 'Uganda Question' had very different reasons for pledging their support. Some, influenced by the missionary lobby, believed that continued control of Uganda was essential if that country's slave trade were to be stamped out once and for all; some were convinced that 'the Pearl of Africa' had a potential commercial value which should not be overlooked; and others were determined to counter the expansionist intentions of 'Germany's Rhodes', Carl Peters. Most influential of all was the voice of those in both political parties, and the Foreign Office, who feared the growing interest of a number of foreign powers in territories which threatened Britain's control of the headwaters of the Nile, its 'Achilles heel, four thousand miles long'.[5] As Grogan had known when he had entertained an ambition to beat Marchand to Fashoda in 1898, loss of control of those headwaters would threaten Egypt, and therefore Suez, and therefore the vital trade route to India – without which there might be no Empire.

Rosebery's strategy for consolidating control of Uganda centred on the building of a 'political' railway, a characteristic 'toy' of Victorian empire-building with which Grogan was greatly enamoured. This was to be no ordinary railway: although an 1892 survey by Captain Ronald Macdonald concluded that there were 'no insuperable obstacles' along the route from Mombasa to Uganda, it was eventually to cost a staggering £5.5m. Considering that total government expenditure for the closing year of the century was just £133.8m, Henry Labouchère – the railway's most persistent critic in the House of Commons – seemed fully justified in dubbing it 'The Lunatic Line' in his journal *Truth*.

Despite the scepticism of Labouchère and others about the purpose and financial viability of the railway, the first construction staff arrived in Mombasa in December 1895. All rolling stock and labour had to be imported from India; 1.2 million sleepers and more than 200,000 30-foot rails, weighing 500 lbs each, had to be landed at the severely over-stretched port; and then, before construction could even begin in earnest, the 1,700-foot Salisbury bridge had to be built to connect the island of Mombasa to the mainland. Thereafter the problems multiplied. The construction process was continually hampered by disease, shortages of water and supplies, shortages of materials and strikes. At one stage work was even halted for ten months by two man-eating lions which claimed the lives of twenty-eight Indian labourers and uncounted scores of Africans in the vicinity of the Tsavo river. By January 1898, however, the rails extended across the scrubland of the Taru desert to a point 133 miles inland.

A year and a half later a railhead had been established at Nairobi, despite further supply problems caused by the outbreak of war in

South Africa. From there the indefatigable engineer R. O. Preston drove the line on down the hazardously steep Kikuyu escarpment, along the floor of the Rift Valley and up the equally challenging Mau escarpment. Mau Summit, 8,000 feet above sea level, was reached early in 1901. By this time, over 18,000 Indian labourers were at work on the line and despite repeated confrontations with the Nandi – the only tribe to pose any serious threat to the railway's progress – Lake Victoria was finally reached in December 1901. The sturdy, no-nonsense Mrs Preston, who had accompanied her husband all the way from Mombasa, was accorded the honour of laying the last track.

Act of lunacy though the project may have been, it was one of the most staggering feats of engineering ever carried out on the African continent. The total length of the line after six years' work was 582 miles; and it boasted forty-three stations, thirty-five viaducts negotiating the Mau and Kikuyu escarpments, and 1,280 bridges and culverts. Preston, George Whitehouse (the chief engineer) and Colonel Patterson (the vanquisher, after many months of frustration, of the man-eating lions of Tsavo) were all hailed as heroes. Even Grogan's friend Lawley, the builder of most of southern Africa's railways, was impressed – although he noted that the speed of construction was just one third of his customary rate of a mile a day. Of the Herculean efforts of the Indian labourers (some 2,500 of whom had given their lives for the railway) little was said that was complimentary.

By the time it was completed the railway appeared to be a colossal white elephant, much to the satisfaction of Henry Labouchère. The safety of the headwaters of the Nile (and therefore the route through Suez to India) had been secured fully three years earlier with Kitchener's recapture of the Sudan and his forestalment of Marchand's thrust at Fashoda; slavery had all but died out in Uganda; and as there was seemingly no trade worth exploiting along the line it was estimated that the railway would take at least twenty years to break even. A serious dilemma confronted Salisbury's Conservative government, and Colonial Secretary Chamberlain concluded after a visit to East Africa in 1902 that desperate measures were called for to try and recoup the Treasury's investment. That was why Sir Charles Eliot, British East Africa's Commissioner, had despatched his Collector of Customs, Arthur Marsden, to South Africa to attract settlers; and why Grogan

and Gertrude were wandering around the port city of a British protectorate that to all intents and purposes was bankrupt at birth.

What politicians regarded as a dilemma, Grogan regarded as a
challenge. 'The winds of wilderness were calling their people', he
wrote grandiloquently, 'and they tell the tale of Empire, do these
winds; wild calling to wild, and the urge and surge of blood which
must carry our people willy nilly into the last attainable confines of a
finite earth, there to persist, absorb, dictate, boss and impose our Will.
Here is no insolence, but the essential Must of things.'[6]

The day after he arrived in Mombasa Grogan was taken by Bowring
to meet Sir Charles Eliot, British East Africa's forty-one-year-old
Commissioner. Eliot was outwardly as curious a choice for an administrator as his South African counterpart, Milner: both men looked as
if they would have been more at home as dons at their shared alma
mater, Balliol, than determining the future of the Empire in Africa.

Eliot, with his scholarly gaze, thick moustache and severely parted
hair possessed a formidable intellect. At Oxford he had won the Hert-
ford, Boden, Ireland, Craven and Derby scholarships and the Syriac
prize before embarking on a diplomatic career. He spoke twenty-four
languages fluently, read Chinese verse in the evenings and was the
world's leading authority on the sea slug. Being unusual, brilliant, and
a fellow nonconformist, he and Grogan hit it off immediately; Eliot,
having inspected Grogan's bank certificate and heard that he had
understudied Milner on the Johannesburg Town Council, knew
immediately that this was just the sort of settler he was trying to
attract. When he invited Grogan and Gertrude to join him in his
carriage for the journey to Nairobi, Grogan had no hesitation in
accepting.

The Lunatic Line, it soon became obvious, was no Orient Express.
It left Mombasa twice weekly at noon and the 327-mile journey to
Nairobi took anything from twenty-four to thirty-six hours. The roofs
of the coaches, which carried four passengers (bed linen not provided),

were prone to leakage; the carriages shook to such an extent that all were advised to remove their false teeth for the journey; and sparks from the engine and red dust from the surrounding countryside poured in through the windows and doors. Harry Sharp, who four years earlier had made the trip in the reverse direction after leaving Grogan in Uganda to continue his trek to Cairo alone, had remarked that 'for dust or discomfort the journey to the coast would be hard to beat. Everything is covered inches deep in reddish dust, which seems to penetrate even one's skin.'[7]

The train stopped for meals at corrugated iron *dak* bungalows operated by a Goan contractor, Mr J. A. Nazareth, where revolting meals of soup, stringy goat and tinned beef or salmon would be served up accompanied by tepid beer. But beyond the confines of the train the illusion of romance persisted. At night a powerful lamp shone out ahead of the train to warn of elephant or rhinos on the line, and by day honoured passengers like Grogan were able to sit on a wooden bench atop the engine's cowcatcher to take in the view.

Due to various delays it was dark by the time the train entered the Taru desert. Grogan had encountered worse natural hazards, but if Gertrude had been able to see what lay beyond the confines of the train she would have been fully justified in wondering what her thrusting husband was leading her into this time. Eliot used to refer to the desert as 'the vegetable image of democracy' on account of 'its formlessness, its utter want of distinction, and its terrible strength'.[8] His words echoed those of Ernest Gedge, an IBEA officer, who a decade earlier had described the Taru thus:

> The heat as a rule is intense in these forbidding wastes, the red barren soil reflecting back the glare and heat of the sun like a furnace, whilst the deformed and leafless acacia and thorn trees, with their blanched and withered branches, look like so many grim skeletons through which the wind sighs mournfully, seeming to speak to the traveller and to say; 'Turn back, for this is truly the valley of the shadow of Death.'[9]

When dawn broke, however, the train was almost through 'the valley of the shadow of Death' and Grogan and Gertrude were confronted by the magnificent sight of the two peaks of Mount Kilimanjaro, 'the dome of Kibo a pink crust floating on a sea of cloud and Mawenzi pointing heavenward like a black fang'.[10] Still further up the line the Athi and Kapiti plains literally teemed with wildlife, and many stations were occupied by lions which displayed no interest in the passing train as it was neither human nor edible. As the train started to climb towards the highlands the air became fresher, and by the time it reached Nairobi – despite all the discomfort of the journey – Gertrude had, like her husband, 'already come to the conclusion that this was the land for us'.[11]

No one was ever quite able to explain satisfactorily why Nairobi, or 'Nyarobe', existed. Lord Hindlip, one of the Protectorate's early settlers, was convinced that it was the result of some 'momentary mental aberration',[12] a dismal site which had had greatness thrust upon it. The best that could be said about the place was that it was a bastard child of the railway. Situated on a vast flat plain with the Nairobi river running along its northern boundary, it was a dust bowl in the dry season; when the rains came the whole place became a swamp, the 'home of frogs innumerable'[13] and a perfect breeding ground for malarial mosquitoes. Nowhere could have been less suitable for human habitation.

Nairobi's station consisted of a low wooden platform and a corrugated iron office with a kitchen clock suspended over the door. It was, on the face of it, an even more uninspiring sight than the tin shanties of Johannesburg in its infancy, or Bulawayo and Salisbury as Grogan had known them a decade earlier. But 'all the world', as Grogan was fond of recounting later, turned out to greet the new arrivals. There was Ali Khan, a Pathan horse-dealer who sported a huge whip, breeches and gaiters and provided Nairobi's taxi service, Newland and Tarlton, settlers from Australia via South Africa who had started a safari outfitting and land agency business, and that was it. After introductions had been effected, the Grogans were escorted by this welcoming party to Fred and Mayence Bent's Stanley Hotel, a flimsy structure of corrugated iron and wood on stilts with nothing but cloth for its internal partitions.

Mayence Bent was rather taken aback by the sudden rush of visitors. She already had two guests, a pair of farmers from South Africa looking for land, and had to persuade them to vacate their room and pitch a tent outside in order to give the (married) Grogans some privacy. The Stanley's sanitation system consisted of a bucket and the great outdoors, and dinner usually consisted of tins of pickled herrings which brought back painful memories of the Digby chicks that Grogan had seized with such enterprise in Hartley Hill during the Matabele War. Even had Grogan wished for such a thing on his wife's behalf, alternative accommodation was virtually non-existent. Tommy Wood, an auctioneer, ran a two-storey hostelry known as the Victoria Hotel (or simply Wood's), which boasted four rooms for guests, a bar and seating for twelve for meals. Wood's and the Stanley aside, there were no other options until the Norfolk Hotel opened that Christmas of 1904. There were, after all, few calls for much more. Only thirty or so Europeans had settled in the highlands, and the whole country's European population did not exceed 500, of whom the great majority were railway and administrative officials. Few were aware that Grogan was in the vanguard of an influx of 600 settlers responding to Eliot's recruitment campaign in South Africa.

Undeterred by the dearth of facilities Grogan soon set out to have a look around. Although the town appeared to have been zoned, in the loosest sense of the word, there were no proper roads: Victoria Street was little more than a 'hypothetical thoroughfare'.[14] There was also no sanitation system except the river, no streetlights, no electricity, no white policemen, and not even a Town Clerk for Grogan to call on. All water had to be collected from the river, and at night lions and other animals strolled the streets. In the newly founded cemetery six of the headstones bore the simple inscription 'killed by a lion'. The combination of hazards kept the portly Dr Rosendo Ribeiro on permanent standby, and Grogan was told that if the good doctor could not be found in his premises behind Victoria Street he was easily spotted riding his tame zebra around town.

To the south-east of the Stanley was 'Railwayville' which consisted of the station, long rows of white-painted tin and wooden shacks and the Railway Institute which doubled as Nairobi's church. To the north-east lay the putrid-smelling purple- and yellow-painted Indian bazaar, the town's commercial centre in which conditions were so appalling that it had already been burnt down twice, in 1899 and 1902, to eradicate outbreaks of bubonic plague. A missionary captured its idiosyncratic ambience thus:

> one cannot move for the intermingling streams of humanity. The noise is as appalling as the smell. Bells ring, men shout and quarrel, women beckon. Merchants cry the merits of anything: a tusk or a box of cartridges, a bag of hippopotamus teeth or a bolt of cloth; a knife or a gun or a leaf-shaped pear, a handful of *bhang* or a pellet of poison. The stalls are hung with kerosene cans filled with *pombe*, a brew distilled from sugar cane or honey, and into these men dip their mussucks and gulp until their brains are stupefied. There is much depravity . . . A Somali girl costs 5 rupees, a Seychelloise 4, a Masai 3, and a half-cast 1.[15]

The only trees poking out of the featureless landscape were a few eucalypti imported from Australia by John ('Johnny Gumtree') Ainsworth, the sub-commissioner for Nairobi.

Shops stocking European goods were still thin on the ground as demand was limited by the paltry number of settlers and supplies were difficult and expensive to obtain. There was Newland and Tarlton's general store, which sold almost everything from cartridges to tins of sardines; George Stewart & Company, also a general store; Wardle was preparing to start a pharmacy; Dobbie's the jewellers and Elliott the baker were open for business; 'Pop' Binks had abandoned an attempt at farming and was planning a photographic studio; Jeevanjee had started his soda factory; and there were rumours of a bank – the National Bank of India – setting up shop in Bowring's tin Treasury building.

North of the Indian bazaar on the banks of the Nairobi river, which formed a natural boundary between the Kikuyu and Masai tribes, was 'The Swamp', and beyond that rose wooded hills which encircled the centre of town on its northern and western edges. It was in these hills that Europeans had started to build residences. Ainsworth had a white bungalow called Daraja overlooking the river from the site of today's National Museum; a little to the west Reverend 'Pa' Bennett lived in 'The Manse'; nearby was 'Tentfontein', the area where the growing ranks of new arrivals from South Africa camped;

and south of that was the Nairobi Club, a bar perched atop 'The Hill' with a collection of sofas reserved for 'officers and gentlemen'. All looked down on the town, as hideous and unprepossessing a sight as man could imagine. But for all its drawbacks, Grogan regarded Nairobi as full of opportunity. He had the distinct feeling that boom-time was just around the corner, and rapidly succumbed to one of his acute bouts of development fever – from which he would never recover.

Soon after his arrival Grogan was out walking one day with Russell Bowker, a huge South African settler of advancing years but prodigious physical strength. Bowker asked him whether he thought the town would ever amount to anything and, if so, where Grogan thought its centre would be. Grogan pondered this one for a while. He had already discovered that there was a place by the river where ancient paths and tracks used by animals converged and, reasoning that 'every living thing needs a drink and every moving thing from an elephant to a field mouse subconsciously moves along the line of least resistance',[16] he declared that that would be the centre of what one day would be a city.

Grogan was substantially correct: the spot that he had in mind was soon to be bordered by Government Road, Bazaar Road, River Road and Victoria Street.[17] What's more, when the two men went to inspect it they met a railway worker by the name of Cross who immediately offered Grogan eighteen acres of the swamp before them for the princely sum of £100. Cross had bought it to try and cultivate vegetables, but had given up when he found that the frogs and other beasties consumed whatever he planted. A deal was struck there and then, and the 'Cross Estate' was Grogan's.[18]

Grogan thought nothing of Cross's difficulties in making something of the land. His fascination with controlling water and enhancing its potential was by now well known both to his New Zealand friends and to the readers of *From The Cape To Cairo*. Indeed one of his book's concluding chapters was a highly regarded and very erudite study of 'The Swamps of The Upper Nile, And Their Effect on The Water-Supply Of Egypt'. What others saw as a useless swamp, Grogan saw as a goldmine. He trusted his instinct that if the area was drained properly it would make an ideal spot for market gardening, and knew that if he was wrong its value would be underpinned by being in the centre of the city of the future. Bowker, realizing by now – as in time would everyone else in the country – that he was in the company of a 'very cunning fellow', asked Grogan if he would lend him some money so that he could be cut in on the deal. He was met with a polite but firm refusal.

Within a matter of days Grogan also purchased 'Pa' Bennett's homestead, 'the Manse', and its surrounding eighty acres for £600.[19] He then wasted no time in suggesting to Charles Eliot that what Nairobi needed was a town planner to ensure orderly development. Eliot agreed, confessing that 'the beauty of a view of Nairobi depends on the more or less thorough elimination of the town from the landscape',[20] but said that there were no funds available for such a position. That was by no means the end of the matter. Grogan, with his experience of helping to clean up Johannesburg, merely determined to do the job himself.

With his foot firmly in the door of Nairobi's nascent real estate market, Grogan turned his attention to the principal purpose of his visit – an inspection of the forest concession for Lingham. Bowring, excited because he had managed to obtain some Brussels sprouts, asked Grogan to lunch to discuss the matter, and Eliot's enthusiasm for Grogan's suggestion that he should found a timber industry grew by the day. The only problem was that the district in which the concession lay was 'closed' as there was 'unrest' among the Nandi, but Eliot saw no harm in Grogan taking the train and making an inspection of the forests closest to the railway. As soon as Lingham's managing director, Neame, arrived from South Africa he and Grogan boarded the train and headed west.

At Mau Summit, Grogan caught his first sight of mile upon mile of cedar forest stretching north from the railway line as far as the eye could see. It was an exhilarating sight, made all the more attractive to Grogan by the fact that there was absolutely no one about: only one intrepid settler had so far bought land in the area, and that was the magnificently named Major Drought. A little further along the line Grogan was also able to gather more information about the Nandi 'problem' when he met Lieutenant Richard Meinertzhagen of the 3rd King's African Rifles at Londiani. It soon transpired that Grogan ('of Cape to Cairo fame' as Meinertzhagen admiringly commented) knew

Meinertzhagen's Uncle Ernie – and the two men established an immediate rapport. Meinertzhagen recorded in his diary 'on meeting Grogan I was immediately attracted to him; he has great charm, a brain as clear as crystal and a strong character. On parting he said he had heard the most flattering things about me and he hoped we would meet again. He is a great man and will be even greater some day.'[21]

Meinertzhagen told Grogan all he needed to know about the military campaign being undertaken against the resilient Nandi, and advised him not to explore too far from the railway line. Without unlimited access to the area Grogan and Neame wanted to survey there was a limit to what could be achieved in a short space of time, but a few days' march north of Londiani Grogan saw something which he was convinced would make the trip more than worthwhile: the beginning of the grasslands of the Uasin Gishu plateau.

The plateau began about seventy miles north-west of Londiani and was bordered on its west side by Nandi Hills, and to the east by the Elgeyo escarpment. Its southern edge, as Eliot had told Grogan, consisted of 'rolling downs, rushing brooks, many trees and flowers, [which] give one a sense of homely, comfortable, English summer day beauty';[22] and further north it opened out into an almost tree-less expanse which to Grogan spelt cattle country. It did not take him long to discover that 'Uasin Gishu' in fact meant 'striped cattle' in Masai, and while the plateau Masai had largely been exterminated by internecine wars and conflicts with the Nandi decades earlier, Grogan sensed that a people so famed for their expertise with cattle would not have inhabited the area without good reason.

At this point his plans to establish a timber industry began to assume very much greater proportions. Returning through the forest to the railway he did not need Neame, a timber expert, to tell him that establishing a timber business as a stand-alone enterprise would not be easy. There would, he was sure, be considerable difficulties in recruiting labour in such a sparsely populated area, and transporting the wood from the concession to the railway line would be a nightmare, especially in the wet season. But Grogan was convinced that if a forest concession could somehow be linked with development of the Uasin Gishu then he would be in business. With his optimism for the commercial prospects offered by British East Africa reaching new heights, he boarded the train for the journey back to Nairobi, Gertrude, and an all-important chat with Eliot.

The Nairobi to which Grogan returned was not as peaceful as the one he had left a fortnight earlier. He had been so preoccupied with his rapidly multiplying business schemes that he had paid little attention to the Protectorate's politics; but politics now occupied the minds of everyone from Wood's Hotel to the government offices.

The talk of the town was the 'Jewish Question', which had a history running back eighteen months to Chamberlain's visit to the Protectorate. In the absence of any Foreign Office plan for the colonization of British East Africa or for making the railway pay its way, Chamberlain had decided to offer up to 5,000 square miles of the country as a possible Jewish homeland. A Jewish settlement in Africa would, he reasoned, solve a pressing humanitarian problem: in Russia, Rumania and Galicia the persecution of Jews was getting steadily worse. Such an initiative might also make the railway pay, and would protect Britain's workers from competition from an influx of refugee labourers from eastern Europe.

Conservative Jews were not greatly enamoured of the idea when it was put to the 1903 Zionist Congress in Basle by Theodor Herzl. The only homeland they were interested in was Palestine, not some 'African swamp', but just as Grogan returned to Nairobi news had reached the town that Herzl was nevertheless sending a commission to the Protectorate later in the year to investigate its potential. As a result the settlers, missionaries and most government officials were up in arms and extremely virulent anti-semitic language started to taint the pages of the *African Standard*.

Grogan was not remotely concerned about sharing his new home with Jews, and no evidence has ever been offered of his having made a single pronouncement objecting to the Zionist Organization's settlement scheme in general. What *did* concern him was that the area earmarked for settlement was the Uasin Gishu plateau, for which he now had his own, very ambitious ideas. Grogan's plan was to instigate and manage a settlement of New Zealand stockmen on 500,000 acres (750 square miles) of the plateau in partnership with Eddie Watt and his New Zealand friend Carl Teschmaker.[23] Watt and Teschmaker, who visited the plateau in late 1904, were to act as recruiting agents in the Antipodes, offering 5,000-acre smallholdings rent-free to suitably qualified applicants who could deposit £1,000 as surety with the Protectorate's government.[24] Financing for the scheme, including the construction of a suitable infrastructure on the plateau, was promised by Grogan's Johannesburg friend, C. S. Goldmann.

Grogan's boldness and breadth of vision was, quite simply, breathtaking – and was to prove far too bold and broad for most of his contemporaries to comprehend. The Foreign Office, for example, in assessing the merits of a Zionist settlement with its habitual obsession with matters strategic had not – until Grogan put forward his plan – even begun to consider the possibility that the Uasin Gishu might be valuable, and it would be years before anyone else realized this either. Later that summer Grogan's plan was dismissed by the Foreign Office out of hand, a rejection which he considered to be indisputable proof that the corridors of Whitehall were peopled by men of no vision – those whom Rhodes had called the 'little ones who feared to be great'. The fact that for years the plateau was destined not to end up in the hands of the Zionists – or anyone else – was to be scant consolation.

Grogan thrived on opposition, and before leaving East Africa he made it quite clear to all who came across him that he was a law unto himself and quite unstoppable. He informed Eliot in various letters that he had submitted applications for 10,000 acres on the Ndabibi plains, between the spur of the Mau escarpment and the western side of Lake Naivasha; for 25,000 acres elsewhere in the Rift Valley (if they were not taken up by two other applicants); and for 50,000 acres in either Laikipia, the southern Mau or between Nairobi and Fort Hall.[25] Then in mid-June, when he and Gertrude were back in the Grand Hotel in Mombasa and preparing to sail home, he delivered his most audacious 'request' to Eliot in person.

Grogan began by telling the Commissioner that he and Lingham were most certainly interested in exploiting the forest concession. Eliot was delighted by this news, and on 9 July he agreed to a fifty-year least made out in Grogan's name for 64,000 acres at a rent of Rs2000 per annum.[26] But before he signed, the silver-tongued Grogan also told Eliot that he would only take up the concession if he could lease 100 acres of prime land in Mombasa from which to export his timber. He had, he said, noticed the lamentable state of the port the minute he had arrived in BEA, and had now determined that the best course of action was to build a port himself that was as magnificent as Lingham's development at Port Matolla.

To the horror of Whitehall officials who struggled for the next two decades to renege on the agreement by fair means or foul, Eliot had been charmed out of his wits by Grogan and agreed to his demands. Terms were agreed on the spot for a fifty-year lease at a rental of Rs1,500 per annum on four adjacent 25-acre blocks, two with water frontage and two without. This was the crowning achievement of Grogan's two-month tour of British East Africa, following which he and Gertrude joined Eliot on board ship for the journey back to England.

The passage was pleasant enough, but uneventful until the steamer reached Naples. There, Grogan and Eliot decided to visit the famous aquarium and when their tour was complete they were asked to sign the visitors' book. The Italian curator duly inspected their signatures and then threw his arms round Grogan's neck, exclaiming ' "Ah! So I meet the great sea-slug Eliot." ' Grogan hastily redirected the man to the world's leading authority on nudibranchiates, who was gazing pensively into a tank of his 'loved ones'.[27] Eliot had every reason to be reflective: he had just resigned as Commissioner of the East Africa Protectorate.

ELEVEN

Imperial Dreams and 'Official Minds'

Eliot's resignation initially attracted little attention. Most settlers had regarded him as an aloof, even despotic, figure who was not prepared to stand four square behind them. In the memorable words of one historian the situation was, in the eyes of the settlers, like 'Bertrand Russell commanding a platoon of Green Berets',[1] and when Eliot left the editors of the *African Standard* judged that despite his great ability he had 'not made his mark on the Protectorate either socially or politically'.[2]

This was not Grogan's view of his new benefactor. In his brief time in the Protectorate he had forged a close friendship with Eliot and believed that his only 'diversions' from tireless work on behalf of the settlers were 'drinking light claret and reading Chinese verse'.[3] He was also one of only a handful of people who knew the contents of an important cable sent on 5 April by Eliot to Lord Lansdowne, the Foreign Secretary, in which he wrote 'you cannot invite people to dinner and then lock the dining-room door'.[4] This was an unequivocal statement of support for the settlers, and a condemnation of the lack of support being given to them by Lansdowne's Foreign Office. In Grogan's opinion this cable, and Eliot's wholehearted encouragement of his business plans, proved that Eliot was much misunderstood. With that in mind, it was Grogan who had organized a dinner in the Commissioner's honour before the two men had sailed from Mombasa; it was Grogan who called for a full inquiry into the circumstances of Eliot's departure; and it was Grogan who was determined to uncover what he regarded as 'sinister goings-on' at the Foreign Office. Within just months of setting foot in East Africa he had emerged as a powerful and irrepressible force in politics, and also demonstrated that he was a loyal friend and champion of any underdog on whom Whitehall tried to trample.

The events leading up to Eliot's downfall were significant in that, although they were not of earth-shattering import in themselves, they foreshadowed enduring tensions between Whitehall, its government officials in East Africa and the settlers. Eliot's 'mistake' was refusing to back down when ordered by the Foreign Office to withdraw grants of land to two South African settlers – land which the FO had itself earmarked to form part of a 500-square-mile concession that it was offering to the East Africa Syndicate, a group of London and Johannesburg entrepreneurs that Grogan described as 'a mysterious organization ... exploiting the country to the practical exclusion of anyone else'.[5] Eliot's reason for standing his ground was not favouritism but a simple point of principle: he, the Commissioner, had made a promise and he intended abiding by it.

Eliot's intractability should not, if taken in isolation, have proved an insoluble problem for the Foreign Office, but it brought out into the open an intense personal animosity between him and Sir Clement Hill, the high-handed head of the FO's African Protectorates Department. Hill was determined that the Protectorate should, in effect, be run by diktat from far-off Whitehall. He also had a more personal reason for opposing Eliot – his nephew had been lined up to manage the East Africa Syndicate's properties in the Protectorate. Hill resolved to get rid of Eliot, but first he needed a cast-iron excuse which would satisfy his political masters in London.

A suitable pretext was not long in coming. Two of Eliot's subordinates, Jackson and Bagge, complained to Hill behind Eliot's back that the Commissioner was not doing as much as he could to protect the rights of the Masai in the Rift Valley. The accusation was a serious one – quite serious enough to enable Hill to make a lunge for the moral high ground and force Eliot to resign. It was also disingenuous: once Hill was rid of Eliot it was he and Eliot's successor, Sir Donald Stewart, who ordered the Masai to be moved out of the Rift Valley to make way for European settlement. Furthermore, the two settlers whose rights Eliot had defended were eventually granted the very land for which they had originally applied. The 'defence of native interests' card had been played by Hill with only his own interests, rather than those of the Masai, in mind.

During conversations with Eliot on the way back to London Grogan became increasingly certain that the whiff of hypocrisy was in the air. He knew instinctively how to wield the politician's tools – the press and public opinion – and wield them he did when he arrived home, like a Viking with a battle-axe. In a letter to *The Times* he stated that while in the process of acquiring 'considerable interests' in East Africa he had been 'met with the greatest kindness, every possible assistance, and no obstruction whatever' from Eliot, who in his view had 'thrown up a great career ... for the principle of "without fear or favour"'.[6] In addition to writing to *The Times*, he also rapped on the editor's door. Access to the Empire's mouthpiece was always open to the man who had made the first south–north traverse of Africa and was widely known to be a protégé of Milner's, and a deferential letter of 23 October from the paper's Hugh Blakiston to Grogan provides further evidence of his efforts on Eliot's behalf:

> Mr. Chirol wishes me to tell you that he was much impressed by what you told him the other day, and that he has since taken occasion to go carefully through your annotated copy of the correspondence in Eliot's case. If ... you care to write us a [further] letter ... setting forth your view of the case and your impressions of the feeling it has created in the Protectorate, it will be very carefully considered here with a view to publication ... If you could see your way to do this we should be rather glad.[7]

Grogan positively revelled in pursuing what had now become one of his favourite pastimes, namely having a pop at 'Bumbledom' in general – and hypocrisy in particular. Sir Clement Hill was a sitting duck in the face of such an onslaught, and Grogan took great delight in crowing publicly about the events which he described as 'not one of the brightest pages in the history of the Foreign Office'.[8] Indeed, in Grogan's opinion those pages grew still dimmer later in the year when it transpired that the Parliamentary Command Paper[9] covering Eliot's resignation 'omitted' (i.e. censored) another particularly significant cable from Eliot to Lord Lansdowne. In this cable Eliot not only made plain the extent of Hill's haughty and dictatorial leanings but also provided further evidence that Hill's, and the Foreign Office's, avowed support for 'native interests' was a sham. In uncompromisingly imperialist terms, Eliot wrote that 'no doubt on platforms and in reports we declare we have no intention of depriving natives of their lands, but this has never prevented us from taking what we want' and reminded Lansdowne that it was after all he, as Foreign Secretary, who had 'opened the Protectorate to white colonization'.[10]

However uncomfortable Grogan made Hill's life in the latter half of 1904 he did not ultimately prevail. He was, after all, still only twenty-nine years old and, despite his fame and influential contacts in the corridors of power, no match as yet for a megalithic government department that was quite content not only to lie in public but to doctor official publications. The 'great sea slug' Eliot was not reinstated, and his diplomatic career was over for the time being,[11] but it was due to Grogan, who many years later would still describe Eliot as 'the one really brilliant ruler of our destinies',[12] that the settlers in East Africa reconsidered their verdict on the departing Commissioner and would in years to come remember him fondly as their 'champion'. Furthermore, Grogan – the Protectorate's new firebrand – regarded it as a victory of sorts when it was announced that from April 1905 British East Africa's affairs were to be transferred from the Foreign Office, which Eliot had accused of having 'lost all touch with reality',[13] to the Colonial Office. This seemed to confirm what Lord Salisbury had often remarked: namely that Africa seemed to be the plague of a Foreign Office which considered its remit to be strategic and not administrative.

Eliot never forgot the loyalty that Grogan displayed at a time when he appeared to have few friends either in Africa or London; and when Grogan's own career hit its nadir three years later, Eliot was among the first to write to him saying that he would 'always be glad to make some return for the sympathy and help which you have so often shown me'.[14]

Grogan returned to East Africa on the SS *Bohemia* from Trieste on 13 November 1904 to continue his personal scramble for assets in the Protectorate. As the process of constructing a home on the land bought so expeditiously from the Reverend 'Pa' Bennett had only just begun the Grogan entourage – Gertrude, little Dorothy, and sundry servants – were installed in a rented house on the Hill. That done, Grogan marched off to seek out Sir Donald Stewart.

He immediately recognized that Eliot's successor as Commissioner of the Protectorate was not a man who would stand in his way. Stewart was a soldier, a veteran of campaigns in Afghanistan, India, the Transvaal, Sudan and Ashanti, and a man whom one of his subordinates described as possessed 'of considerable force of character and shrewd common sense'. But as the same official observed he lacked 'business experience or training, except perhaps in the racing world' and was 'what might be termed an illiterate man, having no knowledge of other than the material side of life. His powers of application were undeveloped; he rarely read files, and as he went late to bed and rose late the affairs of the country had scant attention.'[15]

Stewart's fondness for 'the material side of life' was a euphemistic reference to his love of the grape, the grain and all their derivative products which would kill him at the age of just forty-five – only sixteen months after taking up his post. His principal leisure pursuit was, however, of no concern to Grogan; what mattered to him was that Stewart shared Eliot's enthusiasm for his ambitions and agreed at the outset to give him 'every assistance'.[16] With that assurance in the bag, Grogan cabled Lingham to join him in East Africa and he was in Mombasa to greet his partner when he arrived from South Africa on the homebound SS *Bohemia* in the third week of December.

Lingham was accompanied by a surveyor, Coryell, a 'timbercruiser' and two engineers. Encouraged by Grogan's initial survey of their concession, and by the astonishing rapidity with which his partner had established the name of the 'Grogan and Lingham syndicate' in the Protectorate, Lingham was now intent on taking a closer look at what they were investing in before drawing up a master-plan for working the concession. What none of this optimistic band knew as they made their way to Nairobi was how complex a process this was to prove – even with Stewart's support. Akin to wading through a tray of official treacle, it would test Grogan's patience, bank balance and extensive reserves of ingenuity to the limit.

Christmas was spent with Gertrude in Nairobi, the tin shanty town being considerably enlivened by the opening that day of Major Ringer and 'Pop' Winearls's new hotel, the Norfolk. It was a considerable improvement on the Stanley and Wood's, even though conditions at the latter were better since Tommy had 'fetched' a wife – Emilie – from England. But despite boasting forty bedrooms with solid walls instead of board partitions, proper chairs (as opposed to packing cases), five European staff and a French chef, the Norfolk was still far from luxurious. The ever-adventurous Quentin, having been fired by Clement Talbot Motors for doing 45 mph in a 15 mph limit on the Portsmouth Road, had arrived to 'help my brother look for new forests' and described the hotel as 'very simple, consisting of two lines of what appeared to be loose boxes facing each other'.[17] Its official opening was briefly interrupted when someone had to go and shoot an elephant that was on the rampage nearby.

The festivities over, Grogan and Lingham swung into action. Their first demand of Stewart was that he double the size of their concession to 128,000 acres. Grogan argued that this was necessary in order to make the forest workable, and the bibulous and avuncular Stewart took his word for it. He wanted his tenure as Commissioner to be as trouble-free as possible. To his way of thinking, Lingham was 'well known [and] successful', while Grogan was 'very famous [and] also a man of means'[18] – and those were good enough qualifications to coax him into handing over a further 100 square miles of the Protectorate.[19]

Stewart also agreed to an important amendment to the terms of the deal: that the two concessions should each *enclose* 64,000 acres of 'workable forest', and that the excess land should be rented to Grogan and Lingham as grazing land. 'All' that remained to be done, as far as Stewart was concerned, was for Grogan to survey the forest thoroughly to establish the boundaries of the two concessions. He was content to let others take care of the minutiae of the agreement, an oversight for which the Colonial Office would not subsequently thank him: the minutiae were in fact the substance of Grogan's bold plans, as they were soon to discover. Stewart, like Eliot before him, had let

Grogan put a foot in the door and before long he meant to prise that door from its hinges.

In a letter to Stewart dated 8 January 1905 Grogan began to reveal the full extent of his ambitions. He began to demand that the concession be granted as freehold land – a demand which even Stewart could see 'ought not . . . to be given'[20] – and declared that in order to extract the timber he or the government would need to construct a branch line of the railway running from either Nakuru or Londiani through the concession to the Uasin Gishu plateau. It did not take someone of Grogan's business acumen to realize that the concession would only be workable if it could be accessed by a railway. But no one had considered that any *individual* would be so bold as to offer to build that railway themselves. The costs were, after all, colossal.

Grogan estimated that the shorter Londiani route to his forests would cost £180,000 to build, but that it would be a backwater line. The route he favoured, at a cost of £450,000, was the one from Nakuru which could subsequently be extended right across the plateau. Uppermost in his mind was an ambition eventually to create a 'much needed trunk' right through to the north-east tip of Lake Albert – an arterial line which would eventually connect with the main Cape-to-Cairo railway.

While in London Grogan had secured backing from investors to the tune of £150,000 for his railway, and knew that if he could obtain governmental approval for the project the additional funds he required would be forthcoming. In return for building the railway he demanded that the government should pay the interest on the loans from his investors or grant him further land in lieu. Some form of government guarantee was essential as, in Grogan's words, 'no timber company could be expected to pay for it [the railway] *gratis*'.[21]

This point was indisputable: Grogan, with Lawley as his consultant, knew his railways. Indeed he had devoted a whole chapter of *From The Cape To Cairo* to an erudite rebuttal of criticisms of Rhodes's dream of a trans-continental railway, the construction of which he regarded as Britain's 'moral obligation . . . inseparable from [its] bounden duty to develop [Africa]'.[22] He also knew that if he could secure land grants for his railway on the same basis as those given to the Canadian Pacific railway he would get 32,000 acres of land for every mile of railway built – or 2,500 square miles of British East Africa. In return he was offering a branch line which opened up the whole of the Uasin Gishu plateau for settlement; and sixty-four train-loads of timber per month within three years.

Stewart was like a rabbit caught in the beam of a lamp. He knew that one of his main priorities was to encourage the economic development of the Protectorate in the hope of making the Lunatic Line profitable, and he had never come across anyone as persuasive as Grogan. To Grogan's delight, he agreed in principle to Grogan's demands. What does not seem to have occurred to him was that British East Africa was not Canada, and that to agree to hand over a lease for 1.6 million acres of its best land to a private syndicate was bound to provoke a storm of protest in Whitehall.

While Stewart forwarded to Whitehall Grogan and Lingham's plan to create what amounted to their own principality, the two men decided to head west to take a further look at their ever-growing concession. Quentin was deputed to buy guns and all the necessary supplies and soon the party was ready to board the train which 'puffed and struggled'²³ its way up to Kijabe before descending to Naivasha on the floor of the Rift Valley. There everyone disembarked to secure the permission of the Provincial Commissioner, William Hobley, to continue on their way. The accommodation in Naivasha was rudimentary to say the least: Seymour's 'hotel' was remarkable only for the fact its proprietor always insisted on tossing a coin to go double or quits on his guests' bills.

Armed with Hobley's permission to enter the forest Grogan's survey party boarded the train once again and disembarked at Mau Summit, from where they set out on foot. Everything they saw confirmed Grogan and Neame's earlier impressions. Progress through the hilly terrain was tough enough on foot which raised the question of what it would be like for teams of oxen, especially in the rainy season. The forest was also very broken, and although there were plenty of good trees these were interspersed with countless glades of poor grass and scrubland. The further they penetrated into the forest, the more Grogan became convinced that it was only with government approval for his massive scheme – combining a forestry business, a railway and a port – that he and Lingham would be able to make something of the forest. Lingham, as the developer of Port Matolla and the 'Lumber King of the Transvaal', agreed; and after a month in the forest he and Grogan returned to Nairobi intent on pressing their claims.

As Grogan stepped off the train he found that Nairobi was once again preoccupied by the 'Jewish Question'. Theodor Herzl's Zionist Organization had, during 1904, raised enough money to send its commission to evaluate the Uasin Gishu as a potential settlement area for large numbers of Eastern Europe's beleaguered Jews. The commission comprised three men: the explorer and soldier Major A. St Hill Gibbons;[24] a Swiss professor called Kaiser; and a man by the name of Wilbusch. By coincidence, this party had arrived in Nairobi just as Lingham and Grogan had left the town and then followed them west, arriving in Nakuru on 17 January to commence their two-month examination of the plateau.

The commission's expedition was a disaster almost from the outset. Vital luggage was left behind in Nairobi, oxen escaped from their *kraal* at night, a Masai guide had to be dismissed, the three men argued, and the rear of their caravan was at one point attacked by Nandi tribesmen. These were the facts contained in the commission's report. But so rapidly was Grogan's stature in the Protectorate growing that many years later an altogether more dramatic myth was born.

The myth was dependent on the geographical proximity of the two survey parties (Grogan's and Gibbons's), and predicated upon the European settlers' antipathy to the idea of a Jewish homeland being created in the midst of what they regarded as 'their' country. According to this myth, two settlers accompanied Gibbons's party and by various means ensured that his expedition was a failure. The two settlers were never publicly named, but in settler lore Grogan was always held to be one of them – based solely on the fact that he was in roughly the same neck of the woods at the same time and that he too had an interest in the Uasin Gishu plateau.

In reality, Grogan was busy about his own business in the forest with Lingham; the settler 'conspiracy' was a *canard*;[25] and Grogan had left the country by the time the commission had completed its survey. In June 1905 it reported to Herzl that immigration would be too expensive, that the land was pastoral not agricultural, and that there were insufficient raw materials available to support a settlement of more than 15–20,000 Jews. This was a far cry from Chamberlain's fanciful hope that a home could be found for 'a million souls', and Wilbusch's view was that 'where nothing exists, nothing can be done'. As a result, the British government's offer to provide an 'ante-chamber' to the Holy Land was turned down at the seventh Zionist Congress in Basle. The scheme failed for reasons that had nothing to do with Grogan, but the myth that he was involved in frustrating the commission's survey is significant in that it shows the extent to which he had already emerged as one of the, if not the, leading lights in the political life of East Africa.

Lingham sailed back to South Africa in the second week of February. A week later Grogan also left the Protectorate, bound for London, where he intended joining battle with the Colonial Office, which was due to assume full responsibility for the administration of British East Africa at the beginning of April. Even if he had wished to stay longer in Africa, pursuing other plans, his departure had become a necessity: Gertrude, to his great delight, was expecting their second child.

In London the initial reaction to Grogan's combined railway and forest scheme was one of indignation. The Colonial Office's W. D. Ellis, in the time-honoured tradition of Whitehall's distaste for entrepreneurs and buccaneers of any description, was unable to 'see that we need to pay people for cutting down our forests' and added that he could not envisage 'any necessity for further railway building unless it is of the nature of a trunk line of communication until the land near the Uganda railway has been more developed'. He also remarked that he had noticed that Grogan, whose *chutzpah* he dismissed as being 'simply outrageous', had 'been writing to *The Times* . . . [and] is one of those persons who will try by such means and by approaching MPs to bounce us into granting concessions'.[26]

This latter accusation was, of course, correct. Grogan was fully intend on mobilizing his enormous influence and influential contacts against those – inside and outside Whitehall – who stood in his way. He knew instinctively how to negotiate, and his 'outrageous' proposal was a classic opening gambit by a natural entrepreneur. Panache, however, was a public nuisance in the eyes of most civil servants and while Ellis huffed and puffed it was only the worldly Stewart who could see that Grogan had merely put down a marker and probably 'would take a great deal less'[27] than he seemed to be demanding.

That the Ellis view did not prevail completely was partly due to Stewart's counsel, and partly to the fact that Ellis represented only one strand of thought in the Colonial Office. He was the most junior of the three men who made policy recommendations to Sir Montague Ommaney, the permanent under-secretary, and through him to Alfred Lyttelton, Chamberlain's successor as Colonial Secretary. Ellis's two colleagues in the new East Africa Department were its head, R. W. Antrobus, and Herbert Read, both of whom were what Grogan would have termed rather more 'enlightened' in their views of how the Protectorate's economy should be developed. Over the next three years the official view of Grogan's massive ambitions was directly related to which of these three men's opinions was in the ascendant at any particular time, and the degree to which he managed to enlist the support of successive governors and senior figures in the Houses of Parliament to put pressure on them.

By the end of the summer Grogan had reacted to Whitehall's reticence by modifying some details of his proposals, but substantively they remained the same. In a letter to Lyttelton,[28] whose Cabinet career was about to end as a result of his having sanctioned Milner's Chinese labour initiative, he offered to survey the branch line route from Nakuru through Eldama Ravine to the Uasin Gishu plateau at his own expense; he also responded to Whitehall's suspicions that he might actually make a profit from his railway by offering to make it a joint venture with the government. The real sticking point was that Grogan still demanded his land grants – amounting to 'all or part of the land comprised in the Uasin Gishu plateau'[29] – as the governmental guarantee for the half a million pounds or so he would be raising from his investors. In other words he was set on building the railway, either on his own or in partnership with the government, but demanded that the government should underwrite the enterprise in the same manner as it had done with railways in Canada, Australia and all over the Empire.

The reply to this letter was not very warm. Lyttelton regretted that he was 'unable to entertain your proposals', as he claimed that the value of the land grants demanded by Grogan was greater than if the government undertook to build the railway itself and that 'such grants' were not in any case 'the policy of HMG in the Protectorate'.[30] As far as Grogan was concerned this was a dubious line of argument. For one thing no one was at all sure whether 'HMG' actually had 'a policy for the Protectorate', and for another he knew that having spent £5.5m on the Lunatic Line the government was in no position to broach the subject of further railway building in the House of Commons. What better then, Grogan reasoned, than to let private enterprise do a job which had to be done if the inaccessible Uasin Gishu plateau was to be opened up for the considerable economic benefit of the Protectorate as a whole?

Lyttelton did at least concede that there was *some* logic in this line of argument, and he tried to meet Grogan half way by offering up to 10,000 acres of land for every mile of railway built (as opposed to the 32,000 acres per mile of railway that Grogan had originally demanded). At this stage of the negotiations one fact stands out above all: Grogan's vision was matched by his stubbornness. He had the opportunity to strike a deal which would have secured for his syndicate a land grant of up to 780 square miles of the Uasin Gishu plateau – certainly sufficient to have yielded a colossal profit on building the railway. But Grogan did not accept the offer, and it is impossible to avoid the conclusion that the cause of his reticence was simply that Lyttelton thought the deal would 'not be bad business'. In other words, Grogan's ego dictated that the government had to accept – and be seen to be accepting – *his* terms, not the other way round. This illustrates that, as was true of that other young thruster Churchill, Grogan's unquestionable ability was not always matched by his powers of judgement.

Furthermore, he chose not only to snub Lyttelton but to astonish him by upping the ante considerably.

In the same way that Grogan had secured the backing of C. S. Goldmann, whose pockets were known to be very deep, and who was married to the daughter of Viscount Peel (a former Speaker of the House of Commons), he now set off in pursuit of one of the very few veterans of the Scramble whom no one in Whitehall could ignore. That man was Sir George Taubman Goldie, who had recently delivered into the grateful hands of the Crown one of its most lucrative territories – Nigeria.

Goldie was an imperial buccaneer, the stuff of legends, whose achievements were comparable in scale with those of Rhodes. His colourful career had not started auspiciously: he was drunk when he took his finals at the Royal Military Academy at Woolwich and, although he still managed to pass, he took off for Egypt and a three-year love affair with an Arab girl rather than take up his commission. An equally scandalous affair with the family governess ensued after his return to the family seat on the Isle of Man. Only in 1875, when he was twenty-nine (and Grogan was one), did he settle down to the serious business of Empire building. He shared with Grogan a desire to paint the map pink; an eccentric and at times aggressive character; a hypnotic charm; a persuasive and at times explosive nature; an aversion to authority, particularly when it was dressed in the colours of the Foreign or Colonial Offices; the drive and business acumen of Rhodes; the same zealous vision of a proactive Empire; and a pair of startlingly phosphorescent eyes. Goldie's autocratic rule in Nigeria, like that of the White Rajahs in Sarawak, also epitomized to Grogan what could be achieved in the name of the Empire. Grogan shared Goldie's conviction that trade was the most effective tool of development in the colonies, and that power should be devolved to as great an extent as possible to local African potentates – a system known as 'indirect administration'.[31]

Much to the alarm of many in Whitehall, Goldie was widely credited with having proved the point that an African colony could make money – lots of it – if men such as he were entrusted with the task of ruling rather than civil servants likely to cause 'the Empire's dropping to pieces from the want of adequate organisation'.[32] Having thwarted German and French territorial ambitions on the Niger for two decades he had finally surrendered his Royal Niger Company's charter to the British government in 1900 and was consequently casting around for something suitably gigantic to get involved in. Not only did he know Africa as well as any European, but he also knew every detail of the Lunatic Line – which he agreed with Grogan was 'the alimentary canal of East Africa'[33] – and whose full length he had travelled in 1901.

In September 1905, to the great consternation of the CO, Goldie – who had just assumed the presidency of the Royal Geographical Society – agreed to join Grogan, Lingham and Goldmann's syndicate and immediately expounded his views on the stalemate to Lyttelton. He countered the Colonial Office's unwillingness to make any further large land grants in the Protectorate by pointing out that they had come within a whisker of doing exactly that with the Zionist Offer, which – unlike Grogan's railway – had given no prospect of a guaranteed return. Furthermore, Goldie added that in his opinion 'land in the hands of such a Company as I propose is more likely to be dealt with in the interests of the country than if it were thrown open to speculators'.[34]

Goldie's dramatic entrance into the negotiations forced the Colonial Office to recognize that the big guns were now ranged on it – guns even bigger than Grogan's – and it decided that the pragmatic course of action was to scuttle for cover. On 21 December 1905 Sir Montague Ommaney wrote to Grogan's syndicate saying that its plans were to be handed over to the Crown Agents for appraisal by what he regarded as 'more commercially experienced minds'.

In addition to securing the support of Goldie, Grogan spent the summer of 1905 doing exactly what Mr Ellis of the Colonial Office disliked: he used his considerable influence with the Press to try and bounce the CO into doing what he wanted. In one particularly scathing letter to *The Times* he was forthright about bringing to the public's attention the fact that the FO had for a decade pursued a 'policy of drift' in the Protectorate, the result of which was that no one knew whether the country was being governed with the interests of Africans to the fore (as was perceived to be the case with Uganda), or as a satellite of India (Indians were established on the coast long before the arrival of European settlers, and it was Indians who had built the railway), or as a country that would continue to encourage the arrival of European colonists. Such indecision was, in Grogan's opinion, a recipe for disaster and had put enormous pressure on the Protectorate's 'small [governmental] staff, essentially sound' which the FO had considered 'sufficient to deal with a position the most important features of which were a few sporadically fractious natives and infinite hosts of antelope' but which had 'suddenly been called upon to handle a rapidly developing colony'.

Grogan also criticized the Treasury's failure 'to supply the comparatively trifling sums which are necessary to render the past expenditure [on the Uganda railway] . . . effective'. Furthermore, it appeared to him from his experience of negotiating with Whitehall that its civil servants loathed any development initiative that smacked of speculation. Yet without speculation, which Grogan called 'the very essence of modern business', he argued that there was a risk of 'no business at all'.[35] Grogan's message to the CO was clear: if they wouldn't pay for development they had to open the field to entrepreneurs. Then, and only then, was there any chance of the Treasury recouping its investment in the railway.

Grogan's letter concluded with a call for three new administrative appointments in the Protectorate. He wanted an agricultural expert and a railway engineer with experience of constructing railways in Canada, but most of all he wanted a governor who knew Africa – a request which must have thrilled the incumbent Stewart after all he had done to help Grogan. Eventually all his wishes were granted, but in the short term the CO's reaction to Grogan's protests was one of haughty insouciance – even though *The Times* wholeheartedly endorsed his arguments.

In June Grogan's attention was momentarily diverted from filibustering when Gertrude gave birth to a second daughter, Joyce. This was some recompense for the early death, in February, of her beloved uncle and Grogan's sturdy companion on the trek – Harry Sharp. By midsummer Grogan had also fully recovered from a further attack of malaria and another burst liver abscess which had temporarily reduced him to 'a shadow of his former self'[36] (and quite possibly exacerbated his petulance during negotiations with the Colonial Office). But he had to wait until New Year, when Joyce was old enough to travel, to return to Africa, and by then his attention was concentrated firmly on a matter of greater import to him than the conduct of the CO: the future of the entire British Empire. With the arrival of winter the final act in a political saga in which he had played a part while in South Africa, and which had led to Milner's downfall, had just been played out.

Balfour, Lord Salisbury's nephew and successor as leader of the Conservatives, delivered his resignation to the King on 4 December. Pressure had been mounting on his coalition government all year, indeed ever since Chamberlain had resigned from the Cabinet in 1903 to campaign vociferously for Tariff Reform – the imposition of protective trade tariffs by the British Empire. This controversial issue had rapidly replaced Irish Home Rule as the political hot potato of the day, and it had also led to what Grogan and many others considered to be Churchill's 'treacherous' and 'opportunistic' defection to Campbell-Bannerman's Liberals.

Grogan believed passionately in Chamberlain's campaign. Trade bankrolled the Empire and, at a time of rapidly increasing competition from the United States and Germany, he believed that it had to be protected at all costs in order to stimulate trade in the colonies and tackle poverty in the Empire's heartland. It had become a considerable embarrassment to all but the most myopic occupants of Westminster that over thirty per cent of the population of Great Britain had been found, in a number of highly publicized reports, to be living in abject poverty. The belief of the Victorian ruling class that the man in the street could prosper through simple hard work and probity had been exposed as radically flawed.

The Liberals, and indeed plenty of Tories, agreed with Chamberlain's tariff reformers about the magnitude of the domestic problem but advocated a radically different solution: Free Trade. Tariff Reform, they believed, would backfire and lead to a rise in the cost of foodstuffs and the loss of untold numbers of jobs at home. Meanwhile, behind the lines, there was an equally potent source of conflict: ever since the unsatisfactory end to the Boer War the belief of the majority of Liberals that their Conservative counterparts were mismanaging the Empire had strengthened. And nowhere, with the possible exception of the appalling treatment of the Australian Aboriginals, did this appear to be more apparent than in the controversy over the use of Chinese labourers in the mines of South Africa – a controversy in which Churchill, now a standard bearer for the Liberals, played a leading role.

When it was discovered that floggings had been meted out to the Chinese labourers working on the Rand in strict contravention of the terms of their contracts – which Grogan had had a hand in drafting – Milner was forced to resign as Governor of South Africa. Despite the fact that Churchill's rise to fame during the Boer War had been greatly facilitated by Milner, his was one of the loudest voices condemning Milner's use of 'slavery'. By the time he admitted that this accusation was a 'terminological inexactitude' it was too late for Milner, who was forced into semi-retirement. For over a decade thereafter he devoted most of his energies to a career in investment banking, to the House of Lords and to supporting the activities of the Rhodes Trust. When he eventually returned to the political frontline, however, he did not forget the qualities that Grogan had displayed during his brief stint in the Kindergarten.

The Liberals' concern about their opponents' management of the Empire increased the more it became apparent that Britain was by no means the worst offender when it came to mistreatment of its subject peoples. The Herero and Witboi in South West Africa had rebelled against barbaric treatment by their German overlords; 'Tiger' Casement and 'Bulldog' Morel's efforts to inform the world of Leopold's regime of terror in the Congo – where literally millions of Africans had perished – were finally meeting with success; and in Russia there was revolution at the end of 1905. It seemed to many that the warning signs of a major catastrophe for the Empire were all there, and the Liberals decided that it was time to rescue what they perceived as being the floundering ship of Empire.

The consequences of all this political ferment were dramatic. In January, just before Grogan set sail for Africa, the electorate comprehensively rejected Tariff Reform and expressed huge indignation at the use and abuse of Chinese labour on the Rand. So great was the support for the Liberals that they did not even have to rely on their traditional allies, the Irish Nationalists. They won 377 seats on their own to the Conservatives' paltry 157. It was a rout, and Chamberlain – the champion of Tariff Reform – suffered a massive stroke. Although he lived on until 1914 his active political career was effectively over.

On board ship Grogan had plenty of time to contemplate the outcome of the election. He was not by instinct illiberal; he harboured an Irishman's sympathy for any underdog; and he was as angry as anyone about German and Belgian excesses in Africa. His experience of what he regarded as Whitehall's ineptitude in determining policy for the colonies under the Conservatives also initially predisposed him to look upon the change of government philosophically. There were, after all, plenty of avowed imperialists in the Liberal camp. But the more he thought about the new government, the more worried he became. Foremost in his mind was his godfather Gladstone, whom he regarded as an arch-hypocrite who had done his best at every turn to frustrate the extension of the Empire, and he became increasingly convinced that the Liberals were naturally inclined to say one thing but do whatever was politically expedient. In this context his suspicions immediately alighted on Churchill, who was being variously described by his many opponents as a 'turncoat', a 'bounder' and a 'jumped-up subaltern', but who had just been appointed Under-Secretary of State for the Colonies by Campbell-Bannerman as a reward for his defection from the Conservatives.

Grogan's resolve hardened as a result of his musings. If, he reasoned, the Empire *was* under threat in its own back yard then the immediate imperative was to launch a massive rearguard action from its outposts against any indecision or humbug on the part of the new government. As if to underscore how he himself intended to proceed he penned the following, ebullient words in a new edition of *From The Cape To Cairo*:

> The world writhes with a quickening life of change. The tide of our supreme ascendancy is on the ebb. Nations, like men, are subject to disease. Let us beware of fatty

degeneration of the heart. Luxury is sweeping away the influences which formed our character. It is as though our climate has been changed from the bleak northern winds to the tropic's indolent ease. Yet we still have a chance. While we sleep, broad tracks have been cut for us by those whom we revile. Far and wide our outposts are awake, beckoning to the great army to sweep along the tracks. Let each man with means and muscle for the fray go forth at least to see what Empire is. Clive, Hastings, Rhodes, a thousand lesser men whose tombs are known only to the forest breeze, have left us legacies of which we barely dream. Millions of miles of timber, metals, coal, lie waiting for the breath of life, 'pegged out' for Britain's sons. In these our destiny lies.

With this impassioned call to arms, Grogan himself 'went forth'.

TWELVE

Sceptics and Speculators

WHEN THE GROGANS stepped off the train in Nairobi they no longer had any need of hotels, not even the 'luxurious' new Norfolk. In his absence Grogan had left the construction of their new home in the hands of a London architect, H. O. Cresswell, and a firm of local Indian contractors – and now it was finished. His brother Quentin had kept half an eye on progress while also working in Gailey and Roberts' wines and spirits department, an occupation he preferred over anything that England could offer. He relished the freedom of life in the Protectorate, and with his easy charm was much adored by everyone he came across. His special friends, however, were the Church brothers (known respectively as 'High' and 'Low').

'Chiromo' was built on the site that Grogan had bought from 'Pa' Bennett, and was named after the Nyasaland settlement at the junction of the Ruo and Shiré rivers through which Grogan had passed on his trek. Nyasaland, known as the 'Cinderella of Africa', was to him the embodiment of what British rule in Africa should stand for: a well-ordered, well-run and prosperous colony in which European and African industries could thrive side by side.

Although Grogan was, and would remain, something of an ascetic he intended Gertrude and their offspring to enjoy the same comforts offered by that other house on a hill in which he had first met her – the Coleman residence in Napier. With that in mind Chiromo was built in gabled Cape Dutch style with a broad, bougainvillaea-clad *stoep* (verandah) looking out over the town to the Ngong hills and Athi plains in the far distance. The front door was fashioned from thick mahogany with a leaded window bearing the initials 'ESG'; and inside was a huge entrance hall with Canadian pine flooring, flanked by reception rooms. Specially imported beams bore the stamp 'Grogan Mombasa'.

A small hunting lodge was built in the grounds as well as a guest house whose main room was of such generous proportions that it was used by Sir James Hayes Sadler, Stewart's successor as commissioner, for entertaining. Few in the town failed to notice that Chiromo was an altogether more substantial residence than the makeshift Government House. By African standards it was a palace; by Nairobi standards it was, and was intended to be, *the* palace. Nairobi's Africans called it the *shamba ya bwana simba* – 'the lion's den'.

Gertrude soon set to creating extensive gardens with imported plants and she planned a beautiful ornamental lake fed by springs on the eighty-acre property. Keeping busy was regarded by womenfolk as the *sine qua non* of an enjoyable life continually under threat from 'danger, discomfort and dullness'. Lady Cranworth, dispensing advice to all new female arrivals, alerted them to the fact that 'nearly every settler is a busy man . . . his whole day is occupied, and when he is not working, he is planning the next step to posterity'. In her view it was up to the womenfolk to run a tight ship, doing 'lots of cooking, washing, poultry-farming, gardening, household pursuits and care of stables'. It was also their responsibility to oversee the servants who were prone unwittingly to commit such offences as rubbing the family silver on a gravel path to clean it; but, she haughtily conceded, 'when one becomes accustomed to the sight of black faces, native servants will be found very fairly good'. All in all a lady, it was generally believed, could look forward to 'a thoroughly good time'[1] if she was well acquainted with the challenges of daily life in the Protectorate.

Gertrude obviously rose to those challenges. Lady Cranworth's eccentric and enterprising husband, who wrote the first comprehensive account of a pioneer's life in the Protectorate, later leased Chiromo from the Grogans and described it as

> a charming house . . . by local standards most luxurious . . . after amply accommodating ourselves and family, there were two or three spare bedrooms, an excellent kitchen, servants' quarters and ample stables; while, best of all, there were two baths in which one could count on the water being

really hot ... At night after dinner in the dry season one could usually hear the deep grunts of a hunting lion in the distance. The site backed on to a patch of forest ... from which duiker and bushbuck made frequent and voracious visitations on our roses and vegetables, and which at that time still harboured a few leopards.[2]'

It is instructive that the Cranworths could support themselves for 'some of the happiest years of [their] lives at Chiromo'[3] on £1,200 a year; Grogan, on the other hand, had expended a colossal £6,000 simply on buying the land and building the house.[4]

Before long he and Gertrude had immersed themselves in Nairobi life. By 1906 there were almost 2,000 European settlers in the country of whom over 500 lived in Nairobi, whose social life had consequently blossomed. Residing in the town had also become rather more pleasant since a system for disposing of 'night soil' had finally been devised, whereby buckets were collected in carts each morning and the contents buried some distance from town[5] – although this had not prevented yet another outbreak of plague in the Indian bazaar in late January. Grogan was made a steward of the Turf Club and elected to the committee of the Agricultural and Horticultural Society; while in March he and Gertrude were presented to the visiting Duke and Duchess of Connaught and their daughter Princess Patricia, who 'accepted bouquets from the little Misses Grogan and Braidwood'.[6] In charge of the duke's official retinue was Baden-Powell, whose brother Frank had married Gertrude's sister Florence, and who had written to Grogan declaring that he 'should like to see as much of the country' as possible and wanted to 'get a shot at something – any kind of beast would do me'.[7]

Grogan's view of hunting had, however, undergone a radical transformation. After returning from the trek he had spent a good deal of time discussing the need to set up wildlife reserves in Africa with his friend von Wissman, dubbed – like Carl Peters – the 'Rhodes of German East Africa'. He had also been asked by *The Times* to contribute a series of articles on the subject, and when the 1902 edition of *From The Cape To Cairo* was published his original chapter entitled 'Big Game And Its Pursuit' was replaced with one headed 'Collections of New Species'. It seems, in other words, that Grogan the over-zealous hunter – having fulfilled his childhood ambitions with the rifle – had become Grogan the naturalist. The Department of Zoology at Cambridge University, the Natural History Museum and Regent's Park Zoo – as opposed to the walls of Chiromo – were the recipients of most of his vast collection of trophies, and after the trek he never hunted again. In Grogan's case this metamorphosis would appear to justify the assertion of one historian of Victorian explorers, namely that 'there [was] a very clear inverse relationship between intellectual calibre and enthusiasm for the hunting of big game'.[8] Out of politeness he did agree, all the same, to act as Baden-Powell's guide for a brief expedition out on to the Athi Plains.

A month after his return Gertrude made her first foray on to the Nairobi stage in the Amateur Dramatic Club's production of *Ici On Parle Français* at the Railway Institute. By a strange coincidence this piece was well known to Grogan, as it had been the showpiece for the final meeting of the Halliwell Shakespeare Society that he attended before being sent down from Cambridge almost exactly ten years earlier. Gertrude, it seems, made a rather better Mrs Spruggins than had Grogan's fellow (male) undergraduate, Broadbent, and her rendition was accorded considerable praise: 'her stately carriage and elderly make-up,' wrote one reviewer, 'suited the part exactly. Her mellow dramatic appeals to the shades of her illustrious ancestors were kept right up against the line of pure farce, without once stepping over to the burlesque – no easy accomplishment.'[9] Indeed Gertrude's ability to make people laugh was one of her greatest attributes and one that she used to good effect at Chiromo, where she charmed all guests and hosted innumerable children's parties and even the first *proper* balls to be held in the country. Whatever clouds Grogan perceived to be gathering over the 'fatty, degenerated' heart of the Empire, he would always remember these early days in far-off East Africa as 'the sunshine days' – a happy time during which anything seemed possible in the new Protectorate if one had the zest to strive for success.

But beneath the carefree surface always lurked frustrations with 'Bumbledom'. No sooner had Grogan settled in the family and turned his mind to the forest concession than he ran up, once again, against official obstruction. This time he was frustrated not by the CO, which was still awaiting the Crown Agents' verdict on the railway scheme, but by security problems.

Whereas the numerically superior Masai, Kikuyu and Luo peoples had for the most part accepted the arrival of the *muzungu* with astonishing equanimity, the obdurate and courageous Nandi had continued to defy British attempts to subjugate them. In November the previous year the fifth 'punitive expedition' in ten years had been mounted against the 25,000-strong tribe, and their leader was killed. Despite this setback, and the fact that most of the Nandi's cattle and sheep were rounded up and their crops burned, Grogan's friend Meinertzhagen admitted that the Nandi had 'not suffered so severely as we thought'.[10] Only military personnel were allowed into the western part of Grogan's forest concession – which left him entertaining a sizeable party of surveyors in Nairobi rather than in the forest. Again led by the South African Coryell, their salaries alone amounted to £120 per month. Grogan told the local administration that he was happy to take full responsibility for any adverse consequences of visiting the forest, but was categorically instructed that he had to stay put. The frustration caused by this soon paled into insignificance, however, when compared with the inconveniences caused by the arrival of the Protectorate's new commissioner.

Whatever Stewart's drawbacks, bibulous and otherwise, Grogan had at least regarded him as a man of action who talked his language. His successor could not have been more different, and the fifty-year-old Sir James Hayes Sadler's three-year stay in the Protectorate was to achieve renown only for the two near-rebellions that it prompted – one led by Grogan and the other by Lord Delamare.

When Grogan had, in his letter to *The Times*, called on the CO to send out a governor with African experience Hayes Sadler, despite his four-year stint as Commissioner of Uganda, was far from being what he had in mind. A weak if genteel man who had great difficulty looking anyone in the eye, he was soon unpopular even with his own administrators and his complete inability to make any sort of decision earned him the nickname 'Old Flannelfoot'. By March, just three months into his tenure, Meinertzhagen was not alone in remarking that 'matters are as bad and inefficient in Nairobi as they were two years ago' and that 'many settlers . . . have gone home disgusted'.[11]

'Flannelfoot', a man who, as Grogan put it, would 'argue for a minute or two with his lady whether his breakfast egg should be boiled or poached',[12] infuriated the latter by continually giving permission for him to go to survey the forest and then withdrawing it. By midsummer Grogan had no choice but to give up and discharge his survey team, but no sooner had he done this than a new Commissioner of Lands was appointed by the Colonial Office, a Colonel Montgomery, who immediately got off on the wrong foot with Grogan by asking him to pay survey fees so that his own men could survey the forest. Although Grogan had at the outset fulfilled all his legal obligations on the concession by depositing £140 with the government survey department, the government had hitherto asserted that it had no one available to carry out the survey. That was why, at great expense, he had brought his own surveyors. It was like waving a red rag at a bull for Montgomery suddenly to request fees that Grogan had already paid and to say that it was time a survey was done. By now Grogan and Lingham had spent over £3,000 (and the best part of two years) trying to lay the groundwork for a much-needed timber industry for the country, and within another two years these costs would rise to a colossal £20,000. Yet for all this Grogan was being treated, in his opinion, 'like a burglar'[13] by many a government official.

By the end of 1906 Goldmann, even more frustrated than Grogan by the impenetrable wall of official obstruction, was on the verge of selling out of Grogan and Lingham's syndicate. That he, and Grogan for that matter, persevered was due to the dogged determination of the latter and a ray of light beamed from a most unlikely source – the Colonial Office itself. It was the affable if bumbling Herbert Read who sought to break the deadlock, and as he was senior to the troublesome Ellis, who had denounced Grogan's plans as 'simply outrageous', Read was a valuable ally.

Read argued that Grogan's aspirations 'ought not, I think, to be dismissed so contemptuously', and that he had been treated in a way that was reminiscent of 'the extremely unsatisfactory manner in which the Protectorate has been administered under the Foreign Office in the past'. Although sceptical about how soon the Uasin Gishu plateau would become a paying prospect, Read was sure that it needed a railway and asserted that Grogan's 'adaptability' in suggesting alternative means for financing its construction 'deserved recognition even in people of his stamp'.[14]

At last Grogan seemed to have found a man inside the CO with whom he could do business, and in no time a government surveyor – Mr Hutchins – was appointed to inspect the concession. Grogan offered to accompany him personally, and secured further support from the fact that when Cathcart Watson, MP, rose to his feet in Parliament to ask for details of Grogan's 'large timber concession' Churchill replied that progress was 'a question of the construction of a railway', and that whether funds were found privately or by the Treasury it was 'important for the development of East Africa, full of ripe possibilities, that the railway should be provided'.[15] Sensing that the Colonial Office now seemed to be preparing to give his scheme the serious attention he thought it merited, Grogan at last moderated his demands considerably: he declared that if the government was prepared to guarantee the interest on his investors' loans his syndicate was willing to build the railway in return for the freehold over 178,000 acres of forest plus 50,000 acres of farming land in areas to be selected by him.[16]

Grogan's new-found (and only temporary) reasonableness was due to a combination of factors. Firstly, he realized that most of the staid occupants of the Colonial Office were finding him, the charmer with the piercing eyes and formidable financial brain, altogether too 'fast' to handle, and that unless he compromised to some degree there was a risk he would never strike a deal with them at all. Secondly, he knew that unless he kept negotiations moving forward his backers might give up on him: by the end of 1906 he was not only facing the fact that Goldmann's crucial support was wavering but was informed that George Goldie wished to sever his links with the syndicate.

Although Goldie was still a formidable personality he was now in his sixties and, since handing over Nigeria to the British government, his sure-footedness had diminished. He had considered an offer to take over Rhodes's British South Africa Company for two years, only to baulk at the last minute; and now he was doing the same to Grogan and Lingham. His excuse was that Lingham insisted on being managing director of the syndicate for ten years and Goldie refused to accede to this demand 'on account of his record in South Africa'.[17] It is uncertain quite what he meant by this, but his objection may well have related to the fact that Lingham was considered even 'faster' than Grogan and had done very well out of the Boer War. Port Matolla had operated at full throttle throughout the conflict, importing essential goods and soldiers for the war effort, and to the old-school Goldie this may have smacked of profiteering. An equally likely cause for his decision is the obvious one that the inclusion of Goldie, Grogan, Lingham and Goldmann in the syndicate was to have at least one too many buccaneers in the same railway carriage.

The extent to which Grogan was forced to compromise should not, however, be over-estimated. Goldie had largely served his purpose simply by pointing out to the floundering CO that the railway scheme was not only not insane, but laudable and economically viable. Goldmann too was replaceable: Grogan had already entered into encouraging negotiations to sell his interest, should he decide to abandon ship, to Churchill's uncle, Moreton Frewen (otherwise known as 'Mortal Ruin' for one of his less than dazzlingly successful investments in a scheme to extract gold from paving stones). A 'brilliant conversationalist'[18] and intimate of King Edward, Frewen struck Grogan as being the perfect standby for Goldmann. Last, but by no means least, Grogan was convinced that the future value of 228,000 acres freehold would be worth more in the long run than the income from sub-letting 1.6 million acres of leasehold land which would revert at some stage to the Crown. This conclusion he based on his unshakeable faith in the economic prospects of the Protectorate: he was utterly convinced, unlike the sceptical majority in the Colonial Office, that it would succeed for the very simple reason that he, Grogan, was going to make it succeed – and with success would come rapidly rising land prices. With that in mind he left the CO to mull over his compromise.

Grogan's boldness and self-assurance at this juncture were remarkable. In 1906 there *was* no land market worth speaking of in the Protectorate, because there were few settlers and precious little development going on. Furthermore a majority of medical experts were still of the opinion that it was doubtful whether white men could survive on the equator for any length of time; and even if they could survive it was considered most unlikely that it would be safe for them to work under the burning equatorial sun at altitude. In Britain, in other words, the success of European settlement was regarded by many as anything but a foregone conclusion. But to the great annoyance of sceptics, Grogan's optimism would in time prove well-founded.

Grogan was not the only visionary pioneer in the Protectorate, nor was he the first visionary to have settled there. That distinction belonged to Hugh Cholmondeley, the 3rd Baron Delamere. The two men's love of Africa and optimism for its prospects were equally boundless. Like Grogan, Delamere was also a passionate believer in what they both perceived as being Rhodes's vision of Empire, and both were, in the opinion of Dr Norman Leys, an ardent critic of European settlement, 'the lineal descendants of the old gentleman adventurers, who colonised Virginia, singed the king of Spain's beard, exacted homage from those people who are compendiously called "natives" and ended their careers, some in Westminster Abbey, some at a yard-arm'.[19]

Delamere had won his African spurs with five daring hunting expeditions in Somaliland, one of which had left him with a permanent limp (disguised by wearing a built-up boot) after being savagely mauled by a lion. In his youth his passion for 'sport' was so great that on the family estate, Vale Royal in Cheshire, 'the English seasons were marked off for him, as for others of his tradition, by the species of animal it was appropriate to kill. Success was largely measured in terms of destructive ability.' Delamere had first arrived in the Protectorate from Somaliland in 1897, and the country had made a deep impression on him. In January 1903, over a year before the success of Eliot's South African recruitment drive started to be apparent, he returned to settle permanently. A year later he had installed himself on a 100,000 acre ranch, which he named 'Equator', between the Molo river and Njoro on the floor of the Rift Valley.

Delamere cut a striking figure. Although not as tall as Grogan, he was more thick-set and was easily recognizable by the enormous pith helmet which he habitually wore. Beneath it his ginger hair grew unchecked during months of toiling on the farm and was often shoulder-length by the time he came to visit Nairobi for Race Week, a knees-up at the Norfolk Hotel or a political gathering. His raffish guise caused many a new arrival in the Protectorate to mistake him for a tramp, but never for long: he exuded a natural authority which was backed up by a very quick and often violent temper, a propensity to alternate unpredictably between exquisite charm and biting sarcasm, and a pair of piercing blue eyes with which he would transfix whomever he was addressing. Grogan considered him, somewhat equivocally, to be 'a loveable blend of puckish charm and unpredictable political orientation advantaged by a short-term hereditary title', but fifty years later he also asserted that 'D.', was the only one of the pioneer settlers 'likely to remain [a figure] in history'.[20]

This was a modest, if percipient, observation on Grogan's part: the testimonies of many a pioneer echo the sentiments of Lord Cranworth, who wrote that nobody in the Protectorate 'made more impression' on him 'than Ewart Grogan, a romantic figure to any young man'.

> Grogan was gifted by nature far beyond the ordinary ...
> Good-looking, with a fine physique and an impelling eye,
> he had a presence in full keeping with his reputation. Well
> read and with a gifted pen, he possessed ... the power of
> oratory to a degree unequalled in Kenya and unexcelled in
> my opinion elsewhere ... Politically minded, he had already
> [by the time of Cranworth's arrival in 1906] taken the lead
> of the more politically progressive of the settlers.[21]

The relationship between Grogan and Delamere cannot be described as being a close personal friendship. In many respects they were too similar – like two sticks of dynamite – for any great intimacy to have developed. As political allies they often disagreed, sometimes acrimoniously, on the specifics of how their common aim of making the Protectorate a jewel in the Empire's crown should be pursued. Nonetheless it was clear from the outset that they had no rivals for leadership among the settlers, and for twenty years they co-operated by and large in trying to force successive commissioners and governors, not to mention generations of Colonial Office officials, to implement their own back-of-the-envelope master plan for the economic and political development of British East Asia. And when the British Treasury or Colonial Office would not do their bidding neither man baulked at making their displeasure known in explosive fashion.

In addition to their zealous imperialism, a pathological desire to prove that things were possible was common to both men – with scant regard to the short-term financial consequences. Both looked on life as simply a succession of challenges, and if ever they found themselves without a challenge they would swiftly invent a new one. This, to their way of thinking, was what Empire-building was all about – pushing back boundaries – and Rhodes would no doubt have wholeheartedly approved of their bravura. The scale of Grogan's initial ambitions has been described; Delamere, who had once lost £3,000 on a single bet at Chester races, tackled the challenges of his new African home in equally gung-ho fashion.

As the British government was sceptical about the prospect of large numbers of Europeans surviving on the equator, and was loath to commit funds to investigate East Africa's agricultural potential, Delamere resolved to set himself up as a one-man experimental station. His efforts were heavily influenced, as were Grogan's agricultural aspirations, by experience gained in the antipodes. By the end of 1904 he had over 1,500 head of cattle on his Equator ranch, only to see the herd decimated by East Coast Fever and pleuro-pneumonia. Five hundred merino ewes imported from Australia suffered the same fate, due to the mineral deficiencies in the soil. So Delamere turned to wheat, using a thousand oxen to plough furrows – the first of which was a staggering three miles in length. Without hedgerows and other obstacles characteristic of home there seemed little point doing anything other than just keep going across the vast green expanse of the Rift Valley floor.

By 1909 Delamere was planting 1,200 acres of wheat at Equator, but when rust attacked the shoots the whole lot had to be ploughed in. He eventually succeeded in tackling the threat of rust and the harvest from a single field of 1,750 acres filled two entire trainloads. He also managed to establish 15,000 sheep on another ranch at Soysambu, by the shores of Lake Elmenteita, having erected a network of twenty miles of pipeline which bore 67,000 gallons of water per day to his flocks. The cost of this single venture was more than £25,000. By World War I victory over the environment and its biblically pro-portioned hazards – disease, wild animals, flood, drought and locusts – was inch-by-inch being won by Delamere, but at colossal cost: he had mortgaged Vale Royal, his English estate, to the tune of some £80,000 and had borrowed yet more locally.

Penury was one reward for proving – to himself, the government and settlers struggling to make land-holdings both large and small pay – that large-scale agriculture could bankroll the Protectorate in the future. However, the real reward for Delamere, and indeed for Gro-gan's enterprises, was the proof itself. It did not matter to him that all the while he and the graceful and charming Lady Delamere lived a life of Spartan simplicity in a mud and grass hut, subsisting largely on a diet of what could be shot, and consoling themselves by playing 'All Aboard For Margate' on their gramophone when they rose at dawn.

For most of the first two decades of the century Grogan and Delamere resembled a pair of high-rollers squaring up to each other in a high stakes game of craps, in which the only thing that matched the magnitude of the two men's colossal ambitions was their egos. One particularly famous example of their competitiveness occurred in 1905, when Delamere intimated that he was going to import pigs to prove that they could thrive in the Protectorate, and Grogan immedi-ately countered by declaring that in that case he would prove that the Protectorate's streams were ideal for trout. While such a project was obviously not of great economic importance it was of considerable symbolic importance as one more proof that all they deemed best about 'home' could be replicated in the East African highlands.

The logistical problems involved in Grogan's experiment to see whether 'lusty trout could disport themselves in our babbling streams'[22] were legion, and the story of how Grogan overcame them has been described as 'one of the most romantic episodes in the history of the Colony'.[23] The Loch Leven ova – brown and rainbow – were purchased from Howitoun Fisheries and shipped from Scotland to Mombasa; then they were loaded on the train for Nairobi packed in as much ice as Jeevanjee's factory could produce; and finally they were loaded on ox-wagons (there being no motor transport and no roads) for the journey to Nyeri, 11,000 feet above sea level on the edge of the Aberdare forest. There, with labour provided by the Provincial Commissioner, Hinde, they were introduced into the Gura river near a track leading from Nyeri to Naivasha. A year later it was proudly announced in the *East African Standard* that 'Captain Grogan's first importation of ova has been successful';[24] and twenty-five years later there were, thanks to Grogan, over 1,500 miles of excellent trout waters in the colony.

Given Grogan and Delamere's profligacy, the question of how it could be funded soon arose – in their minds and those of others. Neither man had the infinite resources of a Rockefeller, so their brink-manship required not only amenable bank managers but profit – the pursuit of which caused them both to be looked upon with considerable suspicion in Whitehall. Their problem was that the prevailing late Victorian Establishment view of trade and commerce was that both were rather grubby; as a result the making of profit was regarded, as Grogan was often wont to say, as 'some form of insidious crime against the State'. In his view this was a monstrous hypocrisy: the Empire had been built on the back of speculation and, as he had declared in *The Times*, 'speculation' was 'the very essence of modern business', without which there was 'no business'.[25] For his temerity in speaking a truth that many considered was best left unspoken, Grogan earned a reputation in certain quarters as being 'a little too much ahead of the times',[26] and Delamere was considered by the Colonial Office to be an equally modern 'company monger'.[27] Such was the stigma attached to these allegations that as late as the 1930s Delamere's biographer felt the need forcefully but disingenuously to assert that 'speculation' was an activity in which her subject '*never* indulged'.[28]

Striving to make a profit was a far from easy process in the early days of the Protectorate. In 1906 Delamere optioned the whole of his Equator ranch to the Uplands Syndicate, in which Grogan's friend Goldmann was involved, but the deal was stymied when – due to another of his land sales – he was placed under investigation by the Colonial Office for the fraudulent transfer of land. Two large-scale real estate schemes devised by Grogan and Delamere, aimed at smart-ening up the townships of Nairobi and Nakuru[29] in partnership with the local government, were also thwarted simply because 'there was', in Grogan's words, 'an obvious chance' that he and Delamere 'might make some money out of the deal'.[30] The irony is that, while it was obviously true that Grogan and Delamere would benefit from any rise in land values, a far bigger beneficiary was the British government, which so often sought to counter their plans. It was, after all, the Crown which had claimed the freehold of all land in the country which it (often mistakenly) understood to be 'unoccupied' by Africans and had also bought (often using dubious bargaining tactics) large tracts of prime agricultural land from the Kikuyu and other tribes.

Grogan remained as stubborn as ever in the face of official obstruction of some of his schemes. Indeed, during the second half of 1906 he succeeded in concluding a plethora of deals with breathtaking rapidity. After seeing off a challenge to his ownership of the forest concession in a court case brought by a well-known malcontent by the name of Grant;[31] he bought a further 121.4 acres of the Nairobi Swamp (which he now renamed 'the Gertrude Swamp') in partnership with an Indian company, Shariff Jaffer;[32] and he founded Longonot Ltd, a company whose main asset was a 20,000 acre farm with six miles of frontage on Lake Naivasha on which he installed a New Zealand manager recruited by Eddie Watt with the instructions that he should turn it into a sheep farm.[33] He also bought two farms near Limuru with a view to cultivating black wattle, and at the beginning of October he registered the Kilindini Harbour, Wharves & Estates Company Ltd, with a nominal capital of £100,000.

The timing of this latter initiative was significant in that the government had just announced that it intended to build Mombasa's first deep-water pier, which would enable cargo and passengers to be unloaded direct to shore rather than in lighters or on the 'brawny shoulders of Swahili longshoremen'.[34] Preliminary earthworks began five months later, but Grogan was as sceptical of the government's ability to undertake the project as Henry Labouchère had been of its ability to complete the Lunatic Line on time and within budget.

Grogan therefore determined to try and beat the government to the finishing post by building his own pier on the 100 acres of land that Eliot had so graciously ceded to him adjacent to the government port at Kilindini. Thus began a second battle with the Colonial Office which, like his battle over the forest concession and Uasin Gishu railway, would roll on for fully two decades.

This whirlwind of activity soon made Grogan realize that his business interests were now so extensive, and his ongoing negotiations with the Colonial Office so time consuming, that he needed a trusty lieutenant to oversee his personal Scramble for Africa. The man he chose as his factor was Wilfrid Hunter, who had married Grogan's eldest sister, Dorothy, and could not have been more different to Grogan. Hunter was a rather dour, portly individual with a severe centre-parting, whose only concession to sartorial elegance was his penchant for wearing bow ties. Other than that Hunter defined, in build and temperament, the word 'solid' and was the perfect choice to sweep up behind Grogan. An accountant, civil engineer, Cambridge graduate and Associate of the Chartered Institute of Secretaries, he was also scrupulously honest and for almost thirty years would do his level best in good times and bad to keep the Grogan business empire on the rails – a task which a more excitable mortal would probably have abandoned in the first year. This loyalty and his professionalism were immediately apparent to all who met Hunter, and in no time he became factor to Delamere and a host of other settlers, as well as a pillar of a community whose flamboyance he most certainly did not typify.

Hunter and B. G. Allen, Grogan's legal advisor, were much needed. Scarcely a month passed without one of Grogan's businesses being involved in litigation – sometimes as defendant, sometimes as claimant. These were mostly just cases of a technical nature relating to the daily workings of his rapidly growing business interests. Certainly they had nothing to do with either 'absenteeism' or 'dummying', which the Colonial Office regarded as the twin evils of the commercial world, because Grogan was obviously not an absentee landlord seeking only to profit from rising land prices while safely ensconced at home in London; nor did he have any need to 'dummy' – 'dummying' being the term used for applying for land in someone else's name in order to circumvent restrictive land regulations.[35] But Grogan's omnipresence both in the law courts and the commercial life of the Protectorate increasingly raised fears on the part of those in the local administration whom Grogan would have categorized as 'little ones who feared to be great' that he was uncontrollable.

These fears were not rooted in a suspicion that Grogan actually sought to break the letter of the law, though he habitually sailed very close to the wind; rather it was that he was increasingly recognized as being anti-authoritarian and a law unto himself. This caused his friend Frederick Jackson, a renowned sportsman and naturalist and Hayes Sadler's deputy, considerable unease when in the company of the man he described as 'a dreamer, a man of great ideas, but a little *too* much ahead of the times'. The monocled Jackson also noted that 'no one can sit long in [Grogan's] presence and listen to him talking without becoming aware that all the time, and behind a quizzical smile, he is busy summing-up, and trying to form a verdict'.[36] That verdict, as far as most civil servants were concerned, was invariably a poor one. And although Grogan was a master at mobilizing his formidable vocabulary to convey his disapproval without needing to resort to impoliteness, and could deliver the most crushing put-down with his iridescent eyes still twinkling and a genial smile fixed on his face, sometimes he went to extremely provocative lengths to highlight what he perceived to be the shortcomings of his peers.

Grogan regarded it as his bounden duty as an imperialist to expose governmental incompetence and unproductive rules which jeopardized economic progress in the Protectorate. In late 1906 his particular target was a new Mining Ordinance in which he found a clause which seemed to classify earth as a mineral, thereby implying that if a man simply wanted to dig for clay in his own back yard then he had to apply for a full mining licence. At a time when local building materials were in short supply, and imported ones far beyond the means of most people, Grogan considered this ruling to be absurd and resolved – on a day that went down in the annals of settler lore – to do something about it.

Accompanied by a retinue of staff Grogan marched out of Chiromo and proceeded to peg out 400 acres of the centre of Nairobi in double-quick time. Then, having only excluded Hayes Sadler's garden 'for fear of hurting his feelings',[37] he paid a visit to William Hobley, Ainsworth's successor as sub-commissioner for Nairobi, and registered his claim to excavate the town centre in the search for clay. Hobley, who was generally referred to as 'Hobley Bobbley' on account of his inability to make speedy decisions and penchant for issuing highly ambiguous instructions, recognized immediately that he had been hoisted by his own petard – and the wording of the ordinance was swiftly changed.

At much the same time Grogan threatened the government with legal action when he discovered some workers involved in the construction of a new hospital cutting down trees on the edge of the Chiromo estate, although when he had wrung a confession from the administration that it was technically guilty of trespass and wilful damage he relented and allowed a small portion of the estate to be incorporated into the hospital. Such were the lengths that the man known to local Africans as *bwana simba* was prepared to go to prove a point.

He was far from being the only pioneer who was deeply dissatisfied with the Colonial Office and its local administration, which under 'Flannelfoot' had atrophied to a worrying degree. Indeed by the end of 1906 the settlers had decided that what they needed was a 'big man' to voice their frustrations; someone with influence and authority; someone who would *lead*. And as more and more South Africans arrived to settle in the country the political tide swung away from Delamere, who was deemed by many of the newcomers to be too aristocratic for their liking, and towards the more flamboyant Grogan whom they judged to be a 'people's leader'.

On 23 January 1907 the Colonists' Association, the settlers' mouthpiece, held a ballot for a new president and by an overwhelming majority of 95 votes to 14 Grogan was elected. Now, in addition to everything else on his plate, he was the settlers' official leader.[38]

THIRTEEN

Battle Lines are Drawn

It was Churchill, as Under-Secretary of State for Colonies, who best encapsulated the state of political foment in the Protectorate by declaring that 'every man in Nairobi is a politician; and most of them are leaders of parties'.[1] The only party of any significance, however, was Grogan's extremely voluble Colonists' Association whose members were 'emboldened by the confident hope . . . that the paramount factor in Colonial Office rule is to govern according to the wishes of the governed'.[2] By 'the governed' the European settlers meant, first and foremost, themselves – thereby displaying a degree of chauvinism which was substantially shared by their political masters, but the unabashed expression of which caused the latter considerable unease.

Despite this, the power of the Colonists' Association was formally recognized by Churchill's superior, Lord Elgin, when he conceded to its demand that the Protectorate should have its own Legislative Council, or parliament, combining both settlers and officials. The council was designated for inauguration sometime in 1907 and Grogan, in recognition of his stature and leadership of the Association, was earmarked as one representative of the settler community; Delamere was the natural choice as the other.

Elgin's concession was a very significant victory for Grogan and the settlers. Churchill remarked that 'never before in Colonial experience has a council been granted where the number of settlers is so few',[3] and most of Grogan's supporters regarded this fact as a positive indication that they would at some juncture be granted the self-government enjoyed by their fellow colonials in Canada, Australia and New Zealand. They were united in regarding this as their ultimate goal, although their backgrounds and many of their other aspirations were far from uniform.

The East African settlers had converged on their new home from many different parts of the Empire, but those who were to leave the biggest stamp on the mythology of the Protectorate were the English aristocrats. This was largely down to Delamere, who publicized the attractions of a life in the Protectorate to members of his class back in the 'old country', and by 1907 the Lords Cranworth, Hindlip, Cardross, Howard de Walden and Egerton of Tatton all had extensive interests in the country – as did a large number of equally well-heeled new arrivals like Denys Finch-Hatton, Gilbert Colvile, and Galbraith and Berkeley Cole, younger sons of the Earl of Enniskillen who were also Delamere's brothers-in-law. 'Titles', as Grogan not entirely enthusiastically put it, 'were three a penny in Kenya';[4] the aristocrats were influential beyond their numbers both in the Protectorate and, importantly, in Britain. There, Hindlip (a Conservative Whip from 1908) and Delamere in particular ran an ongoing and increasingly effective campaign promoting the interests of the settlers in the House of Lords.

The aristocrats and public schoolboys went to East Africa in pursuit of profit, sport and adventure. Above all they nostalgically sought the freedom of what Isak Dinesen described as an 'earlier England, a world which no longer existed'[5] and which, arguably, never had existed except in their imaginations. To such men Grogan's introduction of trout to the Protectorate's streams was an achievement of the greatest symbolic importance in their drive to establish a home from home. Their aspirations were those of their class, as was their behaviour: when not engaged in the monumentally challenging task of trying to wrest an income from the soil they would relax in time-honoured public school fashion. The Norfolk Hotel, otherwise known as 'The House of Lords' or the 'Dukery', became particularly riotous during Race Week – the high point (if not the only point) of the social diary. The street-lamps opposite the hotel would be used for target practice, Delamere locked obstructive managers in the meat-safe, mounted revellers competed to jump over the Indian barber's tent in the gardens and rugby matches were fiercely contested in the bar. Such 'good clean fun' could be further enhanced by a spot of cricket or a ride out with Jim Elkington and Jack Riddell's Masara Hunt which boasted its very own pack of foxhounds (but whose principal quarry was jackals).

But until after the Great War the aristocrats, although they made an indelible mark on life in the Protectorate, were far from being in a majority among the settlers. It was the South Africans – mostly British South Africans as opposed to Boers – who dominated numerically and politically, and gave the country the over-riding feel of being a South African colony. These were the pioneers who had answered Eliot's call for immigrants and began arriving in numbers at much the same time as Grogan himself; and like their aristocratic compatriots they brought their own distinct style of behaviour to the Protectorate. They were an altogether more rough and ready lot, used to the hard knocks of the Boer War and the frontiersman's life. Indeed, quite a number were so rough and ready, or so poor, that they were deported straight back whence they had come. Whereas the aristocrats looked to fashion the Protectorate as an England in the tropics, the South Africans sought to create a new South Africa – one with none of the post-war bitterness or economic depression of 'the South'; without the overwhelming power of the Randlords or the complications of living alongside their erstwhile Boer enemies. Like the aristocrats they did not wish to sever completely their links with their own 'old country', and from the outset they campaigned for the Protectorate to be included in the South African Customs Union.

Among both the British and South African groups there were also many pioneers who shared neither the aggressive swagger of the South Africans nor the conspicuity of the aristocrats. On the whole this gentleman (and often ex-military) class of settler got on with life quietly and without ostentation. Although their role in shaping the character of European settlement was less public, whether it involved carving a paying farm out of a wilderness or trying to exert a moderating influence on the political firebrands, it was no less significant – and ultimately it would prove more enduring.

Eccentrics there were aplenty, some of whom – in Grogan's words – were 'so odd that their proper portrayal would require a three volume novel'.[6] A piratical Yorkshireman, John Boyes, had virtually established his own principality among the Kikuyu in the late 1890s. William Northrup McMillan was an American from Missouri (of Canadian parentage) who had made a fortune out of Rumania's Ploesti oilfields and Malayan rubber, and with his sixty-inch girth had earned the name *bwana tumbo* ('The Tummy') among the local African populace. He arrived after trekking down the Nile on foot and camel and was accompanied by 'Uncle Charles' Bulpett, famous in his own right for swimming the Thames at Greenwich in frock coat and top hat for a wager, for subsequently swimming the Hellespont as well, and for having been ruined by a courtesan of legendary beauty and lack of scruples. The genial Abraham Block had begun his commercial career, which culminated with his creation of the country's largest hotel group, by making mattresses out of dried grass and sewing them up with needles fashioned from old bicycle spokes. The bear-like and ebullient Russell Bowker sported a leopard's head on his felt hat, its visage permanently fixed in a snarl, and rode about on a mule called Satan. And so the roll-call went on.

Very few of these pioneers were poor, although the origins of most were a good deal more humble than those of their Lordships. As Quentin Grogan soon discovered, a substantial amount of capital was required in order to thrive in the Protectorate, which was largely devoid of both mineral wealth (and therefore the possibility of getting rich quick) and opportunities for European artisans. In 1904 the minimum capital requirement for a settler was estimated at £500, but this trebled two years later as the magnitude of the difficulties of making a living from agriculture became increasingly apparent. Quentin, not having been as substantial a beneficiary of his father's Will as his eldest brother, was one of many who was forced to leave the country due to a lack of funds and by the end of 1906 was – to his great regret – back in the employ of Clement Talbot Motors in London's Barlby Road.

For his part Grogan defied being pigeon-holed into any one category of settler and instead straddled all groups like a Colossus. He shared a similar upbringing with the aristocrats, although he shunned most of their recreational antics (of which he had had quite enough for one lifetime at Cambridge) and harboured a fiercely meritocratic streak (which inclined him to believe that the success of European settlement depended ultimately on the ordinary farmer or business-man). In turn, his common touch, and the reputation gained by the adventures of his adult life – serving under Rhodes in the Matabele War, the Cape to Cairo trek and membership of Milner's

Kindergarten – bestowed on him an aura which made him an equally acceptable leader to the South Africans. As friends, however, he most enjoyed – and always would – the company of the nascent community's great eccentrics.

Grogan's ability to draw support from such disparate groups was remarkable, and was due to the fact that he possessed so many of the personal traits of leadership. In addition to sharing many of the aspirations of each of his 'constituents', his intellect and physical presence were formidable; he was acknowledged to be far and away the most brilliant orator in the Protectorate; he was known to wield huge influence in Britain; and by now his penetrating yellowy-green eyes radiated the same 'cold gleam of cynicism inseparable from true greatness'[7] that he had once identified in Rhodes. Lord Cranworth was just one of many settlers to extol the achievements of the Colonists' Association, which 'under the presidency of Lord Delamere and Mr Grogan placed the settlers' point of view before the Government again and again', and to conclude that 'the work it did for the country can never be forgotten'.[8]

Bolstered by such adulation, and with his reputation further enhanced among the settlers by deeds such as his embarrassment of 'Hobley Bobbley' over the wording of the Mining Ordinance, Grogan thrived in the political arena. He was prone to theatricality, and increasingly to demagogy, so the confrontational nature of what he perceived as a personal duel with the 'silverfish'[9] of the Colonial Office suited him down to the ground. In one intemperate conversation with his monocled friend Frederick Jackson, the Protectorate's Deputy Commissioner, he even went as far as characterizing his role as being to 'criticise and destroy'. He did not mean by this that he had any intention of 'criticising and destroying' the country which he had made his home, or indeed any part of the Empire; rather it was that he regarded civil servants, even when they were his friends, as enemies of progress whom he intended continually to criticize and, if necessary, destroy. As a result, in the years leading up to and immediately after the Great War, Grogan's rhetoric and actions were to frustrate, infuriate and sometimes horrify what he called the 'bumblers' of Whitehall and the local administration – who rapidly came to the conclusion that there was 'an indefinable something about Kenya Colony that is

very unbalancing'.[10] They also firmly secured Grogan's reputation as
the settlers' champion.

Grogan's single biggest bone of contention with Whitehall was that
the Colonial Office had, by the end of 1906, done nothing to address
the problems caused by the Foreign Office having pursued a 'policy
of drift' in the Protectorate. There were still no signs in Britain of a
public and categoric definition of whether the country was to be principally governed with what were perceived as the interests of the African
population to the fore, as was the case in neighbouring Uganda; or
as a province of India; or as a territory which would continue to
encourage settlement by Europeans. This oversight not only caused
considerable confusion but triggered a competition for rights between
the settlers, the Indians and the African population that was to last
for the fifty years of Grogan's active political career and beyond, to
Independence.

From the outset Grogan believed that such competition was largely
unnecessary. His argument, posited in a letter to *The Times*, was that
the Protectorate simply needed the 'arrangement (of a *modus vivendi*)
[which] would lift the existing plane of unconstitutionalism and racial
antagonism'.[11] By this he meant the definition of 'spheres of influence'
for all, in the same manner as the European Powers had defined
respective 'spheres of influence' in Africa as a whole. Such a philosophy
was not enlightened by today's standards, given that it was predicated
on Grogan's wholehearted support for conquest by Britain of a quarter
of the globe and his belief in the maxim 'to the victor . . . the spoils'.
Nor did he believe in any great degree of power-sharing, and was as
convinced of the supremacy of the Briton as all his countrymen –
liberal and conservative alike. But Grogan did consider it the duty of
the Empire to deploy 'the spoils' responsibly, and to seek to foster a
'reasonable and decent society in Africa'.[12] Unlike more radical colonials
he harboured no ambitions summarily to dispossess the two million
strong African population of all the best land in the Protectorate; or

to undermine what he had observed during his Cape to Cairo trek as being 'in many cases, the admirable state of society in Africa';[13] or to deploy 'the brutality and coercion' of the Boers, who in Grogan's opinion treated Africans 'like vermin'.[14]

Until the 1950s it was not the indigenous Africans but the Protectorate's resident Indian population who provided the European settlers' aspirations with the stiffest opposition. It was Indian labourers who had built the Lunatic Line, nonsensically to the Indian metre gauge as opposed to the 3'6" gauge of African railways – an error later admitted by the Colonial Office to be 'unfortunate',[15] and all supplies necessary for its construction had also been shipped from India. As a result the Foreign Office had, until the arrival of European settlers, largely treated the Protectorate as a province of India. The rupee was introduced as the official currency, as were the Indian civil and penal codes; Indian troops were deployed in the country; and Nairobi's Turf Club, of which Grogan was a steward, even followed the rules of the Calcutta Turf Club. Of the 32,000 Indian labourers involved in building the railway almost 7,000 stayed on in East Africa after the expiry of their contracts, of whom about 2,000 remained in the employ of the railway.[16] At the end of 1906 the Indian population of 3,500 – a figure that would more than treble by 1911 – dwarfed the settler population and, in the words of Shiva Naipaul, 'represented dangerous competition: [they] too wanted a share in the spoils of Empire'.[17]

That the idea of running the Protectorate as a province of India did not prevail after the arrival of the European settlers was principally due to two factors. Firstly, the Indians had neither the influence nor the power in London of men like Grogan, and secondly, they were a heterogeneous community made up of many insular and caste-conscious groupings. This was largely true of the newly arrived Europeans as well, but whereas they substantially subsumed their differences in the pursuit of common political and economic ends, the various Indian factions remained divided and insular. Shiva Naipaul, in describing this phenomenon, even went as far as saying that his fellow Indians made the mistake of '[reacting] neither to the land nor to the people among whom [they] lived',[18] with deleterious effects for their own pursuit of political and economic power.

There was, among the community compendiously referred to as

'the Indians', an aristocracy comprising the great traders and businessmen, some of whose families had been established on the coast for centuries. Most, like Shariff and Jaffer (Grogan's partners in the Gertrude Swamp), were Muslims (although the most vociferous political activist among them was Jeevanjee, a Parsee), and were almost perpetually at loggerheads with the Hindus who made up the bulk of the Indian population as well as the country's artisanal, shopkeeping and clerical classes. In turn, the Hindus were themselves divided by their rigid caste system. Then there were the Christian Goans, much in evidence in the civil service, and the 'martial races' greatly admired by the British – the Baluchis, Pathans, Punjabis and Sikhs who served in visiting regiments. The presence of this diverse collection of peoples was absolutely essential to almost every facet of daily life in the country – Hindu labourers had even built Grogan's house, and Gujarati money-lenders may well have financed it – but it was not united. To complicate matters further certain groups of Indians demonstrably and loyally upheld the system that was imposed upon them by the British Empire: the Ismaili Khojas, for example, were instructed by His Holiness the Aga Khan to be 'obedient and loyal to [their] secular rulers and to adopt the customs of their adopted country'.[19]

Grogan knew perfectly well that the economic life of the Protectorate depended on the Indians, and it was not a fact which concerned him greatly. What did concern him was any attempt on the part of the latter to translate economic power into political power. To counter this he did not stoop to casting aspersions on the Indians' personal and sexual habits, as was the wont of many a settler, but – ever the politician – played on the xenophobic fears of the British public that their own jobs as well as those of their colonial cousins might some day be jeopardized by Asiatic expansionism. This he characterized in a letter to *The Times* as 'the next great threat which the Empire will be called upon to face'.[20]

This line of argument struck a chord not only with the British public, but with politicians and civil servants as well. Even though the Empire was at the peak of its might a sense of caution prevailed in the corridors of power, and a continuing source of that caution was the notion that the Empire might one day be undermined from within. The recent change of government made little difference: while the new Liberal government made lofty pronouncements about its obligations to Britain's 'subject races', its attitude to power-sharing was in reality no more progressive than that of its Conservative predecessors or Grogan. As a result it refused to make any provision for the inclusion of an Indian representative in the Protectorate's new Legislative Council. And in pledges made in 1906 and 1908 by Lord Elgin, the Secretary of State for Colonies, it was made clear that although the Indians would not be barred de jure from making future applications for rural land in what had rapidly and possessively become known as the 'White Highlands' of the Protectorate that, de facto, would largely be the case. The irony in this, which was not lost on Grogan, was that it was Mr Ellis at the Colonial Office – an avowed champion of the 'subject races' – who was the architect of these so-called Elgin pledges, a fact which not only underpinned Grogan's faith in the power of the British taxpayer but also his conviction that the Colonial Office was not to be trusted even when it took action which was seemingly to the considerable advantage of the European settlers.

The societies of the native African peoples, the third competitor in the contest for rights and privileges in the Protectorate, were in most respects every bit as heterogeneous and introspective as those of the settlers and Indians, but their responses to conquest by the British were even more multiform than those of the Indian community to the arrival of European settlers. Indeed the ease with which the country was 'subjugated' was a stark contrast to the horrifying experience wrought on Africans in, for example, Leopold's Belgian Congo or certain of the German territories. There were no mass executions and no enforced slavery. Nor, in contrast to the British 'pacification' of Zululand in the 1870s and Matabeleland in the 1890s, was there much resistance or bloodshed: only in two 'punitive' campaigns, of which there were fewer than thirty in total between 1893 and 1911, did African casualties number over a thousand.

There were many reasons for the apparent ease of the British occupation. Firstly their opponents were poorly armed and with the exception of the proud Masai and their fellow Nilo-Hamites, the Nandi, very few tribes were inherently warlike. Many were also nomadic and had grown accustomed over the centuries to moving on when presented with opportunity or confronted by adversity. Furthermore, the ability of the Protectorate's Africans to wage war had been severely curtailed by the effects of a number of natural disasters as the nineteenth century drew to a close. The herds of the cattle-centric Masai had been decimated by the rinderpest epidemic in the 1880s, and its effects were exacerbated by internecine warfare in the following decade. Similarly the most populous tribe, the highland Kikuyu, had experienced a great famine (the *Ngaa Nere*) at the turn of the century, and this was soon followed by a smallpox epidemic. Simple pragmatism dictated most chiefs' passive response to the arrival of the white man. Indeed for many Africans, especially in southern Kikuyuland, this pragmatism extended to embracing outright collaboration when it was realized that alliance with the British could be a powerful instrument for enhancing their prestige within their tribe or for securing protection. Masai volunteers enthusiastically took part in the campaigns against their decades-old enemies, the Nandi, having spotted the opportunity to augment their own herds with stock confiscated from the Nandi, and large sections of the Luo and Luhya tribes, in the west, also allied themselves to the British in order to gain protection against Nandi cattle-raids (although other factions joined with the Nandi for equally opportunistic reasons).

In the early years of the century it appeared to the British and to many an African that conquest had put an end to large-scale inter-tribal warfare and the worst ravages of famine, and had facilitated rapid population growth, but it had also – with the benefit of hindsight – caused considerable cultural and political turmoil within some tribes and laid the foundations for strife in the not too distant future. It is a moot point whether *any* tribal faction believed that the British had come with the intention of staying permanently, and the longer they stayed, and the more the African population grew, the greater became the discontent about ownership of the Protectorate's main asset – the land itself.

The tone of Grogan's contributions to the debate about what the British government called the 'Native Question' varied considerably. At times he undeniably pandered in public to the racial chauvinism that was endemic to the Britain (and indeed the India) of his time. But he equally often declared himself to be '100% pro-African' and unlike the Protectorate's more bigoted and blinkered settlers he readily acknowledged – and lauded – the fact that it was the African economy which contributed 'a very large proportion of the actual wealth that keeps the whole country going'.[21] His over-riding preoccupation was with economic development and, though some of his suggestions verged on the despotic, he vociferously opposed any of his compatriots whom he considered to be interfering with African customs and traditions and forcefully advocated that the African population was best governed 'through the chiefs ... without injuring their prestige'.[22] There was, in Grogan's ultimately mistaken opinion, plenty of land for all as the Protectorate was one quarter the size of India but had an indigenous population less than one hundredth the size; and he had little time for anyone who called for the introduction of laws as repressive as those that came to be favoured by the Afrikaners in South Africa (which smacked to him of paranoia).

The degrading conditions of the vast labour compounds of the Transvaal gold mines did not become a feature of life in the East Africa Protectorate, but that is not to say that unpopular laws were not introduced. As early as 1902, before the arrival of all but a handful of European settlers, the Conservative government had imposed on the African population a hut tax of 3 rupees per annum (the monetary equivalent of a sheep), and in 1905 this was followed by the Masters' and Servants' Ordinance.[23] In 1915 the Liberal government formulated the most anti-libertarian pieces of legislation so far: the Pass and Registration Ordinances.[24] Successive British governments of whatever political persuasion took their self-appointed duty of 'trusteeship' over the Africans only as seriously as funds or their prejudices would allow. On the other hand, though the European settlers were regularly demonized in Whitehall, most were at worst guilty of working the system and at best sought to live amicably with their African neighbours on whom their success and very survival depended. To have behaved any differently, in rural areas in particular, would – as Grogan well knew from the days of his great trek – have been both counter-productive and foolhardy.

During Grogan's early years in East Africa no issue caused greater controversy than the allocation of land. By the time a Land Committee was convened in 1905 it was generally accepted that the British government's failure to formulate a land policy during the decade since taking control of the Protectorate had led to total confusion, but even then it took a further twelve months for the Colonial Office to appoint a Commissioner of Lands, Colonel Montgomery, to sort out the mess which affected European settlers, Indians and Africans alike.

In almost demonic fashion, Grogan thrived on the chaos. He despatched long memos lecturing the Colonial Office on the economics of European settlement; he heaped criticism on the Protectorate's Land Office and its overworked surveyor, the hapless but ever-cheerful Reginald Barton Wright; and he suggested that the civil servants who slowly and belatedly began to grapple with the formulation of a policy should 'borrow a primer on the subject'.[25] But by 1907 there were still over 650 European land applications outstanding, some of which took a decade to settle, and, despite the Colonial Office's pronounced distaste for 'monopolists' and 'speculators', there were no provisions in the law to curb land dealings – with the one exception that applications for grants over 10,000 acres had to be referred for approval to the Secretary of State.

Amid the chaos Grogan worked the system for all he was worth. If, he reasoned, there were no workable property laws and 'the assets of the country' were – as he declared to the 1905 Land Committee – 'being dealt with most promiscuously', then he might as well deploy his charm, shrewd business sense and ruthless determination to maximum effect. The result was that by the time the Colonial Office proclaimed the 1915 Crown Lands Bill from – as Grogan put it – their 'Augean stables', the horses they sought to tame had long since bolted: by then, in the words of the leading historian of European settlement, 'Delamere, the two Coles, Grogan, the East Africa Syndicate and East Africa Estates, held *one fifth* of the alienated land in the Protectorate'.[26] The Colonial Office had thus been well and truly outmanoeuvred and Grogan dismissed their protests by declaring that land monopolists were nothing more than an illusion 'in the minds of academics'.[27]

Grogan and his fellow 'big men' had every reason to be jubilant at each new victory over the Colonial Office, not least because they were achieved with considerable assistance from its own officials in the Protectorate who were mostly in favour of a quiet life. Such collaboration was, of course, not exactly what some officials at the CO expected from those whom it entrusted with adjudicating evenhandedly the rival claims of settlers, Indians and Africans. But others in Whitehall had discovered what it was like to fall under Grogan's persuasive spell. They also acknowledged that the process of adjudication was fraught with difficulties, and that the realities of daily life for the Protectorate's administrators were bound to expose them on occasion to accusations of favouritism, every bit as much as was true of the CO itself – as Mr Ellis, architect of the discriminatory 'Elgin pledges', discovered. While Grogan made a habit of castigating such double standards, he was in no position to deny that more often than not they substantially benefited him during the first decade of the century.

The Protectorate's administrators, whom Grogan had bewitched almost to a man, comprised – like the three communities that they oversaw – a diverse bunch of characters. With the exception of Commissioner 'Flannelfoot', most of the senior ones were considered, at least by their masters at the CO and the settlers, to be 'as fine a body of men as ever did the pioneer work of Empire-building';[28] in marked contrast to their masters they also had considerable experience of Africa. Prominent among this group were men like the monocled Jackson, 'Hobley Bobbley', and the bulldog-like Ainsworth – all of whom had worn the white jackets and coloured cummerbunds of the Imperial British East Africa Company prior to its demise; and the Prussian-looking Charles Bowring, whom Grogan had first met in Nyasaland while making his way north during the trek. Not all their underlings were of equal calibre, nor did they all share the privileged, public school educated backgrounds of the leading officials and settlers. Indeed, many junior officials had little education of any sort, which meant that their ability to wield authority over the likes of Grogan and Delamere was no greater than that of a corporal trying to issue orders to his regimental colonel. Many could not even claim to be professionally qualified in any way. No exam was required to enter the Protectorate's civil service, until a three-month law course became mandatory in 1907 (thereby answering in part a call made by Grogan in *From The Cape To Cairo* for properly qualified officials). Only in 1909 was a general three-month course introduced, which included classes in surveying and accounting.

Most officials regarded their prime duty to be safeguarding the paramountcy of 'native interests' in the Protectorate, but they also believed, like Grogan, that there was – as Hobley put it – 'space for both [settler and African]',[29] and that there was 'nothing to stop [Africa] from becoming the greatest producer of economic raw materials in the world'.[30] They were continually hampered in their work by the chronic shortage of funds forthcoming from the British Treasury,[31] by the absence of a rigid policy framework within which to operate, and by a shortage of key staff, particularly in the Land Office. These all contributed to a tendency on the part of government to do whatever was expedient, and possible, at any one time in an effort to work towards what Grogan described as 'the arrangement of a *modus vivendi*'. Government policy was therefore as inconsistent as Colonial Office policy, with bewildering consequences. On the one hand officials were distinctly loath to do anything that might smack of coercion in response to the settlers' continual complaints about a shortage of available labourers; they vociferously defended the rights of the African to the land they occupied; most were sceptical about Grogan's hopes of turning the Protectorate into 'a second New Zealand';[32] and to a man they opposed the settlers' ambitions to run the country themselves one day. But on the other hand, while Jackson and Hobley and Bagge strongly defended the rights of the Masai to remain in the Rift Valley, they were also instrumental in moving them to make way for European settlement when ordered to do so by none other than the Colonial Office itself.[33] Officials, like the settlers, also had their favourites among the African tribes, and the martial Masai were unfortunate in being one of a number that were generally held in greater esteem by the latter than the former.

Such inconsistency in the making and execution of policy, born in part of necessity, made the Protectorate's officials a 'safe thing' for Grogan 'to kick'.[34] In public he was wont to accuse them of behaving like 'little tin gods', and to deride the local government for always 'multiplying in numbers [without] accumulating competence in proportion to its increasing obligations'.[35] Despite this, in private the senior officials were also his friends, and most remained so even when he set out to embarrass them. This speaks volumes for their tolerance of a man who, charismatic and charming though he was, was utterly convinced that every one of his opinions was correct and did not suffer gladly those he perceived to be fools. Indeed in his negotiations with officials Grogan tended to issue instructions; if they did not agree to comply with his wishes immediately he would often just sit and stare at them in complete silence, and when really uninterested in the proceedings he would simply fall asleep.

Nevertheless, when Grogan assumed the leadership of the Colonists' Association in January 1907, Jackson spoke for almost all his colleagues when he expressed 'considerable satisfaction' to his superiors at the Colonial Office that 'this gentleman, though to some extent a critic of the Government in the past' was elected. It even led him to entertain 'high hopes ... of a saner and less aggressive policy [on the part of the settlers] in the future.'[36] It was on Grogan that Jackson pinned his hopes of curbing the seditious activities of a gang of South African 'townies' and 'barloafers' who had arrived recently and were, in Jackson's opinion, trying to turn the country into a 'domain of nigger- and game-shooters'.[37] After all, Grogan had a toe in every camp, was considered by the government to be '100% pro-African', and was also a Visiting Justice to the Nairobi gaol and a member of the Town Council.

But within months the settlers' champion, 'carried away by the desire to become a popular hero'[38] as Jackson subsequently put it, was to let his monocled friend down disastrously.

FOURTEEN

The Nairobi Incident

Grogan seemed to have every reason to be satisfied with life at the beginning of March 1907. He was President of the Colonists' Association, a pillar of the community, and had just returned from an interesting three-week tour of the Aberdare Mountains (in which he hoped to acquire a further forest concession). Nonetheless, beneath his usual ebullient exterior he was in a singularly testy frame of mind. Not only was it common knowledge that the end of the dry season was a time of year when 'nerves ... easily [got] on edge',[1] but Grogan was also experiencing the first, excruciatingly painful, symptoms of yet another liver abscess.

Within a fortnight his mood had worsened still further. Although a Legislative Council with settler participation had been promised by Lord Elgin the previous year there was still no news about the date of its inauguration, and Grogan suspected that the Colonial Office was contemplating reneging on its promise. More importantly, he received word on 12 March that Elgin had rejected his scheme for building a railway across the Uasin Gishu plateau. This was a massive setback which compounded the effect of the almost simultaneous publication of a government report concerning his forest concession.

In January Grogan had guided the government surveyor, a man by the name of Hutchins, round his concession. Grogan had taken an instant liking to Hutchins, whom he regarded as 'the oddest of oddities',[2] and had consequently hoped that his findings would be favourable. Instead Hutchins had concluded that the 'terms on which part of the [Eldama Ravine] forest has been leased to Messrs. Lingham and Grogan are unsatisfactory and would mean the destruction of the forest'.[3] Grogan not only thought this was singularly ungrateful behaviour on Hutchins's part after all the hospitality and assistance he had given him; but of greater concern was the fact that he knew that the Colonial Office would seize on Hutchins's words as justification for trying to do him out of his concession.

On the afternoon of 13 March Grogan was pondering his blighted hopes in the grounds of Chiromo when his sister Dorothy suddenly rushed into the garden 'in a state of obvious terror and prostration ... "Ewart! Ewart!" she called out, "you must do something to those rickshaw men. They have been treating me shamefully, jeering in a horrible way and trying to throw me out of the rickshaw. I am terrified. I shall never forget it as long as I live!" '[4] Although the details of what exactly had happened are 'very vague',[5] it seems that Dorothy and a Miss McDonnell, a teacher, had gone down to the town centre in a rickshaw drawn by three of Grogan's Kikuyu staff. On the way back up the hill the rickshaw men had asked the ladies to lean forward as it would make their task easier. As the latter understood no Kikuyu they ignored the request and the men continued as best they could. They did, however, shake the shafts of the rickshaw to indicate their displeasure and their passengers responded by rather ineffectually trying to 'beat the natives with umbrellas'.[6] No harm came to either party.

Grogan listened attentively to his sister's version of events. Gertrude then joined the two of them and agreed that the rickshaw men had been guilty of 'insolent conduct'. There was, however, 'no suggestion' on the part of Dorothy or Miss McDonnell 'that [the] boys had been guilty of an indecent act'. The incident seemed innocuous enough, and despite her melodramatic outburst Dorothy was renowned as something of a *femme formidable* who, though always quick to voice her opinions, was seldom rattled by anything. But Grogan, being 'angry and unwell', was not prepared to let matters rest.

In the grip of what colonists used to refer to as '*furor Africanus*' Grogan marched off in search of his headman and syce to discuss condign punishment for the rickshaw men. Neither was to be found as darkness was descending, so Grogan made for Wilfrid and Dorothy's house to 'discuss the matter' with them further. Halfway there he decided that 'since [Wilfrid] would be as angry as myself over the matter' there was no point calling on him and went to visit another neighbour instead. Grogan's decision to speak to Sydney Fichat, a South African estate agent, was not purely predicated on the fact that he was a neighbour: Fichat was a well-known political agitator and also a ringleader of the group of Nairobi malcontents that Jackson had described as 'nigger- and game-shooters'.

Fichat listened to Grogan's account of what had happened to Dorothy and Miss McDonnell. He then told Grogan about a recent incident in which he claimed that an African had been guilty of 'indecent conduct' towards a member of his own family, and asked Grogan what he proposed to do. Grogan replied that he was considering beating his men in public, and Fichat warned him that if he did so he might get into trouble. There is no record of what else passed between them before Grogan returned home. But during the hours of darkness Grogan took leave of his senses and pondered an act of defiance which his fellow Matabele war veteran Robert Foran, the newly appointed Chief of Police, subsequently called 'the first open revolt of the non-official Europeans against established authority'.[7]

Grogan deliberately chose the emotive question of internal security as the peg on which to hang his general dissatisfaction with the local government and the Colonial Office. Although in his own experience relations between Europeans and Africans were almost entirely peaceable, he knew that Fichat's Nairobi 'barloafers' were up in arms about the Colonial Office's failure to provide Nairobi with a full strength European police force that was 'convenient for deployment elsewhere'.[8] This they regarded as essential to the maintenance of the 'prestige' and safety of white settlers, and it had been promised by the CO as early as 1905.

By March 1907 such a force had still not been deployed when news started to filter into the capital of the massacre by a Turkana raiding party of an entire 500-man trading caravan of Baluchis and Swahilis in the far north of the country.[9] Robert Foran also noted that there was an 'increasing prevalence of crime'[10] in Nairobi itself; and in the light of recent 'native uprisings' both in German South-West Africa and German East Africa he expressed some 'sympathy with the resentment of the European settlers against the weak policy of the Government and the official attitude towards their community'.[11] But the government remained adamant that the prospect of a similar occurrence in a British protectorate was 'a bogey' which existed only 'in the minds of a few speculating Johannesburg gentlemen residing in Nairobi'; and that these 'gentlemen' might actually be bent on 'bringing about a native uprising in order to occupy their lands and seize their cattle'.[12] Conditions in the capital were tense, and Grogan – though not seriously concerned about the likelihood of an imminent uprising – spotted that conditions were perfect for what the CO later called a 'deliberate defiance of settled order and government'.[13]

While Grogan and Gertrude were having breakfast on the morning of 14 March Fichat appeared at Chiromo. Grogan again told him that he intended to make an 'example' of the rickshaw men in public, and would certainly have been aware that the subversive Fichat would proceed to spread the news around Nairobi. Grogan then went off in search of the 'offenders' and found them going about their work in the grounds of Chiromo. He tied their hands behind their backs, and marched them off towards town accompanied by three other servants – a Masai, a Mkamba and a Kavirondo. They were 'selected', Grogan later asserted, 'so as to let the news circulate among the different tribes' that if the government would not ensure the maintenance of law and order then he would. At 9.45 a.m. Grogan and his cortège arrived in the centre of Nairobi.

In parading past the police station and other government offices before deliberately selecting the Court House[14] as the venue for what would become infamously known as 'The Nairobi Incident', Grogan effectively challenged the authorities to stop him. But no one did, and the news spread like wildfire that he was on the warpath. By 10 a.m. a crowd of between 100 and 300 of the town's 600 Europeans had gathered at the Court House. Most were in as fractious a mood as Grogan himself, having been stirred up by inflammatory rumours spread by Fichat that Dorothy and Miss McDonnell had been indecently assaulted.

Standing in a semi-circle formed by the crowd Grogan announced his intentions. The Nairobi magistrate, Mr Logan, and a police reservist, Captain Smith, made extremely half-hearted attempts to make him reconsider what he was about to do, but Grogan brushed their efforts aside and petulantly declared that he was going to beat his servants 'because I want to'.[15] A Mr Cowlie was then called upon to tell the three Kikuyu rickshaw men in their own tongue why they were being punished and to instruct them 'to tell their own fellow natives that white men would not stand any impertinence to their women-folk'. The crowd cheered, and with that Grogan gave the first man twenty-five lashes with a *kiboko*.

When Grogan had finished, the *kiboko* was grabbed from his hand as the crowd closed in and Russell Bowker flogged the next man. Captain Thord Gray, a police reservist and JP for Eastern Transvaal and Natal, flogged the third. Miss McDonnell thanked Grogan for what he had done and the crowd then dispersed.

After the flogging Grogan went to the Travellers' Club, also known as the 'Cads' Club' ('so named,' as Grogan put it, 'to distinguish it from the Club of the High and Mighty [government officials] on the Hill').[16] It seems that he had cooled down considerably because if he had indeed entertained fanciful thoughts of bringing about a full-scale revolt by the country's European population, as was later suggested, he made no attempt to press home the advantage that he had had at 10 a.m. But he was still bent on making trouble: when a police reservist chatted to him in the 'Cads'' Club Grogan told the man that it was 'a lucky thing . . . that the police had not intervened as Tommy Wood . . . had been on an adjoining roof with a Maxim gun to mow them down'.[17] Despite the fact that no one except senior military officers had access to Maxim guns this was, to say the least, a provocative quip.

From the club Grogan went to a meeting of the Colonists' Association at Wood's Hotel. The exact agenda at this meeting is not known, but Grogan certainly reiterated that his 'object' in flogging his men was to show that 'the safety of one's women-folk was a matter of such paramount importance' that he did not consider 'justified as a family man [to leave] such a matter to the mercy of the vagaries of law and the application thereof'. Foremost in his mind was his wish 'to let the authorities know of the discontent I felt in this matter'.

After lunch Grogan and thirty settlers then went to visit Jackson, the Acting Commissioner while 'Flannelfoot' was on leave. They told Jackson that they believed there were widespread fears of an uprising among the Kikuyu, that such an uprising might easily spread to Nairobi itself, and that Grogan intended to sound the call to arms for a 'Colonists' Defence Force' if the government took no action. Grogan had no need to thrust himself to the fore in this meeting: having lit a fuse of dissatisfaction events had now developed a momentum of their own. Nevertheless, it was principally because Grogan was in the room that Jackson took the settlers' expressions of alarm seriously. He immediately agreed to a loan of ammunition to farmers in isolated districts to 'calm [the] excited and hysterical people' in his office. Significantly, only one farmer took up the offer: whatever fears were now rampant in Nairobi, they did not reflect the opinion of outlying farmers.

It was only *after* this meeting with Jackson that Grogan told the Acting Commissioner what he had done that very morning, having realized that his friend was in a state of 'complete ignorance' about the affront to his government's authority four or five hours earlier. Jackson had seemingly been caught napping, but having learnt about the flogging he quickly put two and two together and worked out that the rumours of an impending uprising in Kikuyuland were fabricated. But although Jackson knew Grogan better than anyone in the country and was convinced he knew what *wasn't* going on, he was still far from sure about what *was*.

Jackson waited a full two days before sending a cable about the Nairobi Incident to Lord Elgin, the Colonial Secretary, who by then was extremely alarmed by stories that were already circulating in London. Whatever the cause of his delay in keeping his political master informed, by the time he did respond Jackson had worked out that the whole incident had been 'deliberately engineered and planned by Grogan, Burn, Fichat, Low and others ... with a view to bringing the Administration into contempt'. By then Grogan had effectively confirmed as much by admitting that he too saw 'no cause for alarm'[18] regarding a possible Kikuyu uprising. Not every one of the statements in Jackson's cable were as sound: someone had fed him the story that one of the flogged men was seriously ill in hospital and that many of the crowd that gathered at the time of the flogging were armed. Thus, just when the brouhaha seemed to be dying down, Jackson reignited it with his fears that he might not only be dealing with a case of murder but that there might yet be an armed rebellion by the settlers. The Nairobi Incident acquired a new lease of life, and the trail of havoc in Grogan's wake grew longer still.

Neither of Jackson's new suspicions were well founded, a fact which reflected poorly on the administration's intelligence-gathering skills. The three rickshaw men had returned to work at Chiromo after their ordeal; and Jackson had not a shred of evidence that any settler had been armed during the events of 14 March. Grogan described this second allegation as based on 'idle rumours gleaned in the [Nairobi] Club'[19] – rumours which he had played a prominent part in disseminating through his quip to the police reservist in the Travellers' Club.

That the administration proved inept at establishing exactly what was and wasn't true was disingenuously regarded by Grogan as definitive proof that even if a Kikuyu uprising had been about to take place, the Protectorate's officials would have been the last to know about it. He was also amused by Jackson's realization that if his worst fears came true, and there was armed insurrection by the settlers, the government would be unable to maintain law and order by dint of the fact that the CO had still not provided the full-strength European police force that the settlers themselves had been demanding for so long. Jackson unwittingly admitted as much by telegraphing an immediate request to Churchill for the number of white police promised by the CO to be doubled from twenty to forty.

Despite all the misinformation with which he was being fed by his subordinates Jackson, an old Africa hand and the model for Rider Haggard's dependable Captain Good, kept his nerve. On 19 March, five tense days after the flogging, he issued summonses to Grogan and his South African fellow protagonists – Russell Bowker, Gray, Wilson, Burn, Low, Fichat, Bennett and Dun. A number of charges were brought under sections of the Indian Penal Code including 'riot', 'armed unlawful assembly' and 'unlawful assembly', and Grogan and Russell Bowker were additionally charged with 'resisting the police'.

Jackson also requested that HMS *Hermes* should stand by off the coast in case of further trouble. This Grogan considered to be a laughable over-reaction, and later claimed that the admiral's language – after learning 'the facts which had necessitated the summoning of the Fleet to save the Empire' – was 'too dreadful to repeat'.[20]

Amid widespread accusations among the European settlers that the court case was nothing more than an 'unscrupulous political prosecution' and a 'gross libel on [the] community at large' the trial began on 25 March in Nairobi's tiny Court House. Combe, the Crown's prosecuting counsel, was in severe difficulty from the start. Charges against the Reverend 'Pa' Bennett, Dun and Wilson were dropped for lack of evidence. Combe was unable to prove that any of the crowd had been armed or that there had been a riot. Captain Smith was also deemed not to have made a sufficient effort to stop the flogging for the charges against Grogan and Russell Bowker of 'resisting the police' to hold any water (and Captain Gray, himself a policeman, *was* one of the floggers).

To make matters worse for Combe it was soon established that 'armed unlawful assembly', 'riot' and 'resisting the police' were charges that could only be tried by jury – yet Grogan and his co-accused were being tried only by a magistrate. So they too had to be dropped, and confusion reigned supreme. The only thing that became abundantly clear during the proceedings was that it was Fichat who was responsible for the size of the crowd of onlookers at the flogging, many of whom declared to the court that they would not have been present had they known of the falsity of his insinuations that an 'indecent assault' had been committed against Dorothy and Miss McDonnell.

Judgement was finally delivered by H. O. Dolbey, the magistrate, on 2 April. As a minimum of five people had to be found guilty to constitute an 'unlawful assembly', the only charge that had not been dismissed, Dolbey duly found five guilty. Fichat was sentenced to fourteen days' imprisonment; Low to seven days; and Russell Bowker and Gray to fourteen days' imprisonment and a fine of Rs.250. Grogan, whom Dolbey adjudged to be 'the worst case of all', was ordered to spend one month in prison and fined Rs500. The five men were led from the court, and Jackson's erstwhile hopes that Grogan would curb the reactionary element in settler society were left in ruins. He was even castigated by his friend the Acting Commissioner as 'a serious danger to the community'.[21]

Grogan spent the first night of his sentence in the Nairobi gaol, of which he was ironically a Visiting Justice, but as it had recently been condemned on medical grounds Jackson moved all the prisoners the following day to a government bungalow on the Hill. There they had meals brought in from the Nairobi and Travellers' Clubs, the town band turned out to play outside Grogan's window at dinner times, and a medical officer visited each day to check on his still parlous state of health. The whole thing, observed police chief Robert Foran, 'became a standing joke'.

Grogan's reaction to his trial and imprisonment was initially one of insouciant amusement, but the longer he spent in confinement the more his mood became one of bitterness and resolute obstinacy. He knew that he had over-stepped the mark, but loftily refused to acknowledge any connection between cause and effect by maintaining that his action had been 'purely personal and [had] no more public significance than my inordinate affection for bad cigars'.[22] He also flatly denied allegations that he had sought to carry out 'a sort of Guy Fawkes plot'.[23] However, when Commissioner 'Flannelfoot' returned to the Protectorate at the end of April he was far from convinced by the attempts of a man so renowned for his cunning to play down the wider consequences of his actions. When he interviewed Grogan in the middle of May, Grogan did admit 'that he had made a fool of himself and seemed to regret the part he had played'; but beyond that the Commissioner found him 'quite unreasonable' and 'implacable with regard to the trial and the action of the Administration generally'.

'Flannelfoot's final verdict was that 'the pity of it all is that Captain Grogan is not a man who has the reputation of treating his servants badly, rather the reverse. He has [also] taken considerable interest in Municipal affairs and rightly his experience and energy have been carefully employed for the benefit of the Protectorate.'[24] The

Commissioner requested that Grogan resign as Visiting Justice of the gaol, and Grogan complied. But he remained determined to have the last word about what he called a 'silly farce which reflected credit on nobody except the Club cook and the town band'.[25]

At the end of May he and Gray appealed against Dolbey's verdict, and in July their convictions were 'revised', or quashed, on a technicality: namely, as had become evident during the trial, that in view of the gravity of some of the initial charges the case should have been tried by a jury not a magistrate.[26] It is certainly possible that Grogan, who was much enamoured of legal technicalities, was aware of this flaw in the Crown's case from the outset: it was he who had specifically requested trial by a magistrate, but Jackson had also had good reason to try and avoid a jury trial: he sensed that, 'as was the case in the west of Ireland and parts of the United States',[27] no jury comprised of partisan settlers would have convicted the accused of any wrongdoing.

Even the success of Grogan's appeal failed to bring a definitive end to the turmoil caused by the Nairobi Incident. Fichat, Low and Gray commenced proceedings against the government on various counts, including malicious prosecution. This left the government with no choice but to file an appeal against the appeal, fearing that the decision of the High Court might lead the settlers to believe that 'similar acts of lynch law may be perpetrated in the future'. Matters were only finally brought to a conclusion when the Crown dropped its appeal in exchange for a written undertaking of regret from Grogan, an admission by him of the justifiability of the government's action and an undertaking not to pursue any further action against the government for malicious prosecution. This was deemed by 'Flannelfoot' to be 'as satisfactory [an outcome] as we can expect from so obstinate a man'.[28]

Behind the scenes, however, Grogan continued for three years to try to force the British government to admit in a Command Paper to a number of errors in the handling of the affair. In particular he wanted it publicly to refute that there had been any grounds for initially claiming that an armed riot had taken place, and to make it clear that he had in the end been acquitted of all charges. No such paper was ever laid before Parliament as the government refused to accept that Grogan could prove that his reputation had suffered as a result of the legal proceedings against him.

The debate about the rights and wrongs of the Nairobi Incident raged across the Empire throughout the summer of 1907. Even twenty months later it was still appearing in the pages of *The Times* which declared that 'public opinion naturally ranged itself with the Government in condemning the public flogging ... [by] a few unofficial residents, whose respect for law and order was not quite equal to their proclivity for doing as they pleased'.[29] The editors, however, also expressed some sympathy with accusations levelled by Grogan that Colonial Office misrule triggered his actions; and they admitted to harbouring extreme doubts about the veracity of the official version of events that had been laid before Parliament.

The actual act of the flogging, as opposed to what it symbolized, did not concern *The Times*. Flogging was not illegal and Lord Elgin himself declared that 'when an offence of [insult or assault] is taken red-handed, the infliction of summary punishment might be properly excused'.[30] In other words, few Britons cared overmuch about a form of punishment that was commonly meted out in their own country.

What did divide public opinion was the question of whether Grogan's defiance of the Empire's authority was excusable. There is no doubt that this skirmish was won by Grogan's adherents throughout the Empire, and marked a significant watershed in the relationship between colonists everywhere and their detractors. Headlines in the Protectorate's *Star*, *Times* and *East African Standard* proclaimed 'Grogan Shows The Way', and letters of support poured in to colonial and domestic newspapers. 'If ever there were a sane and heroic mind in a brave man's body it is Grogan's' read one; 'one of those who have made our Empire what it is – not by diplomacy, but by forceful strength of character' read another. Ethel Cockburn, the matron of the Lady Dudley Nursing Home where Grogan had recuperated after his operation in 1903, wrote 'I hope you suffered no ill effects from the gaol, we are all so proud of you here [in South Africa].'[31] Lord Hindlip campaigned vigorously on Grogan's behalf in the Lords, as did Sir Charles Eliot in Whitehall. The pressure was less on Grogan than on the British government's management, or mismanagement, of its colonies.

The main target of the flak fired by Grogan's supporters in Parliament was Churchill, who did not enjoy the experience. On no fewer than three occasions in the middle of April he misled the House of Commons by maintaining even after the court case that many of the crowd had been armed, and that the police had attempted to intervene; that great improvements had been made to the gaol in Nairobi (which had in fact been condemned on medical grounds);[32] and by professing to have 'no official knowledge of Captain Grogan's explorations [in Africa],[33] despite having been asked by Rhodes and Abe Bailey just seven years earlier to follow in Grogan's footsteps through central Africa.

In East Africa the reaction of Churchill's officers on the ground – the local officials – was principally one of disappointment in Grogan. Hobley lamented that 'men of Mr. Grogan's stamp, if so minded, could prove a great assistance to the Administration', and called him 'impulsive and illogical'. But police chief Foran was not alone in government circles in believing that Grogan's 'hot-headed action', though 'ill-advised', had 'produced a good effect' and 'showed that the settlers could take strong steps to maintain their rights and would not be trifled with over major matters of deep concern to the community'.[34]

Among the members of the Colonists' Association support for Grogan remained undiminished. His offer to resign his post of President was refused, and voluble calls were made for a governmental Board of Inquiry to investigate whether his prosecution was political and for intervention on Grogan's behalf by the premiers of the Transvaal, Cape Colony and Natal. Some of the aristocratic settlers thought this was going too far. Lord Cranworth thought it best to draw a line under 'an episode which brought no particular credit on anyone'.[35] Lord Delamere, who stood to retain control of the Colonists' Association were Grogan to stand down, went one step further by writing to Grogan that he felt 'obliged to take the other side in this case' while 'never wavering in my personal friendship for yourself'.[36]

By the end of July the attention of officials and settlers alike became increasingly preoccupied by the news that Churchill was to visit the Protectorate. His status among colonists everywhere had tumbled when he had turned against Milner, his one-time mentor, and it was now in free-fall as a result of his pronouncements on the Nairobi Incident. The settlers relished, and the officials dreaded, the prospect of a head-to-head confrontation between Churchill and Grogan, but it was not to be. Gertrude was gravely ill.

During June and July she was twice on the brink of death, suffering from mastoiditis and attendant complications. Successive operations by 'Daddy' Milne failed to bring about a recovery, as did recuperative trips to the coast and the family farm at Longonot. At times she was in such great pain that her hands had to be tied together to stop her beating them in agonized exasperation against the bedstead. By the end of August the worst seemed to be over but she was then overcome by 'acute mania', or depression, and Grogan decided that he must get her back to England as fast as possible. He placed his business interests in the hands of his brother-in-law and the *East African Standard* recorded that though he remained 'the acknowledged head of the non-official white community'[37] he was handing over the reins of the Colonists' Association to Delamere. On 28 September Gertrude and Grogan sailed for Europe, expecting to be away 'for at least nine months'.[38]

FIFTEEN

To the Shires

WHEN CHURCHILL ARRIVED in East Africa he had not had an easy time of his two years at the Colonial Office. His defection to the Liberals had caused him to be almost universally distrusted as an opportunist. Such blatant political man-oeuvring was simply not regarded as the done thing in British politics. Furthermore, he and his colleagues on the Liberal front benches had found the task of fulfilling their pledge to rectify what they perceived as the mismanagement of the Empire by their predecessors to be a singularly challenging one. As Grogan had always suspected, there appeared to be a yawning gulf between the cant of Liberal politicians, whether imperialists or no, and their ability to translate it into effective action in the colonies, and he increasingly regarded Churchill, whom he was wont to refer to at this stage in his career as 'the hybrid Yank',[1] as the most duplicitous politician of all.

Churchill had been exposed almost the minute he walked through the door of the Colonial Office. Having played a leading role in Milner's downfall over the use, or abuse, of Chinese labourers in the mines of the Rand he had swiftly discovered that what he had con-demned as 'slavery' paid the Empire's bills. Churchill's response to this conundrum was to declare that his use of the term 'slavery' had been a 'terminological inexactitude' – and to perpetuate the use of Chinese labour. No *new* licences were issued to mine-owners to import further labourers from the east, but the 50,000 or so licences issued by Milner were not revoked. By the same token it was not the Liberal government or its Foreign Office which translated its condemnation of Leopold's brutal regime in the Congo into action, but President Roosevelt. In America's first decisive involvement in the colonial affairs of Europe he forced Leopold to disgorge his private fiefdom in Africa while the British government dithered over the dangers of driving Belgium into the Kaiser's paws.

Churchill encountered similar dilemmas all over British Africa. He could do nothing to prevent Lugard from putting down an uprising in Northern Nigeria with considerable force, and when he intervened to condemn the suppression of Zulu insurrection in Natal there was angry protest not just in Africa but from all over the so-called 'White Dominions' of the Empire. Churchill was ignominiously forced to back down, and it looked as though the 'arms' of the Empire were being plunged into a conflict with its 'heart' – as the Nairobi Incident had shown.

Part of the problem facing the Liberal government was the fact that neither Campbell-Bannerman nor his successor, Asquith, possessed the formidable grasp of foreign affairs of their predecessor, Lord Salisbury. As a result they chose to pursue a policy which they believed would assert tighter control over the colonies, but which in reality had exactly the opposite effect.

This policy, with which Churchill was intimately associated, was to grant 'responsible self-government' – or 'partial devolution' – to as many African colonies as possible. This was why in 1906 Lord Elgin had approved the inauguration of a Legislative Council in the East Africa Protectorate, and the same year he moved to devolve power to the colonists in South Africa. The subsequent elections in South Africa demonstrated just how fraught with risk Elgin's initiative was. Like Milner, he hoped that British South Africans would win the elections, but since his ousting of Milner British immigration had all but dried up. The result was that the old enemy, the Boers, swept to power with Botha and Smuts's *Het Volk* party securing thirty-seven of the sixty-seven seats in the Transvaal. The Boers also secured a majority in the Orange River Colony, and in May 1910 all the South African provinces, including British Cape Province and Natal, united under the authority of Afrikaners rather than the British. It was therefore the policy of a Liberal government which aspired to uphold the 'paramountcy' of 'native interests' which ironically led to non-whites being denied the prospect of any political voice whatsoever in South Africa and ultimately paved the way for the imposition of apartheid by Afrikaner Nationalists. The Union of South Africa, a little surprisingly, stood by Britain in two world wars, but it was certainly not the British-controlled country that Churchill fancifully envisaged when he oversaw the elections of 1907.

Whatever difficulties Churchill was having on other fronts he was greeted politely in Nairobi (and treated to some good 'sport'). The European settlers cast aside their annoyance at his treatment of Grogan in Parliament, and soon found that 'the hybrid Yank' was captivating company in spite of his reputation as an opportunist and marked penchant for talking about himself. He had great charisma, was a brilliant conversationalist, and the power of his intellect impressed all who met him. Hobley was not the only official to remark that 'it was at times rather amusing to see the old gentleman ['Flannelfoot'] trying to keep up with Mr Churchill's brain'.[2] All in all there were considerable similarities between the impression left by the under-secretary of state on officials and settlers alike and their opinion of Grogan.

Grogan kept a careful eye out for any news of Churchillian pronouncements during his visit to the Protectorate, and was rather encouraged when Churchill declared that he found the country to be in a state of 'perplexing disarray'. Equally encouraging were his opinions that the best hope for the future lay in ensuring the success of all communities, and that he was a great admirer of the settlers' 'Spartan' lifestyles; that he saw 'no insuperable difficulty ... in assigning spheres to the external activities of different races',[3] by which he meant accommodating the aspirations of all; and that 'much of the irritation and restlessness of the white population arises from the present state of the law and of its administration'.[4] But Grogan did not share Churchill's doubts about the feasibility of extending European colonization in the tropics, and he regarded his avowed support for the Indian community to be motivated by nothing more principled than a desire not to antagonize the India Office. On balance, Grogan decided that it was best to wait and see what Churchill did for the country, as opposed to said about it.

Within a year, however, the Protectorate's affairs were no longer Churchill's responsibility. Campbell-Bannerman resigned in April 1908, and Asquith took the helm of the Liberal government. Churchill, aged just thirty-three, was promoted to the Presidency of the Board of Trade and so to full Cabinet rank. As was the custom he had to offer himself for re-election in his constituency – and lost. He bounced back from this embarrassing setback by taking Dundee, and in his new job set about erecting the first real foundations of a welfare state in partnership with Lloyd George.[5] It would be fourteen years before Churchill returned to the Colonial Office as Secretary of State – having yet again crossed the floor of the House of Commons to rejoin the Conservative party – to face another assault on Whitehall by Grogan.

When the Grogans arrived in Britain they were homeless and rented a large house in London's Palace Gate from Gertrude's sister, Florence, who had married Frank Baden-Powell. Grogan had been seriously alarmed by coming so close to losing Gertrude, as well as by his own ill-health, and decided that they needed a home of their own in the country. He also decided that in future, at least while Gertrude was raising children, it was too risky for her to return to East Africa permanently; 'Daddy' Milne had managed to pull her through her crisis, but it had made Grogan aware just how far Nairobi was from state-of-the-art medical facilities. This decision was sad for both of them because it meant they no longer had any need for Chiromo, their Nairobi 'palace' on which so much attention had been lavished, and by early 1908 they had rented it to a syndicate including Lord and Lady Cranworth. That done, Grogan started to cast around for a suitable home in England.

In the summer of 1908 Grogan and Gertrude moved the family out of London to Newcastle-under-Lyme in the Staffordshire Potteries. Grogan's choice of location was not random. During the winter he had been introduced to Tom Twyford who lived at nearby Whitemore and was 'the prince of sanitary potters'; more importantly as far as Grogan's future was concerned, Twyford was also a confidant of Chamberlain who, though now retired, remained a force in Tory politics. In December Twyford had happened to mention Grogan to Chamberlain, and the Tory grandee wrote to Grogan stating that his 'co-operation [would] be welcomed'.[6] After a few meetings between the two men, Grogan was asked if he would be interested in standing as the Tory candidate for Newcastle-under-Lyme, and he immediately agreed to take up the challenge. It enabled him to be with his family and, with the Protectorate's economy in the doldrums and negotiations with the Colonial Office over his forest concession still stalled, he saw no need for the time being to visit East Africa more than once a year.

Grogan's instructions from the Conservative and Unionist Party Central Office were clear: although a general election was not looming he was required to do as much as possible to pave the way for victory when it was called. This was no easy task: the Potteries were fiercely contested territory and Grogan was pitted against local magnate Josiah Wedgwood in Newcastle-under-Lyme. Wedgwood was high on the list of men the Conservatives most wanted to scalp, a veritable 'Prince of Darkness' in the Liberal camp, and they knew that only a completely indefatigable candidate of great notoriety, like Grogan, would stand any chance of unseating him. In order to help him in his task Grogan was advised to style himself a Liberal Unionist rather than a Conservative, and to refer to the party's core policy by the less emotive handle of Tariff Reform rather than Protectionism. He understood the logic of the advice, and accepted it, but it did not stop him from regarding it as symptomatic of 'the hypocrisy seemingly inseparable from English politics'.

Grogan found such hypocrisy 'a bit of a jar' after the plain-speaking of colonial politics, but he found it marginally less of a 'jar' in the Tory camp than the Liberal. He still considered his godfather Gladstone to have been 'a nasty old humbug', and a couple of years of rule by Gladstone's successors had in his opinion confirmed his suspicions that Liberalism – as opposed to liberalism – was nothing but 'a fraudulent façade behind which lurked the elements of disruption, [and] pursuit of the individual's interest'. He had come to the conclusion that 'the only liberal principle in the Liberal programme was to acquire and distribute for their own benefit the property of others' via a plethora of direct taxes.

The only Liberal policy with which Grogan had any sympathy at all was that of Home Rule for Ireland. This he supported 'by heredity', believing that the two countries 'should work in motherly co-operation but not [be] joined administratively' as 'no Englishman could ever quite understand the happy-go-lucky, coatless outlook of the Irish and no Irishman would ever quite understand the caste worship and the unconscious pomposity of demeanour of the average English person'. But he believed that the time was not yet right formally to split Ireland from Westminster, and so accepted the need to declare himself a Unionist although it made him feel rather as if he too was starting in British politics 'as a fraud'. There were, in his opinion, far more important things to worry about before dealing with Ireland, as the following scathing assessment of his Liberal opponents made clear:

The main planks of the Liberal platform appeared to be as follows. England must stick to her policy of Free Trade; the increasing unemployed could emigrate or survive by picking oakum in the various workhouses; the employed could eke out their scanty wages with cheap bread rather than be safeguarded by a fully-employed, prosperous and highly-protected agriculture from starvation or humble submission in wartime. The Kaiser protected agriculture and was only building himself a great fleet to amuse himself and anyhow it did not matter – there was usually fog in the North Sea. The Tory cry for more cruisers was jingoism worthy of Kipling. The Kaiser would never go to war with England because he loved his grandmother and had a deep affection for his anglicised cousins, especially King Edward. The Germans were a nice people, but poor; and they lived on blood sausage and black bread and burst into tears listening to the music of Chopin. Their goods were non-competitive, notoriously shoddy and were kept out by being compulsorily labelled 'made in Germany' so that even if they were much cheaper no sensible person in England would buy them. The great textile industry of Lancashire was quite secure because no other country had or ever could provide such a nice damp climate; and their Indian market was not allowed by Britain to protect her textile industry. The pottery industry was safe because nobody in their wildest dreams could imagine that the disciples of the Ming period of China or the Satsuma ware of Japan could ever provide articles with such delicacy of texture and night time utility as the mass-produced bed-chamber utensils of Stoke. The sanitary industry was safe because no other countries were sanitary-minded and without a home market they obviously could not compete ... First and foremost all people connected with the land, especially dukes, were nasty people and should be taxed or otherwise evicted from the land to make the land for the people. All good Liberals should learn the 'Land Song' and, in the interest of the Liberal loudly-proclaimed belief in the principle of free speech, should sing it in chorus at Conservative meetings to protect the people from hearing the views of other people.[7]

Grogan sardonically observed that this was 'all very puzzling'.

The Grogans' new home in Newcastle-under-Lyme, from which he was to pursue his political ambitions, was called Camp Hill. It was a small but very beautiful estate, and a former home of Charles Darwin. Far from the frustrations, disease, dust, and heat of Africa Grogan recovered his strength fully after another grisly operation on his liver abscesses, and Gertrude also bounced back from her trials of the previous year. On 27 August 1908 she gave birth to their third child, and for the third time Grogan's ambition to have a son was thwarted. His disappointment was compounded by the fact that the *East African Standard* erroneously congratulated the couple on the birth of their first son, and by the time the editors corrected the mistake a flood of congratulatory letters referring to the new Grogan heir arrived at Camp Hill. Grogan had to content himself with the consoling words of James Coleman who wrote 'no doubt you feel rather sorry it was not a boy, but there is plenty of time yet'.[8] The two men, as a number of letters from Coleman to Grogan show, were now on the best of terms; it seems that Coleman saw in his son-in-law a reflection of his own entrepreneurial, ebullient self, and always signed his missives to Grogan 'yours affectionately'.

The child was christened Cynthia, and her godfathers were Baden-Powell and 'Daddy' Milne, who had saved Gertrude's life the year before. Despite her gender Grogan was as enchanted by her as he was by Dorothy and Joyce – and for that matter all children. He was a doting and spoiling father and, as he had done at Chiromo, held regular children's parties at Camp Hill for which he insisted on being in charge of every last detail. Chestnuts and potatoes would be roasted in the embers of huge bonfires; races were held on the lawns; mountains of cream cakes were produced; and Grogan would do conjuring tricks and draw funny sketches for his young guests to take home. In between parties he behaved no differently. At any opportunity he would tell the girls spell-binding tales of his own invention, sketch for them, and hide cuddly toys between the sheets before they went to bed just as his own father had smuggled chocolates to his offspring, carefully avoiding his wife's censorious attention. This was a supremely happy time for the whole family, and Grogan's great and constant displays of affection for his children must have qualified him as one of the most unusual fathers in Edwardian England.

Ever the doer, Grogan also set himself the task of transforming Camp Hill's grounds and laboured tirelessly cutting down trees, planting new ones, altering flower-beds and generally making the place shipshape. When not at work in the grounds, entertaining the children, or making himself known in the neighbourhood, he also somehow found the time to write his second book. This was an extremely erudite tome entitled *Economic Calculus and its Application to Tariff*; completed in August 1909 it was dedicated to Delamere 'who is responsible for the germination of much of the theory herein contained'. Grogan's motive for writing the book was that most economists were Free Traders and as he rejected their conclusions he felt that it was necessary to refute the soundness of their precepts as well. His 'lines of thought', in his own words, were as follows:

> I realised that economic theory could never claim to be a science until some physical constant could be found as a unit of measurement. African experience had taught me that the only real money is human food because no commerce or need of measure could arise till somebody produced more

food than his family needed and the surplus was available
for exchange with the efforts of others. 'Price' is a variant,
the result of innumerable measures. 'Value' is nothing but
a matter of personal idiosyncrasy. 'Cost' on the other hand
is an absolute measurable, but measurable in terms of what?
Surely only accurately in measurable terms of the food
calories expended in the achievement.

Gold, he argued, was a fickle measure of monetary value; so food
calories should replace it as the unit of value.

This was an eccentric conclusion to reach at the end of a highly
academic and, in parts, brilliant assessment of contemporary economic
thought, and it was incomprehensible to most people. Grogan's
brother Quentin would have dismissed it as a 'bee in his bonnet', and
Philip actually did tell him that he was 'getting near the edge . . . by
seeing pigs not as swine but as storage batteries of potential human
energy'. This judgement rather missed the point of the book: Grogan
was using his idea of an alternative measure of value – food calories
– simply in order to expose what he thought was wrong with the
existing monetary system. Africans, after all, used the 'bimammalian
goat-damsel standard' as an 'efficient social stabiliser over wide areas',
and cowries and elephant meat also 'did the money job quite smoothly
without bump or slump';[9] so, Grogan argued, why could the so-called
'developed' world not find a more efficient and more constant measure
of value?

Never far from the surface, of course, were Grogan's dreams for
Africa. He looked forward to a time when 'millions of whites might
flourish in the production of a mighty tide of food-stuffs, cotton, and
other organic matter which would secure England's industrial future
after the exhaustion of her coal-beds'. This production boom, he
also believed, should fully involve the indigenous inhabitants (and not
merely as labour): he had seen at first hand what could be achieved
by the African economies in both Uganda and Nyasaland and was
convinced that although 'the African native is not readily amenable
to industrialisation'[10] there was no demonstrable reason why there
should not be an effective and mutually beneficial partnership between
African and European production.

Economic Calculus was, in contrast to *From The Cape To Cairo*, of limited popular appeal but Grogan was very proud of it and it did not concern him that he 'never saw people queuing up to buy it or even a copy on the book stalls'.[11] His next book, *Tariff: The Worker's Charter* – a collection of his speeches on tariff reform and its potential benefits for Britain's working classes – was of much wider appeal. Published in 1910 it was altogether more comprehensible and showed that Grogan could successfully compose for any class of reader, from academic to Staffordshire miner.

Grogan had timed his departure from the Protectorate well. No sooner was the Nairobi Incident forgotten than the political situation once again became critical. Even the Colonial Office, which had long entertained severe reservations about their choice of 'Flannelfoot' as Commissioner, started to consider ways of removing him. The European settlers appeared well on their way to securing (with the co-operation of the local officials) a Land Bill of which they approved,[12] and in spite of – or arguably because of – the temperature in the wake of the Nairobi Incident, the new Legislative Council had been inaugurated in August 1907. But very little else was going right. Many a farmer found that the only source of capital was Gujarati money-lenders charging up to 10 per cent per month on loans, and they were hampered by a dearth of markets for their goods when they succeeded in defying the environment by actually producing a surplus. The main grievance of the Indians, led by Jeevanjee, was that they had no voice on Legislative Council, while Africans opposed to having to pay the hut tax frequently showed their dissatisfaction by withholding their labour – an initiative which swiftly led to the second outright rebellion by the European community in less than a year.

This time, with Grogan safely ensconced in Camp Hill, it was Delamere who succumbed to *furor Africanus* after reading a report by the new Secretary for Native Affairs, Claud Hollis. Hollis had been called upon to review the Protectorate's policy for recruiting labour and had concluded that it was far from satisfactory. African labourers hired by the government's own Public Works Department and by the Indian community were deemed by Hollis to be subject to the worst treatment. In seeking to redress this situation he imposed new rules to stamp out coercion and establish standards of care which, in Delamere's opinion, were so stringent that no one would be able to recruit African labourers. As the settlers had not been censured in Hollis's report alongside the Public Works Department and the Indians, and most were conscientious employers by the standards of the time, this was deemed by them to be deeply unfair. As there were less than 450 farmers and planters in the entire settler community they also regarded their labour needs as being far from excessive.

The result was that Delamere called a meeting at the Railway Institute in March 1908, to which 150 settlers turned up. They demanded that the government should set up a Labour Bureau and establish a fixed minimum wage for African workers, but also that Hollis's rules should be revoked if the economy was to be saved. Confronted by these demands, 'Flannelfoot' was like a rabbit caught in the beam of a lantern and did what was his wont to do – nothing. The next day the settlers marched on Government House, led by Delamere and Baillie, his fellow settler representative on the Legislative Council. 'Flannelfoot' again demurred from withdrawing the new labour rules, and there were cries of 'Resign! Resign!' among the crowd. Worse still, Delamere was subsequently reported to have threatened to burn down Government House and was accused in the House of Lords of organizing a demonstration of an 'insulting and disorderly character'. The result was that he and Baillie were immediately suspended for six months from Legco (Legislative Council).

The settlers were outraged, and in England Grogan immediately began a campaign to reinstate Delamere.[13] Using Lord Hindlip as his conduit he set out to put before the House of Lords 'as many facts as possible which [showed] the rottenness of Sadler's administration'.[14] Lady Delamere repaid his loyalty with the words 'if this world were only composed of such spirits as you',[15] but Grogan's efforts on her husband's behalf were to no immediate avail.

'Immediate' is the operative word here: the Colonial Office was severely rattled when it realized that Delamere's rebellion could not be dismissed as the work of bigoted South African 'barloafers'. In addition to Delamere, the majority of the most prominent landowners in the country had taken part, including other peers of the realm like Lord Cardross. The country's aristocrats had proved themselves to be every bit as capable of the 'un-British' behaviour of which some had accused Grogan just a year earlier. Indeed they were lucky not to be tried for unlawful assembly themselves after they all attended a mass meeting on 4 April which rather bizarrely called for Delamere to be made governor. Delamere was, of course, neither a soldier nor a civil servant. But the meeting's message was clear enough and Grogan started casting around for a replacement for 'Flannelfoot' who was acceptable to both the Colonial Office and the settlers.[16]

In the face of such united (and well-heeled) opposition the Colonial Office couldn't do nothing. Locking up peers of the realm was an unthinkable proposition; so it decided that the hapless 'Flannelfoot', the man Gertrude habitually referred to as 'The Old Woman', had to go. First, in order to get rid of him, it had to find a suitable pretext which did not smack of submission to the settlers' demands. Sleaze was the answer, and before long they got it. A scandal broke in the Protectorate which involved some District Officers using their authority to procure African girls as mistresses, and that was that: 'Flannelfoot' was put out to grass as Governor of the Windward Islands. Before long the Colonial Office also compromised over the settlers' call for what they regarded (but many an African did not) as 'reasonable' and workable labour laws.

Grogan briefly visited East Africa at the end of 1908 and in the autumn of 1909, by which time he had been re-elected to the committee of the Colonists' Association. Camp Hill became a sort of unofficial embassy for the Protectorate and, with his relations with the country's officials normalized, Grogan always extended a warm welcome to any who were on leave. Ainsworth, Bowring, Jackson and Hollis always dropped in to 'have a quack' about African affairs, and Hobley and

Grogan even cooked up a scheme in conjunction with the Salvation Army to settle some poor British families in East Africa.[17] It was also from Camp Hill that Grogan redoubled his efforts to persuade the Colonial Office of the merits of his scheme for a railway across the Uasin Gishu plateau.

Despite Elgin's antagonistic ruling two days before the Nairobi Incident, Grogan reiterated that he would be unable to work his forest concession, whatever the terms for its operation, unless a railway was built by somebody. 'It is impossible', he wrote in one letter, 'to carry two thousand trees weighing up to ten tons apiece a distance of forty miles on natives' heads', and by the end of the year his persistence was rewarded when Elgin's successor as Secretary of State for the Colonies, the Earl of Crewe, agreed to reopen the file.

Grogan also turned his attention to countering Mr Ellis's ongoing contention that his forest concession had been granted on 'exceptionally favourable terms',[18] and that it should be forfeited because 'even with a railway the Eldama [forest] timber could not be profitably exported and it will be long before the local market is large enough to make its exploitation on a large scale profitable'.[19] Ellis had never been to the Protectorate, let alone to the forest, and was simply hell-bent on 'getting' Grogan. But once again his two colleagues, Read and Antrobus, supported Grogan's ambitions and a stalemate ensued. This was only broken when Grogan threatened the British government with legal action, which prompted the Earl of Crewe to take his side for the second time in under a year.

East Africa's most redoubtable entrepreneur was not beaten yet.

SIXTEEN

Playing the Game: Agincourt and After

FOR GROGAN, the silver-tongued orator with a marked penchant for theatricality, the general election of January 1910 presented a magnificent challenge. When he had agreed two years earlier to stand as a Unionist candidate not even he could have foreseen the gravity of the situation which unfolded during 1909. By the end of the year Britain was in the depths of a constitutional crisis which threatened to destroy the very heart of the Empire.

The crisis was triggered in April by Lloyd George's 'People's Budget', which Churchill helped to draft. Although the significance of its measures was not immediately appreciated, within days it became clear that the Liberals had raised taxes on everything and introduced a super-tax on those earning over £3,000 annually. Most controversial of all, there were proposals to introduce a land tax.

In the House of Lords the Tory majority threw out the budget, and in so doing defied a 250-year-old tradition not to use the power of veto in matters of finance. Churchill responded swiftly by calling for the abolition of the Upper House and Asquith dissolved Parliament. The stage was set for the 'People versus the Peers' election amid scenes of intense political acrimony (not to mention considerable industrial and civil unrest).

Grogan thrived on the chaos. But, though his family was now well-known in the Potteries, and his charm and Gertrude's maternal manner had won them many friends from all walks of life, he did not underestimate the scale of the task confronting him. Wedgwood had a considerable head start: apart from being a local dignitary he was sitting on a massive 2,207 vote majority from the previous election.[1] Even this did not dampen Grogan's optimism. He knew that if he overhauled his opponent in such a key seat it would almost certainly mean that control of the Empire would be wrested from Liberal hands. Furthermore, he was certain that his opponent had an Achilles heel.

Grogan had first met Wedgwood when both of them were involved in the reconstruction of South Africa: while Grogan had been a member of Milner's 'Kindergarten', Wedgwood had served as a magistrate in the Transvaal town of Ermelo. That, Grogan was convinced, was the sort of man Wedgwood *really* was. He had been at Clifton, that assembly-line of loyal servants of Empire; boasted a distinguished record in the Boer War; and was sitting on pots (literally) of money. In other words, he could not possibly – in Grogan's opinion – be genuine in his support for the land tax or his avowed belief in independence for India, and Grogan determined to expose his opponent for what he thought he was: a fraud.

Despite his large majority Wedgwood was far from complacent about the outcome of what he called 'the finest political fight of my life'. 'My opponent', he later wrote, 'was Captain Grogan, the disciple of Cecil Rhodes, the apostle of protection, and the uncrowned king of East Africa – at thirty-two in his prime ... He had written a book on Protection as I had on Land Values. We ridiculed each other's book; and after that the gloves came off.'[2] This was something of an understatement: during the month-long campaign the entire local populace was mobilized on one side or the other.

The colour of Grogan's camp was red. Even children painted their faces red, tied red ribbons in their hair, wore red clothing and fought running battles in the streets and playgrounds with their blue opponents. Gertrude strode out daily with Grogan's little sister Hilda, who was armed with her violin, to appeal to voters through their vote-less wives.

The Catholic community, some 800 strong, defected to the Grogan camp early on. They were appalled by the secularist Wedgwood's denunciation of compulsory religious education in schools and quickly sensed that the 'Unionist' Grogan had more than a little sympathy for Irish Home Rule. With their support Grogan looked, at a single stroke, to have cut Wedgwood's majority to approximately 500 votes – and the campaign became even more belligerent. Neither candidate went anywhere without bodyguards. Pitched battles were fought in the market squares of the constituency's villages, and both men were regularly heckled off the podium when their meetings were infiltrated by rival supporters. Thirty years later, Wedgwood reflected that 'old men still tell with awe of that great free-for-all fight with Captain Grogan. It took the place of Agincourt.'[3]

The key to Grogan's success was the fact that the voters *wanted* to come and listen to him, for a variety of reasons. He undoubtedly cut a dashing figure on the podium and mesmerized his audiences with his gaze. Moreover his speeches, with their mix of caustic wit and bombast, were both electrifying and hugely entertaining. Always made without the use of notes, they often went on for two hours or more – yet still his audiences would call for more. Above all, though, he spoke from the heart, was transparently honest, and talked *with* people rather than *at* them. Tom Twyford's butler told him that this particularly endeared him to the working classes, whom Grogan considered to be the people who 'made Britain great'.[4] Some of them were disillusioned with Liberal cant; some sensed, approvingly, that Grogan was hardly a lover of 'the Establishment'; and many were instinctively more conservative than the most ardent Tory. Grogan's forceful support for trades unions also struck a chord, and soon earned him a reputation for being 'progressive'.

No matter how magnetic his personality and brilliant his oratory, one key element of the ticket on which Grogan was campaigning was far from universally popular. Tariff Reform, the issue that had greatly contributed to the Tories' losing the previous election, was again one of the – if not *the* – leading issues. Britain's workers were still far from convinced that protectionism (as opposed to free trade) would save jobs, lead to cheaper food and pay for social reforms which the Tories, every bit as much as their Liberal opponents, saw as vital. The sceptics, who were in the Wedgwood camp, took to disrupting Grogan's meetings with voluble renditions of the Land Song – a move which Grogan countered by placing his henchmen next to known agitators. This gave him a free rein to address the voters' doubts, and enabled him to use his favoured tactic of asking people in the audience what their job was so that he could tell them how he believed Tariff Reform would help them (although even he was lost for an answer for the man who rose to his feet and declared that he was a gravedigger, and he was completely nonplussed when asked by another why there was so much fuss about 'traffic reform').

Reasoned opposition, fisticuffs, or being shouted down, Grogan handled with obvious relish. If heckled he would often simply sit down, light his pipe and read the papers until his hecklers became hoarse. Or he would lock the door to the hall and commence his speech by challenging anyone in the audience to relieve him of the key. But when a whispering campaign started, it proved far more difficult to counter than high spirits. Aspersions were cast on his military rank, on his role in introducing Chinese labour into the mines of the Rand, and – most damaging of all – the Nairobi Incident returned to haunt him. The rumbustious but mostly good-natured campaign suddenly turned nasty.

Grogan's entitlement to the honorary rank of Captain, which he himself did not generally use, was not difficult to prove, and of his involvement in importing Chinese labour to the mines he remained defiantly proud. He used as the cornerstone of his defence the fact that it had saved the mines, and that it was not he – or indeed Milner – who had been responsible for mistreating the labourers. All this the Liberals knew to be true, as was Grogan's assertion that a huge number of both white and black jobs had been saved by the importation of Chinese labourers. But his instigation of the Nairobi Incident was not so easily swept aside. At one point Wedgwood and his supporters accused Grogan for days on end of 'hooliganism' and 'armed riot', and only desisted when Grogan threatened a libel action and the election came within a whisker of being declared void on the grounds of foul play. Wedgwood was forced to apologize in person to his opponent, but by then considerable damage had already been done by what the local paper described as 'many grotesque fairy tales [circulating] about Captain Grogan'.[15]

Grogan's dignified reaction in the face of these 'fairy tales' won him many friends, even in the opposition camp. He seldom alluded to the smears while on the podium, choosing instead to make occasional clear statements of rebuttal to the newspapers, and he was determined not to resort to the mud-slinging employed by others. 'In his modesty,' the *Staffordshire Sentinel* remarked, 'and in his belief that political principles and not personalities mattered, it seems that he never cared or it never occurred to him to speak publicly about such details, notwithstanding the annoyance to which he was being subjected'.[6] He just got on with the job, banging the drum for the expansion of the Navy ('the basis of our whole imperial structure')[7] and protectionism, and resolved to let the electors decide his suitability for the seat.

There was one highly influential group which had absolutely no doubts about Grogan's attractions: the constituency's womenfolk. Although still denied the vote, women exerted huge power over their spouses and had proved instrumental in ousting Churchill from his Manchester seat in the by-election of 1908. The Liberals had granted women the right to vote in local elections the previous year but beyond that Asquith would not go: he was already pledged to two pieces of controversial legislation – the Parliament Act and Home Rule – which were testing the party to the limit and he was not keen to risk pushing through universal suffrage as well. 'Votes for Women' was tossed to the winds in the interests of political expediency, thereby giving Grogan a clear opportunity to score over his Liberal opponent. Although he was once heard to quip that the suffragettes were 'hysterical females ... chaining themselves to railings in the hope of being manhandled by the burly police of London',[8] he was in fact four square behind female suffrage and Gertrude dutifully soothed any feathers that were ruffled by her husband's more outrageous jests. The womenfolk of Newcastle-under-Lyme backed their cheeky Unionist candidate to the hilt with the maxim 'No one shall up us but Grogan'.[9]

When polling day came Grogan went on a final tour of the constituency with Gertrude, Nanny Redwood and little Dorothy and Joyce (as well as his heavies) in tow. The children, bedecked in red as usual, carried placards proclaiming 'Vote For Daddy'. Despite all his efforts, Grogan knew he was beaten. Some of the mud flung in the whispering campaign had stuck, and, more importantly, a last-minute order was issued by the Irish Nationalists to the Catholic voters to vote Liberal – no matter how great their fondness for the Anglo-Irish Unionist candidate. On 17 January, despite increasing the Unionist vote by almost half, Grogan was defeated by 5,613 votes to 4,245. If the Catholics had held firm he would have pulled off one of the most dramatic turnarounds in the whole country; instead he was left to muse on the perfidy of his Irish cousins. The first battle for Newcastle-under-Lyme was over.

On a national level there was every reason for Grogan to be jubilant: Asquith's Liberal coalition was hammered. The massive 354-seat majority it had secured in the 1906 election was reduced to just two, thereby demonstrating that the electorate were not quite as keen on 'The People's Party' as the Liberals had assumed. Even the nascent Labour Party, in coalition with the Liberals, failed to improve on its fifty-four seats of the previous election, a dismal performance considering the explosion in trades union membership over the preceding decade. But the threat posed by the Liberal government to Grogan's vision of Empire was not completely vaporized. With the support of the Irish Nationalists and Labour Lloyd George's 'People's Budget' was pushed through Parliament, and the Liberals again resolved to do away with the Tory majority in the House of Lords once and for all. Their monarch, however, intervened.

Edward VII would not agree to allow the Liberals to flood the Lords with appointed peers, nor to wholesale reform of the Upper House, unless there was a general election fought solely on the question of the constitution. Edward died in May, but in the late autumn the second general election of the year was called for December. This presented Grogan and Gertrude with a considerable logistical problem: when they received the news they were 6,000 miles away in East Africa, but Grogan immediately cabled a message to his agent in Newcastle-under-Lyme which unambiguously read 'Am Spoiling For A Fight'. Just a few days later a Marconigram despatched from a steamer somewhere in the Red Sea announced, 'Am hurrying home. I urge all who cherish England's Imperial destiny to strain every nerve to expose radical programme of promises deceptive and unsubstantial as the mirage and barren as the sand of the desert past which I am steaming.'[10]

Three weeks later, after a 6,000-mile dash for home, Grogan arrived in Staffordshire on 2 December with just one day to campaign. Wedgwood, on the other hand, had enjoyed a clear field for the best part of a month. But, in a sporting gesture born of his regret over the muck-raking tactics he had employed in the previous contest, Wedgwood issued clear instructions to his campaign team that Grogan was to be given an absolutely free rein for twenty-four hours. At his last-minute meetings there were no fisticuffs, no egg throwing and no disruptive renditions of the Land Song.

Grogan's platform was the same as in the first contest except for one 'policy'. Whereas many of his fellow Conservative candidates conceded that reform of the House of Lords was inevitable, Grogan went one step further and positively embraced this constitutional change – though he did not think it should entail the Liberals being given carte blanche to flood the Upper House with what he referred to as 'nebulosities and non-entities'.

Despite his progressive stance on the main constitutional issue, Grogan's dash was in vain. He was again defeated, by a margin of 5,281 votes to 4,087, but was touched by the fact that he had lost fewer votes in the course of the year than Wedgwood. The national situation also changed little. The Conservative and Unionist alliance polled 272 seats, the exact same number as the Liberals, who retained power due to their coalition with the 84 Nationalists and 42 Labourites, but Grogan was encouraged by the fact that in England the Tories secured a majority of 239 seats to 226. The main consequence of the election was that a year later Balfour, the Conservative leader, conceded defeat over the issue of reform of the Lords and resigned, and the peers voted through the 1911 Parliament Act, curtailing their powers. Tariff Reform had again been the Tories' undoing and was put on the back-burner for almost two decades. At the time, and subsequently, Grogan regarded this as a huge error; in his opinion 'the experience of the coming war would have put [the Tories] in power for a generation'[11] had they stuck to their guns on this key issue.

Grogan never stood for Parliament again. Although he remained the Unionist candidate for Newcastle-under-Lyme until the end of 1913, there was no further election before the Great War. When he resigned the *Staffordshire Sentinel* warmly praised his 'sense of fun', the 'insight and imagination for which he must in part thank his Irish ancestors' and remarked that 'many opponents pay him the very high compliment of wishing that he were on their side'.[12] The North Staffordshire Unionist Party wrote him an even more glowing commendation, thanking him for his 'untiring and unselfish efforts', for his 'brilliant exposition of the policy of Imperial Preference', and for being 'the type of citizen which has made our Empire great; as scholar, as explorer, as traveller of world-wide fame, as pioneer in the opening up of the great Dark Continent, as colonist of one of the youngest portions of our Empire, as one who has realised the true significance of *Civis Britannicus sum*'.[13] Grogan's affinity with 'those who made the Empire great' was also recognized when, in April 1911, he was elected President of the Working Man's Empire United League.

Wedgwood held Newcastle-under-Lyme until 1942. During the Great War he again served with great distinction in Belgium, Gallipoli and finally Africa. There, he and Grogan were destined to be reunited briefly and stand, as Wedgwood put it, 'arm in arm as twin warriors'.[14] In 1919 Wedgwood joined the Labour Party and thereby provided Grogan with a cast-iron explanation of why during the two contests of 1910 'his replies to questions as to what was his policy tended to be evasive'. Grogan's final, scathing observation regarding his former foe was that 'he ended up a well-intentioned nebulosity in the parliamentary Whipsnade, the House of Lords'.[15]

In the meantime, as the *Staffordshire Sentinel* remarked, 'Captain Grogan has always played the game and will continue to play it.'[16]

When Grogan and Gertrude sailed into Mombasa on 30 June 1910, in between that year's British elections, they found that the atmosphere among their fellow settlers was one of considerable excitement. The country's new governor, Sir Percy Girouard, seemed to have transformed its prospects in a matter of just nine months.

Girouard was a dapper, monocled French-Canadian engineer who had joined the British Army in 1888 and – to Grogan's great satisfaction – had a formidable reputation as an expert on railways. He was a veteran of Kitchener's Nile expedition, had overseen the total reorganization of the Egyptian railways before moving to South Africa to run its railways for Milner, and had served under Grogan's mentor, Lugard, in Northern Nigeria before taking over as governor there in

1907. In short, he was just the sort of governor that Grogan had been calling for – a man of 'vision and boundless energy'[17] – for over five years. To the delight of all settlers, Girouard soon showed that he 'had not the slightest fear of giving offence to the Colonial Office or of the dreadful consequences that might follow his actions'.[18]

Girouard had kicked off his tenure by submitting an interim report to the Colonial Office on the state of affairs in the Protectorate. It took him just two months to produce what the CO nervously referred to as 'this prodigious piece of work',[19] in which Girouard declared himself to be appalled by how little had been achieved by his predecessors and their superiors in Whitehall. He was heavily critical of the absence of *any* defined policy framework for the country, let alone a consistent policy for safeguarding African interests, and he was equally scathing of the local administration. Ainsworth was the only one among senior officials who emerged relatively unscathed (as Grogan's friend Jackson would have done had he not been promoted to the post of Governor of Uganda). As if all this was not enough for the Colonial Office to swallow Girouard expressed a confidence that the settlers would, and should, be granted self-government within a matter of two or three decades.

It is hardly surprising that Grogan was on the best possible terms with the new governor from the outset. After his first year in office a great dinner was given for Girouard at the Nairobi Institute on 7 November 1910, and Grogan was called upon to toast him on behalf of the settlers. When he rose to his feet he announced himself, as if anyone needed reminding, as 'the baddest and boldest of a bold, bad gang' – which gave rise to great hilarity among his fellow diners. He then went on to describe how the country had first been led by a 'brain' (Eliot) and then by a 'man' (Stewart) following which there was a 'period of doubt with the titular leader ['Flannelfoot' Hayes-Sadler] describing his army as a rabble'. But now, Grogan declared, everyone was relieved that the Protectorate had 'a man and brain combined' in Girouard.

Earlier that same day Grogan had presided over another historic moment: the inaugural meeting of the Convention of Associations. This body superseded the Colonists' Association, and Grogan was unanimously elected its first President. It was, in effect, a settlers' parliament in which all smaller political entities – from the Colonists' Association to the Pastoralists' Association to local farmers' groups – were represented. The first meeting lasted two days and according to Lord Cranworth was 'voted a great success, especially by ourselves'.[20] Its important remit was to present a united front of settler opinion to future governors and their administrators. With the approachable Girouard as governor, his officials on a tight rein, and 'bad and bold' Grogan as President of the Convention, the climate of settler–official mistrust disappeared. As Grogan remarked in his after-dinner speech to Girouard it was 'truly a red letter day'.[21]

On the face of it Grogan seemed to have undergone a radical volte-face since his ill-judged 'revolt'. There was now no trace of the Grogan whom government officials had accused of 'ruthless and persistent criticism' of the Administration, but Grogan had not changed: it was Girouard who had changed every aspect of life in the Protectorate.

During 1911, with the political situation stabilized, the country started to improve in leaps and bounds. New settlers arrived, encouraged by the confident atmosphere, and African, Indian and settler alike benefited for the first time from being able to export what they produced in ever-increasing quantities. Girouard personally led negotiations with Whitehall for adequate funding to improve the country's infrastructure, and succeeded in securing its first development loan of £250,000. Mombasa was still in need of a deep-water pier, and Girouard was also determined to build a forty-mile railway from Nairobi to the rich agricultural land around Thika.

This railway brought immediate benefits to both the Kikuyu and European settlers. Men like Charles Taylor, one of many who had been encouraged by Grogan to settle in East Africa, no longer needed to transport everything to and from their farms by ox-wagon and had ready access to distant markets; within a decade coffee exports, chiefly from this highland region, were worth over £1m per annum to the Protectorate's coffers. The sisal industry, pioneered by Swift and Rutherfoord, was also given a much-needed boost and the optimism felt in Kikuyuland started to spread elsewhere. Delamere's master-plan for a wheat industry achieved a significant lift-off. Crop experimentation began to yield positive results. Most dramatic of all was the headway made by the African economy.[22] At last it seemed as though Grogan's dream of adding another jewel to the Empire's crown might be realized, and everyone had good reason to be grateful to the man who had so doggedly and unwaveringly campaigned on their behalf in the corridors of power.

The Colonial Office was somewhat bemused by the rapid progress. It was also distinctly alarmed by the new alliance between settlers and officials forged by Girouard, and by the conduct of the Convention of Associations – which was universally referred to as Grogan's 'Big Noise'. The Convention was emboldened by Girouard's support for self-government for the Protectorate, and soon began to call for settlers to be elected to the country's Legislative Council as opposed to being nominated by the governor. This demand grew more voluble after the settlers started to pay poll tax, as Grogan was adamant that there should be 'no taxation without elected representation'. His case received a significant boost when, in 1911, the Treasury's last grant for the support of the 'Lunatic Line' was paid. Despite all the official scepticism the country had, in effect, begun to support itself just eleven years after the completion of the railway – a decade earlier than the most optimistic forecast in the Final Report of the 1904 Railway Committee. It was a formidable achievement, and was in no small measure attributable to the efforts of Grogan, Delamere and the other 'big men' in the Protectorate.

In the summer of 1911 Grogan joined Lords Erroll, Hindlip and Cardross on the British East Africa Committee for the Coronation Exhibition at White City, but he decided to relinquish the presidency of the Convention of Associations as he was keener on the 'big occasion' than on the grind of committee work. Besides, it was time for him to confront the ongoing threat from the Colonial Office to his business empire.

Grogan had invested huge amounts of money in a wide range of assets in the Protectorate, and was perpetually short of ready cash. He habitually referred to the country as 'the happy hunting-ground of those whose heart, ideas and ambitions outrun the balance at the bank',[23] and by 1911 it looked as though the cost of his pioneering activities had caught up with him.

The gravity of the situation can be surmised from correspondence between Grogan and Coleman in which, as early as 1908, Grogan was asking to borrow money against the final settlement of Gertrude's share of her father's Trust which was due to be paid in 1912. Coleman was completely sympathetic to his needs, as he shared Grogan's belief that 'the Colonial is not much better than the Foreign Office for practical knowledge of the real requirements which the various countries under its control are always trying to make them understand'.[24] He was also so enthused by his son-in-law's career that he had the *East African Standard* sent weekly to New Zealand. But, having recently advanced Grogan £5,000 and sent Gertrude a dividend of £1,800, Coleman was unable to oblige further and at one point Grogan was even reduced to borrowing £1,600 from his brother Philip in his attempt to keep his businesses afloat.

It was a matter of paramount importance for Grogan to reach an agreement with the Colonial Office over the terms of his forest concession so that he could start to earn a return on it. Bit by bit, the pieces started to fall into place. The Colonial Office's Concessions Committee admitted that 'the difficulties which have arisen are not entirely the fault of the concessionaires' and that 'Mr. Grogan has acted very openly in the matter'; Grogan's *bête noire* at the Colonial Office, Mr Ellis, was replaced, and Lingham, the Lumber King of the Transvaal, went into voluntary liquidation. By the end of 1911 Grogan had not only established title in the courts to Lingham's share of the business but had bought out Goldmann. He was therefore the sole concessionaire and was free to negotiate only on his own behalf. Thereafter events moved swiftly, and when he visited the Protectorate in February 1912 the *Leader* was able to welcome him back with the words: 'it is encouraging to learn that Captain Grogan has had a very successful business tour in England, having doubled his interests in BEA'.[25] Terms for the forest concession had been agreed, and Grogan's astonishing tenacity in dealing with the CO had finally paid off.

His stay in East Africa lasted just long enough for him to put in train his massive plans for the Eldama Forest. Gertrude did not accompany him on this occasion for a very good reason: she had, on 22 December 1911, given birth to her fourth child. It was another girl, christened Jane. Grogan was by now despairing of ever producing an heir, but had precious little time to dwell on the matter. On safari out in the forest equipment was ordered; plans were drawn up for sawmills; the logistics of extracting the timber were discussed with his new managers over and over again; and the enterprise was proudly named Equator Saw Mills. Equator was not the first company to mill timber in the Protectorate, but it was destined, with astonishing rapidity, to be its largest by far and to earn Grogan the hard-won and fully justified accolade of founder of East Africa's timber industry.

After two months of frenetic activity in the forest Grogan sailed back to England to be with Gertrude and the children at Camp Hill for the summer. No sooner had he arrived home than he received disturbing news. Girouard, who had done so much to create a workable development plan for the Protectorate, had proved too much for the Colonial Office. Right from the moment that he had set to work the Earl of Crewe's successor as Secretary of State, Lewis Harcourt, was dismissive of Girouard's conspicuous success in East Africa. So 'Lulu', as Grogan irreverently referred to Harcourt, resolved to be rid of Girouard the minute he exceeded his authority.

Like Eliot before him, Girouard's nemesis proved to be the Masai. Having been moved out of the Rift Valley in 1904 by order of the Colonial Office, in order to make way for intensive cultivation by European settlers, the Masai were again moved by Girouard in 1911. His plan was to reunite those Masai who had been moved north to the Laikipia plateau with those who had been moved south in a new, enlarged territory in the south of the country. This action was beset by problems, but that fact alone was not enough to have precipitated Girouard's resignation. The Colonial Office was suspicious about Girouard's insistence that he was not motivated by a desire to open up the Laikipia plateau for European settlement.

By May 1912 Harcourt had amassed enough evidence to confront Girouard, who admitted that he had indeed promised land in Laikipia to a number of settlers. Girouard was required to fall on his sword; Harcourt was able to feed the erratic moral vanity of the Colonial

Office; and Grogan expressed his extreme annoyance that such a constructive governor had been 'quite wrongly driven by the Home Government to resignation'.[26]

The settlers waited anxiously for the smoke to rise from the Colonial Office's chimney, signalling the announcement of Girouard's successor, and soon received the news that they were to be governed by a man of whom none of them had ever heard. At fifty-seven, Sir Henry Conway Belfield was hardly in his prime; moreover he had no experience of governing in Africa. He was a barrister, not an administrator, by profession and had spent most of his career in the Malay States. The message from the Colonial Office to the settlers was a clear one: progress had been indecently rapid under Girouard and Whitehall meant to put a brake on it by using legal – or any other – means.

Grogan was, as usual, deputed to welcome the new governor at a dinner for eighty-five at the Connaught Rooms in London on 3 September. His speech was polite but to the point. He described the Protectorate as having graduated from its 'lurid past in which he [Grogan] and many others had featured', a period characterized by a 'condition of heat . . . generated by friction', and how this graduation had been effected by the country's 'greatest governor', Girouard. In effect, Grogan warned Belfield that he had a hard act to follow, but 'could depend upon being received with open arms'.[27]

Initially the doubts about Belfield, who appeared to be what Lord Cranworth scathingly called 'a typically loyal servant of the Crown',[28] seemed to be well founded. He was not a great mixer, unlike Girouard, and – although by no means the first nor the last to do so – he dismissed an over-petulant Delamere from Legislative Council early in his tenure. But bit by bit his popularity grew, helped no end by his 'game' wife who didn't even bat an eyelid when Delamere's brother-in-law, Berkeley Cole, inserted a banana into her ear trumpet during dinner one evening. Belfield also proved himself to be an adept and patient administrator, despite his lack of charisma, and soon Grogan personally 'passed' him as 'a highly efficient governor'.[29]

One key issue on which Belfield was unable to make any headway was the 'Indian Question'. As the demands of nationalists in India itself grew ever more voluble, so did those of Indians in the Protectorate. Such protests were not confined to the East Africa Protectorate. No sooner had the Liberals granted self-government to the Transvaal than an attempt had been made by Jan Smuts to expel all Indians who had entered South Africa 'illegally'. His argument was that if uncontrolled immigration continued the Indians would overwhelm both Europeans and Africans in number. But resistance to Smuts was strong, and led by M. K. Gandhi, who was sentenced to two months in jail with hard labour for his efforts. Undeterred, Gandhi continued the fight and in 1912 was instrumental in forming the South African Native National Congress, the forerunner of the ANC. In Australia too there was opposition from Indians to the imposition of an educational test as a means of restricting immigration.

Indian agitation in the East Africa Protectorate was thus part of a wider movement, and achieved a measure of early success. A. M. Jeevanjee gained a seat in Legco in 1910, but resigned a year later when it became obvious that his desire to see the country federated to India was not one that the Colonial Office was likely to fulfil. He did not, however, give up the fight, and as the Protectorate's politics became increasingly linked to those of India the European settlers, as well as many an African chief, started to suspect they were under siege. Outbreaks of plague in the Indian markets of Nairobi in 1911, 1912 and 1913 did little to improve the prevailing atmosphere in the capital.

Grogan, Gertrude and young Dorothy sailed back to East Africa in January 1913, leaving the other three girls in the care of Nanny Redwood. They were joined at the end of February by the Colemans, who had come to inspect what the 'youngsters' were up to, and Gertrude returned with them to Camp Hill in midsummer. Although Grogan was as optimistic and indefatigable as ever during his parents-in-law's stay, the truth was that the birth of his timber business was proving troublesome.

During 1912 he had spent £8,000 on a state-of-the-art saw mill in the Eldalat Pass at Maji Mazuri, but, as he had always foreseen, getting the timber to the mill proved a nightmare: he could not find sufficient workers, or oxen, for love nor money. The problem was compounded by the fact that what timber he could get to the mill could not be shipped on in the absence of any branch line linking the concession to the main line. He had no choice but to lay his own twenty-mile tramway from Maji Mazuri to the main-line station at Mau Summit. It was a major feat of engineering, and as such cost a colossal £20,000, but without it his mill was inoperable.

A tramway was, however, no substitute for a railway through his concession to the Uasin Gishu plateau – the line that he had always offered to build. Even Grogan had to admit that he, for the time being, had shot his bolt as far as railway-building was concerned; he needed someone else to conduct the campaign against Whitehall's 'silverfish', in much the same way as he had hoped Goldie would back in 1906.

The ideal candidate for the job was already a close friend. George Lloyd, later Lord Lloyd of Dolobran, hailed from the great banking family of the same name and had first visited the Protectorate in 1906, but his lifelong friendship with Grogan, who was five years his senior, had begun when he stood as the Tory candidate in the West Stafford-shire constituency in 1910. Unlike Grogan, Lloyd had won his seat and in the new parliament's very first session he was on his feet pressing the government to allow Grogan to get on with working his forest concession. In the summer of 1913 he stayed with Grogan and Gert-rude in Nairobi, and it was then that the plan was hatched for Lloyd to launch an assault on the CO.

Whitehall's initial response was predictably deflating. Mr Read and Sir George Fiddes reiterated that their policy in the Protectorate was to 'mark time', told Lloyd that in their opinion economic develop-ment in the Protectorate was moving much too quickly, and declared themselves to be 'not concerned about transport for the future'.[30] Lloyd was no more easily deflected than Grogan, however, and by the autumn of 1913 three things had moved dramatically in favour of their railway.

The first was that the CO had underestimated the strength of the boom that Girouard had stimulated in the Protectorate. Just as Grogan had always said it would, European settlement on the empty grasslands of the Uasin Gishu plateau had proved an enormous success and more and more settlers were arriving there each month to farm wheat. To the north of the plateau, Trans-Nzoia district had also been 'opened up' with equal success. All these farmers to the north of Grogan's forest concession were as desperate as he for a branch railway to ship out their harvests. Finally, at a meeting in London in October, Lloyd and Grogan managed to enlist the influential and enthusiastic support of Ainsworth, who had, as Provincial Commissioner of Nyanza, personally orchestrated a boom in African sugar production around Mumias, between the Uasin Gishu plateau and Lake Victoria. The case for a branch line could no longer be ignored in Whitehall.

By the middle of 1914 Lloyd had everything in place. Neither the CO nor the Treasury would agree to finance the £1m needed for a railway from Nakuru through Grogan's forest to the plateau and then west through the sugar regions to Lake Victoria, but they were, they now decided to Grogan's great amusement, prepared to see it built privately, and from the wings Grogan advised Lloyd every step of the way. Belfield was kept enthusiastically onside by Grogan's persuasive charm, and Grogan even wrote the governor's speeches relating to the railway; Bowring, the Treasurer, he told 'quite bluntly what we wanted and why';[31] financiers – principally Barrington Kennett of Helbert Wagg & Co. – were won over to the tune of £1m.; Lawley and Paulings were taken on as the contractor; and mass meetings of support for the railway were organized by farmers at Nakuru. There was not a single pie into which Grogan did not stick his finger.

Although everyone knew that the railway would take three years to build, and was no instant panacea to the farmers' transport problems, the optimism that Lloyd and Grogan's efforts generated was huge. Like a 'disgorging gannet',[32] as Grogan put it, Delamere started to subdivide and sell off 500-acre plots on his Equator Ranch, through which the railway would have to run prior to reaching Grogan's forest concession, and Grogan was himself able to turn his mind again to developing his landholding in Mombasa into a proper deep-water port. The local government, beset by technical difficulties, was for the umpteenth time reconsidering its own scheme – leaving the field open for Grogan to pursue his own ambitions.

Grogan's letters to Lloyd also began to show that, even without adequate transport, his timber business had achieved lift-off. In February 1914 he wrote:

> I do wish you could get out here. The apple is ripe for dropping on so many trees. We are getting a big move on against gigantic odds – I have orders (mostly government) for £30,000 worth of timber ... and my Nairobi yard is selling stuff at the rate of £1,200 a month ... There are vast fortunes in these timbers and you and I could grab the lot. Down your toy drum politics – this is the real game. Down this end of the telescope you look like kids with tin whistles playing at soldiers.[33]

Later the same month he added, 'you must keep your hand on the Kenia position. I am sure you and I could corner the timber industry of this country and you'll never never never get such a chance again. It is better by far than the hot air game.'[34]

There is an almost manic euphoric about these letters to Lloyd. For over a decade Grogan and Gertrude had pumped every penny they possessed, not to mention a good deal of the banks' and co-investors'[35] money, into the Protectorate, and now, at last, he was scenting the sweet smell of success. It could not come soon enough. His assets in 1913 included his land in Mombasa, a 19,000-acre farm on the Kapiti Plains growing maize, linseed and millet, a half share in the Kenani fibre company already growing 300 acres of sisal near Athi River station, Chiromo, the Swamp, a large plot in Sadler Street and various other properties in Nairobi, a controlling interest in the Longonot sheep farm, now enlarged to 35,000 acres and boasting six miles of frontage on to Lake Naivasha, his two farms at Limuru, one growing black wattle, the other oranges and coffee, a 6,000 acre farm at Ravine adjacent to one of his timber mills, and 20,000 acres between Turi and Molo, which was the headquarters of his timber business and where he had built an eccentric new home called Molo House, universally referred to as the 'Pagoda'. Built on stilts, with a corrugated iron roof but beautiful wood-panelled interior, it looked out over the Turi swamp. The then current market value of these assets was £278,000 – without assigning any value to the potential of the forest concession – though few, if any, of them were producing a single penny of cash.

With land values soaring and the timber business requiring constant investment Grogan decided, like Delamere, to do a bit of 'disgorging'. Quite apart from anything else he had more on his plate than he and his trusty brother-in-law, Wilfrid Hunter, could effectively oversee. In June 1913 he sold forty-four small plots on the Swamp Estate for £11,500, having bought out Shariff Jaffer & Co. (his Indian partner). Not all his negotiations ended successfully. He briefly considered a government offer of £200 per acre for his 100-acre landholding in Mombasa, but swiftly terminated discussions when a Dr Charlesworth succeeded in selling fifty acres nearby for £450 per acre; a similar thing happened when officials offered to buy 18 acres of the Cross Estate with the intention of providing an extension to the Indian Bazaar. In this case too the local government underbid, because it had rather conveniently declared the area unfit for human habitation. That was hardly Grogan's fault: the Public Works Department had still failed to put in roads and sanitary lanes promised a decade earlier and until they did Grogan could not install his own specially designed drainage and sewage treatment plant on the estate.[36] Grogan resolved to make the government wait until it was prepared to pay a proper price, and all the while the Colonial Office looked on aghast as Grogan and Delamere rearranged their assets.

With his attention increasingly focused on Africa, and having relinquished his political responsibilities in the Potteries, Grogan also decided that some domestic rearrangements were called for. The beautiful Camp Hill was sold and an enormous London house bought as the family's base in England. Four-storeyed 52 Draycott Place, a former dance academy, soon came to be known to visitors simply as 'Number Ten'. The ground-floor ballroom was kept intact for entertaining; tusks, trophies and animal skins from Grogan's Cape-to-Cairo trek adorned the walls and corridors; but most important to Grogan was his eyrie on the top floor. This he transformed into a study and library, housing his enormous collection of books, and it was eccentrically painted grey so that the dust which gathered during his absences in Africa would not show. Maids were strictly barred from this inner sanctum.

Grogan did not consider Equator Saw Mills' headquarters at Turi to be an ideal place for bringing up the children. There was no school for Dorothy, who was now eleven, and even in Nairobi schooling was inadequate (which precluded the family from living at Chiromo). Furthermore he knew from bitter personal experience about the health risks of a life in the middle of nowhere, and Gertrude's narrow escape from death in 1907 was never far from his mind. Grogan decided that he and Gertrude would continue to shuttle to and from Africa according to school terms, spending as much time with each other and the children as was possible given his frenetic activity, and Gertrude agreed with the plan. Like her mother before her, she was gamely 'prepared to go anywhere at any time'.[37]

Draycott Place was evidently as happy a home as Camp Hill before it. When Grogan was in residence it became the scene of many a children's party, at which he continued to delight in performing his repertoire of conjuring tricks and melodies on the banjo. As ever, he doted on his little charges and when he was away the children would wait expectantly for 'the thrill of his return'. 'I remember it vividly,' Joyce would later say,

> he always brought us presents: Turkish delight, little black elephants, bangles made out of the hair of an elephant's tail. Then on Sunday afternoon he would take us all to the Zoo, to which he had presented six or seven lions; he would buy buns for the elephants and nuts for the monkeys; and as a grand finale, he would take us to tea and allow us to eat as much as we liked. I can remember those éclairs, still: full of rich cream, so that as you bit one end it squirted out the other – whereupon Father would laugh and say 'Get under the table, little pig!'

When Grogan, Gertrude and Dorothy sailed for East Africa in November 1913 on the *Carisbrooke Castle* it was, however, to be a very long time before the other three children saw their father again. And when they did, he seemed to have changed almost beyond recognition.

In July 1914 Gertrude and Dorothy left the Protectorate to return home, just after the jaunty Quentin sailed in on the *Matiana* to lend Grogan a hand at the Turi sawmills. Having found life unbearable in

the 'old country', he had spent six years building a formidable reputation as an elephant hunter in the Lado enclave on the Upper Nile,
and then worked for two years on a rubber plantation in Sudan before
deciding to rejoin his brother. When he arrived he found his old
friends in the Protectorate in buoyant mood. Settlers visited the bank
manager with confidence not in trepidation; everywhere stories circu-
lated of how so-and-so was succeeding with this, how so-and-so had
received so much for such-and-such a crop. And since New Year's
Eve the settlers had even had their own club as a counterpoise to the
officials' Nairobi Club.

Grogan had had quite a hand in the birth of Muthaiga Country
Club,[38] set in the hills three miles to the north of Nairobi's city centre.
In 1912 the fabulously wealthy (and generous) Major Archie Morrison
had breezed into the Protectorate on safari and, while staying with
Grogan at Chiromo, had been introduced by his host to a business
agent by the name of Freddie Ward. Morrison, schooled by Grogan,
was much taken with the prospects for business in East Africa and
soon committed himself to investments worth hundreds of thousands
of pounds. But he insisted that his investments were conditional on
there being a *proper* club. To finance it he wrote out a cheque for
£60,000 to Ward saying he would return in five weeks' time to check
on progress – and never visited the Protectorate again.

When Muthaiga Club, never to be seen by Morrison, opened it
had the best cellar in Africa, a shop which boasted dreamy luxuries
like Charbonnel et Walker chocolates and a head chef from the
Bombay Yacht Club. Dinner cost Rs5 and bachelor rooms were Rs60
per month. Although only fourteen settlers sat down to dinner on its
opening night, by July 1914 – when a fancy dress ball was held for
150 guests – it had come into its own. Miss Henderson was much
admired for her Apache outfit, as were Mrs Hodgkinson as Bo-Peep
and Mrs Gilkes who came as a magpie.[39] Just two weeks after this
great event, at ten to four on 4 August, the order was given in Britain
for mobilization.

The Empire was at war.

SEVENTEEN

The Leopard's War

THE PROTECTORATE was completely unprepared for an outbreak of hostilities with its German neighbours to the south, and for the first month confusion reigned. There were just seventeen companies of the 1st, 3rd, and 4th Battalions of the King's African Rifles, comprising some 2,400 officers and *askaris*, available for the defence of British East Africa. Worse still, these units were widely scattered: the six companies of the 3rd KAR were in Jubaland, the north-eastern extremity of the country, and the 4th KAR were in Uganda. Less than 150 men were stationed in Nairobi, and the 500-mile border with German East Africa – not to mention the country's lifeline, the Uganda Railway – lay undefended.

From all corners of the country settlers converged on Nairobi. Grogan and Quentin left Turi by train, reaching town on 5 August, and were met by a scene which reminded Grogan of the Bulawayo *laager* eighteen years earlier. The streets were filled with men on horseback or astride mules wearing just what they had left their farms in: khaki trousers or shorts; slouch hats, *terais* or *topees* atop their heads; and coloured handkerchiefs knotted around their unshaven necks. Uniforms were non-existent. Their weapons were those of the frontiersman: hunting rifles and shotguns, with bandoliers of ammunition slung about the shoulders. There was a marked absence of discipline, and as the bars of the town were open all hours in spite of the declaration of martial law, chaos reigned. Above all, no one knew what was going on or where to go. There was scant intelligence from anywhere – only dark, whispered rumours of impending invasion by legions of 'squareheads', and an inexplicable obsession with the possibility of impending air attack.

The settlers' gung-ho spirit was not shared by the civil authorities either side of the border. Dr Schnee, the Governor of German East Africa, was keen to avoid a scrap, believing that East Africa would be better off leaving the war to be fought in Europe. He knew that he could only mobilize some 3,000 white fighting men – approximately the same number as could be mustered by the British – which limited his ability either to attack or defend, and the presence of the Royal Navy in the Indian Ocean cut him off from supplies and reinforcements from home. Governor Belfield was equally ambivalent about the prospect of open hostilities. In addition to his lack of the necessary manpower the heaviest weaponry in the country was believed to consist of two machine guns, one of which was out of order, and, like Schnee, Belfield harboured an unease about the reaction of 'the natives' to the sight of two armies of white men slugging it out in the bush. Grogan considered both men's attempts to keep the peace to be 'wise and humane', as the 'African peoples were unconcerned with the quarrels of Europe'.[1]

Their hopes of averting a clash were dealt their first blow when the British cruisers *Pegasus* and *Astraea* bombarded Dar-es-Salaam on 8 August as a 'warning' to the German colony's coastal towns to remain neutral. The Germans then invaded the strategically vital area around Taveta by mid-August, although their first attempt to mount an offensive against the railway at Tsavo was beaten back by a KAR detachment. On 20 September the sole German cruiser in the Indian Ocean, the *Königsberg*, sank HMS *Pegasus* in Zanzibar harbour before hot-footing it to seek refuge in the Rufiji delta, and hopes of avoiding a full-scale conflict all but disappeared.

Back in Nairobi the irregulars, having reported for duty to Nairobi House – the Sixth Avenue headquarters of Grogan's business empire – organized themselves into bands in a manner reminiscent of the Crusading era. The indomitable and now aged Russell Bowker, sporting his snarling leopard's head cap, rallied his followers into 'Bowker's Horse'; the Boer settlers from the Uasin Gishu plateau demonstrated their determination to protect their new homes by forming the 'Plateau South Africans'; Berkeley Cole gathered 800 Somali volunteers into his 'Cole's Scouts'; and some of the more aristocratic settlers formed 'Monica's Own', named after the Governor's daughter and intended to resemble a detachment of lancers. These wholly untrained units, plus 'Arnoldi's', 'Ross's' and 'Wessels's Scouts', were all then placed under the new banner of the East African Mounted Rifles. But the EAMR was not for the headstrong and independent Grogan brothers. They took one look at the pantomimic fray in Nairobi and returned to the saw mills at Turi to await developments. Grogan, now forty years old, had no intention of joining anyone else's 'Horse' or 'Scouts', and Quentin disliked riding.

Delamere also side-stepped the EAMR by organizing an invaluable intelligence network along the southern border of Masailand. Spending up to twelve hours a day in the saddle, the following six months were the hardest of his life. When he returned to his farm at Soysambu he was half dead, wracked by malaria and suffering from a 'strained heart' which left him bed-ridden for several months. The Irish doctor, Roland 'Kill or Cure' Burkitt, could do little for him and he had no option but to return to England for treatment. Although he returned to Africa in 1916, he would be dogged by ill-health for the rest of his life. Meanwhile the EAMR scored some early successes. Bowker's Horse pushed the Germans out of Karungu, on Lake Victoria, while the main body of the EAMR moved down to the borderlands. They derailed at Kajiado and set off through dense bush towards the front.

Like their comrades on the Western Front the volunteers, although all old African hands, soon discovered that German soldiers were only one of a plethora of enemies. They were chronically under-equipped and under-supplied, and confronted by a perpetual threat of attack by wild animals, malaria, blackwater and dysentery. Most of their horses succumbed to tsetse fly, and nowhere was there anything for man or beast to drink. Transport for the sick, communications and a strategic reserve were non-existent. The sun beat down on them relentlessly and before long every man's dream of emulating the swashbuckling achievements of Rhodes's 'bloody troopers' of 1896 became a nightmare. Yet for a crucial two months, the only period in the war when the Germans might realistically have been able to invade the Protectorate, the settler units succeeded in holding the border.

At the beginning of November they went on the offensive. Joined by the first regular troops to have arrived from India, led by General Stewart, the EAMR launched an attack on a heavily fortified hill at Longido, just inside German East Africa. The aim was to dislodge

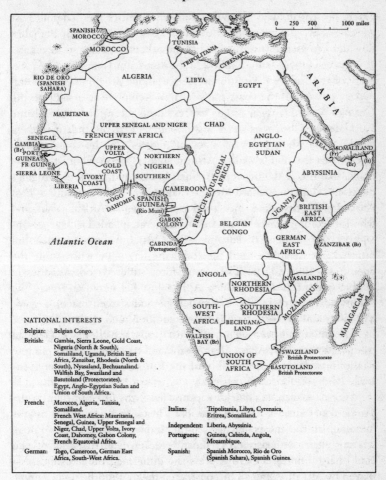

NATIONAL INTERESTS

Belgian:	Belgian Congo.
British:	Gambia, Sierra Leone, Gold Coast, Nigeria (North & South), Somaliland, Uganda, British East Africa, Zanzibar, Rhodesia (North & South), Nyasaland, Bechuanaland. Walfish Bay, Swaziland and Basutoland (Protectorates). Egypt, Anglo-Egyptian Sudan and Union of South Africa.
French:	Morocco, Algeria, Tunisia, Somaliland. French West Africa: Mauritania, Senegal, Guinea, Upper Senegal and Niger, Chad, Upper Volta, Ivory Coast, Dahomey, Gabon Colony, French Equatorial Africa.
German:	Togo, Cameroon, German East Africa, South-West Africa.
Italian:	Tripolitania, Libya, Cyrenaica, Eritrea, Somaliland.
Independent:	Liberia, Abyssinia.
Portuguese:	Guinea, Cabinda, Angola, Mozambique.
Spanish:	Spanish Morocco, Rio de Oro (Spanish Sahara), Spanish Guinea.

Africa on the Eve of War, 1914

the enemy and mount a flanking operation round the south side of Kilimanjaro against the German forces in the Taveta Gap. But the enemy were too well dug in at Longido. What ensued was a fiasco, during which Bowker's Horse suffered the indignity of having most of its horses rustled at night (thereby becoming 'Bowker's Foot').

Quentin Grogan, who by now had joined a unit of the fledgling East Africa Supply Corps attached to the recently arrived 29th Punjabis, was lucky to escape with his life.[2] Many others were not so fortunate.

An even graver setback followed the disaster at Longido. The main body of the Indian Expeditionary Force under the blimpish General Aitken arrived off the coast and prepared to mount an assault on the German port of Tanga. Aitken expressed his intention to 'thrash the Germans by Christmas'[3] and was confident that his Indian soldiers would 'make short work of a lot of niggers'[4] (as he disparagingly referred to the highly skilled African soldiers upon whom the Germans, like the KAR, depended). Such bluster did not fool Grogan's old friend Captain Richard Meinertzhagen, who was returning to East Africa for the first time since 1906 as a member of Aitken's staff, and who looked on in disbelief as Aitken deliberately failed to take advantage of the element of surprise. Two battalions were landed but ordered not to attack until the following day – by which time the enemy was fully dug in. The assault force suffered 300 casualties in double-quick time, after which Aitken lost his nerve and gave the command to retreat. The British left behind sixteen machine guns, 455 rifles and 600,000 rounds of ammunition, and their strike force of 8,000 men had been seen off by just 1,000, mostly black, German troops. For the East Africa High Command this was the first glimpse of the formidable tactical ability of the Prussian Colonel (later General), Paul von Lettow-Vorbeck.

Meinertzhagen was quick to acknowledge the discipline and courage of von Lettow's *Schutztruppe*, both black and white, but he was horrified at the incompetence of the Indian Expeditionary Force, whose soldiers he described as 'mostly chicken-hearted Hindus',[5] and could hardly find words to express the dithering and arrogance displayed by Aitken. All in all he considered the assault 'the best example ... of how a battle should not be fought'.[6] Had it succeeded, and von Lettow been captured, the war in East Africa might indeed have been over by Christmas, but instead yet another deadly enemy now confronted the Protectorate: the arrogance of its own British generals.

Von Lettow could not believe his good fortune at Tanga. Aitken's Christmas present of arms vitally underpinned the Prussian general's ability to sustain the fight and he would receive just one more such stroke of luck during the conflict, when two German ships broke through the British naval blockade in the spring of 1915. Thereafter he received nothing from the outside world. He knew that it was impossible to defeat the ever-increasing force pitted against him, but the British performance at Tanga had shown him that he had a chance of holding out in the vast territory of German East Africa almost indefinitely. He resolved to carry out his duty to the Kaiser by tying down as many imperial troops as possible for as long as possible, thereby keeping them away from Europe's Western Front. His chosen tactic was to leave his main force concentrated in areas like the Taveta Gap where natural defences made them well-nigh unassailable, and from the safety of these strongholds to instigate an elaborate and supremely courageous game of what Grogan called 'tip and run'[7] guerrilla tactics. Between April 1915 and May 1916 he despatched no less than fifty-seven raiding parties to attempt sabotage of the Uganda railway. But, these raids aside, the war in East Africa – like the conflict on the Western Front – soon became a stalemate.

After Tanga the East Africa High Command was not minded to take any risks: a stalemate was as good a situation as they could hope for. Aitken was ignominiously dismissed and his baton passed to the affable if inept General Wapshare – 'Old Wappy' – for whom caution was the watchword. Wapshare, who was transferred to Basra in April 1915, was not the only cause of inertia. In a speech delivered on 10 January 1915 Belfield, the Protectorate's governor, astonished both the settlers and the military by declaring that now imperial reinforcements had arrived the local defence force was no longer required; and he added that he wished to 'make it abundantly clear that this colony has no interest in the present war except in so far as its unfortunate geographical position places it in such close proximity to German East Africa'. Meinertzhagen noted in his diary that 'someone should shoot the man'[8] for such an unpatriotic display; and it was small wonder that most of the EAMR volunteers drifted back to their farms, deciding that if that was the view at the top then they might as well leave the fighting to the KAR and Indian troops.

Meanwhile Grogan, predictably, had followed his own war agenda. After the rout at Tanga Meinertzhagen had been charged with organizing an Intelligence Corps and immediately called on his services. Ten years had passed since the two men had last met, but Meinertzhagen had certainly not forgotten the impression left on him by the man who '[knew] British East Africa better than most'.[9] Together they set to work, and their attention soon alighted on the Congo. Despite what Britain was committed to doing on behalf of their countrymen at home the Belgians were proving 'troublesome' and 'unco-operative'. Little had been done to involve them actively in the conflict because 'Lulu' Harcourt and others at the Colonial Office feared their territorial ambitions, yet without their help there was no hope of surrounding von Lettow's forces. Someone, therefore, needed to go and square the Belgians, and Meinertzhagen was adamant that there was no better man for this challenging task than the 'encyclopaedia Africana'.[10] Grogan knew the perilous Congo border country from his great trek, and the Belgian commanding officer was none other than his friend Commandant (now Colonel) Henry, whom he had first heard of when the latter was stranded on the Nile with 'Daddy' Milne and Captain Gage in 1899.

Meinertzhagen's choice of Grogan for this delicate mission was heartily endorsed by all his superiors. Sir Frederick Jackson, the Governor of Uganda, wrote that there could not have been 'a better selection [as liaison officer], as quite apart from his speaking French fluently, Grogan's own resolute fighting spirit was a useful standby and had taught him when to sprinkle oil on troubled waters'. The 'little rift' and 'feeling of soreness' between Jackson and Grogan caused by the Nairobi Incident had, in Jackson's own words, 'all passed away long ago'.[11]

Grogan set off from Turi for the Congo with Ibrahim, his fiercely loyal Somali headman, and a small band of porters. He intended to travel fast and light to make contact with Henri and tap his 'unlimited supply of cannibals, [who were] very suitable raw material for the making of awe-inspiring African soldiers'.[12] The first hazard, successfully negotiated, was to cross Lake Victoria, which was controlled by the Germans with a single steamer – the *Muansa* – until it was sunk in March 1915.[13] Then, from Bukakata, Grogan's troop marched a hundred miles west to Mbarara to investigate wild rumours that the Watutsi or the Germans might be about to invade Jackson's undefended Uganda.

It did not take Grogan long to quell the fears of the townsfolk of Mbarara: he pointed out that the nearest Watutsi were over 200 miles to the south and the intervening area was fly-infested. As he knew that no self-respecting Tutsi would go anywhere without his cattle there was, in effect an impregnable barrier protecting the south-western corner of Uganda. The Germans were a different matter, and Grogan turned south, following the Kagera river, to investigate the border country.

After crossing the river into German East Africa Grogan knew that, if found, he would be shot. But he thrived on the hardship and constant danger and relied on the tactics of his fellow intelligence officers, who were universally lauded as 'men as sound in body as they were dauntless in spirit':[14] once he was behind enemy lines he avoided water-holes, never lit fires or shot for the pot and travelled mostly by night. His survival, and that of his men, depended solely on their bushcraft skills, and the fact that Grogan carried with him detailed maps procured in more peaceful times during a visit to Carl Wiese, the 'Lumber King' of German East Africa. Not wishing to leave anything to chance, Grogan also captured a German *ruga-ruga* (volunteer), and with the help of the man's local knowledge marched fifty miles west to Chilwe on the Ruanda border. He saw no Germans along the way and concluded that as there was no immediate danger of an offensive in the area, it was time to enter the Congo. Having no further use for his *ruga-ruga* guide he handed back the man's rifle and released him, advising him that it was probably in his interests 'not to mention his little trip'[15] to his German commanding officer. With that farewell caution, Grogan and his men recrossed the Kagera back into Uganda and yomped fifty miles north-east to Kigezi.

Back in Nairobi Meinertzhagen carefully scrutinized the reports sent by runner from his 'very lovable' friend, whose 'ability and courage, both moral and physical, placed him very high in my estimation', and pronounced them to be 'masterpieces'.[16] All were signed '*Chui*' (Leopard), the name that had been assigned to Grogan by Ruandans due to the colour and dazzling luminescence of his eyes. In return Grogan received news of the war while in Kigezi – and in particular of a successful push on the Western Front in which a large number of Germans were captured. When he related this to Ibrahim, who had ridden in Queen Victoria's Golden Jubilee procession, the man disappeared only to return moments later with a pen and paper. 'Write to Kitchener,' Ibrahim solemnly instructed Grogan, 'and tell him that Ibrahim, the old Somali, advises him to kill the lot or they will only breed more Germans for another war.'[17]

From Kigezi Grogan headed west until he reached the Rutchuru valley, and then followed it all the way south to the volcanoes and Lake Kivu. Old memories were stirred of his escape from the Baleka cannibals to the west of Mount Götzen, and just a few miles from where Harry Sharp had pitched camp on the lake shore Grogan found Henry's camp. Sixteen years after their first meeting the two old friends were reunited 'like lost brothers',[18] but it did not take Grogan long to discover that Henry's troops were not in great shape. Some detachments had marched for six months from Stanleyville to reach Otter Bay and had sustained casualties of over fifty per cent due to the inhospitable climate and terrain. Most of the *askaris* were Man-yema, like Grogan's porters on the trek; and he noted that their culinary predilections had obviously not changed in his absence as they eyed him 'as if I might be a tempting morsel'.[19] Indeed, so nervous was Henry of his men's poor morale and state of near-starvation that he had set up a machine-gun facing their camp.

Grogan immediately took steps to address the situation. He gave an extremely grateful Henry £100 and told him to send a revictualling party to Mbarara. Then he led a Scandinavian officer and fifty porters back up the seventy-five-mile length of the Rutchuru valley to shoot hippos on Lake Edward, returning ten days later with meat for the troops. Camp was then moved out of the 'veritable death-trap'[20] in which it was situated to the Rutchuru valley itself, and Grogan set about establishing proper lines of communication and supply between the new camp and Mbarara. In so doing he was helped by the fact that the District Officer at Masaka was a former Jesus College man, and the one at Kigezi was Irish. With the Belgian force put on a war footing, Grogan bade a fond farewell to Henry and set out on the 500-mile journey via Entebbe back to Nairobi. No sooner had he reached Uganda than he received new orders to 'lose' a general for as long as possible in the Congo without impairing the good relations he had established with the Belgians. Grogan immediately smelled a rat, but agreed to escort the man to a rendezvous with Henry at his new encampment.

Grogan's 'pet general' was Wilfrid Malleson, variously described by Meinertzhagen as 'a bad man', 'clever as a monkey but hopelessly unreliable', and 'a snake in the grass ... who comes from a class which would wreck the Empire to advance himself'.[21] Grogan found Malleson 'rather wearisome' from the outset, but took his mission seriously: when he received a message from Meinertzhagen that the Germans had got wind of it he changed his route lest the general be captured. Privately he wondered 'how much general agreement there would be as to the measure of the disaster' if Malleson were captured, and whether the Germans 'when they discovered the identity of their captive, would not hurriedly return him with all honours across the border'.[22]

To make matters worse, Malleson insisted that he and Grogan travel disguised as rubber merchants, which Grogan thought unduly provocative considering the horrific cost in African lives of Leopold's Congo rubber trade. Again he kept his thoughts to himself and went along with the ruse, dutifully delivering Malleson to Henry for discussions. As he had expected the meeting was not a success. The Belgians regarded Malleson with 'thinly veiled suspicion and, because of his Poona Poona attitude, with distaste'.[23] Within days it looked as though all Grogan's efforts to establish good relations with the Belgians would be undone, so he despatched a runner with a message to Meinertzhagen telling him to recall the general for 'urgent consultations'. Without waiting for the answer Grogan informed Malleson that they had received orders to set off for Nairobi.[24]

When Grogan returned exhausted to the Protectorate it was to the adulation of the British High Command. He had almost single-handedly ensured that the Belgians would stay in the war and shore up their front for the British, and was informed that he would be recommended for a decoration. But, to his great amusement, no one saw fit to offer repayment of the £100 he had given to Henry. That bothered him little; what did cause him concern was that during his six-month absence the atmosphere in the capital had gone from bad to worse. Tension between the officers of the Indian army detachments and non-combatant government officials was mounting, and most settlers had ceased to play any active role in the fighting. Meinertzhagen, with his penchant for pungent criticism, bemoaned the fact that 'patriotism [did] not exist'[25] in the country.

The military situation was, however, not without its bright moments – dug in and dangerous though von Lettow's men remained. In March the 500-strong 2nd Rhodesian Regiment, acknowledged as 'real fighting men', arrived; and they were soon followed by a battalion raised by the Legion of Frontiersmen, the adult version of the Boy Scouts of which Grogan was still a central committee member. Officially gazetted as the 25th Battalion Royal Fusiliers, or 'Boozaliers' as Grogan was wont to refer to them, this was in his opinion 'the most extraordinary military unit in British history'.[26] Its combatants included the twenty-seven-stone Northrup McMillan, whose swordbelt measured all of sixty-four inches, the sixty-three-year-old hunter and naturalist Frederick Courtenay Selous, Grogan's fellow veteran of the war in Matabeleland, several former members of the French Foreign Legion, a footman from Buckingham Palace, Texan cowboys, publicans, a former colonel in the Honduran army, seal-poachers from the Arctic Circle, a Scottish lighthouse keeper, American soldiers, and a number of circus acrobats and clowns. Led by the South African Colonel Dan Driscoll they soon proved themselves to be lethal in battle, but wholly undisciplined in between times. After a successful attack in June on Bukoba, on the east side of Lake Victoria, Driscoll lost control of his men altogether after they captured the town and reports of the resultant looting, boozing and consorting with local African girls considerably alarmed Meinertzhagen. But he could not deny their courage, or its cost: nineteen months after their arrival only sixty of the original 1,166 'Boozaliers' were left alive. The legendary Selous himself fell at Behobeho on 4 January 1917.

*　　*　　*

The success at Bukoba briefly raised morale, as did the sinking of the *Königsberg* in the Rufiji Delta in July and the replacement of Old Wappy by General Mickey Tighe. Tighe was a 'thruster' who referred to all Germans as 'sausage-makers'.[27] At last it seemed to the 10,000 troops in the Protectorate that they were commanded by a man who, despite a pronounced penchant for the odd tipple, was worthy of their respect. This was all the more important since Belfield, according to Meinertzhagen, had taken to spending his war sea-fishing off Mombasa. Tighe insisted that what was needed was some great event to rouse the settlers once again, and to galvanize everyone – official, soldier and settler alike – into a unified and effective fighting force. Once again Meinertzhagen called on Grogan's services: he knew that if anyone could whip the Protectorate into a patriotic frenzy it was Grogan, the Protectorate's master orator – and master of theatricality.

Grogan obligingly returned to the soap-box as only he could. On 7 September 1915 Nairobi's Theatre Royal was packed out for what the newspapers subsequently called 'the greatest meeting in the history of British East Africa'. The evening began with a stirring performance from the orchestra and the singing of patriotic songs. Then Grogan, immaculate in his captain's uniform, rose to his feet. The cheer from the 1,500-strong audience was deafening, and it was many minutes before he could start his hour-long call-to-arms (delivered, as was his wont, without the assistance of a single note).

Grogan began with a resumé of the war. He fulsomely praised the 'magnificent work' being done by fellow colonists from Australia, New Zealand, Canada and South Africa – which brought further cheers – and reminded his audience that the conflict in East Africa was 'but a small part' of the whole. Many in the Protectorate, he declared, had done what was expected of them, whereupon he singled out the exemplary bravery and loyalty of the African soldiers. But there were many, he added, fixing on his audience a rapier-like gaze, who had not. There were settlers who were 'chaffering in the market, dodging about attending to twopenny-halfpenny bits of business and thinking of *shambas*' instead of fighting, and there were officials happily tending their gardens and playing tennis on the Hill while continuing to draw salaries far in excess of the bob a day to which enlisted men were entitled. It was possible, Grogan mocked, 'to walk into any club and see half a dozen men between twenty and twenty-five passively reclining in chairs with illustrated papers on their knees', and he poured scorn on the Public Works Department, accusing it of doing nothing to help anyone at the front. Given this situation, in which so many were behaving like 'white rabbits', he asked whether it was any wonder that Bonar Law, leader of the Unionist party and the Secretary of State for Colonies in Lloyd George's coalition cabinet, had pointed out that British East Africa was the only protectorate in the Empire that had called on outside help. This deplorable state of affairs, thundered Grogan, had to change.

His rebuke was received with ecstatic acclaim. Then, carrying the crowd with him, Grogan turned to exhortation. It was time for everyone to realize that 'these were times of war, war – red war; not games'. *Everyone*, he stressed, had to be prepared to assume responsibility for some part of the war effort. Conscription had to be imposed, Provincial Commissioners had to help run the farms of absent farmers, and women had to play their part to the full since it was well known that they were indispensable 'if you want anything well done'. In short, it was time for sacrifice by all. He gestured to the chairman of the meeting, Northrup McMillan, and pointed out that he had offered Chiromo – which he had leased from Grogan – as well as his farm at Juja for use as hospitals; Grogan declared that he was ready to follow this magnificent example by offering his estate at Turi as a camp for women and children.

Grogan saved the most emotional appeal for his finale: he asked everyone to realize that they were facing the 'ultimate challenge', and to ensure that 'when the history of the war comes to be written and the children ask "what did your Daddy do in the war?", let no man shrink from having the question asked. When we pass on our account of what we have done, let us be sure the answer from home will be "Well done thou babe of Empire."' With that, he stood down.

It was several minutes before the clapping, hollering, and stamping of feet abated, causing Mr Radley, the manager of the Theatre Royal, to worry that the roof might cave in. The meeting was then thrown open to the audience. Mr Narayandass rose to his feet and expressed the support of the Indian community for Grogan's speech, and an affirmation of loyalty from the Goan community – of which Grogan was an ardent supporter – was offered by J. M. Campos. The latter was deemed by the audience to be rather more genuine than the former, since Indians had left the country in droves since the outbreak of hostilities. Russell Bowker, plain-speaking as ever and soon to die in the field, of double pneumonia, answered on behalf of the settlers and declared that it was indeed time to 'shoot straight and stick together'.[28] Three cheers were given to Grogan and, with a rousing rendition of the National Anthem, the meeting drew to a close. That same evening Meinertzhagen wrote in his diary: 'I look on this moment as being the turning point in the history of British East Africa. The colony has found itself.'[29] Many years later, after Churchill's famous exhortations during World War II, old men and women in the colony would look back to that night in the Theatre Royal and respectfully bestow upon Grogan the title of 'Kenya's Churchill'.

Only one dissenting voice was heard. In the local government's Secretariat lurked a very bright 'little freak' by the name of W. J. Monson. A languid and sardonic old Etonian, his principal pastime was penning poems poking fun at others from the safety of an armchair in the Nairobi Club. In attacking Grogan's call-to-arms, however, he badly misjudged the country's mood. Belfield remarked that it was 'a pity that Monson is not man enough to wear the King's uniform when his country is at war',[30] and General Tighe wanted him shot, or at least deported. Grogan had other ideas. He explained to his commanding officer that 'as one sometimes finds with sedentary civil servants, Monson's soul is jaundiced, possibly due to a lack of exercise and a traditional dislike of anything factually positive',[31] and he asked Tighe to let him deal with Monson himself. Tighe agreed.

Grogan's response was to write a devastating open letter to Monson, informing him that 'what may be pardonable and even welcome impertinence in youth may, in middle age, be deemed mere flatulence', and advising him to 'take the next chance . . . of making direct contact with the world, and after a while come back to us . . . maybe a useful civil servant'.[32] The letter was distributed throughout the country by Tighe's staff and, to Grogan's great satisfaction, 'Monsoon' 'ceased to appear at any party where a member of the forces was likely to be present'[33] for the duration of the war.

For once, the response of the local government to Grogan's accusa-

tions of inactivity was swift and positive. Belfield immediately summoned Grogan and Northrup McMillan for talks, and one week after
the meeting in the Theatre Royal he agreed to their demands for a
War Council and conscription.³⁴ The War Council was an immensely
powerful body, chaired by Charles Bowring and empowered to rule
virtually by *diktat*. Meeting daily and passing resolutions at the rate
of more than one a day, it comprised three officials, two soldiers and
three unofficials: Grogan, Northrup McMillan and J. J. Toogood, the
general manager of the Standard Bank. All civilians, men and women
alike, were immediately registered by the Council and sent to the
front or designated essential jobs, and a great deal of attention was
devoted to longer-term measures like drawing up the blueprints for
an ambitious programme of infrastructure development and a scheme
to attract demobbed soldiers to settle in the country when the war
was over. At last it seemed to Grogan that the country was being run
in a proactive manner with proper settler representation, and that the
Protectorate was being seen to do the right thing by the mother
country.

For three months Grogan remained in Nairobi, devoting his full attention to Council business. As he was again chronically short of cash he
took up residence in a cottage at Muthaiga Club and sold Chiromo
to Northrup McMillan 'to the temporary relief of my bank manager
and the welcome reinforcement of the provendor which I had managed
to send to my family in England'.³⁵ Northrup McMillan could count
on a secure income of £70,000 per annum and regarded it as part of
his war duty to help out Grogan, whom he nicknamed 'Tommy', as
the embodiment of British fighting spirit.

By Christmas 1915, Grogan received news that his services were
once again required elsewhere. Kitchener and the Imperial General
Staff were casting about for any front which offered the possibility of
a morale-boosting victory and, in the wake of the Dardanelles fiasco,
their attention alighted on East Africa. Sir Horace Smith-Dorrien,

veteran of the Zulu War of 1879, Omdurman and the Boer War was quickly appointed to lead a new offensive against von Lettow's forces, but the East Africa High Command knew that such an offensive could only succeed if the co-operation of the Belgians was guaranteed. So Grogan, now promoted to Major, set off once again for Uganda to secure it.

Grogan's base in Entebbe was Government House, placed at his disposal by Frederick Jackson, who thoroughly enjoyed the company of his one-time sparring partner. Both men, in Jackson's words, 'loved Africa for itself, its vastness and its free life . . . [and] the call of the wild'; they also shared a passion for ornithology, and took regular birding walks together during Grogan's 'rests between battlings to keep the peace'[36] with the Belgians. After much to-ing and fro-ing, in February 1916 Grogan finally managed to arrange a meeting between Jackson and the Belgian High Command in a remote valley outside Entebbe. The location had to be secret, not only because of German spies in Entebbe but also because Uganda was regarded by both sides as being uninvolved in the conflict. At the meeting Jackson offered to provide arms, equipment, medical back-up, food and transport for the Belgians – provided they made no territorial claims at the end of the war. The Belgians agreed to Jackson's terms, and preparations began for their advance into German East Africa.

Grogan was instrumental in these preparations. He brought in Oulton, an old friend from the Potteries who had been persuaded by him to settle near Northrup McMillan's farm at Juja, to drive a telegraph line from Uganda to the Congo border. This he succeeded in doing in record time, and earned the Military Cross for his achievement. Grogan's Equator Saw Mills built, free of charge, 100 huge carts for the Belgians as 'relying on human porterage alone through a foodless area was impossible unless the *askaris* at the extremity of the chain ate the porters'. Other friends were also co-opted to help Grogan. Among them were Trevor Sheen, an Irish farmer from Njoro, who was given the task of training Ankole oxen to pull Grogan's carts, and the highly respected and resourceful Donald Seth-Smith, who had already won the Military Cross at Longido and who further developed Grogan's intelligence network. As important a task as any in these months of feverish activity was Grogan's instruction to keep General

Sir Charles Crewet, 'a Natal journalist with the rank of general'[37] whom Grogan and everyone else disliked intensely, well away from the Belgians lest they renege on their agreement. All the while Grogan busied hither and thither on foot or, where possible, in a much-loved 'Tin Lizzie' – a Model T Ford, with the registration number 404.

To the west in BEA the preparations were no less frantic. Smith-Dorrien fell ill before arriving to take command, so the baton passed to an equally illustrious soldier – and former enemy of the Empire – the fearless Jan Smuts, known to all as '*ons Jan*' (our Jan) or '*slim* Janie' (cunning Janie). Although much of the credit for the six-month military build-up lay with the bibulous Tighe, the contribution of the forces of the Union of South Africa over the next two years was decisive. With Smuts's arrival, fresh from putting down a Boer rebellion led by De La Rey and de Wet, then forcing the surrender of German South-West Africa, the course of the war would start to turn. He was, in Grogan's opinion, the 'catalyst', who ensured that 'the muddied waters crystallised into some sort of war purpose'.[38] The 'natural simplicity . . . and ruthless determination' of his old, and much-admired Cambridge contemporary Grogan found 'a striking contrast with the mannerisms of the British regular officer'.[39]

Bedevilled in its latter stages by torrential rain, disease and starvation, the huge offensive began in early 1916. Smuts's South Africans were instrumental in finally dislodging the Germans from their strategic stronghold in the Taveta Gap in March; Moshi and the Tanga–Taveta railway were captured soon afterwards and the process of sweeping the Usambara mountains began. By July, von Lettow was forced to withdraw first to Kondoa Irangi and then Dodoma – but he was still far from defeated. His aim at the outset had been to occupy as many Imperial troops as possible with a force of just 2,000 white troops and 14,000 African *askaris*. That remained his intention, but his enemy was growing more powerful by the month: at the peak of the offensive the Imperial force comprised over 30,000 troops in three field divisions, two of them South African, supported by 190,000 African porters of the East Africa Carrier Corps. Against such opposition his 'tip and run' guerrilla tactics became increasingly hazardous, and digging in anywhere for too long was to court disaster.

At last the day came for the Belgians to advance as well, and with the benefit of Grogan's carts, maps and logistical preparations they did so at lightning speed. Covering between twenty and thirty miles a day they crossed the Kagera river and soon reached Biharamulo inside German East Africa. A small German force retreated before them, and on entering the town Grogan discovered an explanation for the ease of their advance: abandoned German staff records referred to a number of soldiers as being 'missing, believed eaten'. Such was the reputation of the Belgians' Manyema soldiers. Mwanza was captured next, then the Belgians turned south and the race with General Crewe's own force for Tabora, the seat of government, was on.

As Grogan had always feared, Tombeur – the Belgian general who had replaced Henry – and Crewe bickered continuously after linking up at Mwanza. At one point Grogan even had to call in Jackson to broker a truce between the two men. After that, exhausted and sick, he returned to Nairobi for a rest. Much to his personal satisfaction Tombeur won the race to Tabora, reaching German East Africa's second most important town after Dar-es-Salaam on 19 September 1916. General Northey advanced simultaneously from Nyasaland, capturing Iringa in August, and with this successful thrust two-thirds of the country was nominally in the hands of the Allies. As Grogan put it, 'the first, more important phase of the campaign was coming to a close and we were entering the last, desultory phase of clearing up'.[40]

The clearing up was to last two years. After a four-month lull in the fighting in early 1917, caused by the worst rains in living memory, detachments of von Lettow's army fought yet another heroic rearguard action. Although vastly outnumbered, the indefatigable Prussian general relied on his extraordinary resourcefulness, his ferociously loyal African troops, and the ten huge guns salvaged from the *Königsberg* before it was sunk in 1915 – each of which required manning by a team of 400 porters.

After he had recuperated Grogan returned to active duty in his capacity as, in the words of one of his superiors, 'the one who got things done, but suffered fools not gladly'.[41] Early in 1917 he and Northrup McMillan, who although an American citizen received the DSO and was knighted for his war service, were sent on a mission to collect abandoned enemy supplies along the Tanga–Taveta railway.

Then, after Smuts had been summoned to Europe to attend the Imperial War Conference and General Hoskins had assumed overall command, the latter called Grogan to Dar-es-Salaam. There he was informed that once again Belgian co-operation was faltering and that a flattering condition of their continued support was Grogan's return as liaison officer.

Grogan embarked on the hazardous journey across German East Africa 'in a train marked bait',[42] but arrived safely at Ujiji to rendezvous with General Huyghe. There, on the shores of Lake Tanganyika, were most of his carts from the first Belgian offensive – still in working order, and Huyghe, charmed by Grogan, soon agreed to embark on what turned into a 1,600-mile pursuit round the north of the country of one of von Lettow's columns, led by Captain Heinrich Naumann. Naumann and his fourteen officers, 115 *askaris* and 250 porters eventually capitulated on 17 October, thus removing a lethal arrow from von Lettow's quiver.

Grogan's final assignment of the war was to join the staff of the giant General Jacob van Deventer, who succeeded Hoskins, at Lindi. This was a task he greatly enjoyed. He regarded 'Van Splosh', a dyed-in-the-wool Boer and formidable fighter, as a 'splendid specimen of humanity'[43] and although the South African's English was limited the two men often sat up late at night chatting about the finer points of farming.

Responsibility for the final pursuit of the Germans fell to van Deventer. By the end of 1917 von Lettow had been driven across the Rovuma river into Portuguese East Africa, but once there he promptly captured large quantities of arms and supplies and resolved to carry on the fight. For a whole year von Lettow and his dwindling band avoided capture, always keeping one step ahead of van Deventer's troops. From Portuguese East Africa he re-entered German East Africa and marched through Songea, round the north end of Lake Nyasa, and 'invaded' Northern Rhodesia. When Armistice was declared he was craftily considering whether to strike out for the Atlantic, 1,300 miles to the west, or to go and blow up the Belgian copper mines in Katanga, and did not receive news of the German surrender until two days later.

On 25 November, eleven days after Grogan delivered a moving

address to an open service of Thanksgiving in Nairobi, von Lettow formally surrendered at Abercorn. His survivors – thirty officers, 125 white troops and 1,165 *askaris* – lined up, saluted the British flag and were called upon to lay down their arms. Van Deventer had, however, issued explicit instructions that von Lettow himself and his German officers should be allowed to retain their weapons as a mark of respect to this most remarkable guerrilla army.[44]

After four years of combat the Allied casualty list was a long one: 976 officers and 17,650 men were killed; and 44,572 African porters out of a total of 261,000 who had become embroiled in the so-called 'white man's war' had died. Of the 2,321 settlers of fighting age two thirds had seen active service. The 'babe of Empire', stirred into action at a crucial juncture by Grogan, had thus – eventually – played its part and its efforts were accorded full recognition by Smuts. In a speech to the Royal Geographical Society in January 1918 he declared that 'in the story of human endurance this campaign deserves a very special place, and the heroes who went through it uncomplainingly, doggedly, are entitled to all recognition and reverence. Their commander-in-chief will remain eternally proud of them.'

Of many lasting memories of the war two left a particularly deep impression on Grogan. The first was of spending a few days with Selous, his fellow veteran of the Matabele campaign and 'modest, entrancing raconteur of his life of romance and constructive endeavour'. When Grogan saw him off to the front the sixty-six-year-old Selous turned to him and said, with a smile, 'Old friend, I am beginning to feel my age.'[45] Just days later he was dead.

The second was of a torchlight march-past by Huyghe's troops on the shore of Lake Tanganyika, organized by the Belgian general to raise morale amongst his men:

> It was a dark night, and we took our stand midway to take the salute. In the rising dust and smoky glare of the torches the impression was of some immense, half-seen submarine monster coming out of the depths. Except for an occasional word of command there was no other sound other than . . . the soft pad, in perfect unison, of thousands of naked feet. The only clearly visible feature of this monster was the

glaring white eyeballs and glistening white teeth as it passed the saluting point. I was stirred to the depths.[46]

Grogan was greatly, if paternalistically, concerned about the effect that the war had had on Africa – a concern shared by Smuts when he declared to the Royal Geographical Society its likely consequence was that 'tropical Africa [would become] one of the great problems of future world politics'.[47] Not only had it involved 'the slaughter of the innocents . . . [and] the fall of the mighty', and provided the 'creative factors of World War number two',[48] but, most importantly in Grogan's opinion, it had fatally exposed the fallibility of the colonial powers.

Grogan refused to accept a single penny for his services during the war: he never pushed for repayment of considerable disbursements or even drew the pay to which he was entitled as a volunteer. It was a characteristic display of idiosyncrasy, or what his brother Quentin called 'bees in his bonnet', and he stuck to his principle even though the personal cost of fulfilling his duty was enormous. The war had virtually bankrupted Equator Saw Mills, and his many other business interests, on the verge of lift-off at the start of the war, lay – like the Protectorate's economy – in tatters; it would take him six years of battle and persistent worry before he restored a semblance of order to his financial affairs. Ruination faced many a settler returned home from the front, but Grogan believed that any money owed to him was better spent rebuilding the Protectorate than making a small dent in his gargantuan overdraft. He did, however, receive two mentions in despatches and the DSO;[49] the Belgians also conferred upon him the title of Officer of the Order of Leopold which, he remarked in a wry and self-deprecating manner, 'entitled me to free travel on the Belgian railways'.[50]

He had also suffered physically. Although over twenty years younger than Selous when he marched off to battle for the last time, and younger than von Lettow, he was nevertheless only three weeks short of his forty-fourth birthday when the war ended; and his time in the bush had triggered recurrent bouts of malaria. Twice the malaria developed into blackwater fever, usually a fatal condition, and saw him hospitalized. But he had survived those ordeals just as he had survived several brushes with death in hand-to-hand combat while attached to the Belgian army. Whatever criticisms were levelled at him in his life, no one ever sought to deny that he was a man of immense physical and mental strength.

In the spring of 1919 'Tommy' Grogan boarded a troop ship home. At Southampton he shared the experience of many returning from the war: there was no flag-waving, no band, and no cheering crowd. Just 'the soft tone of the south English porters saying "this way, gentlemen, for the London troop train."'[51]

Grogan devoted fully one sixth of his memoirs to the four years of war. Those he deemed incompetent or unpatriotic he belittled with acerbic wit, but he accorded fulsome praise to those, like Northrup McMillan and Selous, whom he deemed to have 'played the game'. After the war he gave the largest individual contribution to a fund formed to present Smuts with a Sword of Honour; and he was on the Committee for the Selous Memorial. Reading his account of events it is clear that, above all, he *enjoyed* the war despite its terrible hardships.

His war service, and in particular his performance at the Theatre Royal, provided further proof that he was a man temperamentally best suited to emergencies. He revelled in the freedom of his role as a lone operator charged with missions that he, and those commanders like Smuts whom he respected, regarded as being of the utmost importance to the war effort; and he revelled in being back in the African bush for prolonged periods, far from what others called the 'civilized' world. While perfectly at home in London's clubland, there would always be a part of him that was most content when sitting by the camp fire with a Manyema sergeant.

As he stepped off the train in London he looked like the same old Grogan. Flecks of grey had appeared in his jet-black hair, and he was a little leaner, but his eyes still shone as keenly as ever. In character he was also much the same. A single, insightful, piece of evidence demonstrates this beyond a shadow of doubt. In September 1918 one Nora Strange wrote a satirical play for performance in Nairobi in aid of the Star & Garter Hospital Appeal. It was entitled 'Potted Personalities: A Masque of Modern Nairobi'. Chief among the six characters were 'Lord D-L-M-R' (representing 'landed interests') and 'E.S.G.' (representing 'politics'). The narrator introduced E.S.G. as

> an arresting personality, one with vast visions of empire, restricted and hampered by non elasticity of purse. A man who finds on occasion a difficulty in reconciling the Dream and the Business. An orator of no mean eloquence . . . Possesses in common with women a Sixth Sense, and is gifted with a great charm of manner, which at times is marred by his adoption of an attitude of intimidation. He is capable of great generosity, even of self-sacrifice, provided the cause or individual stimulates the imagination. He takes his relaxation in the formation of companies, the promoting of which he leaves to others, and in the giving of children's parties, the arranging of which he keeps entirely in his own hands. If he has one prejudice, it is the existing Government of British East Africa.[52]

But, although his character had not fundamentally altered, he was unrecognizable to his children with whom he 'renewed . . . acquaintance'[53] after five years apart. During his absence *they* had changed: with the exception of eight-year-old Jane they were no longer little children, of whom he was so enamoured. The 'Daddy' who had left them was frozen in their imaginations as a conjuror, artist, mimic, story-teller, party-giver and purveyor of chocolates, but the one who returned treated the older girls as young women, and expected them to behave as such. This change in their relationship with their father was traumatic for the girls, and as adults they arguably never really came to terms with it. In later life they described Grogan's behaviour at this time as 'very odd', and often intimidating. Cynthia was wont to cite a story about her father having likened her to a tapir at a lunch party, which reduced her to tears. There were even suspicions that he had a nervous breakdown, the evidence for this being dim memories of an incident in which Grogan drove off in his Model T Ford, stopped in the middle of London, and told a policeman that he could go no further.

By no stretch of the imagination can Grogan have been an easy father to teenage (as opposed to preteen) children, but such recollections reveal as much about the children – and what was to happen in their own lives – as they do about Grogan. For example, Cynthia was very sensitive, the least robust of the four girls, and saw only cruelty in what were otherwise recognized by long-suffering government officials and business associates as typical Groganesque quips. As for the 'driving incident' there is a rational explanation for this, of which either the girls were not aware or which they simply chose to ignore. Model T Fords – 'Tin Lizzies' – of the period were prone to a sudden electrification of their whole body, and this is precisely what happened to Grogan one day as he motored under Admiralty Arch towards Trafalgar Square. It was his being 'allergic to, and suspicious of, every active form of electrical phenomena'[54] that caused him to abandon the vehicle – not a nervous breakdown.

To revert to the picture of Grogan painted in other sections of Nora Strange's satire, what the children were having to come to terms with – with mixed results – was Grogan in the round. As little children they had only known his 'great charm of manner', 'great generosity', 'gentleness' and 'Groganesque smile'. Now they received a startling introduction to the 'basilisk stares', a sometimes 'intimidating manner' and 'expression of ogrishness' as well, and they experienced a growing realization – be it conscious or subconscious – that they no longer 'stimulated his imagination' as much as clearing 'vast primeval forest', making 'desert tracts habitable' or turning 'neglected creeks into busy ports'.[55] Each girl also grew up with the uncomfortable knowledge that one of them 'ought' to have been a boy; none of them could match their father's encyclopaedic knowledge of politics, economics, business or current affairs; and none would in any way match their father's great fame. By – or perhaps because of – their father's standards, the girls were just ordinary mortals, and as such 'management' of them came to be delegated entirely to Gertrude.

Unlike her daughters, Gertrude had no difficulty recognizing her returning husband. She had always known that the man she loved with a passion – and would always love – was far from normal in the first place. After all, it was hardly normal for a man to trek from Cape to Cairo to win the hand of his beloved. He *may* have been a little more strident, a little more hard-edged, than when they had parted, but as a supremely understanding wife and mother that was nothing more than she expected. He had fought a war, brushed with death on several occasions, and was in severe financial difficulties. Gertrude knew that such challenges were her husband's lifeblood, and regarded her role as one of providing support and a much-needed 'grounding influence'.

If recognition was no problem for her, it soon became clear – as it did for millions of wives whose husbands returned from the war – that the nature of their partnership had changed forever during their five-year separation. Gertrude, like her children, had been robbed of the Grogan she had known, but in a different way and for a different reason. Through no fault of her own, but due to the vagaries of European politics, she had fallen foul of the old Victorian adage that said that a lady could let almost anyone look after her children, but that no one else must look after her husband.

Soon after Grogan's return in May, 1919 Gertrude's niece, seven-teen-year-old Gertrude Lowry, came to stay at Draycott Place. She remembers the huge elephant tusks framing a mirror in the entrance hall; that everyone always dressed for dinner; that Grogan had 'perfect manners', and that he was 'the most handsome man [she had] ever seen'. At the time she also suspected that 'he would not do right by Gertrude, as extremely handsome men never treat their ladies well',[56] and she was absolutely right. It soon emerged that Grogan had had at least two wartime affairs, both with nurses. One of them, the widowed Doris Tate-Smith,[57] sixteen years Grogan's junior, had looked after him in Muthaiga Club during one of his attacks of black-water fever. Gentle, kind Gertrude could no doubt have borne such news with magnanimity if that had been the end of the matter. After all she, more than anyone, must have known that her husband, as his friend Ernest Rutherfoord and others used to put it, was 'over-engined'. But it did not end there. In the spring of 1918 Doris sailed home to England knowing that she was pregnant. On board ship she suffered a miscarriage, but soon discovered that she had been carrying twins and that one child – the 'gritty Grogan' in the words of that child – would reach full term.

Grogan faced the problem head on, as he faced every problem. One day he came home to Draycott Place with Doris, and introduced her to Gertrude as 'the lady who is going to have my baby'. Gertrude took to bed for a week in shock, and her children never forgot her hysterical crying. But when the baby girl was born, with hazel eyes every bit as piercing as her father's, Gertrude visited mother and child in hospital in Chelsea. It was a remarkable act of acceptance on the part of the woman who paid the highest price for *bwana chui*'s war.

EIGHTEEN

'Boldest and Baddest of a Bold Bad Gang'

WITHIN WEEKS of returning to England Grogan was summoned to the Colonial Office by the Under-Secretary of State for Colonies, Leo Amery, and informed that Lord Milner had requested his presence as the special adviser on African boundary questions at the Paris Peace Conference. So Grogan hot-footed it across the Channel to rejoin the man for whom he had worked in South Africa fourteen years earlier.

The presence of arch-imperialists Milner and Amery in government attests to the changes wrought by war on the political map of Britain. Grogan's suspicions about the Liberal government's inability to translate words into deeds seemed to have been proved correct, and as early as 1915 public opinion had started to swing decisively against Asquith. The 'Shell Scandal', concerning the government's failure to produce enough artillery shells for the Western Front, seriously undermined his authority and its effect was compounded by the disastrous Dardanelles offensive, the government's impotence in the face of numerous labour disputes, and – to Grogan's great annoyance – its failure to avert civil strife in Ireland. To all intents and purposes it appeared as though the Liberals were simply incapable of coping with national crisis, and Asquith was forced to enter into a coalition with the Conservatives.

In December 1916 Lloyd George – the 'Goat' – ousted Asquith, and by then the influence of what Grogan considered to be the Empire's 'natural party of leadership' was growing steadily. Tariff Reform, forcefully advocated by Conservative leader Bonar Law, was once again back on the political agenda; and, as if to put in bold letters their resurgent fortunes, the Conservatives demanded Churchill's scalp. Churchill was forced out of the Admiralty and the War Cabinet, and ended up as Chancellor of the Duchy of Lancaster, the erstwhile employer of Grogan's father.

Yet Churchill the master politician was no sooner down and out than he began his climb back. For all his 'treachery' in leaving the Conservative Party he had been undeniably successful in readying the fleet for war, and during his political exile he served in the field with fearless distinction. By 1917 he was once again in government as Lloyd George's Minister of Munitions, and, as irrepressible as a rubber ball, he began his climb back to power with whoever would get him there – which would ultimately prove to be the Conservative Party.

On arrival in Paris Grogan was reunited with many old faces. His best man, William Hayes Sadler, was *major domo* of the British delegation and Grogan was allotted the suite adjoining Milner's in the Hotel Majestic. Such preferential treatment, and the fact that Milner made it quite clear that Grogan was to be his eyes and ears when it came to African matters, naturally caused ructions with the Colonial Office. But Sir Herbert Read, described by Grogan as 'that amiable and antediluvian denizen of the CO',[1] had to lump it: Milner had no desire to risk a disproportionate involvement on the part of his civil servants in negotiations that he regarded as being of the utmost importance to the future of the Empire.

Over the next few months Grogan underwent what even he called 'an astounding [education] in how the great international affairs of state are adjusted'.[2] At one point, when Lloyd George was considering ceding Jubaland – 25,000 square miles of today's southern Somalia – to the Italians, Milner asked Grogan 'where is it, and has it any significance?' 'Thus,' remarked Grogan, 'are empires made and unmade.' On another occasion, determined to put the wind up Sir Herbert Read, Milner told Grogan, 'I suppose I shall have to sacrifice one of our little colonies.'[3] The victim was Mauritius, which had been a British naval base since Nelson's time.

Grogan's main task was to prepare a memorandum on the Congo Basin Treaties for Smuts and Botha, whose respective 'sheer force of personality' and 'irresistible personal charm' dominated the scene in Paris and, in Grogan's opinion, made a mockery of the 'tragically weak'[4] Colonial Office team. In his memorandum he made a compelling case

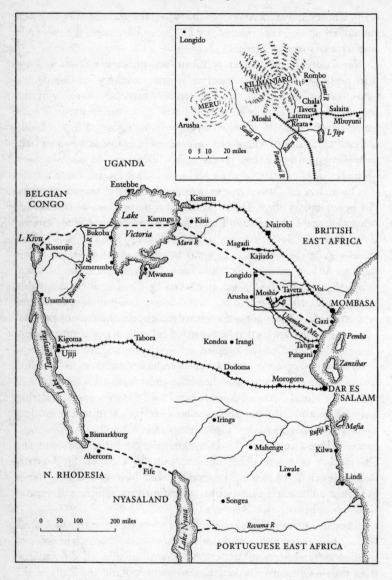

East African Theatre of War, 1914–1918

for a free-trade area comprising the Union of South Africa, Rhodesia, German and British East Africa, and Uganda; and he was instrumental, with fellow delegate Meinertzhagen's support, in persuading Lloyd George to turn down a suggestion that German East Africa be turned into a 'receptacle for the overflow of the population of India'. His reasons were the same as ever: 'my contention', he wrote, 'is that it would be a disaster for the Africans; that the function of whites and blacks in tropical Africa is 99% complementary and not competitive; whereas the part played by the Asian is competitive with both – preventing the whites from expanding and the blacks from rising in the economic sphere'.[5]

Grogan's greatest regret, on the other hand, was that he failed to prevent the former German colonies, Ruanda and Urundi, being placed under Belgian trusteeship. This was in direct contravention of the agreement he had brokered between the Belgians and Jackson in the valley outside Entebbe, and he was convinced that it would lead to misery for the African population of those two territories. However useful the Belgian contribution had been to the war effort in East Africa, Grogan could not forget the horrors inflicted on the people of the Congo by Leopold's henchmen, and he warned Milner that in Ruanda 'Billygee, the native name for the Belgians, is the synonym for Bogeyman. Mothers use it to horrify their babes.'[6] Politicking prevailed, and against his better judgement Grogan was instructed to draft the new treaty.

Although the peace negotiations, collectively embodied in the Treaty of Versailles, rumbled on into 1920 Grogan stayed in Paris just long enough to see the African questions settled. Whatever the cost to the Empire in lives and in hard cash, he believed there were good grounds for optimism: Milner and Amery were exercising a controlling influence on colonial affairs, and with a few strokes of the pen the Empire increased in size by almost one million square miles. In no time his thoughts therefore returned to the reconstruction of British East Africa where, as he put it, 'the settler's foot, a bit crushed perhaps, [was] still in the door'.[7]

Even before the fighting in East Africa was over Grogan had resumed, with redoubled vigour, his political crusade. Indeed in post-war colonial politics the name Grogan became ever more synonymous with controversy. This bothered him not one jot: he saw no room for sentimentality in his fight to establish the Protectorate as a country with an economy that was the envy of all in Africa – including her colonial cousin, Smuts's auriferous South Africa.

This remained an uphill task, as the war had left the colony bankrupt. As Grogan put it, the country's finances had 'sunk to a state where the tape worm (the railway) and the ticks (the Civil Service) were glaring at each other with bared teeth through the diaphanous film (the farmers) which had once been their host'.[8] In 1919–20 the Protectorate's expenditure exceeded revenue by a colossal £0.5m; less than 200,000 acres of the land occupied by European settlers, many of whom had had to start again from scratch, was being cultivated; and the British Treasury was not prepared to consider a grant to bail out the country's finances. In many ways it seemed to Grogan that the settlers, having rightly or wrongly been encouraged by Sir Charles Eliot to make East Africa their home, were being abandoned to an impecunious fate by the British government.

On the political scene, by contrast, the formation of the War Council had imbued Grogan with a degree of optimism. Its authority was almost as great as that of a Chartered Company and it was vested with a remarkable degree of autonomy by the Colonial Office. Resolutions were discussed and rapidly implemented by a small group of men whom Grogan regarded as qualified, without the interference of civil servants. It was just the sort of body, reminiscent of Milner's Kindergarten, that he considered appropriate for the administration of African colonies both in war- and peace-time, but in his opinion its constitution had one important flaw. It provided for the election, rather than nomination, of its settler members. Furthermore, the British government had agreed to the principle of post-war elections in which the settlers were to compete for ten (later increased to eleven) seats in an enlarged Legislative Council.

Grogan was extremely sceptical about the merits of an elective system, for many reasons. As early as 1914 he had written to his friend George Lloyd, observing that 'the diffused nature of the community

. . . means that political dominance [following any elections] will surely fall to the townee toughs who have facilities in the local bars for meeting and combining'. A rabble of independent-minded frontiersmen, however, could be controlled and Grogan was a past master at so doing. What he was more alarmed about was that elections would increase 'the risk of the Indian vote being established' given 'the present position in India',[9] where the nationalist cause grew stronger by the month. As the Indian population outnumbered the settlers by a considerable margin the grant of equal voting rights to the former would, Grogan realized sooner than anyone else in the Protectorate, mean that the latter were consigned to political – and possibly economic – oblivion.

Soon after Belfield retired as governor in April 1917 Grogan had initiated a behind-the-scenes campaign to ensure that seats on the new, enlarged Legislative Council would be allocated by interest group. 'One value, one vote' (as opposed to one man, one vote) was the maxim he used in an open letter to the *Leader* written while he was on active service in German East Africa at the end of 1917. A month later, having returned to Nairobi, he followed this up by organizing a mass meeting to call for the appointment of a military governor, preferably Girouard. Grogan's objective is clear: he was seeking to ensure the country was ruled by an autocratic government of 'national reconstruction' as opposed to some 'tin-pot' parliament. Not surprisingly, Lord Delamere agreed with this strategy, and the settlers who attended the Nairobi meeting appointed a committee under his chairmanship which sent telegrams forcibly stating the case for a military governor to Prime Minister Lloyd George. Smuts, who was regarded as East Africa's saviour during the war, was also approached for support.

Grogan's friend – and Acting Governor – Bowring was livid at this political manoeuvring, which he regarded as undermining his authority. In one confidential despatch to the Colonial Office he wrote in exasperation: 'Grogan is a man of considerable gifts, [but he] combines a colossal egotism with a passion for political intrigue. A fluent speaker, he is never happy off the platform. To speak colloquially, he must always be in the limelight.' The affable and bumbling new head of the East Africa Department, Sir Cecil Bottomley, noted in the margin of Bowring's despatch: 'Major Grogan has been a thorn in the side of the local government for many years', and added nervously, 'he may be a megalomaniac'.[10]

Bowring briefly considered disbanding the War Council, on which Grogan sat, in an effort to control him. But Grogan countered him by buying the *East African Standard* in partnership with Delamere and Northrup Macmillan and thereby ensured the loyalty of the most influential organ of the local press. By the end of the war the political situation in the Protectorate was so explosive that the Colonial Office, after twelve months of pencil-chewing, decided to take action by appointing Major-General Sir Edward Northey as Belfield's successor.

The logic behind this decision was that a 'strongman' was needed to reassert control over Grogan and Delamere after a twenty-two month interregnum in which they had seemingly been allowed to run amok. Northey was a Khyber Pass veteran, and had commanded the 2nd KAR and other battalions in Nyasaland and Northern Rhodesia during the war. But he was also very much his own man, and within months demonstrated that Whitehall's civil servants had shot themselves in the foot every bit as much as they had done when they had appointed Girouard as governor.

The tall, long-necked and moustachioed Northey arrived in East Africa in January 1919. Pending the inauguration of the newly elected Legislative Council, Grogan's 'Big Noise' – the Convention of Associations – had reconvened; and, as its president, Grogan was nominated to deliver the main speech at Northey's welcome dinner. Describing himself as usual as 'the boldest and baddest of a bold bad gang', Grogan had something very combustible up his sleeve for Northey.

Delamere's biographer claimed that Northey was 'greeted warmly by the settlers',[11] which he was if ordeal by fire is synonymous with warm. The Grogan who delivered the speech was the Grogan of the Nairobi Incident, not the Grogan of the universally acclaimed Potteries campaigns of 1910, or of the great call-to-arms of 1915. He was humorous, certainly, but his humour was barbed and the twinkle in his eye was steely. From the outset he demanded to know whether Northey was just another Colonial Office 'telephone girl',[12] and for fully two hours he subjected the new governor to a grilling in what he well knew to be the most public of fora.

In East Africa his diatribe was lauded by the settlers. The odd dissenting voice was heard to criticize Grogan's usually impeccable manners for giving such a 'warm' welcome to Northey, but such dissent was the exception rather than the rule. Back in Britain, on the other hand, the Aborigine Protection Society accused him of delivering a 'barbaric ultimatum'[13] on the increasingly vexed question of whether the African population should, or shouldn't, have to provide sufficient labour to help kick-start the post-war economy; and both the India Office and the Colonial Office were alarmed by his demands for a lasting solution to the 'Indian Question'. His words were also referred to in the House of Lords as nothing less than a 'violent and insolent tirade',[14] indicating that he had either badly misjudged the situation or knew exactly what he was doing.

Northey himself showed that he was up to Grogan's challenge. He sat out the two-hour rant with true military insouciance, before rising to his feet to thank 'the gallant and talkative Major' for his welcome and declare that from now on he would look upon Grogan as his 'godfather'.[15] In double-quick time he also ruled that Indian 'agitators' would not be granted equal representation in the new elected Legislative Council, and that two settlers were to be included in his Executive Council, or cabinet, with immediate effect. Northey's response to Grogan's 'tirade' was therefore to show that he was a hawk who was pinning his colours to the settlers' mast.

It was at this point, in May 1919, that Grogan returned to London for the first time since the end of the war and was soon mired in further controversy. Not only did he drop his bombshell to Gertrude regarding the fact that he now had two families, but his return coincided with the publication of the Final Report of an Economic Commission charged with laying the foundations for the post-war economic development of the Protectorate. The Commission comprised two officials, Grogan, and four other settlers – Delamere, Edward Powys Cobb, Tommy Wood and Wilfrid Hunter – but Grogan was very much its dominant force.

In addition to a comprehensive survey of the state of the nation, the Commission made wide-ranging recommendations. Its Report contained ambitious proposals to connect the East African railway network to the main Cape-to-Cairo system which looked to be nearing completion, a call for protective tariffs to be introduced, and a call for a government study of what could be done to help develop the country's timber industry. There were also suggestions that an industrial apprentice scheme should be set up for Africans, as well as a scheme for encouraging Africans to leave their reserves and farm land alongside European settlers. None of this, nor the Commission's aspirations that the country should seek to prepare itself for 'responsible government'[16] of its own affairs, caused a stir in Britain. What was contentious was the call for a cessation of Indian immigration and the gradual transfer of governmental jobs currently occupied by Indians to Africans and Europeans. This was not due to any great sympathy with the Indian population on the part of the Colonial Office, whose senior civil servant scathingly remarked that 'the Indian immigrant [in Kenya] is almost invariably of a type which does not do any good either to the country or to the nation',[17] rather it was that holding on to India was becoming an increasingly complex political challenge, and no one in Whitehall wanted the waters muddied by expressions of xenophobia emanating from East Africa.

Grogan certainly understood the predicament that Milner, as Colonial Secretary, was presented with by his civil servants, but his preferred solution did not involve compromise. He had seen that the British government had been prepared to grant self-government to South Africa rather than become bogged down by its complex internal politics, and was preparing to do the same in Southern Rhodesia. He was convinced that Westminster would also disgorge the Protectorate if it was politically expedient to do so. Such was the logic underpinning the more strident demands and sporadically vituperative language of the Economic Commission's Final Report.

Milner gave Grogan a good deal of covert, and indeed overt, support. Both men knew that 'closer' settlement was a vital precursor to the latter's quest to secure self-government for the Protectorate, or Kenya Colony as it became known from 1920. A mere 3,500 male settlers were not considered to constitute a responsible body to which to grant charge of the country's affairs, and the War Council had admitted as much by planning to launch a post-war Soldier Settlement Scheme. Milner gave this scheme his official blessing, and appointed Grogan its spokesman in London just prior to their departure for the

Paris Peace Conference. It was a task which Grogan threw himself
into with great gusto.

On 8 July 1919 hundreds of former combatants interested in settling in Kenya turned up to hear him speak at Caxton Hall, and
Grogan did not disappoint them. Deploying his charm, his amusing
rather than barbed wit and his intimate knowledge of life as a settler
he gave a display of the sort of straight-talking for which he was
famous throughout Africa. He declared Kenya to be 'in the fortunate
position that, as distinct from South Africa, with their tragic racial
history, there is no antagonism or real dislike [between the European
and the African]', and he added that he was 'perfectly certain' that
this would facilitate 'the most stupendous development'.[18]

Grogan's optimism was infectious: the word spread quickly about
his lecture – the transcript of which ran to twenty-eight pages of small
type – and so great was its appeal that he had to give a repeat performance a week later. The result was that the settlers' ranks were swelled
by almost 700 families who could prove they had over £5,000 capital
and an annual income of not less than £200 (and would therefore
never need to rely on any state support). Some 550 of the men were
former officers, including forty-six generals, 105 Majors and 160 cap-
tains, and this ensured that the distinctly South African character of
the European community of the pre-war days became overwhelmingly
British, military and upper-middle-class after the war. Most of this
new generation of settlers left England on the *Garth Castle* in November 1919, and were intent on seeking a better life than that offered
by depressed, post-war Britain. They were in for a rude awakening:
as they arrived in East Africa the currency started to appreciate dramatically, and within a year world-wide commodity prices started to
tumble.

The causes of Kenya's great Currency Crisis were complex,[19] but the
effects of a 50 per cent appreciation in the value of the East African
rupee were all too obvious. For the farmer – black or white – who

sold his products for sterling in the British market, but paid his workers and living costs locally in rupees, the effect was an immediate 50 per cent diminution in his profits (which in most cases meant no profit at all). By the same token the sterling cost of rupee overdrafts extended to European farmers and businessmen increased by 50 per cent. For Grogan, and many others who had borrowed very large sums locally, bankruptcy seemed imminent. On the other hand the country's shopkeepers found the rupees paid for their goods were worth 50 per cent more when they bought their supplies in sterling from Britain. Government officials, to Grogan's great annoyance, also benefited as their rupee salaries were in theory worth 50 per cent more when they returned to Britain on leave (or permanently) and could convert their rupees back to sterling. The Currency Crisis therefore split the country in two: there were those, like officials and shopkeepers, who stood to benefit from the rise in the value of the rupee; and those, like Grogan and all farmers, who were faced with ruin.

As the crisis deepened it was to Grogan, his 'godfather', that Northey turned for assistance. No one else connected with the colony's affairs had such a formidable grasp of economics, and Grogan revelled in being put in to bat against a British banking system whose 'main principle' he regarded as being 'to swallow, and absorb itself, like a boa constrictor, much of the wealth of their clients without rendering reciprocal service'.[20]

Everyone involved in the acrimonious debate – in which Grogan took up his favoured position centre-stage – agreed on one thing. With the Kenyan currency fluctuating wildly according to whether Indian silver merchants were buying silver or not, urgent stabilization measures were called for in order, as Grogan put it, to avert landing 'the East Africa Government in a morass of absurdity from which there is no retreat'.[21] At the Colonial Office, Grogan's friend Leo Amery favoured stabilization at a rate of two Kenyan shillings to the rupee, but to Grogan this smacked of panic and would crystallize for all time the 50 per cent losses being suffered by farmers and those with local overdrafts. With this in mind he wrote to Amery stating that his proposals were frankly appalling – legally unsound and economically NIHILIST. If imposed they would leave British East Africa and Uganda (though potentially the richest part of Africa) a withered waste . . . my mind boggles at the thought of the unfathomable conditions they would generate, and the Pelion of Ridicule that they would pile on the Ossa of Hate upon the Colonial Office back.

Grogan added, for good measure, that the blame for such dire consequences would fall squarely on the shoulders of the British government, as it had 'made no attempt to control its currency as every other government has had to do'.[22]

What is most striking about the Colonial Office records for the duration of the crisis is that it is abundantly clear that Grogan knew – and was tacitly acknowledged to know – a good deal more about what was going on than almost anybody else involved, and that included the Treasury, the Crown Agents and the Bank of England. But only one man – Northey – was courageous enough to side with him throughout his attempts to propose a workable return to the old rate of exchange.[23] Despite an initial lack of support Grogan had very nearly won the argument in London when on 13 February – a Friday as luck would have it – the value of the East African rupee leapt to 2s. 10d. The Colonial Office, fearing that this was a permanent appreciation, panicked.

Neither Northey nor Grogan was asked to the meeting at which their country's fate was decided by stabilizing the Kenyan rupee at the two shilling rate favoured by Amery. Grogan's worst fears for the colony were realized. A 50 per cent increase in settlers' overdrafts, the running costs of most farms and the salaries of European government officials became cast in stone, as did a 50 per cent reduction in the value of exports and the cost of sterling imports. Worse still, within months of the stabilization, the Indian rupee fell – just as Grogan had predicted it would – to its old rate of 1s. 4d., and left the East African rupee high and dry at a value of 2s.: 1 rupee. The immediate consequence of this was that Indian currency traders on both sides of the Indian Ocean indulged in currency smuggling on a massive scale, a fact readily admitted to by local magnate Jeevanjee.

Grogan was outraged by the Colonial Office's action, and never forgave its perpetration of a wrong which he regarded as tantamount to drowning Kenya, the 'babe of Empire'. In his opinion the European settlers, particularly those who had participated with Colonial Office encouragement in the Soldier Settler Scheme, had been 'in ordinary language . . . sold to the banks'.[24] This was undeniably true, and led pioneer settler Arnold Paice to dub the settlement initiative 'the Soldier Robbery Scheme'. It was also tacitly admitted in confidential memos circulating within the Colonial Office a decade later: 'a large body of people', reads one, 'believe that both the basis of conversion of the EA shilling and, even more important, the post-war policy in relation to sterling were mistaken'.[25] The fact that a 'large body of people' later conceded that Grogan had been right all along was, however, of no use to him when he was embroiled in the fight to save the Kenyan economy. In London he set about campaigning vigorously for compensation for farmers, as did Delamere in Kenya itself. The official attitude was much as they had expected; they were told to 'cut the cackle and get to work'. Far less predictable was the opposition they encountered from a most unexpected direction.

The Currency Crisis had not only bankrupted the colony at a time of worldwide depression, but also split the ranks of European settlers into a beleaguered farming camp and a commercial camp which was, as long as people were still able to shop, a beneficiary of the new rate of exchange. Thus, just at a time when Grogan considered it to be of paramount importance that settlers should stand shoulder-to-shoulder in an attempt to push for the economic revival of the colony, political unity among the European community seemed to have dissolved.

NINETEEN

'Comet of Political Agitation'

THE DIVISIONS IN the settlers' ranks caused by the Currency Crisis widened in the run-up to the first elections for seats in the new Legislative Council. There was something quintessentially British about this surprising development, in that it was underpinned by a groundswell of distrust of those, like Grogan and Delamere, who were conspicuously more powerful and successful than others. Age-old jealous accusations that the two men were little more than a pair of robber barons with over-large business empires gathered momentum, and harsh words were muttered in the bars of Nairobi to the effect that they had only ever sought to feather their own nests. Intoxicated by the prospect of their ability to influence the outcome of the colony's first elections, many among the settler rank and file simply chose to forget – or reinterpret – the efforts of their leaders to establish a thriving colony. Amid the prevailing atmosphere of suspicion, Grogan reflected that 'one man, one vote' was – as he had always maintained, indeed a dangerous thing.

The correspondence pages of the *Leader*, fighting its own battle with Grogan and Delamere's *East African Standard*, illustrated the increasing level of popular discontent with the 'big men'. After Grogan's nomination to stand for the Kyambu constituency was officially filed in January 1920 one farmer wrote to the paper lamenting that 'Major Grogan's supporters intend to try and push him on us . . . all we ask for is to be left alone and allowed to choose our man in our own way'. Another declared that 'the old groove is worn out . . . Empire-building is a very attractive occupation but there is still some virtue in looking after one's own cabbage patch',[1] and one malcontent complained that Kyambu was being used as a 'dumping ground for Major Grogan . . . who isn't even resident in the colony'.[2] It was true that, at the time of the election, Grogan was not in the colony. He was in the midst of fighting the settlers' corner in the Currency Crisis and giving extensive evidence relating to the colony's future, and its ability to support a loan, to Milner's Colonial Economic Development Committee. He was in other words fully preoccupied with affairs of state, but that cut little ice in the parochial atmosphere of the bars of Nairobi.

Grogan was unruffled by the criticisms levelled against him. He could see that 'rabble rule' was the most likely outcome of the elections, and declared himself 'not anxious to stand' despite his nomination. 'It is a thankless task . . .' he added,

> as there is every prospect of a long, arduous and bitter struggle before we procure for East Africa the necessary voice in the control of our own affairs, and the necessary protection from unintelligent and not always benevolent interference from the CO in purely local matters . . . Such a fight can only be maintained by a person of my temperament if and when there is loyal support behind me.

Throughout January and February of 1920 the question of 'loyal support' remained finely balanced. 'It would be nothing short of a disaster', the editors of Grogan's *East African Standard* thundered, 'to the political fortune of the country if Major Grogan is not elected',[3] but their rivals at the *Leader* were more ambivalent:

> Grogan's name is probably more spoken of and discussed in political circles here than [that of] any other man. He is faced with a good deal more criticism in local circles than Lord Delamere . . . But the intellectual and more intelligent men of the land are keen upon securing Major Grogan's election. If Lord Delamere may be termed the doyen and father of political thought here Major Grogan is the comet and life of political agitation.[4]

In the middle of March, the votes were cast in what was the most acrimonious of six pre-World War II elections. By then Grogan was unable to make a last-minute dash from London to the colony, and left his campaign in the hands of agents. His absence, and the fact that one of those agents was a rather murky character by the name of Arthur Tannahill,[5] did not go down well with the electors and he was defeated by an unknown named Collings-Wells. The result of a vote by less than fifty men was hardly a major setback for Grogan, though it pricked his pride and seemingly confirmed his scepticism about the fickle loyalties of the European community.

Across the country results followed a similar pattern, although the turn-out was less than 50 per cent, which implies that lack of interest was at least as big a feature of the election as the Grogan and Delamere witch hunt. Delamere would have lost in his Rift Valley constituency had he not agreed to the demands of small farmers around Naivasha to campaign in the future for its incorporation as a separate constituency. His brother-in-law, Berkeley Cole, was rejected in the Kenya Province constituency and fellow 'big man' A. C. Hoey lost to a soldier-settler in Plateau South. The enormous (in girth and wallet) Northrup McMillan just secured his seat. All in all the colony's 'big men' won just three of the eleven seats contested and when the first elected Legislative Council sat it was a singularly uninspiring entity. Dominated by commercial men and those whom Grogan referred to as 'verandah farmers', what had been intended as a thrusting assembly of powerful men of the world appeared to many to resemble nothing more awe-inspiring than a meeting of village bell-ringers. Furthermore, when a fractious and now white-haired Delamere resigned over a trivial matter, as he was wont to do when crossed, the settler benches in Legco were left leaderless. Then, if not before, it became obvious that the colony's first election had been a farce.

The *Leader* could not resist cocking a snook at Grogan's defeat. It published a cartoon depicting Grogan's *East African Standard* as a grieving widow staring at a gravestone which bore the words: 'In loving memory of Ewart S Grogan, author, speech maker, Office Légion D'honneur Belge etc who departed our political life on March 25th 1920.' Below the cartoon was printed a merry jingle, one verse of which ran as follows:

> And now the Major's dead
> How grieved we are to shout it
> Electors can't be led
> That's all there is about it.

The chorus lamented the death of 'poor cock Grogan'.[6]

'Cock' Grogan ignored the jibe. A lot of hot air, 'the privilege and pleasure of the British race',[7] as his friend Lord Cranworth put it, had been let off by a minuscule electorate but otherwise nothing had changed. Grogan knew that the future of the colony, and of the Empire in Africa, would be decided in London, so it was there that he decided to stay. During the next five years, like some leader in exile, he only visited the colony when it was necessary to oversee his business affairs.

The rank and file's hour of glory in Legco was soon cut short by the final act of the Currency Crisis, which had done so much to put them there in the first place. Northey, on the advice of Grogan and Delamere, decided to offer the settlers a chance to return to the old exchange rate of 1*s*. 4*d*.: 1 rupee. He prevailed upon government officials in Legco to vote in favour of the measure, provided that there was a similar 'yes' vote by the unofficial members. A return to normality was within the settlers' grasp – but to Grogan's disgust (and the well-intentioned Northey's amazement) the unofficial members meekly threw away the opportunity, saying in effect that such a course of action might antagonize the Colonial Office and jeopardize the colony's chances of raising loans in Britain. Nothing more clearly illustrated the parochialism of the men who had swept the board in the 1920 elections. The result was that their continued participation in Council became untenable and the path was open for the return of the country's 'natural leaders'.

Delamere led the way. His Reform Party won six by-elections in 1921 for seats vacated by 'small men' and the old guard – including Delamere, Berkeley Cole, Freddie Ward, Powys Cobb and Northrup McMillan – took control of Legco's unofficial bench. Despite his now deeply embedded disdain for Legco, Grogan was persuaded by Delamere to stand for the Plateau South constituency. A. C. Hoey wrote to the *Leader* telling its readers that 'it is up to us to put up . . . men who will be a real asset to the country' in the by-elections; 'some of you', he added, 'might shudder at his [Grogan's] name, but what is it that makes you shudder? Is it the feeling of petty jealousies, or what is it? . . . Some of you may say he only grinds his own axe, but he grinds yours with it and his interests are yours.'[8]

The *Leader*'s editors had sensed that opposition to Grogan no longer made good copy, and promptly executed a volte-face:

> Major Grogan's return is not without its importance to Kenya Colony. Truth to tell, than Major Grogan (we do not even except Lord Delamere) there is no more outstanding personality connected with non-official affairs in East Africa. In many ways he remains a man of mystery. That he is rather elusive, somewhat ambiguous in his attitude, and not a little Sphinx-like, despite his frank and open manner, in his general demeanour towards the people of this country, is sometimes admitted. But that he is a man of high intellectual powers, forceful, compelling, domineering we might also say, a strategist, diplomat, and a shrewd man of the world, is also recognised. Added to these characteristics the gift of oratory and personal magnetism . . . [and his] tall, slim, lithe, virile figure; a bright keen animated face . . . and fiery appeal . . . Major Grogan undoubtedly stands out as a man amongst the men of Kenya with a man's faults and a man's weaknesses but withal possessed of a strength and vitality granted by nature to few.[9]

'The gallant major', once again the darling of the fickle public and press, was duly voted into Legco.

Grogan's first appearance in Legco was on 24 March 1922. When Northey said the usual opening prayers, and began 'Oh Lord . . .', it is said that Delamere rose to his feet and bowed. Northey then continued, '. . . God Almighty', and Grogan is reputed to have risen to his feet and bowed. Whether or not the story is true, these two men dominated Legco as they dominated life in the colony. Within two months steps were taken to raise large sums of money for infrastructure development, and protective tariffs were imposed on various agricultural imports (most notably wheat imports, thereby protecting Delamere's milling company Unga Ltd). 'Every effort', Grogan declared on 25 May, 'should be made to stimulate the proper industries of this country.'[10] Some of those industries were, of course, controlled by Delamere and Grogan – but they also provided the lifeline for any number of smaller settlers. And when a two-year experiment with income tax was abandoned by the local government, due to pressure from Grogan, all settlers benefited. One of them even wrote a ditty for the *Standard* saying as much; it read as follows:

> God moves in a most mysterious way
> His wonders to perform,
> He plants his footsteps on the sea
> And sends our Grogan alone.[11]

At the end of May Grogan sailed again for London. During 1921 he had, according to the *Leader*, continued to perform 'yeoman service . . . in connection with the Indians',[12] but by the middle of 1922 the Indian Crisis had reached boiling point.

After the war Indian nationalism had become one of the central problems for the British Empire, and tensions were greatly exacerbated by the now infamous massacre of 379 Indians by General Dyer in Amritsar on 13 April 1919. By the end of 1921 an Indian uprising looked to be a distinct possibility, and Kenya had been thrust centre-stage in the fight by Indian nationalists for political concessions.

The elections for Legislative Council accentuated the Colonial Office's Kenyan dilemma. By 1921 the colony's heterogeneous Indian population numbered over 25,000, almost three times the size of the European population including government officials. To grant Indians equal political rights on the basis of a common roll franchise would therefore have had the immediate effect of ceding control of the colony to the Indians – and thereby set what was regarded as a dangerous precedent for India itself. On the other hand, to dismiss out of hand the demands of Indian activists for greater political rights in East Africa was regarded by Whitehall as an equally dangerous strategy.

Grogan had a good many friends among the most prominent Indians in the colony, among them the business magnate Jeevanjee and the moderate, intellectual Shams-ud-Deen, Secretary of the Indian Association. He fully recognized their vital contribution to the economic prosperity of the colony, just as he readily acknowledged the heroic and fanatically loyal service rendered by the 'martial

races' of India, predominantly Muslims and Sikhs, to the Empire's
war effort. But, in common with all but a small minority of Britons,
he did not believe such 'yeoman service' merited equal political representation.

Grogan's petulance on this latter point was not prompted by the
behaviour of India's 'martial' races, but by his dismay as a patriot at
the reaction of Kenya's Indians to the recent war. Out of an adult
male Indian population of just over 12,000 in the colony, just 227 had
volunteered to fight and forty-five were briefly conscripted into the
East Africa Mechanical Transport Corps.[13] In Grogan's opinion such
facts rather made a mockery of Mr Narayandass's expression of support
for his great call-to-arms in the Theatre Royal in 1915, as did the fact
that eight of the Protectorate's Indian civilians had been executed for
treason and hundreds were court-martialled and imprisoned for spying
for the Germans. Furthermore, most of the colony's Indian population– with the exception of shopkeepers and railway and government
workers – seemed to have proved themselves to be economic migrants:
many thousands had fled East Africa at the start of the conflict, and
only returned when it was safe to do so. This migratory trend continued after the war: in the five years between 1918 and 1923 17,000
Indians left the colony and 19,000 entered it. Grogan, while lauding
the obvious loyalty of groups such as the Aga Khan's Ismaili Khojas
to their country of domicile, was profoundly sceptical about the rights
of the majority of Indians to claim anything but a token political voice
in Kenya.

Indian activists, of course, saw things rather differently. Some
resented the disproportionate power wielded by the European settlers;
some objected to being barred by the Elgin pledges from applying for
farmland in the colony's highland regions; and others denounced on
principle the residential segregation imposed in towns between the
Indian and European populations (though few in practice wanted to
live cheek-by-jowl with Europeans any more than Hindus in the
colony wanted to live cheek-by-jowl with Muslims). What united them
was the increasingly voluble call from the settlers for immigration
restrictions to be imposed as a means of curtailing Indian numerical
superiority and dominance of the non-agricultural economy.

By the time Grogan returned to London in the summer of 1922

he had already come to a decision which was – for him – both characteristically contrary and perceptive, and unusually pessimistic. During the previous year he had consulted everyone in the corridors of power that he could collar, and the result was that he came to see Kenya's 'Indian Question' in its wider context to a far greater extent than any of his fellow settlers. On the basis of what he learnt he decided that Kenya's situation was insoluble in the short term: the Empire simply could not hang on to India, its crown jewel, without to some degree appeasing the Indians in Kenya. In public he zealously maintained in a piece he wrote for the *National Review* that 'history' had proclaimed 'the British people a ruling people', and provocatively added that 'no Indian has ever conquered any part of Africa by the sword, no Indian ever played in Africa the part of a Livingstone or a Rajah Brooke, no Indian ever moved to Africa to tame the wilderness, and no Indian ever touched African soil except and until some other race had imposed safe and ordered existence upon the spot'.[14] But in private he could see and, in the case of the Muslim Indians in particular could accept, that some form of accommodation was necessary.

In October 1922, having completed his stint on Bowring's Economic and Financial Committee (whose reforms were widely credited with saving the colony from economic collapse), Grogan resigned his seat in Kenya's Legislative Council. There were a number of reasons underpinning his decision to watch from the sidelines as what became the Indian Crisis unfolded. The British government's handling of the Currency Crisis had prompted Grogan radically to reappraise his view of Kenya's future, and to his considerable chagrin he concluded that when push came to shove the interests of the colony were always likely to be regarded as – at best – of secondary importance in Whitehall. In other words, Grogan underwent something of a political transformation in 1922, and his instinctively rebellious streak began to be less a characteristic of his politics than what might be termed intelligent non-conformity. Repeated, and severe, bouts of malaria and sporadic recurrences of his agonizing liver problems may have played a part in this change. Either way, the Grogan whom officials regularly feared might march on Government House as a means of expressing his disgust at some particular policy was gone for ever, and in its place appeared a politician who was above all a logician, motivated by a desire continually to challenge orthodoxy and the assumptions of others more than by a desire to make trouble.

In many respects this transformation showed that Grogan had come of age as a politician, but, ironically, it also led to his political isolation – a position in which he was not uncomfortable. His quasi-Socratic intelligent nonconformity was too similar to Churchill's own creed for the two men to be able to co-operate after the latter succeeded Milner at the Colonial Office in 1921, despite Churchill's assurance that 'the British settler in Kenya is one of our greatest responsibilities, one of our greatest difficulties, and one of our highest hopes'.[15] It was also antithetical in spirit to the formation of Delamere's Reform Party. Indeed, many a settler failed to understand Grogan's new approach altogether: he appeared to them to be a cynic or deliberately obstructive or simply an outsider of whom it was best to be suspicious. But, as his friend A. C. Hoey had written, 'the intellectual and more intelligent' were able to recognize – and appreciate – the new role as Kenya's most authoritative and challenging 'back-bencher'-cum-'special adviser' in which Grogan cast himself.

In his new guise Grogan stood aloof from the slanging match which soon came to characterize the antagonism between European settlers and their Indian compatriots. As the crisis worsened, the settlers vilified the allegedly unsanitary living habits of the colony's Hindus, their lying and scheming, their caste-consciousness, the barbarity of their practice of taking child-brides and so forth, and they habitually referred to 'their' Hindus as the 'Bombay failed'. Hindu nationalists countered by proclaiming that incest was endemic in Britain, that most Englishwomen were 'loose' and had to have abortions before they could be led to the altar, and that the reason most English aristocrats were so simple was that they had been conceived out of wedlock and their mothers had, in desperate and futile attempts to induce a miscarriage, spent every hour of their pregnancies on horseback. The gloves were well and truly off.

The Indian Crisis lasted throughout 1922 and well into 1923 – by which time Churchill had recalled Northey as governor for siding too openly with the settlers. His own earlier assurances to the settlers he cast aside in favour of what he described as a 'nicely balanced agreement'[16] between the warring factions – but which the settlers regarded as nothing less than an attempt to offer them up as a sacrifice to the India Office. By early 1923 the settlers were on the brink of an all-out revolt and Northey's replacement, Sir Robert Coryndon, was forced to inform the Colonial Office that his commanding officer and police chief could no longer count on the loyalty of their men if the settlers did rebel.[17] Few in number though the settlers were after the war, they included a disproportionate number of former soldiers, and Coryndon knew that the more radical among them had laid complete plans to seize all major government installations, to deport all Nairobi's Indians to Mombasa and to kidnap him (thereafter secreting him in a location with particularly fine fishing).

Such was the situation when, in the autumn of 1922, the Conservative Party ended its coalition with Lloyd George over the civil war in the Irish Free State, his handling of a near war in Turkey, not to mention his sale of honours. The Liberal Party never recovered. Andrew Bonar Law led the Tories to their first general election victory in almost two decades, and Churchill's replacement as Colonial Secretary, into whose lap the sorry mess left by the *bouleversements* of his predecessor fell, was the Duke of Devonshire.

Outwardly the plum-faced and white-haired duke seemed to treat the whole crisis with the insouciant hauteur much favoured by British diplomats, but he was no fool. Blimpish though the settlers' army of majors may have appeared, Devonshire took Coryndon's advice that they were more than able to carry out their threats and that if they did so there was a very real danger of provoking rebellion in volatile India itself. He also took at face value thinly veiled secessionist threats made by Delamere in words that deliberately echoed those used by the Ulstermen in 1914.[18] At the end of March 1923 the Colonial Secretary summoned delegations representing the Indians and the settlers to London; and the Revd J. W. Arthur, a missionary, was nominated to represent the views of the African population.

Even at the eleventh hour of the negotiations in London it looked as though Delamere and Kenneth Archer, the blunt-speaking President of the Convention of Associations, might reject the compromise proposed by Devonshire and that the settlers' militant Vigilance Committee might implement its plans for a rebellion. But support sought by the latter from Smuts's South Africa was not forthcoming, and hot heads were cooled by very heavy rains in Kenya in March and April. Devonshire was able to secure grudging agreement from the main protagonists to various proposals. Delamere and Archer secured guarantees that the Elgin pledges banning Indians from holding agricultural land in the highlands would remain in force, that the possibility of restricting Indian immigration in order to protect 'native interests' would be looked into, and that the Indians' demand for a common roll franchise was being rejected. On the other hand, self-government for Kenya – as Grogan had suspected would be the case – was dismissed as being 'out of the question within any period of time which need now be taken into consideration',[18] racial segregation in townships was ended, and the Indians were granted five seats in Legco, to be decided on a communal franchise, against the settlers' eleven. The large coastal Arab community was also given one seat on Legco, as was a missionary to advise on 'native affairs'.

Neither the Indian delegates nor the settlers were in any way satisfied. The ire of the former was so great that the settlers decided that they must have won a victory of sorts: Indians began an immediate campaign of non-co-operation in the colony, and did not even take up all their seats in Legco until 1931.

Grogan's silence regarding the edicts of the Devonshire White Paper was deafening. In his opinion strife could have been averted two decades earlier if the Foreign Office had formulated a clear settlement policy for Kenya, but he had also now resigned himself to the fact that, in politics, today's edict prompted tomorrow's volte-face, and that if the growing crisis in Britain's relations with its subjects on the Indian mainland was resolved then Kenya's constitutional turmoil might also evaporate. What caused him altogether greater concern was that the Duke of Devonshire had reiterated the fact that 'native interests' should remain paramount in Kenya. Grogan found this disturbing not because he disagreed with the sentiment expressed by Whitehall: after all, Covenant XXII of the recently formed League of

Nations asserted that it was the 'sacred trust of civilization' to govern and guide those 'not yet able to stand by themselves under the strenuous conditions of the modern world'. Rather it was because, in his view, British civil servants were being profoundly dishonest, and the evidence backed him up.

Although in 1920–21 African production was still the mainstay of the Kenyan economy, and Africans provided 25 per cent of the government's revenue through taxation, the local government was spending just £30,000 annually on the administration of 'native affairs' and £36,000 on 'native education' – out of a total budget of £3.2m. *That*, in Grogan's opinion, was how seriously the Colonial Office, for all its high-minded rhetoric, took its duty of 'trusteeship' over the 2.5 million indigenous inhabitants of the country. In striking contrast to the millions invested by the Germans in their colonies before the war, the only capital forthcoming from London in the early 1920s was loan capital – not grants.

Grogan believed that such parsimony jeopardized the economic future (and therefore the political future) of the colony every bit as much as the fact that the Colonial Office was attempting 'the governance of a very considerable fraction of the earth's surface' with what he knew to be 'a staff no bigger than that employed on [his] timber estates'.[19] Furthermore, in the post-war years African hut and poll taxes had been increased by one third (measures which Grogan had criticized as wholly counterproductive), and wages had been cut by a third in the wake of the Currency Crisis. This was hardly what Grogan had hoped would happen when, in a speech in 1919 to the Convention of Associations, he had called for the African population to be 'given reasonable education, especially technical, industrial and agricultural',[20] for the setting up of a mechanical training school for Africans and for the provision of proper medical facilities. All these demands were ignored by the government, and Grogan was convinced that its insouciance would have ramifications.

He was, in fact, sure that there were *already* ramifications. Although the Devonshire White Paper had pronounced that 'no articulate expression of opinion can be expected from the African tribes of Kenya', the experience of the more alert in the colony told a different story. More than fifty chiefs had visited Coryndon during the 'Indian

Crisis' to make plain their feelings about the Hindu population; one had even gone so far as to state menacingly that 'if the *wazungu* (Europeans) will only sleep for two days, there would be no Indian Question'.[21] 1922 had also witnessed the first riot by Africans in Nairobi, during which twenty-five participants were shot. The message to those prepared to listen was clear: the tolerance of poor government by an emerging cadre of African activists was no greater than Grogan's.

Grogan's old friend Meinertzhagen was arguably the first person to spot where organized resistance would begin. As early as 1904 he had written that 'the Kikuyu are the most intelligent of the African tribes I have met ... They will be one of the first tribes to demand freedom from European influence.'[22] Though many a black Kenyan would have disagreed with the first statement, Meinertzhagen's second was correct. In the 1920s Harry Thuku (a government telephone operator) and Jomo Kenyatta (a clerk at the Municipal Waterworks) formed the vanguard of a group of literate, mission-educated Africans who, aided by Indian Nationalists and a few sympathizers in Britain, took the first tentative steps towards fostering Kikuyu nationalism and the rejection of colonial rule.

Not even they, however, would have believed in their wildest dreams that in a matter of decades they would help to bring about the almost complete fulfilment of an astonishing prophesy written by an amateur European scribe for the *Leader* in 1913:

ANNALS OF BEA

Being the deciphered and translated portion of a manuscript discovered at the excavation near Mount Longonot, 5001 AD

'this time came the British Administration who established rule as servants and trustees of the various coloured peoples and tribes. Industry was established throughout the land ... as the country waxed rich the presence of the white man became no more necessary and the native and Indian laws which were imposed by the combined nation in the Legislative Council marked the era of the European exodus ... many European settlers and their families perished during the Great Rebellion; the remainder left the country, with the exception being a few which became absorbed in the nation . . . Thus did the early European settlers perish. The land reverted to the ideal life of the native *shamba*, the chiefs regained their lost power and in AD 1968 the last of the British left these shores.'

[*Discoverer's note: the period of this British debacle synchronised with the great political disturbances in Great Britain, due to the peculiarities of the 'Faddist' party and the loss of prestige in the Colonies, consummating in the break-up of the great Imperial Power.*][23]

TWENTY

Bold Dreams Fulfilled

IN ADDITION TO bringing Kenyan settlers to the brink of rebellion, the Indian Crisis crystallized certain far-reaching changes in the character of settler society. Post-war soldier-settlers had laid the plans for rebellion as well as hijacking Grogan's one-time 'Big Noise', the Convention of Associations; and the colony's 'small men' had briefly, and with less than dazzling results, pushed themselves to the fore in the election of 1920. Furthermore, Nairobi became the global capital of jealous tittle-tattle as well as of the safari. Both Grogan and Delamere found themselves to some degree victims of the adage that Kenya was 'a country of no steady devotion to its would-be leaders . . . the hero of today [is] more often than not the rejected of tomorrow'.[1]

Grogan carried on his business unconcerned by any jibes emanating from those whom Kipling had derided as 'little ones who fear to be great'. Apart from dealing with affairs of state, there is no doubt that he enjoyed spending long periods in England with Gertrude and his children – however much his relationship with them had changed during his long wartime absence.

There was also his second family to attend to. After Doris gave birth to their daughter in 1919, he had bought her a small but very beautiful estate in the East Sussex village of Burnt Oak. The large, high-chimneyed farmhouse was set near the bottom of a small valley and surrounded by tall trees; within a mile were woods with quaint names like Wilding, Pickreed, Oaky and Marlpit; and just a dozen miles to the south lay the Sussex Downs. It was to this idyllic spot that Grogan regularly retreated when he wanted to escape the confines of the city or sought a change of scene from 'Number Ten', his palatial home in Chelsea.

Grogan was extremely attached to the feisty Doris, sixteen years his junior, and to their child. For her part, their daughter fondly remembers the visits of her mother's friend 'Bun', so-called because he used to conjure for her by saying that if she peered through the holes in the sides of his hat she would see a bunny (which he fashioned from a handkerchief). At any opportunity Grogan would perch her on his knee and cuddle her, and he opposed her going away to school in Seaford because he could see that she loved her horses – and knew that he would miss her. When her mother insisted she did go, however, it was Grogan who paid the school fees. As she grew up, his daughter found him – unsurprisingly – both dazzlingly charming and *very* obstinate, but it was not until the evening before her wedding in 1953 that she learnt from her mother that 'Bun' was in fact her father.

On his trips to Sussex Grogan, ever the doer, worked slavishly on scheme after scheme. A succession of rather useless farm managers came and went, seldom able to keep up with their employer's exacting and usually unachievable standards or to adapt to the fact that Grogan always preferred to do things himself. With his daughter ferrying him glasses of his favoured tipple – the same creamy milk that he had been plied with at prep school to increase his strength – he constructed trout ponds in the garden and connected them via waterfalls with the stream below; he dug ditches, trimmed hedges, planted trees and put in fences; and he built an over-optimistically enormous concrete wheat silo in the farmyard which stands to this day. All in all Grogan spent a lot of time in Sussex, and it is remarkable that Gertrude – and indeed Doris – tolerated this 'division of the spoils'. That they did was down to both women's pragmatism and good nature, and the fact that – however trying life with the 'over-engined' Grogan may have been – it was better than life without him.

While in the process of casting himself slightly adrift from mainstream Kenyan politics and attending to affairs of state, Grogan also focused the full force of his attention on his business interests. The post-war depression and the Currency Crisis had cost him dear: all his enterprises were founded on colossal sums of money borrowed from banks (for which he used Gertrude's wealth and his other assets as collateral), and the revaluation of the rupee had caused those debts to increase in value by 50 per cent overnight. Grogan summed up his predicament by quipping that 'the needle of my financial compass was standing on its head – indicating polar conditions'.[2] As a matter of urgency he needed to make some money, and his attention alighted first on the continuing need for a railway running through his timber concession to the Uasin Gishu plateau. Its construction, he well knew, held the key to enhancing the efficiency, and therefore the value, of his Equator Saw Mills.

Grogan had, of course, originally offered to build the Uasin Gishu railway himself, but his offer had been rejected largely on the basis that the Colonial Office had ruled that it would be decades before such a railway was needed. Grogan's optimism about agricultural prospects on the Uasin Gishu plateau had been proved correct by Boer and British settlers in a matter of a few years, and in 1913 the CO had been forced to reopen its files on the railway. During this second phase of the long-running saga Grogan had again spearheaded the campaign for the railway's construction, putting forward Lawley as the contractor and George Lloyd as its political sponsor. He had also won the wholehearted support of the local Kenyan government, who had all but secured a loan from Britain to finance the railway when war broke out and scuppered any further progress.

In February 1918 the third phase of the Uasin Gishu saga began with Grogan's determination to revive the pre-war plan to build the railway. Lawley, that grizzled veteran of African railway-building, was again put forward as the contractor and, knowing that Britain's coffers were drained by the war, Grogan secured private finance from Erlanger's, the merchant bank. Support for the railway was so great among farmers who had settled on the plateau and in the Rift Valley in the pre-war years that Bowring, the acting governor, informed the Colonial Office that 'great disappointment will be caused if [the railway] is not considered'.[3] Farmers on the plateau, in particular, were experiencing acute transport difficulties when trying to get the produce from Kenya's 'breadbasket' to market as the nearest mainline station was many days by ox-wagon. Furthermore, Bowring was taken aback to discover when he went to the plateau that the farmers on the Uasin Gishu had not received a single visit from a government land or medical officer in the ten years they had been there, and that settlers in Trans-Nzoia, to the north-west of the plateau, had neither a Post Office, nor a dispensary, nor even a District Officer. This was, as Grogan had long maintained, a damning indictment both of the efficiency of the local government and the Colonial Office's failure to encourage the economic development of the colony.

By the middle of 1919 the Colonial Office took Bowring's advice and gave initial approval for the railway, although it rejected out of hand Grogan's private initiative in favour of one proposed by the Crown Agents. Grogan expressed no disappointment about this decision: all he wanted was the railway, and it didn't matter to him who built it. He was, in fact, more than happy when the Crown Agents appointed as contractor the renowned engineer Sir John 'Empire Jack' Norton-Griffiths, whom Grogan had first met in the Bulawayo *laager* during the Matabele War, but he also knew from experience that the Colonial Office might yet seek to renege on their approval for the railway, and sought to keep up the pressure on Whitehall.

At the Paris Peace Conference Milner and Grogan discussed railways at length, and subsequently Grogan was summoned by his erstwhile mentor to give evidence to Milner's Colonial Economic Development Committee in early 1920. The nub of Grogan's argument was that 'British East Africa made a bigger war effort in proportion to its white and black populations and its developed resources than any other part of the British Empire', that 'the war had sucked the white and black populations dry', and that what was needed was 'a hand over the stile, a dose of oxygen, [which] we will soon repay with a flood of raw material'.[4] The 'hand over the stile' to which Grogan alluded was the Uasin Gishu railway, and the 'flood of raw material' included the wheat harvest from the Uasin Gishu, the African-grown sugar crop from Mumias district, and the African-grown cotton crop from Uganda as well as what Grogan anticipated to be huge quantities of timber from his forest concession. Milner stood four square behind Grogan and, as he was Colonial Secretary, his civil servants had no choice but to reaffirm their initial endorsement of the Uasin Gishu line.

There remained the thorny question of deciding the exact route the new railway should take. The choice was between branching off from the main line at Nakuru and following a route north-west up the Mau escarpment to Maji Mazuri, the new headquarters of Grogan's timber business, and thence to the plateau, or branching off from the main line at Mau Summit, thereby avoiding the expense of building two railways up the escarpment. This latter route, just eleven miles long and therefore forty-two miles shorter than the Nakuru route, was calculated by the Kenyan government's Public Works Department's engineers to cost a mere £200,000 – fully £900,000 less than the route through Grogan's land. The PWD's findings caused a huge stir in the colony, though many 'old hands' who were well acquainted with local rivalries were immediately suspicious about being offered what looked like a free lunch when Legislative Council was asked to vote on the merits of two routes in July 1920.

It was very significant that at the time Legco comprised the men who had ensured that Grogan was denied a seat in the colony's first elective assembly and done their level best to exclude Delamere. The Nakuru route was voted against not just on the basis of cost, but because it ran directly through Delamere's Njoro farm and would include no less than six stations within Grogan's forest concession (as opposed to three with the Mau Summit route). It seemed that the 'small men', and a majority of officials, were united in their reluctance to do *anything* that might advantage either Delamere or Grogan. Feeling himself to be politically isolated, and having already sold off much of his Njoro farm, even Delamere voted with his less than inspired colleagues on the Council (though he subsequently executed a swift volte-face).

Legco made a serious mistake in pursuing its Grogan and Delamere 'hunt' by voting for the Mau Summit route. In doing so the councillors not only ignored the pleas for the Nakuru route of wheat growers in the Rongai and Molo areas, but they paid far too much attention to an 'expert' with a very big axe to grind: one William McGregor Ross.

McGregor Ross had been director of the Public Works department since 1906, and had a reputation as a chippy Scottish Labourite. For the best part of two decades he had waged a personal vendetta against

Grogan, Delamere and any European settler who, consciously or unconsciously, did anything to agitate his giant-sized inferiority complex. In 1914 Belfield, the governor, had written of him that

> the value of his service is discounted by his apparent inability
> to work harmoniously with other departments. The range
> of his official vision is too circumscribed and his interest
> appears to be limited to projects of his own promoting. His
> usual attitude is that of opposition and his arguments are
> presented with a tedious prolixity.[5]

Even the meek and hesitant 'Flannelfoot' Hayes Sadler had remarked that McGregor Ross 'is too much inclined to take a purely partisan view on matters ... and [is] naturally very obstinate and not gifted with much tact'.[6] In short, McGregor Ross was not exactly well liked by the vast majority of either the settlers or his fellow officials, but in 1920 Legco was dominated by newcomers who were as yet unaware of his unpopularity or the reasons for it.

In the case of the Uasin Gishu railway McGregor Ross's gripe stemmed from the fact that he had not been asked by the local government to survey either of the alternative routes, nor to tender for the construction contract, nor to tender for the construction of another branch line from Nyeri to Thika. His estimate of the costs of the two possible routes for the Uasin Gishu railway was therefore produced entirely off his own bat and was, to say the least, influenced by personal bias. Having been officially cut out of the project his prime aim was to get back at those who had most to gain if the Nakuru route was chosen by Legco – his old adversaries Grogan and Delamere – and as was his wont he pursued his vendetta with a 'tedious prolixity'.

McGregor Ross was deemed to be a competent enough engineer, which gave his findings a good deal of credence among new arrivals in the colony who knew nothing of his hidden agenda. But he, and they, ignored important facts. For a start, the Nakuru route had been surveyed not once, but twice before, by men with considerably better qualifications as railway surveyors than McGregor Ross. On both occasions the route was favoured over any alternatives, and it was with that in mind that Grogan had positioned his saw mills where they stood. After Legco's decision to support the shorter Mau Summit route Grogan appealed to the Colonial Office for a second opinion and Milner despatched an independent surveyor, Colonel Hammond, to investigate. Towards the end of 1920 Hammond submitted his report in which he criticized Legco's decision and pronounced that the difficulties involved in building the Mau Summit route were far greater than McGregor Ross had anticipated. He also pointed out that although money might be saved in constructing it, rather than the Nakuru route, this saving would be more than offset by higher running costs. The 'battle of the surveys' thus became a stalemate.

The stalemate was broken when, in 1921, the Kenyan government ordered a Public Inquiry into McGregor Ross's Public Works Department. Many of his staff were singled out for criticism as 'incompetents' and for seeking to benefit personally from PWD tenders; the department as a whole was censured for its deplorable treatment of African workers (which irked McGregor Ross no end as he had always liked to pose as a champion of 'native interests'); and McGregor Ross was personally censured for attempting to run the department as a personal fiefdom. The final recommendation of the Chairman of the Inquiry, Major J. Kerr Robertson, was that McGregor Ross's PWD should be abolished immediately. This did not happen, although the Department was henceforth limited to calling for tenders and preparing estimates rather than undertaking construction work. McGregor Ross's case for the Mau Summit route was thoroughly discredited, and the government's chief railway engineer publicly declared the Scot 'not capable' of surveying let alone building a railway. The Nakuru route was settled on once and for all,[7] and following the election of Grogan and other leading settlers to Legco in March 1922, steps were taken to raise a £3m loan for the development of the railway – half of which was spent on the Uasin Gishu line.

'Empire Jack' Norton-Griffiths finally began construction of the Uasin Gishu railway in 1922, thereby bringing to an end a twenty-year saga in which Grogan had played the leading part. It was true, of course, that the railway benefited Grogan and Delamere. It enabled Grogan to transport his timber to market, and Delamere was able to sell the remaining plots on his Equator Farm at better prices than he might otherwise have done. Moreover, it facilitated the transport from far afield of milk to his new dairy business at Naivasha and of wheat to his milling company. But the railway had to be to someone's advantage to merit consideration in the first place, and the bigger the traffic it carried the more logical its route.

By the time it was completed five years later it proved, as Grogan had always maintained it would, a lifeline to many others as well. Boom times came to the wheat growers of Molo and Rongai (most of whom were within easy reach either of the main line or the branch line), and to the farmers of the Uasin Gishu plateau and Trans-Nzoia. By 1928, in a remarkable transformation of the colony's economic structure, European settlers were producing some 80 per cent of the country's exports, but the African cotton growers in Uganda had every bit as much reason to be grateful to Grogan, the man whose obstinacy and tenacity over two decades had ensured that distant markets became accessible for their harvests.

In those quarters where envy of Grogan had taken hold, tongues started to wag even more furiously when it emerged that he was still bent on not only seeing the Uasin Gishu railway built but also on building a modern port at Mombasa. Even his friends wondered whether he had taken leave of his senses in the days of the post-war depression, but Grogan was adamant that the depression would end sooner than anyone expected, and that then the colony would be crying out for suitable export and import facilities. With this in mind he set out to fulfil what he called 'one of the great ambitions of my life'.[8] It very nearly killed him.

On Mombasa Island Grogan still owned the valuable parcel of land – known as Mbaraki – which Sir Charles Eliot had granted him in what the Colonial Office regarded as an ill-judged fit of generosity. He had been unable to do anything with it for much the same reason that had delayed the foundation of Equator Saw Mills for almost a decade: the CO's policy of 'marking time' did not exactly imbue the colony's commercial life with a spirit of dynamism. It had taken Grogan eight years to agree terms for his lease with Whitehall, and when he did so, in view of the dearth of prime real estate on the island, he had to settle for fifty acres instead of the hundred acres he had been promised. The CO for once conceded that Grogan had behaved with 'admirable reasonableness' and instructed the local Land Office to issue Grogan with his lease. Pulling out all the stops, the Land Office took eight years to draw up this lease and, after a sixteen-year wait in total, Grogan was finally free as of November 1920 to commence the development of Mbaraki.

He had not entirely ignored Mbaraki in the meantime. Long though his wait for the lease had been, he always knew that the CO would eventually have to honour Eliot's promise or risk a very public scandal. With that in mind he had, over time, purchased a further 150 acres of private land adjacent to the initial grant. Most plots were charmed from the clutches of Sheikh Ali bin Salim, the *Liwali* of the Arab community, of which Grogan was an ardent admirer and whose interests he always staunchly defended. Once again Grogan's partner in this venture was the financier C. S. Goldmann, who had backed him in the early days of negotiation for his forest concession.

As a result of his purchases from the *Liwali*, when Grogan was granted his fifty-acre lease by the government his total land holding around Mbaraki amounted to 200 acres. The land leased from the government included just under a mile of frontage onto the deep water to the south of Mbaraki creek, and just over a mile of frontage on the creek itself. This land was 'free of all conditions', as were his foreshore rights – a favourable stipulation made at the specific behest of Milner (who considered that Grogan should be given carte blanche to do as he wished with the land after waiting so long for a lease). Misunderstandings about the all-embracing nature of this official blessing given by Milner were, however, soon to cause the most acrimonious dispute that Grogan ever had with the Kenyan government.

As soon as the ink was dry on the Mbaraki lease Grogan set about planning something comparable to his erstwhile partner, Lingham's, magnificent development at Port Matolla in Portuguese East Africa. The war had revealed to Grogan chronic deficiencies in the working of the existing port facilities, which had almost collapsed under the strain of importing vast numbers of soldiers and even vaster tonnages of supplies. The crux of the problem was that without a deep-water facility ships were unable to lie alongside a quay to unload. Instead, they anchored off-shore and lighters were used to ferry cargo and passengers from ship to shore – a process which was as time-consuming as it was costly.

Grogan was not alone in wanting to rectify this parlous state of affairs. Before the war the government had twice begun work on a deep-water facility only to be thwarted by engineering difficulties in the first instance, and in the second instance by the war itself. In 1920 some far-sighted officials again started to draw up plans for a deep-water port at Kilindini, 1¼ miles to the north-west of Mbaraki. But Grogan believed that Mbaraki had significant natural advantages over Kilindini, and wasted no time in pointing them out to anyone who would listen.

That same year the government's and Grogan's schemes were put before Legco. It was as important, in terms of the consequences, as it had proved with the Uasin Gishu railway that this was the year in which the unofficial benches of the council were dominated by men who envied or feared Grogan. Rather than dwell on his 'yeoman service' in connection with the Currency Crisis, then at its height, or his attention to affairs of state, a majority of councillors were far more preoccupied with the fact that Grogan was known to be spending a lot of time with his old friend Milner. Furthermore, their suspicions seemed to be confirmed when Grogan returned to the colony brandishing a licence from Milner to do exactly as he liked at Mbaraki; and as Grogan was not at the time a member of Legco he had no way of countering the whispering campaign against him.

Two plans of Grogan's were put before Legco as rivals to the government scheme at Kilindini. Plan A was drawn up with Lawley's assistance and proposed developing Mbaraki as quickly as possible so that, at a cost of £350,000, Mombasa could be rid of congestion within a year. Plan B was altogether more ambitious and was fashioned to serve the long-term needs of the colony. It cost £1m and was devised with the help of the renowned civil engineer, Sir George Buchanan. Buchanan had spent twenty years running the ports of Rangoon and Basra and, to the considerable chagrin of the local government and the Colonial Office, it took only the most cursory of glances at Mombasa for him to comment that 'port facilities is another subject illustrating the past lack of policy and economic vision [in Kenya]'.[9]

The merits of these two plans were only given hasty consideration in Legco in the closing months of 1920. Work had already begun by then on the government's deep-water port at Kilindini, which greatly influenced the decision of official members of Council: to abandon Kilindini in favour of Mbaraki would have left many of them with egg on their faces. Furthermore, McGregor Ross was hell-bent on preventing Grogan from turning Mbaraki into a 'private lake' and on this occasion, to Grogan's great disappointment, the influential Bowring (the colony's Treasurer) concurred. The settler members were equally opposed to the Mbaraki schemes because many were convinced that Grogan must be trying to put one over on them. An overwhelming majority in Legco decided that Grogan should be given 'no encouragement' for his Mbaraki schemes, a thinly disguised way of saying that an almost unanimous Council was determined to do everything in its power to thwart Grogan's ambitions.

There was one dissenting voice in Legco, and that – to his considerable credit – was Delamere's. By the end of 1920 he had not only smelt a rat in Legco's treatment of the Uasin Gishu railway proposals, but had also realized just how intent McGregor Ross was on 'getting' him and Grogan. As if to declare that he was far from happy about the level of impartiality being displayed by both settler and official members of the council, he insisted on it being put on record that promises made to Grogan by Milner – namely that he could do what he liked at Mbaraki – must be honoured in full. Delamere added that if the government could release much-needed funds for other developments in the colony by entering into partnership with Grogan, then it should carefully consider so doing. But his wise words went unheeded, and the government headed off along a path marked 'disaster'.

Delamere was not the only one to hold reservations about Legco's conduct. Even in the government's own Secretariat there were those who were certain that, as had happened during the Uasin Gishu railway saga, too much credence had been attached to engineering advice prejudicial to Grogan's Mbaraki schemes delivered by the far from unbiased McGregor Ross. Major Dutton, for one, expressed his unease in a letter to Robert Coryndon, who at the time was still Governor of Uganda. 'A number of people', wrote Dutton, 'are not convinced that the "Grogan scheme" . . . should have been turned down.'[10]

Grogan, as was often his wont, had split public opinion down the middle. But on one thing almost everyone who knew him well was agreed: telling Grogan that he was being given 'no encouragement', and thereby implying that he would not dare to raise the sums of money needed to build his port as a rival to that of the government, was akin to waving a red rag at a bull.

Grogan was certainly disappointed by Legco's rebuff as he set out to prove his opponents not just wrong, but imbecilic. He knew there was no chance of raising the £1m necessary for the execution of Sir George Buchanan's plan without government backing, but by the end of 1921 he had employed his own engineer – Major Hickes – and begun work on Lawley's more modest plan. With each passing month he grew more convinced that the government had blundered, and that the economy was on the verge of rebounding so rapidly that the government's rival Kilindini scheme would not be ready in time to handle an explosion of both exports and imports.

McGregor Ross (publicly) and his cronies (privately) declared Grogan insane, and after six months of construction work even Northey, usually a supporter of Grogan, judged the prospects for Mbaraki to be 'most unpromising'. That same month – April 1922 – the Colonial Office also adjudged the rapidly developing private port to be 'amateurish and inadequate'.[11] There was, in other words, still no sign of alarm in the highest echelons of government that Grogan might be outflanking them. By the end of the year they were in for a nasty surprise.

In December 1922 an astonishing, if makeshift, feat of engineering had been completed under Grogan's watchful eye. At the foot of the cliff overlooking Mbaraki creek, on the water's edge, a 445 ft concrete and wood pile wharf fronted directly on to deep water. Extending from the wharf were three pontoons equipped with the latest three ton electric 'Goliath' cranes for the loading and unloading of ships;

behind it, between the water and the cliff, was the largest transit shed in Africa with ten more electric cranes inside. Two miles of railway had been built below and on top of the cliff, linked by conveyors – direct access to and from the Uganda Railway was thus assured for cargo. Roads and warehouses were complete, and a new lighter wharf, to complement the deep-water pier, had been built on the creek itself.

Just before Christmas, as the Indian Crisis approached its denouement, not one but *two* steamers tied up alongside Grogan's deep-water pontoons and became the first ocean-going vessels to load directly from Kenya's shores. After decades of waiting, and two failed attempts by the government, Kenya at last had its first deep-water port. *The African World*, the British public's handbook on matters African, duly paid tribute to 'one very clever man'.[12] More prosaically, Grogan observed that 'my personal position was a peculiar one, because I could sit and dangle my legs over the deep water but could not afford to go to the Club as I had not enough cash to pay for a drink'.[13] Undeterred by this minor problem he declared himself ready for the *next* stage of development at Mbaraki, and with its own facilities at Kilindini nowhere near completion the government panicked.

Work on the £1.5m 'official' port at Kilindini had proceeded at a snail's pace and, to add insult to injury, had been declared by an eminent visiting engineer to be 'grossly extravagant'.[14] Robert Coryndon, who had by now succeeded Northey as governor, faced a nightmare of which Delamere had once warned in Legco: namely that as Grogan was allowed to build his own port, he would, and that there was a significant danger that Kilindini would prove to be a white elephant. The potential consequences of what Coryndon criticized as a 'complete absence' of governmental 'pre-vision in business affairs in Kenya in the past'[15] were far greater than a simple and perhaps temporary loss of face. It had become clear that the jealous machinations of McGregor Ross and his cronies threatened the economic survival of the entire colony.

Grogan had been right all along in his optimism for the East African economy and his claim that Mombasa of necessity would be the biggest port north of Durban – an opinion with which Coryndon had always agreed. 'All produce', he recorded in a memo, 'from Kenya, from a large part of the eastern Congo Belge, a large part of Belgian

Ruanda and Urundi and that rich Mwanza area of Tanganyika Territory *must* come out at [Mombasa].'[16] Between 1914 and 1924 the volumes of that produce grew exponentially: notwithstanding the effect of the post-war depression on worldwide commodity prices, the value of agricultural exports from East Africa rose from just under £0.5m to over £5m, and imports rose from c.£2m to over £6m. Increases in the production of maize, cotton and coffee were gargantuan. In the absence of any sign of imminent completion of the deepwater port at Kilindini only Grogan's Mbaraki stood between the African and European farmer and bankruptcy at the end of 1922. Coryndon heaped praise on his old Matabele War comrade-in-arms as fulsomely as he derided the myopia and petty-mindedness of the anti-Grogan factions among officials and settlers.

Grogan was cock-a-hoop that Mbaraki had proved his detractors wrong, but he also appreciated Coryndon's dilemma and did not want to see him – or the colony – further embarrassed just because Legco had backed the wrong horse in the 'battle of the ports'. Coryndon had a reputation as a brilliant administrator, could tear a deck of cards in half with his bare hands, and personified for Grogan the spirit of 'the old jolly African days'.[17] He resolved to present the Kenyan government with a way out which upheld everybody's honour.

Grogan proposed that in order for Coryndon to reassert governmental control over the workings of Mombasa as a whole, it should buy Mbaraki from him for £150,000. This was roughly what he had spent developing it, but in case he should be turned down Grogan wisely opted to take out an insurance policy by leasing Mbaraki to the African Wharfage Company for £1,000 per month and offering the company the option of buying him out at any time for £120,000. This deal still left him free to sell to the government if they accepted his offer, and the value that it placed on his port should have silenced those who suspected that he might be asking an unreasonable price from the government. But it did not. William McGregor Ross had not yet given up on trying to 'get' Grogan.

McGregor Ross was by now smarting from his defeat and humiliation over the Uasin Gishu railway – construction of which had just commenced straight through the middle of Grogan's timber concession. He laid into Grogan's offer to sell Mbaraki to the best of his splenetic ability, calling it 'an act of piracy'. The cornerstone of McGregor Ross's argument was that the quality of the Mbaraki deep-water wharf and piers was so poor that they would fall apart in less than six years – so there was nothing worth buying.

Despite the fact that Grogan, Delamere and the other 'big men' of the settler community were back in Legco, on the government benches a majority were still prepared to listen to McGregor Ross's views. The Council therefore turned down Grogan's offer to sell Mbaraki. Coryndon was aghast but, as an exceptionally fair man, he was not in the habit of over-ruling his own officials. His disapproval of their decision was nonetheless plain for all to see: he publicly praised Grogan's 'boldness' in developing Mbaraki, and said that he now had 'every right to deal elsewhere and earn some financial profit'.[18]

By the middle of 1923 Legco's refusal to sanction the purchase of Mbaraki was proving more expensive to the colony by the day. Grogan's facilities at Mbaraki were handling fully half of Mombasa's exports,[19] including the entire Ugandan cotton crop and a substantial proportion of East Africa's maize crop – both the mainstays of the African economy. With Kilindini still nowhere near completion, Coryndon finally decided to call time. He had had enough of McGregor Ross's vendetta against Grogan, and ordered that Mbaraki had to be purchased forthwith by the government to counter the dire economic consequences of congestion in Mombasa. Furthermore, in order to avoid any future conflicts between government and private interests on Mombasa Island, he was determined to buy not only Grogan's port but all the adjacent land that Grogan had bought from the *Liwali*. Again Grogan agreed to 'play the game' and asked for £400,000 for the whole 200-acre estate.

Coryndon's decision should have been followed by hasty resolution of the matter. Instead it presaged almost *three years* of negotiations which, for the only time in his life, brought Grogan to his knees. One of the backers of his Kilindini Harbour, Wharves and Estate Company (KHW&E) which owned Mbaraki went bankrupt, owing the company

£50,000, and the business agent of one of his partners in the enterprise, Lord Howard de Walden,[20] motivated either by a desire either to protect his employer's minority interest in Mbaraki or to see the company bankrupted (thereby enabling him to repurchase Mbaraki for a song), started to furnish the government with confidential information behind Grogan's back.

Whatever his motives the agent acted without Lord Howard de Walden's knowledge, and as he was Managing Director of both KHW&E and Equator Saw Mills, his decision to pass company secrets relating to the strength of Grogan's negotiating position was at best unethical and at worse illegal. By revealing to certain officials that Grogan was on the verge of bankruptcy he not only undermined his chairman, but made the government aware that if it dragged its feet long enough Mbaraki would cease to belong to Grogan without a penny changing hands.

The result was that during 1923 a powerful group of officials in the Kenyan government increased the pressure on Grogan by a variety of underhanded means. They approached the directors of the African Wharfage Company to try to spoil Grogan's agreement with them; they jacked up the railway rates on the Mbaraki siding in an attempt to render it unprofitable; McGregor Ross disputed Grogan's right to ownership of land that he was reclaiming in the creek, and contested the proven validity of his foreshore rights; and so the list went on. Grogan found himself in the unwelcome position of being not only the builder of the colony's first deep-water port, but also one of the founders of its legal profession: law suits flew in all directions, including one brought at the behest of Lord Howard de Walden's agent by Grogan's own company, KHW&E, against Grogan himself. In time it would transpire that none of these suits had any legal justification, but time was just what the heavily indebted Grogan did not have, and for many months even his old friend Coryndon was unable to help him while each and every allegation against Grogan was disproved.[21]

Grogan guessed exactly what was going on well before he learnt what Lord Howard de Walden's agent had been up to. The minute Mbaraki's railway tariffs were raised he wrote to Coryndon stating that the action was 'thoroughly dishonest ... and unquestionably illegal', and he added, 'believe me you are heading for an absolutely impossible position ... I am very bitter about it [and] cannot believe that you personally intend to join in the Grogan hunt to the extent of using State funds in an attempt to ruin a private enterprise which was a mere execution of the rights given me by Government'. As he edged closer to bankruptcy the tone of his letters became yet more desperate, and he was even reduced to threatening Coryndon with legal action while declaring that he was 'sick to death of your d——d country and your people and [I] only want to get out'. 'Why don't we do things in a decent way?' he beseeched his old friend, 'do you intend to do me in?'[22]

By the autumn of 1923, Grogan's suspicions were confirmed beyond any doubt when he heard privately – and on good authority – that his opponents in the government were determined to 'not do anything out of which the accursed Grogan might conceivably be supposed to make a penny'. With the big guns at the Colonial Office also seemingly ranged on him, Grogan finally appealed to Coryndon for help. He revealed that he was 'devilish ill' with another burst liver abscess and unsure whether he could 'stand much more'. Finally, he rather meekly requested 'a decent resolution' to the Mbaraki saga so that he might tackle one more project 'before I die'.[23]

At the end of 1923 Grogan's luck changed, when he discovered what Lord Howard de Walden's agent had been up to. Exactly how he did this is unclear, but his contacts and influence were as extensive as ever and someone – quite possibly Coryndon himself – must finally have spilled the beans. Grogan was livid, not just with the agent but with Coryndon, who had allowed his civil servants to believe all that the man had told them without giving him a chance to clear his name. With the agent and the government exposed, Grogan came back with a vengeance. In a KHW&E board meeting held during the night of 13 March 1924, the agent was voted off the board and Grogan prepared to take on the government. His good relations with Howard de Walden, who it seems remained wholly unaware of his henchman's shenanigans, were unaffected.

Coryndon – and indeed the whole Kenyan government – were even more embarrassed by the industrial espionage indulged in by some of its less scrupulous officials than they had been by the success of Mbaraki port. Furthermore, they discovered soon after Grogan had ousted his malevolent co-director that he had succeeded in borrowing another £100,000 of capital from 'nice Mr Toogood' at the Standard Bank. This new loan led Grogan modestly to quip that by comparison with the stellar careers of his two old Matabele War friends – 'Empire Jack' Norton-Griffiths and Coryndon – his own 'only claim to distinction was the possession of the biggest overdraft in the history of Kenya'.[24] More seriously for his enemies, the raising of further funds meant that so long as Mbaraki remained busy and could pay the interest on the loan there was no longer any prospect of driving Grogan into bankruptcy. In addition, McGregor Ross's allegations about the invalidity of Grogan's claim to reclaimed land and to foreshore rights were shown to be hot air, and Grogan personally demonstrated to the Attorney General's complete satisfaction that all law suits filed against him were unjustified. No case was ever brought to court.

Having put himself back on surer ground Grogan – with breathtaking audacity – decided to up the stakes considerably in 1924 by starting work on a second larger wharf at Mbaraki. It was planned to add 3,000 tons per day to the handling capacity of his port, thereby multiplying it almost tenfold, and, when completed, he knew that it would render the government's £1.5m Kilindini site, with its planned capacity of 800 tons per day, wholly redundant. With each passing month the pressure mounted on Grogan's opponents as his men worked around the clock to finish the new wharf on time, and finally they buckled.

At the Colonial Office Sir Cecil Bottomley announced meekly that now he 'knew the facts' about the local government's handling of the affair – as if he hadn't all along – it was clear that Grogan was 'not yet beaten' and was 'quite right about the [£400,000] price'[25] he had asked for Mbaraki. Bottomley suggested to Coryndon that he try to settle for £350,000, a bargaining ploy countered by a threat from Grogan to go to arbitration. This the cornered CO and, in particular, the Kenyan government's Attorney General regarded as 'dangerous',[26] all the more so if anything were to emerge publicly about the way some of its members had deliberately tried to force Grogan into bankruptcy. But one last attempt was made to break Grogan: just as the contract for the sale of Mbaraki was being signed his local adversaries tried to have his port condemned on health grounds.[27] As the Public Works Department had itself still not completed the main sewers of substantial parts of Nairobi and Mombasa, the Ministry of Health's initiative predictably failed.

Grogan was sickened by this final attempt to undo him. In February 1925, trusting no one in the Kenyan government after Coryndon died during an operation, he wrote to his friend Leo Amery who was conveniently the new Colonial Secretary in the Tory Cabinet. In his letter he uncharacteristically appealed to Amery 'for protection', as he had done to Coryndon, and he ruefully declared 'they [the Kenyan government] waged war on the venture and have now waged it so successfully that they have disgusted the Bank, ruined the Company, and reduced me to a state of negligent and bitter despair ... There must,' he concluded, 'be some ethics in Government transactions of business.'[28]

Amery's response was rapidly to consult the files relating to the five-year saga. They did not make for pleasant reading. He found that Bottomley, as head of the Colonial Office's East Africa department, had personally admitted late in 1924 that 'certain aspects' of the CO's handling of the affair were 'bad business on our part', and that on the question of the increased railway tariff imposed on Mbaraki early in 1923 Bottomley had also written the following: 'while none of us like the special haulage charge ... it is our last line of defence'.[29] The new General Manager of the Uganda Railway, Christian Ludolph Neethling Felling (whom Grogan considered 'a first class man', who would – as he did – sweep clean 'the Augean stable of the railway'[30]) had gone one step further once he had familiarized himself with the details of the case: he was adamant that the government 'could not contemplate [maintaining] any crushing charge on Mbaraki, first because [it is] improper, and only bare necessity could justify the action already taken by my predecessor.'[31] Amery could smell the very strong whiff of scandal, and ordered the immediate purchase of Mbaraki for an agreed price of £350,000 – approximately £9m in today's money.

Grogan finally received his money in December 1925. It is a moot point how much the other shareholders in his KHW&E company eventually received as it was so deep in debt, but what mattered to him was that he had pulled off a feat of mind-boggling brinkmanship in proving the impossible possible. He derived huge satisfaction from the fact that – at a time when there was no government deep-water pier and the economy began to boom – he, Grogan, had kept both African and European farmers in business by exporting their produce quickly and efficiently from Mbaraki rather than leave it to rot on the docks.

There is no record of just how many individuals actually thanked Grogan for this service, but it was recognized by the Public Inquiry into the 'Mbaraki Affair' ordered by Coryndon just before his death. In a carefully worded statement, which in a very British way alluded to the local government's scandalous treatment of Grogan, the Inquiry's report concluded that 'the facilities afforded by [Mbaraki] have greatly relieved the position so far as handling exports at the port is concerned; in fact, it is difficult to imagine how it would have been possible to cope with the continually increasing volume of traffic had these facilities not been available'.[32] In Legco most councillors, official and unofficial, blamed the handling of the affair on their predecessors, but the soldier-settler J. E. Coney at least had the good grace to pay tribute to 'Major Grogan's foresight [to which] in this and many other matters the Colony owes a very great deal', and Geoffrey Northcote, the Acting Chief Secretary of the government asked all councillors to 'honour the man whose imagination and whose sagacity and energy caused that port to be built'.[33] Such sentiments were only marred by North-cote's further suggestion that a monument be erected at Mbaraki to Coryndon, for having insisted on buying it. No one suggested erecting a monument to Grogan, its visionary builder.

Grogan still managed to have the last laugh. By 1926 his port was collapsing under the strain of handling more cargo than it was built for, and the government had to rebuild large parts of it. And, as he reflected on the whole saga, best of all was the fact that in April 1923 Coryndon had demanded the resignation of one William McGregor Ross.[34]

TWENTY-ONE

Changing Times

As Grogan's remarkable Houdini act approached its denouement his strength, badly debilitated by the burst liver abscess, returned and he threw himself into another of his periodic rearrangements of the family's residences. In 1923 he had rented a country house in the East Sussex village of Mayfield so that Gertrude could be near Cynthia and Jane, who were attending its convent school. Sending the girls to St Leonard's had been, at a time of great uncertainty in Grogan's life, one relatively straightforward decision: his little sister Hilda was teaching there, having – in contrast to her agnostic brother – taken her vows.[1]

Hilda's faith, and that of Mildred (Philip's wife), had quite an effect on the Grogan girls; so too did her determination to pursue a career. When Dorothy and Joyce finished attending North Foreland Lodge in Hampshire, Grogan believed that both girls' destiny was to marry as soon as they met eligible suitors. But he was in for a shock: Joyce announced that she wanted to follow her aunt into the Catholic Church. She had never been a 'thruster' and it is a distinct possibility that taking her vows represented the most effective way of escaping her over-bearing father. This she duly did, being received into the community at St Leonard's soon after her twenty-first birthday in 1926.

Grogan was certainly disappointed at the news but accepted Joyce's decision philosophically. He was, however, far from cheerful about Dorothy's ambition to study medicine at Oxford. She was much more of a chip off the old block than Joyce, but was still largely regarded as mere marriage fodder by her father. Besides, Dorothy had made the fatal – and probably quite deliberate – mistake of nominating Oxford as her chosen place of study rather than her father's own alma mater, of which he remained fiercely proud. Grogan gave Dorothy no encouragement, and the idea was dropped.

The choice of Mayfield as a country residence was not only predicated on being close to Cynthia and Jane: it happened to be just four miles from Grogan's other family at Burnt Oak, thus enabling him to shuttle merrily between the two. East Sussex was also home to many a friend: Kipling was at Burwash, Lawley had a farm in Hawkhurst, and Grogan's long-standing business partner, C. S. Goldmann, had a country residence at Rottingdean. By the end of 1924, however, the rented house in Mayfield no longer met Grogan's needs. His interest in farming – whether in Africa or England – was as keen as ever and, spurred on by his development of the Burnt Oak estate, he decided that what he wanted was a farm where he could keep his first family as well. With that in mind, and taking an optimistic view of the outcome of his negotiations over Mbaraki, he bought Venters on the edge of the village of Rusper, near Horsham.

Venters was a magnificent country house. It boasted an all-important library, a ballroom, numerous bedrooms each with their own sitting room, hard and grass tennis courts, and an enormous garden which, under Gertrude's stewardship, was transformed into something every bit as glorious as her creations at Chiromo and Camp Hill. Four servants kept the place in order. Of greatest interest to Grogan was the adjoining 100-acre Peter's Farm on which he set to work with his customary zeal, and when he desired a change of scene Burnt Oak was only twenty miles away as the crow flew.

There is no doubt that when the Mbaraki Affair hit its enervating nadir, and on at least one other occasion in the mid 1920s, Grogan seriously considered turning his back on Africa. He was, with ample justification, very bitter about (and battered by) the British government's handling of the Currency Crisis and the Kenyan government's underhand tactics when negotiating to buy Mbaraki. In the December 1923 General Election which followed Bonar Law's resignation on health grounds, Grogan briefly flirted with the idea of returning to British politics while masterminding George Lloyd's campaign in Eastbourne. Despite impetuously describing Lloyd's constituency as 'a parasitic excrescence on the body politic',[2] Grogan threw himself into this task with obvious relish and helped his old friend to victory.

But the overall election result persuaded him that he had better not burn all his bridges with Kenya. For the first time the 'Labourites' took power, albeit only for a single year, and Grogan took just one look at Ramsay Macdonald before pronouncing him 'the greatest Prime Ministerial joke in all England's history'.[3]

Grogan saw a lot of Lloyd and his much-admired wife, Blanche, over the next year or so and the two men regularly discussed the state of the Empire. A first Labour government was not exactly good news for old school imperialists, even though Macdonald proved – in Grogan's opinion – to be little more than 'a puppet and loudspeaker for our wise Tory leader, Baldwin'.[4] Equally uninspiring were Lloyd's tales from India. For six years after the war Lloyd had been Governor of the Bombay Presidency and it was he who had been responsible for imprisoning Gandhi in 1922. The intelligence Lloyd fed Grogan during Kenya's own Indian Crisis had been instrumental in enabling the latter to see the crisis in the wider context of Empire. Lloyd's tenure in Bombay seemed to Grogan to symbolize a growing challenge to the Empire. On the one hand Lloyd had built, and given his name to, a massive irrigation barrage across the Indus which transformed for the better the lives of hundreds of thousands of Indians, but on the other, Indian nationalists and their supporters in London – including Grogan's old opponent Wedgwood – were growing bolder and more vociferous by the day.

Both Grogan and Lloyd believed, however, that Africa did not pose the same problem as India. Both were certain that Rhodes's dream of a vast imperial federation stretching all the way from Cape to Cairo might yet be realized, and on the face of it their optimism seemed justified: Egypt, the Sudan, Uganda, Kenya, Tanganyika, Northern and Southern Rhodesia, Bechuanaland and the Union of South Africa were all either British colonies, mandates, or within the British 'sphere of influence'. Fighting for what was termed 'Closer Union' between these territories became a major preoccupation of imperialists during the second half of the 1920s, and it was with this in mind that Grogan actively campaigned to have Lloyd installed as Governor of Kenya following Coryndon's death. This was not his first attempt to lure Lloyd to the colony,[5] but once again Lloyd's prodigious talents as a statesman and diplomat slipped from Grogan's usually persuasive grasp when he was appointed High Commissioner in Egypt.

This setback, and the conclusion of the Mbaraki affair at the end of 1925, prompted another brief period of doubt on Grogan's part about whether his future lay in Kenya. No sooner had he received his money from the Kenyan government than he tried to off-load most of his other assets on the state – so great was his disgust at the way the colony was being run. In a letter to Sir Christian Felling, that 'first class man' in charge of the Uganda Railway, Grogan listed all his assets and put a price on them of £300,000 (about £7.5m in today's money). The government thought hard about this audacious offer, but by the time it turned it down Grogan had already changed his mind.[6] He had firmly decided that his love affair with Africa was not over, and determined to throw himself back into his businesses there with redoubled zeal. All his companies were reorganized under a single holding company named East Africa Ventures (dubbed 'East Africa Vultures' by his detractors) and he turned the full force of his attention on Equator Saw Mills.

The post-war period had proved disastrous for ESM, for a variety of reasons. Some were, at least in part, directly attributable to Grogan himself. When he was not enthused by the prospects for a particular part of his business empire his tendency was to ignore it altogether and leave all administrative matters to his brother-in-law, Wilfrid Hunter, to his agent, Tannahill, or to managers on the spot. This staccato approach was not, it must be said, very successful. Grogan was on the whole a poor chooser of managers, preferring mavericks whose eccentricity appealed to him rather than ones with proven track records, and there was never enough cash in his pocket to enable the highly capable, if dour, Hunter, or Tannahill to do much more than fight fires. This they found extremely frustrating, as is attested to by an uncharacteristically contrite, rather touching, wartime letter from Grogan to his long-suffering brother-in-law:

Venters, the Grogan estate in West Sussex.

Prospective Unionist candidate Grogan with Gertrude and daughters Dorothy, Joyce and Cynthia in Newcastle-under-Lyme during the tempestuous first General Election of 1910: 'it took the place of Agincourt'.

Nairobi, the result of 'some momentary mental abberation' and 'the home of frogs innumerable', in 1917.

A picture of the four Grogan girls taken in September 1916 and sent to their father while he was earning two mentions in despatches and the DSO in German East Africa.

'Kenya's Churchill': it was to Grogan that the East African military authorities turned for a rallying-cry in 1915.

Grogan with his gimlet eye (centre) surrounded by friends.

'Dear old Nanny Redwood'.

James and Hannah Coleman, the grandees of Hawke's Bay.

Viscount Milner – 'an outstanding character'.

Grogan's greatest friend and saviour: Alfred 'Mile-A-Day Boys' Lawley.

Cecil Rhodes: 'give yourself to Africa'.

Grogan's fellow 'bloody troopers' Bobby (later Sir Robert) Coryndon and Sir John 'Empire Jack' Norton-Griffiths, right.

Indomitable Kenya pioneer William Russell Bowker, sporting his snarling leopard's-head cap.

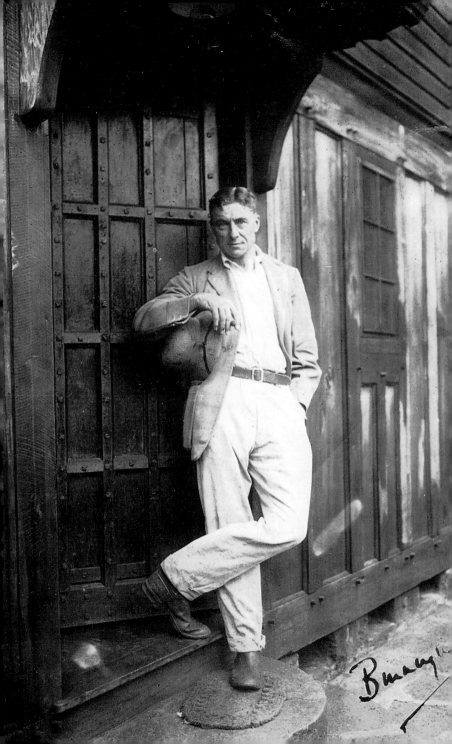

Grogan's Torr's Hotel in 1928 – 'the Carlton of East Africa'.

Mbaraki, 1925: Grogan builds Kenya's first deep-water harbour.

OPPOSITE *Bwana Chui* – The Leopard.

LEFT Grogan climbs aboard Imperial Airways' first commercial trans-Africa flight in 1932, thereby completing a unique double.

ABOVE Awarding the Grogan prize for East African history – Duke of York's School speech day December 1959.

BELOW 'Grogan's Castle' with Mount Kilimanjaro in the background.

Grogan and Gertrude at Muthaiga Club,

Camilla Towers.

With his Pekinese in Nairobi in 1961.
Grogan was wishing for 'the application
kindly method now used in farewell to
and too aged dogs'.

Grogan on patrol on the Taveta estates
where he was credited with 'turning
semi-desert into productive fields'.

Grogan shares a joke with Kenyatta (left) and Tom Mboya on the eve of Kenyan independence.

Grogan's adventures ended where they had begun seventy-one years earlier – in Cape Town.

IN LOVING MEMORY
OF
LT. COL.
EWART SCOTT GROGAN D.S.O.
BORN 12TH DEC. 1874
DIED 16TH AUG. 1967.
R. I. P.

I fully realize the enormous amount of work you have done . . . in the past and the inadequate cash remunerations your firm has received therefor. I have always looked upon the present status as a temporary one and merely the stepping stone towards a final adjustment wherein you would reap the harvest for your unremitting toil and staunchness to me. An occasionally repellent manner (of which I am fully cognizant) has, I sometimes think, disguised from you the immense affection and sincere gratitude which I feel towards you. I also recognized that you from the beginning have looked upon me as a wild impractical dreamer. I am not. I am really exceptionally world wise in the wider fields but am hopelessly negligent of details and irremediably spasmodic in my methods of work. I have always seen in you the exact complement of myself, and have an almost childish confidence in your judgement in all the manifold matters where I know my own incompetence.[7]

During the post-war depression, matters were made worse by an increase in the poll tax levied on the African population (which Grogan had strongly, but unsuccessfully, opposed), a diminution in Africans' wages in the wake of the Currency Crisis, and by the government's introduction of the much-hated *kipande* (pass) laws for Africans. These created an acute shortage of Africans willing to work for Europeans – government and settler alike – at a time when there was also a significantly reduced demand for timber in the colony, caused by economic hardship. Total timber throughput at Grogan's mills at Maji Mazuri and Eldama Ravine in the years 1921–3 fell to a mere 700,000 cubic feet.

In late 1926 Grogan sailed for the colony trailing Dorothy and Cynthia in his wake and determined to address the problems at ESM (Equator Saw Mills) personally. His sudden resurgence of interest was attributable to a number of factors: the Mbaraki Affair was over, so Grogan was once again in funds; the colony's economy was booming (largely due to the measures implemented by the 1922 Economic and Finance Committee, whose proceedings Grogan and Delamere had dominated), and the Uasin Gishu railway was approaching completion, which meant that Grogan could at last transport timber in meaningful quantities out of his 300-square-mile forest concession by rail. He was confident enough to erect two new saw mills, at Sabatia and Londiani, in 1926, and for each of the next five years he succeeded in milling an average of over half a million cubic feet of timber. In resuscitating the business, however, he courted controversy yet again.

Grogan was heavily criticized for only picking the eyes out of the forest, for hampering replanting and day-to-day management of the forest by the government, for defaulting on paying his timber royalties to the government, and for having a complete lack of control over the contractors employed to fell the timber. All of these allegations were more or less true, and were seized on with alacrity by government officials still smarting from their embarrassment during the Mbaraki Affair. At one point in 1926 it seemed that only the fact that the colony could not do without ESM's timber, that Grogan agreed to pay higher royalties than stipulated in his lease, and that his friend Amery was Colonial Secretary enabled him to avert calls for a Public Inquiry into the workings of the concession. But there were always two sides to the Grogan coin.

Working the concession in such a way that it was not only commercially viable and able to provide over half the country's timber, but also to satisfy the diametrically opposite desires of forestry experts and guardians of African grazing rights was well nigh impossible. Furthermore, much of what Grogan was allowed to 'get away with' was perfectly allowable within the terms of a highly favourable forest licence to which the government had, after all, appended its signature. The nub of the problem was that Grogan was sandwiched between conflicting interests, a fact which is clearly illustrated in a report written in 1928 by J. W. Nicholson, the government's Conservator of Forests. Nicholson was highly critical of the conduct of ESM's contractors and its inefficient forest management, but he added observations that were completely ignored by those caught up in another 'Grogan hunt', namely that ESM's sheer size and preferential royalty rates helped to keep timber prices low and that it was 'undoubtedly an advantage to have ESM [here]'. Grogan, he also remarked, 'has shown considerable enterprise . . . not least in establishing a wood preservation plant',[8] another first for the colony.

As he was by now accustomed to doing, Grogan successfully withstood all attempts to 'get him', and continued to satisfy the colony's – and particularly the Uganda Railway's – timber requirements at a time of rapidly escalating demand. Equally typically, his interest waned as soon as ESM was back on a firm footing. At that point Grogan went in search of a new manager for his and Howard de Walden's company, and found young Ferdinand Cavendish-Bentinck – the future 8th Duke of Portland.

'C-B', as he was always referred to, came fresh from being Private Secretary to the Governor of Uganda to running an enormous business of which he had no experience whatsoever. His sole qualifications were that Grogan liked him, liked his politics and liked employing aristocrats. Nevertheless C-B threw himself into the job with great enthusiasm and was quite happy living out in the wilds of Maji Mazuri, which had superseded Turi as the forest headquarters of ESM. His house, built by Grogan in a beautiful cutting in the forest, even had a hard tennis court, and always within his field of vision was an indestructible concrete bunker which housed Grogan's safe – an idiosyncratic feature of almost every house Grogan built in Africa.

C-B liked his new employer, though he was in awe of him. He considered Grogan – who was always referred to by his 2,000 African employees simply as *bwana chui* – 'the leopard' – to be very far-sighted, courteous and generous, and once installed at Maji Mazuri he was left almost entirely to his own devices.

In the meantime, with Kenya's (and ESM's) financial barometer moving to set fair, Grogan again started to spend longer periods in East Africa and, having sold Chiromo to Northrup Macmillan during the war, decided to build a new townhouse in Nairobi. Known as 'the Gallows' on account of its rather sinister-looking wooden gatehouse, this residence was every bit as eccentric as the 'Pagoda' Grogan had built fifteen years earlier at Turi. Standing just across the road from his favourite watering-hole, Muthaiga Club, this Alpine chalet – for want of a better description – still stands today. It was not large: Grogan did not, after his children's schooling was complete, anticipate having to house any member of his family except Gertrude, and his personal tastes always verged on the ascetic. As with C-B's house at Maji Mazuri, the Gallows' most notable feature was a concrete bunker in the garden, complete with a bed for Grogan and a bath into which he could step straight from the bed. In this cool and silent chamber Grogan whiled away hours reading voraciously, consulting maps and planning his next ventures. In 1928 two suddenly popped out simultaneously. One was to build the most splendid hotel in the colony, if not all Africa; the other was to indulge his passion for farming on a colossal scale.

While these new ambitions were planned in meticulous detail he continued to shuttle to and from England. Dorothy remained with him in Nairobi and, having reconciled herself to her extraordinary father's behaviour to a greater degree than any of the other children, she actually volunteered to work for him – which was probably a good deal more taxing on the patience than studying medicine at Oxford. Although she was well beyond the age of majority he remained the strictest of chaperones: each time they took the boat home he would make her go to bed before the fun started in the evenings (and she would sneak out of her cabin the minute he had left her). On these voyages Dorothy was by no means her father's only charge: any number of his friends used to entrust their daughters, if travelling alone, to Grogan's care. For one who was known to be a ladies' man, this may seem surprising, but his friends' logic was simple enough: J. C. Coverdale, a surveyor, was just one of many who reckoned it took a rogue to recognize a rogue, and that on that basis no one knew better how to look after a young lady than Grogan.

Paternally strict though he was, Grogan also loved to spoil. When Dorothy fell ill in Nairobi with viral pneumonia he visited the hospital every day bearing bottles of 'therapeutic' champagne, much to the doctor's consternation. And when chaperoning Coverdale's daughter, Leslie, on a voyage home the 'astoundingly attractive' Grogan did the same for her when she succumbed to appendicitis. All the way to Naples he looked after her 'like a father' and on arrival took her for waffles and syrup and bought her a beautiful Italian shawl. It is perhaps not surprising that although he kept all would-be boyfriends at bay for the voyage, and gave all aspiring Italian Lotharios in Naples the most forcible of brush-offs, Grogan was himself accompanied all the way home by a '*very* lovely lady',[9] a former girlfriend of the Prince of Wales.

It seemed, as the 1920s started to draw to a close, that everything was going Grogan's way again. He was richer, more relaxed and less cantankerous than he had been for years. Kenya's economy was going from strength to strength and, with Baldwin's Conservatives in power, the Empire – whatever the challenges facing it – seemed to him to be in better hands than with the Liberals or Labourites. But all the while the storm clouds were gathering once more over Kenya's ever-turbulent political landscape.

Having resigned from Legislative Council in October 1922 and opted to become a political outsider, Grogan's always uneasy alliance with Lord Delamere broke down completely. Grogan had no desire to be a part of Delamere's – or anyone else's – Reform Party, and as a result their friendship became characterized by an ever-increasing mutual distrust. On the face of it, this need not have happened, but with both men possessed of what even their friends described as colossal egos, and with Grogan operating entirely as a law unto himself in the political arena, it became obvious that the two giant peas of the colony's formative years could not for ever remain in the same pod.

The underlying cause of the rift was simple enough: it concerned the approach to securing self-government for the colony. By forming his Reform Party in 1922 Delamere demonstrated his intention not only to unite the settlers but to work with the government in what amounted to a coalition. Only by so doing, reasoned Delamere, would the settlers show themselves to be responsible enough citizens to be entrusted with self-government. Grogan and his acolytes had severe misgivings about this approach. Firstly, he considered it politically naive, believing – like Churchill – that it was the duty of an opposition to oppose, because to co-operate in formulating policy was to risk becoming a hostage to fortune. Secondly, his Fenian blood, and recent experiences of the local government's conduct, made him instinctively opposed to supporting it on every count. Grogan thought it was obvious that his approach to securing self-government was the one most likely to triumph. It had worked in the case of South Africa; it had worked in Ireland; and in 1923 it worked in Southern Rhodesia. He was convinced that a weak Colonial Office could be forced to devolve power if put under enough pressure and confronted with permanent non-co-operation by the settlers.

The rift's political dimension was also underpinned by an intense suspicion on Grogan's part of Delamere's motives for trying to pull all parties in Kenya together. It is significant in this context that, while praising his fellow pioneer fulsomely for his momentous achievements in agriculture and affirming that Delamere's main mission in life was 'to make Kenya a great place', Grogan confided to his rival's biographer in 1933 that he suspected Delamere had 'suffered all his life from the psychological handicap of consciousness of his small stature and its lacking dignity'. In this interview he also voiced the opinion that Delamere 'adored adulation' and that this 'in the end . . . brought him to destruction'.[10] These were harsh – even cruel – words from one who himself 'adored adulation', and who less than a decade earlier had said that Delamere was 'on balance one of the Great Things of The Earth . . . he is mighty wise and more than loveable'. But there was more than an element of truth in them: Delamere, like Grogan, could be 'devilish trying at times'.[11] And once confirmed as the settlers' official spokesman he stuck rigidly to the policies that had brought him adulation, he ignored the implications of the tremendous economic upheavals and social transformations occurring in Britain during the 1920s, and he unwittingly led the settlers into a cul-de-sac from which they never emerged as powerful as they had been in the years immediately following the Great War. Whether Grogan's belief in the power of permanent opposition would have produced a different result is a moot point.

There is no doubt that being cast, by himself and others, in the role of outsider suited Grogan's temperament. By the mid 1920s he had had his fill of mainstream politics both in Britain and Kenya, and was far more interested in the economic development of the latter and the pursuit of further dreams, although had his friend George Lloyd accepted the governorship it is more than likely that Grogan would have worked with him rather than boycott Legislative Council. When Lloyd turned down the posting to Kenya in favour of the far more senior post in Egypt, the colony found itself under the sway of a rather less self-effacing imperialist.

In the first decade of the century Lieutenant-Colonel Sir Edward Grigg, later Lord Altrincham, had been just plain old 'Ned' Grigg, a rookie on *The Times* and fellow old Wykehamist, to Grogan. Given that Grigg was another erstwhile protégé of Milner's, and had enjoyed a stellar career as a soldier-statesman which included a stint as private secretary to the Prince of Wales, Grogan might have been expected to approve of Grigg. Indeed, he supported Grigg on initiatives which would have been pursued by Lloyd, such as a (failed) plan to encourage closer settlement by attracting up to 100,000 poorer European settlers to the colony. But he also considered Grigg to be no more than modestly capable, that he tried too hard to be 'Kenya's Milner', and that he was a crashing snob to boot. Even worse, in Grogan's opinion, was that Grigg had been a Liberal MP and therefore instinctively enamoured of double-standards.

Grogan had no gripe with Grigg's desire to put Kenya on the social map by playing host to the safaris of the Prince of Wales and the Duke of Gloucester (not least because they struck a death blow to the theory of East Africa as a white man's grave), but the governor's love of pomp and ceremony seemed to extend beyond what might be considered 'normal'. Civil service salaries were raised by 20 per cent, and when Grigg proposed building a new Government House at a cost of £80,000 Grogan thought that enough was enough – and said so. Trans Nzoia, he was fond of pointing out, was still without a hospital or dispensary. To Grogan's dismay, Delamere prevailed upon the settler members of Legco to support the scheme, claiming that he had in return been promised an unofficial majority in Legco. Grigg's new palace was endorsed by a united Legco – but still Delamere did not get his unofficial majority. He was, however, awarded the KCMG at Grigg's behest in 1930.

The Government House Scandal was not the only target for Grogan's criticism. During Grigg's tenure Kenyan government expenditure, mostly aimed at increasing its own size, rose to grandiose levels and Grogan attacked this in an article in *The Times* entitled 'The March Of The *Siafu*',[12] East Africa's killer ant. This very public and widely praised denunciation of government policy caused Grigg to refer to Grogan ever afterwards as 'that Irish firebrand'. Grogan responded by referring to Grigg as 'a loveable and most awfully dangerous fellow', and thereafter their distaste for each other was cast in stone.

All in all Grigg's tenure was not a peaceful one. Following the declaration of the 1923 Devonshire White Paper that 'native interests' should be the paramount consideration in governing Kenya, numerous Parliamentary Commissions were despatched from Westminster to investigate the 'Kenya Problem'. The result was that Grogan watched from the wings as Delamere's cohorts became increasingly embattled and embittered. Few in Whitehall sought to deny that self-government would one day be granted to Kenya, and frequent compliments were paid by visiting officials to the 'extremely virile and progressive European community', but by the end of the 1920s it was made abundantly clear that self-government was no longer synonymous with control by the European settlers. It seemed to Grogan that Delamere, by pursuing a policy of coalition with the British and Kenyan governments, had boxed himself into the corner of which Grogan had repeatedly warned.

Although a deluded minority of settlers would continue to believe that self-government with settlers in the dominant role might one day be attained, the real end for this ambition came in 1929. Against a background of fierce opposition to settler self-government in the House of Commons, increasing African unrest, the collapse of commodity prices, and the onset of the Great Depression, Delamere's coalition finally collapsed – leaving settler politics utterly discredited.

The following year a twenty-man Joint Parliamentary Commission was convened, further indicating that the metropolitan power's grip on the colony's affairs was tightening, not relaxing. It comprised, in the words of delegate Lord Cranworth, 'those lifelong Imperialists who believed wholeheartedly in the British race and the British Empire, who looked with pride on what that Empire had accomplished for the backward races and believed that its task was far from yet fulfilled ... those to whom the word Empire was as a red rag to a bull ... and the "open-minders"'.[13] The 'lifelong Imperialists' were outnumbered, and could only look on as a framework for the colony's future was laid down. The role of European settlers was acknowledged as important, but it was made clear – among other things – that the British government considered that the settler community as a whole was not to be granted the status of trustees for African interests, that Closer Union was a dead duck, that there should be no settler majority in Legco, and that the interests of the indigenous population were not to be subordinated to any minority – be it European or Indian. An immediate Inquiry was ordered into the needs of the African population.

After almost three decades of marking time it seemed that the Colonial Office was finally being required to *run* the colony proactively, ostensibly in the interests of its indigenous majority not its European or Indian minorities, and so warm was the political temperature in the aftermath of the Commission's findings that the man entrusted with the job as Grigg's successor was Sir Joseph Byrne, a veteran policeman of the Ulster Troubles.

On 11 November 1931, the sixty-one-year-old Lord Delamere died and was buried overlooking the lake on his farm at Soysambu. His health had never fully recovered since his heart trouble in 1915, and it was certainly not helped by the political difficulties of his final years nor by the fact that he was powerless to help his beloved Kenya as it, like the rest of the world, sank into Depression following the Wall Street Crash of 1929. In Kenya, the effects of the latter were exacerbated by drought and successive plagues of locusts, and as the crisis deepened most of the European settlers would come to look back on Delamere's death as the end of an era. It was, in his biographer's words, as if 'the country had lost a part of itself'.[14]

As the young Elspeth Huxley was not at the time considered by the denizens of the Colonial Office to be 'among the ranks of eminent and serious English historians',[15] she was denied access to their files when writing her biography of Delamere, which she entitled *White Man's Country*. This, as well as the fact that she was self-evidently writing about Delamere and not Grogan, partly explains why Grogan features only a handful of times in the book, and Grogan was far from the only larger than life character to be excluded from what was after all a personal account. There is no mention of the economic importance of the soda industry established at Lake Magadi; no mention of the pioneering work with coffee by Grogan's friend, Charles Taylor, and others; no mention of the creation of the sisal industry by Rutherfoord and Swift; and certainly no acknowledgement of the size, and crucial importance, of the African economy in the pre-war years.

Personal animus, however, was also a factor. Huxley's colours were so firmly pinned to Delamere's mast that there was seemingly no room to acknowledge the achievements and stature of the colony's other 'big man' without diminishing Delamere's. After Grogan's death Huxley did write that he was 'a charmer, a cynic, a swashbuckler, a buccaneer born out of time; generous with money, bold in his commercial ventures',[16] but such compliments were usually qualified in vituperative terms.

Grogan also made the 'mistake' – as did others – of not exactly saying to Huxley what she wanted to hear when researching her book. Her notebooks show that, while Grogan graciously acknowledged the deceased Delamere to be 'the symbol of white settlement', he added that it was a 'tragedy that he didn't finish his public career 3 years earlier'; that he was 'an extraordinary combination of pettiness and greatness of vision'; and that 'he had ... *no* consistency ... He was always going back on himself and understood or cared nothing about economics – considered it vulgar.' This interview also reveals that Grogan had taken up a position that, even by his own non-conformist standards, was remarkable: he distanced himself from Delamere's 'dying philosophy – the white domination and the founding of new dominions to speed civilization ... He believed in a fair deal for blacks – raising their standards – but always with the whites predominant,' remarked Grogan, while declaring that for his part he 'no longer believe[d] that whites will forever be dominant', and that the aim of colonial rule should now be to envisage the eventual creation of 'a black state ... with only our better institutions grafted on'.[17]

Grogan did not concern himself with the 'disappearing' job done on him by Huxley. He was used to, and not uncomfortable with, the fact that some people felt that he had 'a streak (as it were) of the battering ram'[18] in him. There were, after all, many more who regarded him as 'an Irishman with much charm, who has invested his capital, also his heart, in Kenya Colony, where he is considered by many as the hope of that much harassed country'.[19] But on the one occasion that Huxley libelled, as opposed to merely 'disappeared' him, Grogan fell on her like a ton of bricks and extracted a full apology.[20]

It was not only the great Lord Delamere's death which alerted Grogan to the extent to which times were changing. By 1930 he knew full well that Kenya had failed to attract enough settlers to have under-pinned either the greatest political ambitions of the European community or his own grandiose visions for the colony's economic future. It was also obvious to him that the very character of white settlement was altering. The Great War and the 1920s had robbed Kenya of many of its pioneer settlers, foremost among them the Cole brothers (Delamere's brothers-in-law), Grogan's great friend Northrup Mac-millan and Denys Finch Hatton, and some of the replacement 'stock' was cut from a rather different cloth. Although the Soldier Settlement Scheme, of which Grogan had been a leading proponent, had intro-duced plenty of 'good colonials' to Kenya it had also brought quite a number of what he derisively called 'verandah farmers'. Worse still for the productivity of the settler economy were the unexpected conse-quences of the royal visits during Grigg's tenure and the establishment of Nairobi as the safari capital of Africa. While both helped to imbue the colony with an even greater social cachet than it already possessed, they did not bring in their wake more Delameres and Coles. Instead a coterie of ne'er-do-well aristocrats appeared on the scene further to tarnish Kenya's battered reputation at home, as well as an alarming number of what many 'old hands' regarded as 'third class people travelling first'.

It was the new aristocratic arrivals, at whose apex was the infamous 'Happy Valley' set, who rapidly established Kenya's infamy for being 'A Place In The Sun For Shady People', and their blatant wife-swapping, cocaine-snorting and amorous intentions towards each other's children did far more damage to the country's reputation than Grogan and Delamere's most pyrotechnic political antics ever did. It was of no consolation to the more industrious and serious-minded in the colony that the publicity this group attracted was out of all proportion to its numbers or that it was generally recognized, as Evelyn Waugh observed during his visit to the country in 1930, that 'of the settler community in general, the great majority are far too busy on their farms to come to Nairobi, except on an occasional predatory expedition to the bank or the Board of Agriculture'.[21] Indeed by the end of the 1930s the high jinks of these so-called 'wastrel heirs' were so well-known among the chattering classes at home that Grogan was prompted to write that 'we badly need some symbolic refutation of the current thesis that Kenya is merely a Lido from Lido or a debauched purlieu of Mayfair'.[22]

The effect of the arrival of the 'third class people travelling first' was also not one of which Grogan approved – not on the basis of class, but because of what he regarded as their lack of economic contribution. Most settled in Nairobi and other towns, thereby causing the proportion of urban-dwellers among the settler population to rise as high as 60 per cent, and Grogan pointed out that 'the point of view of people who do not own land and do not work the land and know nothing about the practice of the land is naturally rather distinct from those who work and live by the land and who, incidentally, support the rest of the community by so doing'.[23] Nairobi, in particular, began to take on the distinctly odd feel of a cross between an outpost in the Wild West and a genteel south of England town, complete with flourishing Freemasonries (about which Grogan was distinctly scathing), vigorous municipal politics and a plethora of worthy women's groups. It also, in the words of former chief of police Robert Foran, became 'obsessed by the cult of suburban snobbery'.[24] This change was even reflected in the way that Grogan was addressed. Old hands still called him 'Ewart', but it was more usually the sign of a newcomer when he was matily, and possessively, referred to as 'Grogs'. All in all, although Grogan persisted in publicly declaring that 'the settler community is of the highest possible quality',[25] he was far from convinced that this was still the case.

It was not only in Kenya that Grogan's world seemed to be changing fast. The 1920s had witnessed the deaths of most of the great imperialists with whom he had 'played the game' at one time or another, including Milner, Coryndon, 'Empire Jack' Norton-Griffiths, Frederick Jackson and Charles Eliot. In 1929 their ranks were joined by two old friends to whom Grogan was particularly attached. Dear, faithful Nanny Redwood passed away at the age of seventy-eight, having raised two generations of Grogan children, as did old Lawley, the acknowledged maestro of African railway-building who had saved Grogan's life after the Matabele War. In Lawley's case Grogan was at least able to draw some consolation from the fact that 'the day before he died, and contrary to doctor's orders, I filled him up with roast grouse and the best bottle of Burgundy from the cellars of the RAC'.[26]

Technology, like death and demographics, also started to play a huge part in transforming Grogan's world – but in this case he wholeheartedly embraced all changes. He was almost ecstatic about any new invention which might bring economic progress in its wake, none more so than in the field of aviation. As early as 1920 he had been asked by *The Times*, on the twentieth anniversary of his completion of the trek from Cape to Cairo, to contribute an article about the future of air travel. In it he wrote that the prospect of commercial air travel was the 'startling epitome of our times', and added that

> in the economic sphere it is impossible to exaggerate the significance of the coming of the aeroplane. Many of Africa's areas only require stimulus to become important contributors to the world stock of essential foods and raw materials and reciprocally consumers of manufactures of Great Britain ... Rapidity of movement and inter-communication between these European stimuli is the first essential of African progress. The car, wireless, telegraphy, and the 'plane are facile means whereby the physical obstructions to progress are overcome; and their advent heralds a new era.[27]

Such enthusiasm was far-sighted. By 1925 the Cape-to-Cairo railway was within 500 miles of completion, having reached Stanleyville (today's Kisangani) in the Belgian Congo and Wau in the southern Sudan, and few would have guessed that air travel would beat the railway to the finishing post. By 1932, in the face of almost universal scepticism, Imperial Airways was ready to attempt the first commercial mail-carrying flight from Cairo to the Cape and the company paid Grogan the considerable compliment of asking him to be its first passenger on the route. On 27 January 1932 the *Heracles* took off from Croydon, bound for Paris; there Grogan boarded another aircraft for Brindisi; and at Brindisi he joined the *Sylvanus* for the crossing of the Mediterranean. In Alexandria the *Hannibal* was waiting for him, and he was whisked down the length of Africa in the blink of an eyelid: the whole journey took just eight and a half days.

It was an historic passage. On reaching Cape Town a telegram from *The Times* awaited Grogan, congratulating him on his 'unique double achievement of being the first man to tramp from Cape to Cairo and the first passenger to fly in the opposite direction on the regular service, thus epitomising 32 years of progress of transport in Africa'. When he returned to London all the newspapers interviewed him, and Grogan observed to the *Daily Express* that things had certainly advanced from the days of the trek when he had used 'every then-known form of transport – except camel: mule, wagon, dhow, canoe, gunboat, but mostly my good two feet, and some part of the way through the Nile Swamp, on my stomach'.[28] 'It was almost impossible,' he told the *East African Standard*, 'to believe that one had left one's own element, the Earth. Four thousand feet into the air and one found oneself in an entirely new world – bright, hot sunshine and below, as far as one could see, an unbroken sea of cloud, resembling the Arctic floes, all frozen cotton wool.'[29] Less poetically, he confided to Lady Cobbold, a fellow passenger on a subsequent flight, that air travel also made him feel a bit like a 'registered parcel'.[30]

On his return to Nairobi, Grogan's praise of air travel remained fulsome, and his defence of it forthright. He told the *East African Standard* that 'Imperial Airways are making a fine effort, and yet you get people beginning to crab because there is a deficiency of one per cent. They have got to about 90 per cent efficiency already. Do you know anything in Kenya that is 50% efficient? Well, I don't.' He appealed to the 'thinking people of Nairobi' (at which point he

chuckled) some of 'whose intelligences seem to embrace a world surrounded by park palings' to stop their 'carping criticism',[31] and see
Imperial Airways' achievement for what it was. Less than a week later
he gave a public lecture on his journey to a packed house at the
Kenya Defence Force Institute, and the paper remarked that 'never
has Nairobi heard her orator – Major E. S. Grogan – speak on a more
fascinating and romantic subject than "Then and Now", which he
delivered with his usual wit and feeling for the picturesque ... and
with a *piquant diablerie*'.[32]

All this change might have caused many a veteran of the Scramble
for Africa simply to retire to a safe place and enjoy a peaceful retirement. Grogan turned sixty in 1934, and less than one tenth of his
memoirs is devoted to the years after 1930. But any impression that
he was contemplating giving up 'playing the game' was well wide of
the mark. George Lloyd, though he resigned as High Commissioner
for Egypt in 1929, was still very much alive (and became Churchill's
Secretary of State for Colonies in 1940); Churchill himself, having
executed what he referred to as his 're-rat' and rejoined the Conservatives in the mid 1920s, was sounding more and more like the dyed-in-
the-wool imperialist that Grogan had always believed him to be
beneath his opportunistic exterior; and Grogan was also widely known
to enjoy easy access to Baldwin, the 4th Marquess of Salisbury, and
Austen Chamberlain. In other words he still had plenty of like-minded
sponsors at home, and had no intention of curtailing his ceaseless
crusade to advance the Empire's fortunes in Kenya.

As Grogan's friend and admirer Lady Cobbold once remarked it
struck many people in London as 'strange that he should have chosen
Kenya wherein to bestow his life's labours, when it is remembered
that he astounded the world by accomplishing the almost impossible
feat of traversing Africa on foot from Cape to Cairo ... But,' she
added, 'one thing is certain – that Africa's strange fascination held
him – particularly Kenya with its immense possibilities and charm.'
Lady Cobbold was right. Grogan loved Kenya, and Africa, with a
passion that was sometimes underestimated. He loved the freedom it
offered; he revelled in the vitality of its political life; and above all it
was a country in which he could indulge his entrepreneurial spirit to
the hilt. Kenya was, quite simply, a playground for Grogan that could

not be bettered elsewhere. This was the reason why he set out in the 1930s to build a mini-Empire all of his own, and in so doing he was to display brinkmanship which, even by his own standards, was breathtaking.

TWENTY-TWO

—>•‹—

Torr's, Taveta and Timber

A s soon as Grogan had finished restoring Equator Saw Mills to health first up on his list of things to do was to build a hotel for Nairobi that would match anything that Africa had to offer. Like his bold trout-importing initiative of 1906 this was a project of great symbolic importance. It was also, like all his schemes, monumentally expensive.

He employed Harold Henderson, who had designed Muthaiga Club and was the former partner of Ronald Tate-Smith (the deceased husband of Grogan's paramour Doris), as the architect and together the two men set to work using Stockholm Town Hall as their inspiration. Grogan decided that his hotel should be built of brick. The only problem was that there was no proper brick-works – most bricks were still imported – but Grogan side-stepped this complication by building one on the edge of his Swamp Estate, and gave the colony its first substantial supplier of bricks, just as his Equator Saw Mills had provided it with its first substantial supplier of timber, tiles and roofing materials. It was this sort of determination that led Heini Lustman, a young architect who worked for Grogan fifteen years later, to declare himself a 'great admirer' of Grogan's and to observe that for 'someone who was not an engineer he had vision and he had ideas'.[1]

In no time Kenya's tallest building dominated the Nairobi skyline and was christened Torr's after Joe and Lilly Torr, to whom Grogan leased the hotel in 1928 for the princely sum of £900 per month. It was said that from its roof both Mount Kenya and Mount Kilimanjaro were visible, and its like had never been seen before between Cairo and Cape Town. Referred to as the 'Carlton of East Africa', it had the appropriate cable address of 'JET'. From the outside the most striking thing were the red bricks, the twenty-foot-tall arched windows of the first and second floors, the massive oak front door and the two first-floor terraces – one looking out over Sixth Avenue and the other over Hardinge Street. And on the inside Torr's, whose advertising boasted 'all the comforts of your house and the gaieties of a West End hotel', was positively palatial.

The reception had a pet storage space, where guests could leave lion and cheetah cubs, mongooses and other exotic visitors from the bush, and the ground floor was dominated by the Palm Court Lounge and Grill Room. In one corner was 'Tom's bar' named after its patron, the roguish Irishman Tom Whiston, a former barman at Ciro's; and *thé dansants* were held each afternoon, with live music provided by Sid Zeigler's band, which was enclosed in an ornate minstrel's gallery.

Two wide circular staircases led from the ground floor to the first-floor dining room, whose balconies overlooked the Palm Court lounge below. Here, chefs imported from France and Switzerland produced sumptuous eight-course dinners, featuring such luxuries as caviar, lobster and aspic of *foie gras*. Then above the dining room were three floors of bedrooms, all sixty-four of them containing their own bathrooms with hot and cold running water. The top floor was vintage Grogan eccentricity. Named the 'Pompeian House', it was a lounge decorated with pictures inspired by Grogan's own drawings of houses in Pompeii, which he had visited while on one of many trysts. To cap it all there were two lifts, Kenya's first, in which children loved to play, a hairdressing salon, the finest chocolate shop in the country and a café with soda fountain.

Grogan's timing was not quite perfect, in that the hotel reputedly lost the Torrs £20,000 in the four years before they admitted defeat and surrendered their lease. But by then the worst days of the Depression which followed the Wall Street Crash were coming to an end, and Nairobi – the safari capital of Africa – needed a hotel with *zing*. It was just six days (and a fare of £109) from London on the new Imperial Airways route, and Torr's offered its guests luxury and it offered them quirks – all the more so after Grogan took back the lease. As with all of his enterprises staff came and went with great rapidity, but those at Torr's were always, above all, characters. Tom Whiston was famed for selling his own cheap brands of spirits over his bar and then telling Grogan's managers what a bad evening he had had; 'Aunty' Turner presided over front of house like an executive nanny; sometime manager Baron Fuchs, a tall and thin German, displayed a markedly authoritarian streak and was wont to 'dismiss' guests for not being properly attired; and Joseph, the highly eccentric Goan head waiter, sported a toupée which he combed in strips from the back of his head straight over the top to the front.

None of these characters could overshadow Torr's biggest attraction – the fact that it was the first hotel in Africa to offer dancing every night. Grogan was determined to have the best, and in Sid Zeigler's five-piece band of jazz musicians he got the best. The sixteen-year-old drummer Mickey Migdoll, born in London's Wardour Street, thought that he must be 'the best paid person in Kenya – £60 a month and all found'[2] – more than double what members of Kenya's Legislative Council were paid.

Presiding over events whenever he so desired was Grogan himself. An enormous topee perched on the end of the bannisters told all and sundry that Ewart, or 'Grogs' was 'in', and a casual glance into the Palm Court lounge would provide further evidence in the shape of a table at which sat up to a dozen women hanging on his every word. 'Words poured from his lips like wine at a Bacchic orgy;' wrote Elspeth Huxley, before adding her customary qualification that the words were 'intoxicating at the time but, when the orgy was over, you wondered what he had actually said'.[3] Now grey-haired, Grogan's good looks had become even more striking with age and over a post-lunch glass of Armagnac and a cigar he liked nothing better than to chat away to his bevy of friends and admirers. On any day this might include anyone from the Governor's wife, to officials, to settlers, to what Daphne Moore, wife of the colony's new Chief Secretary, described as the 'exquisite young fluffs' who served behind the counters in Nairobi's shops.

Even the very game Lady Moore, who had quite a soft spot for 'the world-famous Major Grogan [with his] melting voice',[4] found the atmosphere a little overwhelming. 'The people!' she exclaimed,

> sitting in Torr's about noon the scene is like the Piccadilly Hotel, with slight differences. Coming into the palatial and

> very luxurious lounge are the strangest mixture of God's
> creatures you could see anywhere ... men and women in
> every form of attire that the human brain can imagine ...
> the women are extremely kittenish and almost everyone
> seems to be addressed by his or her Christian name and
> addressed as 'Darling'.[5]

Bright corduroy trousers, silk shirts and broad-rimmed hats were the
fashion for both sexes and in the evenings the atmosphere became
even more racy when the dancing began. This was when Torr's, in
Negley Farson's opinion, made Nairobi 'the Paris of the East African
Coast – all of Africa below Cairo'. He added that it was Paris at 6,500
feet which seemed to make its white inhabitants 'slightly daft with the
altitude'.[6]

As far as Grogan was concerned only one event in the Torr's social
calendar really mattered and that was the children's Christmas party
– at which he naturally played the part of Father Christmas. The first
of these, in 1928, was a huge success. Grogan invited over 300 children
from the richest families to the poorest and kept them entranced with
his conjuring tricks, including his old party piece of showing the
children a bunny, fashioned from a handkerchief, through the holes
in his topee. This soon had his young charges roaring with laughter
and gleefully shrieking 'Bunny Man, Funny Man!' Gertrude, on a rare
visit to the colony, co-presided in her usual endearingly maternal way
and organized the charades. The crowning moment came when all
the children chose a present from beneath the enormous Christmas
tree specially imported from Scandinavia.

The second of these annual extravaganzas was not such a success.
Although Grogan had as usual obtained lists of the colony's poorer
children from the Salvation Army and the League of Mercy, the hotel
staff 'forgot' to send out their invitations and it was only the more
fortunate who turned up with their parents. Lady Moore witnessed
what happened next. The children and their parents ended up 'fighting
like cats' for cake and the presents; the Christmas tree was pulled
down and stripped of its decorations; and no one thanked Grogan,
bedecked in his stick-on beard and red suit. He left in disgust before
it was all over. That evening, Lady Moore recorded in her diary: 'I

improved the shining hour by asking him what the second generation in Kenya would be like if the first were like this. No answer.'[7]

Torr's was initially intended as the first in a chain of hotels in all the major termini of the railway between Mombasa and the Cape to Cairo railway. Grogan never built any others, however, for the simple reason that neither the main railway nor an arterial line extending from the Uganda Railway to join it were ever completed. It did not matter: Grogan had already turned his attention to the potential of a seldom visited corner of the country on which he had first set eyes in World War I.

The timing of Grogan's interest in Taveta was no accident. Concerns were growing in the colony about just how much of its land was agriculturally viable, and Grogan harboured a keen desire to demonstrate both to the Colonial Office and the local government that much of what passed for poor land could in fact, with proper management and a little enterprise, be made to bear fruit.[8] His devotion to this objective was to last some thirty years, without interruption, and the result was arguably his greatest achievement, creating a complete 'enterprise zone' which survives to this day.

Taveta ('the plain' in Kitaveta) and its surrounding area had witnessed the most serious fighting of World War I due to its strategic position in a gap between Mount Kilimanjaro and the Pare mountains, on the border between Kenya and what had been German East Africa. It was hot, dry country some 2,500 feet above sea level, with gently undulating scrub-covered plains only broken by isolated hills which played prominent parts in the conflict. Trees, mostly acacias and baobabs, were scarce due to the lack of water. One particular baobab north of Salaita Hill had achieved great notoriety for housing a German sniper for months during the conflict, and bones, cartridge cases, shell fuses and other detritus of war could still be found around Salaita, Latema, Reata and the other hills.

Taveta township, such as it was, had always been important in an understated sort of way. It had been a major stopping point on the old caravan route to the East African interior – a route which purposely ran south of Mount Kilimanjaro in order to avoid crossing Masailand – and the last slave caravan of Wakamba slavers had been stopped there in 1896 or 1897 and broken up by British Indian troops. Taveta had also briefly been a focus for activity by the Church Missionary Society at the turn of the century and produced Kenya's first newspaper – the Taveta Chronicle. In 1899, a government station had been built as a gesture to the strategic importance of the town. But nothing had ever really taken hold in the area. Even before the war the missionaries had left, and after the war the government station was no longer manned. So, although the main road from the coast to Nairobi ran through the town, and a branch line of the railway also passed through on its way from Voi to Moshi, Taveta had never really become important except in wartime.

There were good reasons for this anomaly. Apart from the Taveta forest, the terrain was extremely inhospitable. Missionaries were the first to discover why the Wataveta population never numbered more than about a few thousand souls: a particularly virulent form of malaria was endemic.[9] Moreover, the plains were infested with tsetse fly, which made cattle-rearing well-nigh impossible. Swarms of locusts, East Coast fever, plague and rinderpest also appeared with alarming regularity. Taveta was a place to break a journey, but most certainly not a place to stay. This was why the government had never considered development of the area possible, except by a madman, coupled with a scepticism about the merits of interfering with the local people.

The Wataveta were a hotch-potch of Kamba, Pare, Chagga, Teita and even Masai refugees. They were divided into five clans ruled by a council of elders, the *njama*, and lived mostly in, or on the fringes of, the 5,500-acre forest through which a man could walk in a matter of a few hours. They were easygoing and peaceful but had a number of customs which alarmed the early missionaries. In particular, they put to death illegitimate children, children who were deformed, children who cut their upper teeth before their lower ones, children born to a mother after her eldest daughter had become a mother and twins. Witchcraft was rife, as was the practice of allowing young girls to live with as many men as they pleased until they were married. As late as the 1930s official reports deemed the Wataveta to be 'generally incapable of sustained and hard physical labour' because of their poor state of health and diet, and it was considered 'doubtful that anything can be done to help them'.[10] It was hardly surprising that when a 'madman', in the shape of Grogan, stepped forward in 1928 and declared that if he was leased sufficient land in the area he would do the impossible – cultivate it on a grand scale – the government, for once, almost bit off his arm in its enthusiasm.

At the time there wasn't a single European living in this arid zone between the Teita Hills and the Tanganyika border, but Grogan had spotted what others had chosen to ignore. There was *plenty* of water available around Taveta for anyone bold enough, and with deep enough pockets, to exploit its potential. Harnessing water resources had been an abiding obsession of his ever since he had put forward his scheme for increasing the flow of the Nile in *From The Cape To Cairo*; at Taveta he knew that he had the basic raw material, because the River Lumi ran past the township and was already used by the locals for small-scale irrigation. More importantly, the Mawenzi peak of majestic Mount Kilimanjaro dominated the area, and Grogan was convinced that as it was snow-covered all year round there must be underground water as well.

Grogan's conclusions may seem obvious if surveying the area today, and even sixty years ago Grogan may not have been the first to draw them, but he was the first person to act on his intuition. The further afield he surveyed the more obvious it became to him that there was huge potential in the area, and that far from being barren semi-desert beyond the confines of the Taveta forest it was, in fact, an area of surpassing beauty. Less than fifteen miles to the south-east, beyond the forest, lay Lake Jipe and the headwaters of the Ruvu river. Fifty miles to the east, beyond what would become Tsavo West National Park in 1948, the rugged outline of the Teita Hills was visible on a clear day. To the north were the Chyulu Hills. And just six miles outside Taveta was Lake Chala, which fascinated Grogan.

This crater lake, through the middle of which ran the national boundary between Kenya and Tanganyika, was one of the most beautiful sights he had ever seen. It was the most prominent example of the extensive volcanic activity that had shaped Taveta's topography, and had been caused by a paroxysmal outburst of ash and slag rather than lava. The effect of this outburst often led people to believe, erroneously, that the 300-foot, 45° crater wall had been caused by a meteorite, a theory backed up by a local Wataveta legend that an evil spirit had caused a village that had once stood on the spot to subside as a punishment for some wrongdoing by the villagers. Certainly it was a mysterious place, especially at dawn and dusk, but the mystery which most interested Grogan was where its water came from.

He soon discovered that the level of the thousand-acre lake hardly altered, yet there were no signs, of how it was recharged. Soundings revealed it to be 275–300 feet deep, and therefore – despite its diminutive appearance – it was the third largest body of water in the colony after Lake Victoria and Lake Rudolph. There could, Grogan decided, be only one answer to the conundrum of its consistent water level: the whole Taveta area was one giant volcanic 'sponge' carrying water which ran off from Kilimanjaro and all the surrounding ranges of hills. That, and that alone, could account for the Lumi, other smaller rivers, and the various springs already being used by the Wataveta. To Grogan, that meant he was sitting on an agricultural goldmine – but the costs of the work needed to build the irrigation schemes he had in mind would be colossal.

Grogan's first grant of land was for 30,000 acres alongside the Wataveta Reserve, which the government dearly hoped would benefit from a trickle-down effect from Grogan's labours. Even before the ink was dry on the agreement with the government, Grogan had set to work creating his own kingdom in the bush. His primary product would, he decided, be sisal, and for once he chose advisers who really were experts as opposed to amiable mavericks: he hired Major Stanley Layzell, MC, to manage his estate, and drew frequently on the advice of his friend Rutherfoord, who had established Kenya's sisal industry at his farm Punda Milia as early as 1907.

It wasn't only the government who thought Grogan must be mad. In 1929, as the first chilling effects of the Depression started to be felt, the price of sisal (whose strong hemp is chiefly used for twine and ropes) fell from £40 per ton to £12. But Grogan knew that it would be between three and four years before his plants were ready to cut: he was therefore planting at what he was sure must be the bottom of the market. He was proved right by the end of the 1930s, but the risk a decade earlier was tremendous: the capital costs alone of clearing the bush, establishing a 2,000-acre plantation complete with factory, equipment and trolley lines throughout the plantation was estimated by Rutherfoord at £20,000. As ever, Grogan was thinking big.

Clearing thousands of acres of completely virgin bush was a monumental task, undertaken by the latest RD6 and RD7 tractors – and by hand. The factory was installed in 1934 and went into production on 1 September, stripping the fibre from 600 acres of sisal. By the following year, Grogan knew his gamble had paid off: that year the price of the top quality (no. 1) sisal produced by the estate rose steadily from £15 to £28 per ton, which was within a whisker of the cost of production. It was just as well. By 1936 Grogan had spent a total of £110,000 at Taveta, employed over 1,000 people, and had cleared and planted an acreage whose output was anticipated to reach 3,000 tons per annum by 1940.

The effect of his efforts on the local economy was so dramatic that in 1935 the government reopened its station at Taveta, closed since the war, and installed a permanent District Officer in recognition of the fact that 'it seems likely in view of the capital and forethought that are being expended that this district will in due course become one of the chief sisal producing areas of Kenya'. By then sisal had become the colony's second most valuable export after coffee, and in one of its remoter corners Grogan had proved that he could turn the semi-desert into productive fields. Furthermore, he remained convinced that the potential of Taveta was almost unlimited: soon the District Commissioner at Teita was writing that 'the activities of this estate are so many and so varied and in addition to the production of sisal fibre experiments in cotton-growing, tepiary beans, maize, pineapples, avocado pears, grape fruit, paw-paws, black mint, lavender and asparagus are underway'[11] – crops that were usually associated with the more temperate conditions of the highlands.

The key to all the bounty, particularly to Grogan's ability to process the White Gold – sisal – was boring for water into the volcanic 'sponge' beneath the estate. The factory was placed above an underground stream which Grogan and his hydrologists had unearthed about twenty feet below the surface and which yielded no less than 100,000 gallons a day. The significance of such finds was immense, not only to Grogan's finances but to his wider political agenda. At Taveta he believed, with considerable justification, that he had demonstrated that thriving economies could be established in any number of Kenya's semi-arid lowland districts, and as if to hammer home the point Grogan even started to cultivate rice.

Grogan's success at Taveta in the early 1930s was all the more astonishing for the fact that Equator Saw Mills also, once again, required a lot of his time and attention. By the end of 1928 Equator Saw Mills, after being nursed back to health by Grogan and his young manager, Ferdinand Cavendish-Bentinck, had executed a remarkable turnaround following the slump at the beginning of the decade. Indeed his boldness in providing a lead to other saw-millers was directly responsible for the fact that over £1m of private money was invested in the industry during the late 1920s, that the industry contributed a colossal £250,000 annually to the colony's economy in the shape of salaries, wages, inputs and royalties,[12] and that timber provided significant year-round traffic for the railway. In the two years following the introduction of protective tariffs in 1927 timber production in the colony trebled. By then ESM's main mill at Maji Mazuri alone had over one and a half miles of air-seasoning bins, and as the market leader it drove down timber prices in the colony by almost a half. But just as ESM's barometer moved to 'set fair' the Wall Street Crash occurred. Depression set in, and its effect on the timber industry was immediate. Demand plummeted and Grogan's seven mills were left with running costs of some £25,000 per annum and precious little revenue.

What happened next is shrouded in mystery, and the dearth of evidence indicates that ESM's demise was a terrible disappointment to Grogan. There are no records of Equator Saw Mills having continued to work the 300-square-mile concession after 1934, and payments of its royalties to the government ceased that year. It seems, quite simply, as though ESM ceased to exist even though Grogan's concession had another twenty-three years left to run.[13]

The tragedy is that Grogan had once again simply shown himself to be, in the words of his old friend Frederick Jackson, 'a little too much ahead of the times'. But in this case he was only, at most, a decade ahead of the times. Had he had the financial wherewithal to weather the collapse in demand and in prices for just a few more years his enormous investment and Herculean efforts would have been rewarded many times over. World War II created boom conditions for the colony's timber industry, and by 1947 four times the quantity of timber was being milled compared to the pre-war years. That year the Assistant Conservator of Forests remarked that

> by the time I'm dead someone may have realised that the answer to most of our problems lies in the development of our forests. They alone could keep the country [if the forests were enlarged and population growth controlled]. A fully developed scheme, with all the sawmills and transport and ancillary industries, could support a total of perhaps 400,000 people.[14]

There is a certain irony in it being a forestry officer, whose department had so often criticized the working methods of Grogan's Equator Saw Mills, who so emphatically endorsed what a substantially ignored Grogan had said for almost half a century.

TWENTY-THREE

A Brobdingnagian in Lilliput

THE DEMISE OF ESM and the first steps to creating his kingdom at Taveta took up more and more of Grogan's time in the early 1930s. His visits to England became less frequent and of shorter duration, and by 1935 he and Gertrude had decided that they should both live permanently in Kenya. It was suggested by some – including at least one of their own daughters – that Grogan only allowed Gertrude to come to Kenya because money was scarce during the Depression, and Venters – their Sussex estate – had to be sold. Money certainly *was* scarce,[1] but to have claimed that this was the sole reason for Grogan and Gertrude's residential rearrangements was erroneous. For one thing, they did not sell their large house in London's Draycott Place at the same time which suggests that a fire-sale of assets was not required, however straitened their circumstances. For another, to accept such a suggestion is fundamentally to misunderstand the nature of their marriage.

The main reason why Gertrude had lived mostly in England from the end of the Great War until 1935 was that she – and Grogan – regarded it as her duty to raise her daughters as young ladies, until such time as they were married off. That entailed giving them a proper schooling in England and access to a rather larger pool of eligible suitors than Kenya could offer. It also involved being near the children: neither she nor Grogan believed that the practice of some other well-to-do colonials of sending their children (especially male children) to school 6,000 miles away at the age of eight, only to reacquaint themselves with them a dozen years later, was appropriate for their girls. Gertrude had not left her parents until it was time to go to finishing school, and Grogan's attitudes to parenting also followed the model pursued by his parents, namely that female members of the family had to be closely supervised. To him that meant providing adoration when they were very young and a decent schooling, but after that it was the girls' 'duty' to get married; his role was reduced to discouraging any too ardent expressions of interest in pursuing a career, and providing the appropriate wherewithal for the girls to pursue their duties. Each daughter had an allowance of £100 per annum – a great deal of money – and when Grogan was flush this was augmented by displays of dazzling generosity such as the dispensing of white £100 notes on their birthdays. In other words both Grogan and Gertrude tried to do the best by their daughters according to what they, like their parents before them, regarded as the norm, but it did mean, because of his peregrinations, that he and Gertrude were often apart.

This was not simply a convenient excuse on Grogan's part for him to pursue extra-marital affairs in Kenya because even Gertrude's presence did not exactly act as a brake on his infidelities. There is no doubt that Gertrude *wanted* to be with her husband more, and she frequently expressed her desire to be at his side in Kenya. But she was as devoted a mother as she was a wife, and she stayed in England for the children's sake. Such devotion to her duty, it must be said, presented Jane and to a certain extent Dorothy with a problem: neither turned out to be particularly maternal, so their mother's sacrifice was completely incomprehensible to them. As they grew older they articulated such frustrations in the form of disapproval of their father. Their annoyance was increased by the fact that their mother would not tolerate criticism of their father in her presence, and – whatever he did – she never ceased to adore him.

Grogan's fame and antics undoubtedly cast a rather oppressive shadow over his daughters' adult lives. Most strident in her opinions was fiery, confident and witty Jane, who adored her mother and had been a much-cosseted youngest child, but Dorothy was also, according to her daughter, 'always more or less at war' with Grogan, fond of him though she was. Cynthia on the other hand, being mild-mannered, exceptionally kind and of somewhat nervous disposition, didn't want to be at war with anyone, but she was often deeply wounded by her father's scabrous wit. It is no surprise that all three girls chose to try and break away from their father at the first opportunity through marriage – just as Joyce had done by 'marrying' the church. But they were marriages to men about whose merits Grogan was distinctly ambivalent.

There were two other reasons that had kept Gertrude in England. The first was that until at least 1926 she and Grogan were still trying to have a son, as is attested to by a specific provision in her Will which was drawn up that year. Had she been successful she would have felt she had to raise the boy, like the girls, in England – so long as her hopes of providing Grogan with an heir remained alive there was little point in upping sticks for Kenya, only to have to return when the boy was old enough to go to school. The second reason relates to Gertrude's own state of health. In 1907, in the wake of the Nairobi Incident and the attack of mastoiditis which almost took her life, she had been diagnosed as suffering from 'acute mania', a euphemism for depression. Then, a decade later, Grogan wrote to his brother-in-law Wilfrid Hunter referring to Gertrude's 'illness' as being one reason why his business affairs had been neglected before the war. Hunter's reply to Grogan was that he had just received a letter from Gertrude saying that she was 'very anxious for you [Grogan] to go home as soon as you can'.[2] Given that Grogan was on active war duty there is something distinctly desperate about this request. It is possible that Gertrude, despite her always cheerful exterior, suffered intermittently – with some justification given her husband's solipsistic behaviour – from bouts of depression. If this were so, it would help to explain the depth of the children's periodic antipathy towards their father.

A susceptibility to depression would have been a good reason, over and above her sense of responsibility to the children, for Gertrude to live mainly in the old country. The altitude, sun and climate in Kenya was 'known' to be unbalancing even for the most solid of citizens, particularly towards the end of the dry seasons, and Nairobi was a very long way from the nearest mania specialist.[3] Once the children were married the risk of her developing mania would have mattered less, again enabling her to move to Kenya. In this context it is significant that after her arrival the once-game Gertrude, who had almost always accompanied her husband on safari during the pioneering days, seldom ventured far outside Nairobi. There is, for example, not a single mention of her ever accompanying Grogan to Taveta in the full and detailed diaries of Margaret Layzell, the daughter of Taveta's manager. Before 1935 this could have been easily explained by Gertrude's dislike of driving: she did not drive herself, and was always ferried around Nairobi by a chauffeur, but in 1935 an airstrip was installed on the estate and Grogan nearly always went down there by plane.

Whether she was intermittently depressive or not, the circumstances of Gertrude's arrival in Nairobi would have tested the patience of a saint. In a small community much devoted to tittle-tattle it took no time for the news to reach her ears that it was common knowledge that Grogan had fathered a second child out of wedlock a full six years earlier and had not two, but three 'families'. His latest *amour*, Doreen, was vivacious, free-spirited and attractive and was often to be seen dancing with him at Torr's, always wearing the same black crushed velvet dress. She was twenty-six years younger than Grogan and had come to Kenya, after wartime Land Girl service as a dairy maid at Windsor Castle, in response to an advertisement for farm help placed by Lord Delamere. On discovering that she was a girl Delamere had tried to send her back whence she had come, but relented when she told him she had no money to go anywhere. Soon after her arrival 'Doreen Of The Shorts', so-called because of her eccentric penchant for wearing shorts, had met and married Grogan's friend and fellow politician, Ernest Hay Wright. 'Sandy' Wright was sixteen years her senior, very Scottish, and – like Grogan – had the gift of the gab. By 1928 the marriage had foundered, and a year later Doreen had a daughter by the fifty-four-year-old Grogan. Grogan and Sandy Wright were both at Doreen's bedside soon after the birth, and jovially speculated as to which of them was the father, but as the girl, christened June, grew up her distinctive appearance left no one in any doubt as to her parentage.

Although Sandy Wright and Doreen subsequently remarried, Grogan lavished as much attention on June as he had on all his daughters when they were little. Doreen was not maternal, and when June, who 'hardly knew' her mother, was sent to school at Limuru it was nearly always Grogan who would appear to take her out at half term. There were many girls at the school whose parents lived too far away to do likewise and June remembers that Grogan would always 'look around to see if anyone was left behind' so that he could gather them up as well and take them off to nearby Brackenhurst Hotel. Sometimes he would even take June back to the Gallows, his house in Muthaiga, where she remembers playing up and down the stairs – and meeting Gertrude.

Grogan's affair with Doreen continued until World War II. It was she, and not Gertrude, who usually accompanied him on his regular visits to Taveta and he built a house for her there near the Kitovo springs (even though she had by then remarried Sandy Wright). Until she was grown up June thought that 'Bunnyman' was her godfather, and even when she knew the truth neither of them ever mentioned it. As he had done with the Tate-Smiths Grogan set up trusts for her and her mother, and in later life he also lent June the money to buy out her partner's share in a Miles Magister so that she could earn her living from flying: both she and her mother were formidable pilots. 'Out of the four fathers I had,' June wrote recently, 'he is definitely the best remembered and did the most for me.'[4] It is striking that her memories of Grogan, and indeed those of his daughter by Doris Tate-Smith, are so much fonder than were those of his daughters by Gertrude.

The news of her 'over-engined' husband's latest affair was an immense shock for Gertrude. Her pain must have been all the greater because by the mid-1930s she had lost her looks and had – as had happened to her mother before her – ballooned in weight to some seventeen stone. Gertrude entering a room or walking down the street was now, in the words of those who knew her at this time, like 'a galleon in full sail'. Her response was to display a level of dignity that was conspicuously absent from her husband's extra-marital behaviour. She welcomed June to the Gallows with the same enveloping kindness that she showed to every other visitor, ignored the tittle-tattle in Nairobi, and threw herself into charitable works with great gusto. This further enhanced her reputation as a truly *good* woman.

Until the 1930s Grogan did not pay any price for his infidelities in Kenya. He did not brag about them, but neither was he discreet. Indeed it was impossible to be discreet in a small community where everyone knew everyone else: even out in the bush, employees at Taveta were hardly likely to mistake Doreen for a visiting sisal expert. But sometime around 1931 his behaviour finally cost him his relationship with his usually laid-back brother Quentin.

During the 1920s Quentin and his wife, Irene, ran a moderately successful butchery at Turi. They lived in the curious house on stilts – the Pagoda – that Grogan had built on his estate there before the war, and Grogan had continued to provide them with financial assistance when Quentin's endearing inability to keep his hands on money got them into difficulties. Grogan had been extremely generous to his youngest brother, so the rift must have been over something very serious. Quentin's daughter Diana remembers Grogan's visits to the Pagoda when she was a child: 'Ewart', she says, 'was a rule unto himself – absolutely. I was terrified of him. He frightened me to death: he would *look* at you with those leonine, yellowy-green eyes.'[5] She also remembers when those visits stopped, and believes that Grogan's affairs may well have been the reason. Quentin may have discovered that the infant daughter of his neighbour, Doreen, was in fact his blood niece, or he might have caught wind of some other tryst. Whatever the cause, the matter was never talked about again and, from the moment that Grogan last set foot in the Pagoda, Irene would not even hear Grogan's name mentioned in the house. Quentin was not quite so emphatic, but when he began to suffer from duodenal ulcers in 1934 he took his family back to England and never saw his brother again.[6]

By the time Quentin departed for England, three of Grogan's daughters were married. Joyce, or Sister Mary Christina, had of course married the Church. She completed a degree at Oxford after her profession in 1929 and then pursued a career as a conscientious, but not brilliant, teacher within the Catholic Church. She did not possess her aunt Hilda's charismatic, powerful personality or share her muscular interpretation of Christianity, but she was much-loved – like her mother – as a wholly unselfish doer of good works, and was particularly devoted to the Girl Guide Movement (inspired by her parents' friendship with the Baden-Powell family). Dorothy was the next off the blocks, marrying Charles 'Lennard' Slater in 1928 following a shipboard romance, after which they went to live in Calcutta where Slater worked for the Union Insurance Company of Canton. Cynthia also met her husband, Jim Crawford, on a sea voyage at a time when she was apparently giving serious consideration to becoming a nun like her sister. The couple were married at Venters in 1934 and followed the Slaters to India, where Crawford was a tea planter.

It was Cynthia's marriage that prompted the sale of Venters and finally enabled Gertrude to join Grogan full-time in Kenya. Only 'baby' Jane was left unmarried, and as she had just been forced to break off an engagement to a man thought to be about to die of tuberculosis her parents thought that moving to Kenya might be a welcome distraction. That was not how she regarded it, as she told Margaret Layzell, whom she met in Nairobi: 'Jane said to me,' her friend wrote in her diary, '"here I am stuck out here for the rest of my life and my young man is in England."'[7] Soon, she met someone else – a Kenyan policeman by the name of Peter Elliot. Mild-mannered and affable Elliot *tried* asking Grogan for Jane's hand in marriage, but in a reprise of his own experience with Gertrude's stepfather Grogan is reputed to have said 'Don't be so stupid young man; go away and be thankful I said no.' That was like waving a red rag at a bull: Jane was as used to, and as skilled, as her father at getting her own way. She and Elliot promptly eloped and married in secret in South Africa. It seemed as though all Grogan's chicks had left the nest – but it was not for long.

Within a decade all the girls, with the exception of Joyce, were for one reason or another back within 'bold, bad' Daddy's orbit in Kenya. It is impossible not to feel considerable sympathy for the girls. Being a Grogan cannot have been easy, but on the other hand, whatever his shortcomings as a father, Grogan never criticized his daughters for their marital or other difficulties and never resorted to telling them 'I told you so', and continued to provide a safety net for them throughout their lives.

Although Grogan's daughters were largely uninterested in his public life, no one else could ignore him. Having decided once and for all to throw in his lot with Kenya he was like a Brobdingnagian in Lilliput, and nowhere is this more obvious than in the political arena. When Delamere was forced out of politics by ill-health in 1929, and the dire results of his 'unholy alliance' with the government were plain for all to see, the settlers turned to Grogan – their man for an emergency, whom many regarded as 'the only man in the Colony who carries any political weight'[8] – for a lead. In the autumn he responded to the call for help by re-entering Legislative Council for the first time in seven years, despite his opinion that Legco had been reduced by Delamere's policy of coalition with the local government to nothing more than 'a pantomimic façade behind which the Colonial Office ruled, or misruled, the Colony'.[9]

Over the next two and a half decades Grogan never lingered in Council longer than he thought necessary to make his point or to tackle an emergency. In 1929 he represented his Nairobi North constituency for just one session – but the impact of his appearances was enormous. His criticism of ballooning, and in his opinion unproductive, governmental expenditure earned him the nickname 'the Westinghouse brake', but his warnings that the government was budgeting for a deficit and that this would end in disaster if the country were invaded from Abyssinia were ignored in official circles. Within a few years, however, his uncanny powers of foresight were proved reliable on all counts. When the effects of the Depression began to be felt in 1930 the government found that it was indeed nursing a budget deficit and it had to plunder the colony's reserves not only that year but in each of the following five years. Grogan's fantastic suggestion of an invasion from Abyssinia took a little longer to be proved prescient. His suspicions were based on the fact that he, unlike anyone in the government, had visited the Italian colony of Eritrea and drawn his own conclusions about Mussolini's ambitions. In 1936 Italy invaded Abyssinia and four years later was poised to overrun Kenya.

Whether he was in or out of Legislative Council, Grogan remained vociferous in his condemnation of Colonial Office policy. During the 1930s it became, in his opinion and that of many a colonist in Africa, 'the most discredited institution in the British Empire'.[10] As the grip of the metropolitan power tightened he accused Whitehall of ruling by *ukase*, or Soviet-style edict, with the result that 'everything that really happens [in Legislative Council] is merely "His Master's Voice"', and that the settlers' political status was reduced to 'that of the well-known picture of the pathetic bow-wow, with its ear cocked on one side, listening to the ultimate discussions of Sir Cecil Bottomley or some other great dignitary in Downing Street'.[11] This was not merely anti-authoritarianism on Grogan's part. He did not dispute that the CO was 'pregnant with tremendous and benevolent intention',[12] but what concerned him most was that the Colonial Office simply 'never . . . got the idea of constructive colonization' in Kenya.[13]

There was more than an element of truth in this assertion. In part it could be attributed to the fact that, though it had many capable officials out in the field, taking a position in the CO's offices in Whitehall was still only the third or fourth career choice for aspiring civil servants; the better young candidates tended to choose a more prestigious career in the Treasury, Home Office, India Office or diplomatic service. This parlous situation did begin to improve in the 1930s, due to the appointment of Sir Ralph Furse as Director of Recruitment at the Colonial Office in 1931,[14] but by then the failure over three decades to deal imaginatively or forcefully with the three abiding sources of conflict in the colony was beginning to prove catastrophic.

All that the CO seemed willing and able to do was rather ineffectually to fight fires. As far as the African population was concerned, land grievances which had festered for three decades were not conclusively dealt with by the 1934 Kenya Land Commission, and 'protected' African land was actually seized by the government during the mini-gold rush near Kakamega in 1931–3. The sort of economic assimilation that Grogan had always believed in was also discouraged. Africans were not allowed to grow coffee for fear of the consequences of the economic power this might give them,[15] and the conditions for African labourers in government service remained more lamentable than those on any settler's farm – a fact which led, for example, to a strike by dock workers in Mombasa in 1939. Similarly, while the rising tide of African political and social aspirations was acknowledged and more money was allocated during the 1930s to 'native interests', the number of district officers the CO deployed in the field to implement reforms actually fell sharply during the course of the decade.

The effect of thirty years of fudging the Indian Question also started to have irreversible consequences for Kenya. Mirroring the situation in India itself, the colony's Indian population campaigned with redoubled vigour for a common roll franchise. They received considerable encouragement when the 1935 Government of India Bill was passed in Westminster, paving the way for self-government in India itself. But – as was also true in India – the Bill fanned the flames of deep and age-old animosities between Muslims and Hindus. All in all, Grogan was convinced that the Colonial Office was failing 'to recognise the realities of life', and that the consequences would be 'social catastrophe'.[16]

Grogan's refusal to run with the hounds caused the gentlemanly, straight-as-an-arrow, but far from swashbuckling Lord Francis Scott, Delamere's successor as 'official' spokesman for the settlers, as much difficulty as it had his predecessor. Scott was, in Grogan's opinion, 'a strange personality [who] suffered from acute pain from a severe wound in the war. He was by nature rather intolerant and the pain of the wound rendered him liable to sudden outbursts of passion and impoliteness which were pardonable.'[17] On one occasion Scott, who was continually frustrated by Grogan's resolute non-conformity, even had the temerity to accuse him in Legco of being a 'senile and silly old man'.[18] But, this outburst aside, no one could deny that Grogan's '*piquant diablerie*' brought much-needed colour to Legco's proceedings and greatly energized the political scene. Always declaiming without notes, with his right hand clasping his lapel in the manner of a barrister, Grogan's presence never failed to raise the standard of debates in which he took part. He would inform anyone who referred too often to notes that he 'did not want to hear a speech read like a sermon'; he invariably addressed the government benches as 'the gramophone side of Council'; he frequently referred to governors as 'telephone girls' for the CO, and to the Attorney General as 'the hon. Member for law and disorder' or 'much law and no order'; and the presentation of the Budget he called 'this annual Hawaiian hula-hula dance'. When he occasionally overstepped the mark he would immediately apologize with the words 'Forgive me – I am an Irishman,' and his regular 'history lessons' – the point of which was always to prove that 'Colonial

Office governance precludes government' – were more often than not taken in the spirit with which they were intended.

Anyone who believed that Grogan was just a character was, however, falling into a trap that had been carefully – and with irresistible charm – laid for them. Maverick though he was, behind the high jinks and provocative jibes Grogan remained deadly serious about his politics. Indeed, he was instrumental in dissuading the Labour government's Colonial Secretary, Cunliffe-Lister, from imposing income tax on the colony at the height of the Depression. And as the man whom George Lloyd described as 'one of only six men in London who know anything worth knowing about finance and economics' it was also Grogan who led the campaign in the mid-30s to devalue the Kenya shilling in an effort to kick-start the colony's economy. In a highly influential series of articles (entitled 'Trusteeship!!!') he argued that British monetary policy was directly undermining the CO's responsibilities to the African population. His old ally, *The Times*, remarked that his arguments were 'a fresh wind from the bush to dispel the London fog',[19] but within the CO his entreaties usually fell on deaf ears. Indeed, in one confidential memo written in 1935 a Mr Flood went as far as haughtily declaring that 'it is really absurd that we should have to waste our time examining this kind of stuff put up by Major Grogan . . . Kenya is not the least important economically, socially, or any other way – except noisily'.[20] It seems that Grogan's unrelenting campaign against the CO, and the seriousness with which it treated its responsibility for Kenya in the first half of the century, was more than a little justified after all.

TWENTY-FOUR

'The Dance of the Gnats
in the Setting Sun'

WHEN WAR BROKE OUT Grogan was staying at Taveta. Although he was well into his sixties he immediately returned to Nairobi and reported for duty to General Dickinson, the senior officer in the East Africa Command, and his staff officer, Brigadier-General WA Dimoline. 'It would have been impossible to find a pair so easy to work under,' wrote Grogan, adding that '"Dimmy" could get a bore out of his office without hurting his feelings quicker than anybody in history – I know from practical observation and personal experience.'[1]

Despite Grogan's 'absurd' warning ten years earlier about the extent of Mussolini's ambitions in Africa, and the Italian invasion of Abyssinia in 1936, and the fact that mounting concerns about Kenya's security had led to its being allotted an air vice-marshal as governor in the pre-war years, war preparations in Kenya were as sorely lacking as they had been in World War I. Italy did not actually enter the war until June 1940, but even then the country was not in a position to defend its borders effectively. After a clash at Moyale between the Italians and a detachment of the highly trained King's African Rifles, Dickinson had to order an immediate withdrawal from the border country of Northern Frontier District in order to avoid being out-flanked by an invasion from Italian Somaliland. Such forces as he had available then formed a defensive line further south, the Italians advanced to take up positions around Dobel and Buna, and Kenya braced itself for an all-out invasion.

Three thousand European settlers out of an adult male population of 8,000 volunteered, like Grogan, and a further 3,000 were gazetted to reserved occupations vital to the war effort. But things had changed since the days when they had ridden into Nairobi on horseback with coloured kerchiefs and bandoliers around their necks. Untrained men were of precious little use to Dickinson, and the defence of the country was built around the KAR and the Kenya Regiment until units from the South, Nigeria and the Gold Coast started to arrive. Grogan wryly observed there was no more damning indictment of the failure of Colonial Office policy in Kenya than the fact that, once again, Smuts's South Africa was called upon to save the colony and lead the 50,000 African troops who loyally volunteered to answer the call to arms.

Grogan was, of course, too old to take the field as a combatant and was soon to be found drawing up his own war agenda. In East Africa all eyes were focused on the threat from the Italian colonies to the north but, in characteristically contrarious fashion, Grogan's attention alighted on his old stomping ground to the west. With Belgium having fallen to the Germans he regarded it as of paramount importance to Kenya that the Belgian Congo be kept on side and argued his case forcefully with General Dickinson. To his great credit, Dickinson saw the logic of Grogan's train of thought and immediately appointed him to his former position of Belgian liaison officer. He also agreed that Grogan should waste no time in crossing the Congolese border to carry out a reconnaissance, both covert and overt.

Grogan was in his element. Once again he was off, alone, to a part of the continent for which he had a deep affection, and he was charged with a vital mission which entitled him to do exactly as he pleased. Technology made his peregrinations easier than thirty-five years earlier in that he mostly flew wherever he wanted to go. But on at least one occasion he drove the 1,500 miles to the Congo for old times' sake – though not in a chuntering old 'Tin Lizzie' – and was alarmed by the extent to which Ruanda and Burundi had altered in twenty years under Belgian rule. 'The bourgeois Belgians', he observed, 'had begun to denigrate, belittle and destroy the authority of those splendid aristocrats, the Watutsi',[2] a development which he prophetically concluded might lead to a fatal destabilization of the fabric of Ruandan society. Certain things, however, had not changed: while wandering around the vast African market in Stanleyville he bumped into a Manyema sergeant-major whom he had known in the previous conflict, and the two old comrades whiled away an enjoyable morning discussing the war.

During the first phase of the conflict Grogan was instrumental in advising on the defence of the mines at Broken Hill in Northern Rhodesia, and in assessing the strength of the German settlements in Angola. His most important discovery was that while the Belgians in the eastern Congo were keen to co-operate with the British in East Africa, their brethren in the west were of a much more independent bent. This he hastily reported back to the War Office where, like many of his reports, it was filed without a response.

Grogan's activities greatly unnerved the War Office. No one was ever quite sure where he was, or what he was up to, until he chose to break cover by issuing unambiguous instructions. One of his communications from Government House in Northern Rhodesia notoriously recommended the dispatch to the West Coast of 'an obsolete warship with a red-whiskered admiral with prominent teeth to show that the British flag still flies on the high seas',[3] and another ordered the immediate placing of an order for £1m of copper to stop the mines closing in the Congo. Sometimes General Dickinson received cables from his military superiors asking the identity of 'the Edgar Wallace character' whom he had unleashed – a man who had seemingly asserted his authority over everyone from British governors to Belgian generals and was trying to chivvy the Congo into declaring itself a Commonwealth Dominion. But the general's faith in Grogan never wavered. The Congolese mines were kept open as a result of an order for copper placed by Britain, and as rumours gathered pace in London that Hitler had entered into a pact with the Vatican to make the French and Belgian African territories over to the Vatican in exchange for the support of the Pope, Grogan's intelligence reports suddenly became regarded as priceless. He received a cable of congratulation from George Lloyd, the Colonial Secretary in Churchill's government – the last communication he was to receive from his old friend before Lloyd's untimely death a year later.

Churchill, needless to say, was wholly rehabilitated in Grogan's opinion. Consigned to the backbenches in the 1930s in part due to his zealous imperialism, his hour had now truly come.

By the end of 1940 Mussolini had missed his chance in Kenya.

The build-up of South African soldiers and materiel was complete, and in January 1941 they crossed into Abyssinia and Italian Somaliland under the command of General Cunningham. Mogadishu fell on 20 February and Addis Ababa on 6 April. The highly eccentric Major Orde Wingate simultaneously entered Abyssinia from the west, preparing the way for Emperor Haile Selassie's return from exile, and General William Platt launched a bold thrust into Eritrea from the Sudan. After victory in a ferocious battle at Keren, the gateway to the Eritrean highlands, Platt relentlessly drove the vastly superior Italian force southwards. Asmara, the Eritrean capital, surrendered on 1 April.

This lightning victory over the Italians in East Africa was more than a little surprising. Confronted by a force of over 300,000 troops, 200 planes and large numbers of tanks, not even the most optimistic Allied general had predicted an end to the offensive in just three months. Success was therefore accompanied by immense logistical problems: Eritrea, Abyssinia and Italian Somaliland had to be administered, and hundreds of thousand of POWs had to be fed and housed.

This challenge provided Grogan with his next assignment. With the eradication of Italy's threat from the north his intelligence work in the Congo was no longer required, so he was promoted to lieutenant-colonel and put in command of three POW camps in Gilgil and Nairobi. There he continued his war as a law unto himself. More than once he put noses out of joint by taking Italian officers from the Gilgil camp to lunch at the Rift Valley Club; when taken to task for his unorthodox conduct by the military authorities Grogan replied that he saw no reason not to behave in a civilized fashion just because there was a war on – and challenged anyone to instruct him otherwise. But however enjoyable his repasts with General Nasi and others, after his rollicking time in the Congo nothing could have been more tedious than running POW camps. So Grogan quickly started work on a plan that would be useful to the war effort, make constructive use of the Italian POWs, and get him back to the bush.

Grogan's kingdom at Taveta had come on in leaps and bounds in the pre-war years – to the extent that even most members of the East Africa Department at the Colonial Office could not deny that he had 'made the desert blossom'.[4] His application for two further tracts of land – one to the north-east of Taveta ('Ziwani') and the other abutting Lake Jipe ('Jipe') – were therefore granted, despite the recommendation of the acerbic Mr Flood to 'stone-wall [Colonel Grogan's] activities where possible'.[5] The new additions gave Grogan contiguous land-holdings of 87,000 acres, fully 136 square miles, and by the beginning of the war the first sisal was already being cut on Ziwani, a second sisal factory had been built at Taveta and Grogan had created over 2,000 jobs – a number that was considerably greater than that of adult male Wataveta in the locality. It was also widely noted that he was determined to set an example by providing 'elaborate' stone housing, a canteen and a welfare centre for his African workers.

All the while Grogan's enthusiasm for a plethora of experiments had continued unabated. He transported black bass from Lake Naivasha and put them in the springs where they thrived; he would not allow a single tree to be cut down without his permission, and planted many new varieties; and he and Layzell, his manager, devised a highly innovative system for composting sisal waste. The latter, in particular, had a marked 'psychological effect' on the local population, who were the recipients of the produce from the 'large area of bananas, sugar cane, citrus trees and potatoes'[6] which were grown on the compost. Grogan, it seems, was intent on proving not only to the government but also to his neighbours what could be achieved with a little ingenuity in what had once been written off as an impossibly hostile environment; and in his wake the government followed, providing schooling, on-the-spot healthcare and agricultural assistance for the Wataveta.

Despite the effects of Grogan's development fever on his 'kingdom', for any European who liked Africa in the raw Taveta remained the real thing. Staff mostly lived in 'Noah's Arks', houses built to Grogan's own eccentric design. They had timber-boarded roofs with a pitch of not less than 45° so that all rain-water would run off; the eaves stopped only two feet above the concrete flooring, and timber posts, wrapped in wire mosquito netting, supported the eaves. The interiors of these 20-foot-wide tent-like structures were dark and airless during the heat of the day. Kitchens (through which waterbuck were liable to crash without warning) and bathrooms (in which a man might reach round the back of the door for his shaving strap only to find that he had grasped a snake) were usually out-houses. As was the case with anything he did there was 'Grogan logic' – not always appreciated by his managers' wives – behind the creation of such austere living conditions. Grogan wanted *workers*, not 'verandah farmers' or 'bush cowboys', and his own home in Taveta in the pre-war years was a two-room concrete bunker.

The Spartan living arrangements aside, Taveta was a magical place, especially for young children allowed to run free. Wildlife was more than plentiful (rhinos, in particular, were two-a-penny); Lakes Chala and Jipe, and the beautiful springs at Mzima were all on the doorstep; and the whole area was dominated by the brooding presence of majestic Mount Kilimanjaro. Social life was rudimentary, so visits from successive governors interested in what Grogan had achieved in his kingdom were as eagerly anticipated as events like the huge party held to celebrate the Coronation of George VI in May 1937. Then, the local Wateita and Wataveta had taken on the estates' 'Kavirondo'[7] workers in a football tournament, the European children played sports and planted trees while their fathers contested a tug-of-war, and as darkness descended Africans from hundreds of miles around vied to better each other's displays of tribal dancing. Bonfires were lit, fireworks were loosed off, and prize oxen were roasted for the visiting chiefs and their subjects. Such social highlights were rare. Most of the time hunting was the favourite pursuit for the European menfolk, or occasional visits to Moshi, and picnics for the women and children. Young Margaret Layzell's diary attests to the splendour of these outings:

> us women went on about 5.30 . . . and found a marvellous spot just the other side of Salaita, where we could see the mountain, [Lake] Gyppe, the Pares and the moon as it got up. We collected wood before it got dark and set the supper out and the moon came up – first with a bar of blue cloud across it and then into a sky full of sheep . . . the mountain stood up, a huge dark shape, its snow looking like a white cloud, settled on its shoulders.[8]

No one on the Taveta estates ever knew quite when Grogan would turn up, which kept them all on their toes. Sometimes he arrived in the middle of the night and Margaret Layzell would awake at dawn to hear his voice in her father's bedroom, discussing plans and issuing instructions. Then he would don overalls and disappear, to be seen later digging trenches or grubbing about with his prospecting pick or talking sisal machinery in the factory. His zeal was plain for all to see, and it put people off-balance: not only did he have very eccentric ideas but he would often change his mind and decide there was a *better* place to lay the foundations of a new building (when it was already half-complete), or a *better* way of doing something than he had suggested the previous week. Margaret Layzell had a keen sense of the strain his presence put on her parents: her diary is littered with entries recording that 'Grogs is still here, alas. Daddy will go potty'; that 'Grogs is cross because 4 pathetic little trees have been cut down'; and that 'it is funny that whenever he's here for more than a certain time Ma goes sick.' 'Still,' she often added affectionately, 'he's really no trouble, though he's tiring.'[9]

By the end of 1938 Grogan, and ten years in the isolated community at Taveta, had proved too 'tiring' for the conscientious Stanley Layzell and he resigned. His departure marked the end of the first phase of development at Taveta, but with the recent addition of the Jipe and Ziwani estates Grogan was intent on achieving considerably more. As usual, the fulfilment of his ambitions needed huge sums of money – a requirement which he took care of by enticing into partnership two very rich men indeed who fortuitously liked spending money as much as he did: Sir John Ramsden and the eccentric Maurice Egerton, fourth Baron of Tatton.[10] Together these three pumped in the funds for the next stage of development of Kilimanjaro's hinterland.[11] Major Conrad Walsh, the 'Sisal King' of Tanganyika, was drafted in as a special adviser after Layzell's departure; and, bored by his job as a POW camp Commandant, by 1942 Grogan was determined to return to Taveta.

In March Grogan approached the wartime governor, Sir Henry Moore, with plans to construct two gigantic irrigation schemes on his estates and adjacent African land. They would, he argued, make more productive use of his skills than running POW camps and help to counter the threat to the Empire's sources of rice posed by the Japanese sweep through the Pacific Basin. Moore duly approved Grogan's plan, as did Cavendish-Bentinck, the colony's wartime Director of Production, and by July a budget had been agreed for growing over 10,000 acres of rice and vegetables in the Taveta area. Grogan suggested that this should be financed as a joint venture between his companies and the government, organized along the lines of the legendarily successful exemplars of African irrigation systems, the Sudan Plantation Company, but as development included African-owned land the government decided that it should finance the scheme alone and that Grogan's role should be solely managerial. Throwing Grogan, civil servants and regular soldiers into the same paddy field was not a recipe for unqualified success.

The real problem with the irrigation schemes was one of control: there were simply too many chiefs. A steering committee sat in Nairobi, received reports from government and military hydrologists and surveyors at Taveta, and sent out one set of instructions; while down at Taveta no one was able to do anything without Grogan's say-so, not least because he out-ranked anyone working on the schemes, owned much of the land that was being cleared for irrigation, and provided (and paid for) most of the workers and machinery on which the Public Works Department depended. By the middle of 1943 a serious rift had occurred between Grogan and the 'Taveta Committee', with Grogan convinced that they should be pushing ahead with a cheaper plan that would produce food that same year and the latter sticking to its more ambitious original plan which, as far as Grogan could tell, would take over five years to come to fruition. As Grogan's criticism of the government's inept handling of the scheme became increasingly strident, compromise became the order of the day, but in 1944 Grogan washed his hands of any further involvement in the project.

Brigadier Bednall, who was latterly in charge of purchasing what Grogan produced at Taveta, was not the first person to find 'co-operation with him is a most difficult matter' nor that, as he was 'generally admitted to have many of the attributes of genius' and was known to be 'a political friend of the Earl of Baldwin and of many other influential people at home',[12] discretion was the best course of action when dealing with Taveta's paramount chief. But it was usually the case that when Grogan became wholly intractable there was some underlying cause over and above his ongoing crusade against governmental incompetence. Often the explanation was that he was suffering a recurrence of his liver abscesses, or was on the verge of bankruptcy. In the middle of 1943, something altogether more tragic darkened his mood.

Since the outbreak of war Gertrude had worked tirelessly in support of the visiting forces and had been made President of the East Africa Women's League, taking the reins from Lady Baden-Powell. In so doing, according to the *East African Standard*, she 'neither spared herself nor begrudged her time in the long and often very onerous tasks so cheerfully and gladly discharged at the busiest war period'.[13] In the end the strain had proved too great, and in June 1943 she suffered a heart attack.

For two weeks Grogan spent each day at Gertrude's bedside in the Maia Carberry nursing home, and she appeared to be making good progress. By the morning of 5 July, when Kit Taylor visited, she even found her friend sitting up in bed and 'beaming . . . *beaming*'.[14] The catalyst for her greatly improved spirits was that Grogan had just been with her and had promised that as soon as she was better they would go away somewhere, just the two of them, while she completed her convalescence. That same afternoon, Gertrude had another heart attack and Grogan lost the big-hearted woman whom he always referred to as his 'one and only true love'.

Hundreds of people turned out for the funeral of 'Kenya's universal mother', who was buried in Nairobi's Forest Road Cemetery. The *East African Standard* spoke for all of them in saying that Gertrude 'had a straightforward and simple faith in Kenya as a home for British settlers and that faith and confidence illumined all her words and acts'. The newspaper added, in her obituary, that

> she saw in the Women's League and in such institutions as the Lady Northey Home the means by which her faith could be given practical expression . . . She also presided over many a happy Christmas party for Nairobi children when they gathered together at Torr's Hotel as the guests

of herself and her husband and she always saw in those
gatherings of the new generation more than just a few hundreds of children enjoying life. They were to her evidence
of the happy place that Kenya was meant to be. [Mrs Gro-
gan] was in her quiet way an unperturbed and imperturbable
champion of Kenya.[15]

Grogan was devastated by Gertrude's death and was well aware
that 'nobody [had] ever loved me so unselfishly'.[16] In her own practical,
unflustered way she had been her husband's greatest supporter, in
much the same way as 'Clemmie' supported Grogan's fellow maverick,
Churchill. For both women a sense of duty, and a love whose depth
many others could not fathom, underpinned their tolerance of their
remarkable husbands' foibles and shortcomings. For Grogan the effect
of the loss was compounded by the fact that he had always, given his
own recurrent health problems, assumed that he would pre-decease
Gertrude.

With his usual enthusiasm for life severely dented by the loss of
Gertrude, Grogan lost out in the 1944 Kenyan election. He had represented the constituency of Kiambu since 1939, but with the war
approaching its end the settlers decided they no longer needed their
'man for an emergency' and opted to replace him with a less controversial, and temperate, dairy farmer by the name of Francis Horatio
de Vere Joyce. Settler ambitions were once again riding high: during
the war government had resembled a coalition between officials and
unofficials with the result that much of the influence the latter had
lost during the 1930s was regained. Grogan's former employee, Cavendish-Bentinck became the first settler to gain ministerial rank in 1944,
and deluded talk of securing self-government once again started to be
heard in European circles. As Grogan was not only convinced that such
an aspiration was a dead duck but remained determined to continue to
highlight the shortfalls in Colonial Office policy, he was – as the war

neared its end – the last person the settlers wanted on the hustings when pursuing a strategy of moderation and appeasement.

If Grogan wanted to talk it made little difference whether he was in or out of Legislative Council, and in a series of articles written in 1945 for the *East African Standard* under the collective title of 'Ruminations on Monetary Hysteria' Grogan set out not only to deride the structural shortcomings of the Kenyan economy but to deliver another lesson in history to the newspapers' readers. In general his use of language and the complexity of his arguments were so far above most people's heads that they dismissed the articles as reactionary piffle on the part of a man who had reacted rather badly to the loss of his wife. But in the years to come they would remember his words, and wish they had paid more attention.

In his articles the prime butt of Grogan's criticism was his usual bête noire, the Colonial Office. 'In spirit the whole place is pregnant with tremendous and benevolent intention,' he wrote, 'but it lacks sufficient stimuli from the periphery of the ectodermic activities which it is supposed to provoke and coordinate.' As an example of this he slammed what he called the 'Zoo Theory of State Planning' being deployed by the CO to sort out problems in the 'Native Reserves' caused by rapid population growth and the consequent degradation of the land. 'Let us in God's name face the music,' he implored, and characterized the CO's response to rising discontent in the reserves as the administration of 'little dabs of eyewash'.

Grogan was also heavily critical of what seemed to him to be a policy of infantilizing Africans, and the tendency of Whitehall to regard them as 'melanistic pets'. He regarded the African as being different from the Briton in the same way as, say, a Frenchman was different from a Briton. Colour was not the issue for him, but the 'psyche of widely differentiated peoples ... the acquired momentum of age-old habit, custom, tradition and practice' was. To illustrate this point he argued that 'with the British, bribery, secret commissions, law-dodging and the like subversive habits though practised are instinctively regarded as a matter of SHAME. But in many lands, and the East in particular, such a method is recognised customary procedure provoking only PITY for the unsuccessful practitioner.' The consequences, he iterated, of not appreciating that African society was different from British society when formulating policy would be 'the tragic sight . . . of the pathetic Kikuyu who roams the streets of Nairobi in plus fours, Homburg hat, dark spectacles and the like sartorial incongruities', and 'the rather pathetic dusky beauties you see . . . suffering intolerable agony as a result of using footgear to which they are not habituated, and obviously deriving their sustenance from the practice of the ancient craft'.

What Grogan proposed as the counter to the Colonial Office's 'abysmal failure' in dealing with 'Native Affairs' was 'mass education', 'disciplined co-operation not snarling segregation', and he insisted that 'the road of advancement *must* be open to *all* Africans'. Only then did he believe that his vision of a 'reasonable and decent society in Africa' could be fulfilled; to pursue any different course of action would, he warned, 'surely lead to terrible trouble'.[17]

Grogan's warnings were as usual substantially ignored in official circles, or – at best – misunderstood. It was true that Sir Philip Mitchell, the post-war governor, was a professed adherent of a progressive policy of multi-racialism, but bankrupt post-war Britain simply did not have the funds – nor, arguably, the political will – to back its rhetoric with plenty of good, hard cash. Grogan suspected as much, and decided to put the Colonial Office's honesty to the test.

Even before the war was over Grogan set out to develop his Jipe estate as an agricultural training centre for Africans, preferably ex-combatants who could boast distinguished war records, and then to turn it over to the government so that it could become a state-sponsored initiative. With that in mind he began building an extraordinary 'college' on a hill on the estate known as Girigan, a windswept site which commanded spectacular 360° views of the area. Lake Jipe and the Pare mountains lay to the south and Kilimanjaro to the north-west.

The huge white building which gradually took shape atop the hill was certainly striking. Courtesy of Grogan's own idiosyncratic architectural input it was part monastery, part Moorish fort and part hacienda. It was approached via a road which snaked its way up the hill and deposited visitors at the foot of broad steps leading to an arch in which wrought-iron entrance gates were later set. A large bell stood to the left of the entrance. Beyond the gates was a central courtyard with a fountain and flower beds surrounded by cloisters which contained the rooms for the students. In the south-western corner was a staircase leading to a tower, the first floor of which was a vast circular sitting room with semi-circular openings looking out over the surrounding plains. In the middle of the room was a thick column which supported the floor above, another sitting room, which had steep stairs up to Grogan's 'look-out' on the roof. Quirky touches were to be found everywhere in the fifty-eight room structure: baths were in bedrooms – unpartitioned, as Grogan didn't see why anyone 'needed to hide'; beds were enclosed in cages covered with wire mosquito netting; and many of the ceilings and floors were made from sisal poles.[18]

When Grogan completed his 'college', he duly wrote to Sir Philip Mitchell offering it to the government – and never even received a reply. This left him with an extremely expensive folly on his hands. But, more importantly to Grogan, the rejection of his offer seemed to prove that, at a time when the government's pursuit of multi-racial policies did not extend to providing the African population with universal primary education (let alone a comprehensive programme for technical education along the lines he had proposed at Jipe), 'terrible trouble' really did lie ahead. It also seemingly confirmed his long-held belief that it was individual 'European settlers who had built up Kenya' more than successive British or local governments, and that they had done so 'not at the expense of the African, but very much to his advantage'.[19]

After marking everybody's cards in typically forthright manner Grogan, in political terms, went to ground to wait and see what would happen. For seven years he stayed out of politics, and even dropped out of *Who's Who*. When he returned to Legislative Council it was to confront the fulfilment of many of his most dire prophecies and the greatest crisis to have yet befallen colonial Kenya.

The late 1940s and early 1950s were certainly not idle years for Grogan, despite his withdrawal from politics. One of his first priorities was to fill the gap left by Gertrude's death. She was irreplaceable, of course, but he wanted someone around – if only as a housekeeper – and began by casting his net over familiar territory. It is not known in quite what order the invitations to join him were sent out, but they were received by the mothers of his two illegitimate daughters (Doris Tate-Smith, in Sussex, and Doreen Wright), by another former lover in Hove and yet another known as 'Dilly-Dally'. All declined for one reason or another, except for the lady from Hove who had the misfortune to arrive in Nairobi after the vacancy had already been filled by one Camilla Towers, Grogan's junior by approximately thirty years.

Grogan had always had something of a penchant for lovers who were not generally regarded by the socially aware as equals, but in forging a partnership with the petite, red-headed and immaculately made-up Mrs Towers he astounded his friends and all of Nairobi society by definitively going 'below stairs'. Everyone knew that she had worked behind the counter at Wardle's the chemists, but of other details about her provenance no one was quite certain. Some friends of Grogan's were told by Towers that her husband had been a general who died of a heart attack on receipt of a particularly unpleasant communication from the tax authorities, some believed her to have been a Mother Superior in India, and some had memories of her having worked as a housekeeper at Torr's. Others, confusing her with Doris Tate-Smith, thought that her husband had been an architect. One particularly astounding story that did the rounds was that she had been rescued by a passing Grogan after escaping, stark naked, from a Nairobi nursing home where she was confined while suffering from a bout of depression. Which of these tales is true, or whether the truth is a combination, is impossible to verify. But on two points Nairobi society was agreed: Camilla Towers was no intellectual; and she was at best 'governess class' and at worst '*extremely* common'.

Towers's role as consort-housekeeper to 'Kenya's Churchill', its 'Grand Old Man', cannot have been an easy one to fill, a fact of which she was well aware. In order to try and explain the inexplicable pairing she often resorted to calling herself not only Grogan's housekeeper but 'Grogs's adopted daughter'. This, of course, did little to help his uneasy relationship with his real daughters: Dorothy and Jane loathed Towers with a passion from the outset, and suspected her of being a gold-digger. And it did little to counter the allegations of those who said that after Gertrude's death 'Grogs' had temporarily taken leave of his senses.

Whatever criticism she attracted, Camilla Towers was to stay loyally with Grogan until his death, no mean feat, and did her best to keep his life in order. Her first assignment was to help him make a home out of his folly at Girigan after the government had refused to accept it as an agricultural college for Africans. But – almost inevitably – her input swiftly became peripheral as things had to be done exactly the way Grogan wanted them done, and that did not include bringing costly and garish Indian rugs back from a shopping trip in Moshi or spending money on fripperies of any sort. The man to whom the real responsibility for the task fell was young architect Heini Lustman. Lustman had some idea of what he might be in for: when he was doing some work before the war for Nairobi's leading contractor, George Blowers, Gertrude had arrived in Blowers's office one day to ask if he could help with something at the Gallows, the Grogan house in Muthaiga. It was *urgent*, she had stressed, because her husband was away, and if he came back before the work was complete he was liable to pull it all down and do the job himself.

When Lustman arrived at Taveta by train it was to be greeted by a new-look Grogan. In October 1947 he had had a tooth removed and developed osteomyelitis, which required a section of his rotting jaw to be cut out. This gave his face a slightly pinched look and also left him with a scar which he sought to cover with a Smuts-like goatee beard. But apart from the physical indignity he had suffered (which pricked his vanity as did the fact that he was going slightly deaf) he was the same old Grogan – 'full of fabulous and interesting ideas ... a man of great, great vision'. Staying with him, Lustman said, was 'really quite an experience – a revelation. He was a magnificent raconteur; I don't know that he always told you the whole truth and nothing but the truth, but that made it all the more interesting.'[20]

Lustman was not overpowered by Grogan's presence, for the simple reason that he had no need to contradict him: he just had to try and make a livable home out of the shell that Grogan had constructed at Girigan. He installed windows (despite Grogan's initial opposition), partitioned open floor spaces, commissioned some magnificent wrought-iron grilles for the entrance arch and some of the windows, put in a kitchen, and had a single-slab dining table and sheep's hide leather chairs for twenty-eight made in Moshi. With that, Grogan deemed the job done and he and Camilla Towers moved in to what was thenceforth referred to as 'Grogan's Castle'.

The Taveta estates were, as they had never stopped being, a hive of activity. Each now had its own manager and bevies of consultants came and went to advise on Grogan's experiments. There were Jewish experts from Palestine who helped him to grow the largest and best avocados and grapefruit in all Kenya; a charming Polish refugee, Baron Gostkowski, who started work on creating fish ponds covering hundreds of acres with the aim of breeding tilapia for the 'Kavirondo' workforce; Italian former POW irrigation experts and surveyors who decided to stay on for a while after the war; and a number of pre-war Jewish refugees from Europe whom Grogan employed by dint of his friendship with Lord Rothschild.[21] Some of these advisers and managers were good, others were not, but the community at Taveta was nothing if not eclectic. Considerable attention was also paid to innovative labour relations: in November 1947 the workforce was treated, or subjected, to the first cinema performance on any estate in the country. *Tarzan* and *Crime Does Not Pay* were the films shown, but despite the good intentions, the District Commissioner at Teita recorded in his Monthly Intelligence Report that the workers 'did not seem to have been very impressed by either'.[22]

Water remained the key to the future of all Grogan's experiments – and the workforce. The wartime irrigation schemes on Taveta and Ziwani had never fulfilled their potential and had ended in bitter recriminations which needed to be laid to rest before any further work could be done. Some officials castigated Grogan for having been too autocratic and then for severing his connections with the project in 1944. Others detected irregularities in the way that the government itself had handled the whole affair – irregularities which they felt were 'embarrassing' and best not revealed to an official inquiry. The similarities with the local government's underhanded treatment of Grogan during the Mbaraki affair are striking. Indeed in a letter to the Secretary of State for Colonies, Oliver Stanley, Surridge – the deputy governor in 1945 – had the courage to speak up for Grogan

and accuse his fellow officials of incompetence. In his letter Surridge
wrote that

> I should point out that [Grogan's] estates have rendered
> very considerable assistance to the development of the irri-
> gation schemes . . . These services include the making avail-
> able of heavy machinery at the nominal cost of £1 per unit
> per day as against the ordinary commercial charge of £3
> per unit per hour; the allocation free of estate houses for
> the use of government staff; and permission to utilise build-
> ing and other materials free of charge and royalty.

All in all Surridge calculated the extent of Grogan's personal subsidy
to the scheme as being 'of the order of £4,000'.[23]

The challenge facing the government following this tacit admission
of guilt in its handling of the Taveta schemes was to unscramble what,
of the extensive work done on the estates, technically 'belonged' to
Grogan and what 'belonged' to the government. This was a very
protracted process, but by 1948 the government was desperate to
effect a cover-up and effectively gifted to Grogan most of the work
that it had done. However great Grogan's annoyance with the way
that he had been treated, this was an extremely favourable agreement
for him, and he fully capitalized on the opportunities that the improved
irrigation on his estates afforded. He was able to plant hundreds of
acres of citrus, linseed and experimental fibres on Ziwani, and introduce the first Zebu cattle; on Taveta estate he gained almost free
access to tens of millions of gallons of water gushing from the Njoro
Kubwa springs; and on Jipe estate he was able to start work on a new
canal, some ten miles in length, to carry water by gravity from the
left bank of the Lumi River to his fish ponds. By 1950 this canal was
complete, and the water flow to the ponds was an impressive eight
million gallons per day.

When all this irrigation work was complete it demonstrated that
a decade earlier the water resources of the area, even after ten years
of work by Grogan, had scarcely been touched. It also showed what
might have been achieved during the war if Grogan and his managers
had been left to their own devices by the government. Harnessing the
'liquid gold' made money, and also saved lives and jobs for hundreds

of miles around during the terrible drought of 1949. Foodstuffs, particularly maize and citrus, was made available at knock-down prices to Africans whose crops failed, and when the sisal became affected Grogan managed to keep his factories running (and labourers employed) by cropping sansevieira – bowstring hemp – which grew wild on some 20,000 acres of Jipe and Ziwani. This not only eradicated a natural harbour for tsetse fly but the sansevieira fetched £65 a ton in the international markets at a time of global shortage. Through such initiatives Grogan proved that he had not only made the desert bloom, but that his estates were flexible when afflicted by adverse climatic conditions. It was, by any standards, a remarkable achievement.

Overseeing the work on the estates took all Grogan's energies and attention. Indeed by the end of the 1940s, Taveta was Grogan's life. His share of the ranch at Longonot, his stake in the *East African Standard*, Equator Saw Mills, a rice mill and factory in Mwanza, the land at Turi, the ranch on the Athi plains, his Kingatori coffee farm – all these ventures, and much else besides, had been sold (or passed to the bank) during lean times in the preceding thirty years with the exception of Torr's Hotel which was kept on as an amusing diversion. Just one major asset from the early days remained in Grogan's hands, and that was his 136-acre Swamp Estate in downtown Nairobi. In 1948 this too was sold for the massive sum of £210,000 to two enterprising young Bohra Muslim Indians, Ahmedali and Fidaali Hebatullah.

Grogan thoroughly approved of the Hebatullahs, and their brinkmanship impressed him no end. Although well on their way to establishing East Africa's foremost glassworks, they had no capital and asked if they could pay in instalments. Grogan proved amenable; he accepted 10 per cent of the purchase price as a deposit and agreed terms whereby the total consideration would be paid by 1954. But, as an act of faith, he transferred title to the whole estate immediately. For this the Hebatullah brothers were eternally grateful: Ahmedali said that he 'would have lost everything if Colonel Grogan had not been so reasonable' and believed him to be 'a very courageous man'[24] to have trusted him and his brother. Under their watchful eye, and with colossal investment, the Swamp was finally – over the next two decades – transformed into a developed part of central Nairobi, as Grogan had maintained it would be when standing on the banks of the Nairobi river almost half a century earlier.

The money realized from the fortuitous sale of the Swamp was mostly poured into the estates at Taveta over the next decade, but even before Grogan received the deposit from the Hebatullahs he was determined to fulfil an ambition very dear to his heart: he wanted to construct a fitting, and lasting, memorial to Gertrude. His first idea, inspired by their shared love of children, was to build an orphanage. This soon developed into an altogether more elaborate scheme to construct East Africa's first children's hospital. Trustees were appointed and endowed with seventeen acres of land adjacent to Grogan's Muthaiga house, the Gallows; Grogan agreed to pay the £20,000 building costs; and the East Africa Women's League managed the remarkable feat of raising £10,000 to equip the hospital. After two years of frantic preparations 'Gertrude's Garden' opened in 1948 for its first patients, offering thirty-two beds in four wards. The Gallows had been turned into the matron's house and outside it stood a limousine donated by Grogan as a welcome present to the nurses.[25]

Losing Gertrude was never far from Grogan's mind. After the war he had instructed his daughter, Dorothy, to sell Draycott Place 'to some confiding citizen', and thereby severed his last links with England. He had not visited the magnificent residence known as 'Number 10' since 1935, and had even less desire to do so after it was badly damaged in the Blitz. All its contents were also sold or thrown away at his insistence as if they, like the house itself, were too painful a reminder of Gertrude. That he did continue to miss her greatly is attested to, as is Grogan's mindset in the post-war years, by one of the very few pieces of his personal correspondence to have survived. The letter, dated August 1949, was written to a friend by the name of 'Oliver':

My dear Oliver,

I have been meaning to write to you for some time ...
Alas my dear Gertrude died suddenly of a heart attack some
few years ago and I now live a life of solitude in the real
wilds of Africa ... I had a year or so with surgeons hacking
my skull about – osteomyelitis – in vulgar parlance a rotting
jaw – due to an incompetent dentist. Two five-hour sculp-
ture efforts on one's brain [?] casket at 75 does not help
much but I am all well again now – kicking old Ma Africa
a final one on the panties even though I can only absorb
soup and such-like infantile pabulum.

Have built myself a Moorish home on the top of a hill
with a 70 miles view all round and a mass view of Kilimanjaro as the pièce de resistance ... Have not been to England
for 14 years and doubt if I ever shall again – getting set and
reluctant to move out of one's organized nest of convenience. Have lots of creative work to do here which keeps
me amused and active. Fish farming on a grand scale –
fighting tsetse and an irrigation scheme to deal with a few
thousand acres. The normal Government obstruction
rather spoils the tarte and renders one more bitter than one
should be when one ought to be emulating the medlar. I
wish you could come and have a good laugh with me – only
a day from England now! What about your next leave –
can make you quite comfortable here as a base. Why don't
you collect this Governorship? You could have lots of fun
and perhaps do some good.

This Colony is drifting into social and financial chaos.
No discipline – oceans of eyewash – financial innocents
believing that we are getting richer because of a flood of
funk money and Government inflationary bumph; and the
ground nut scheme is creating monetary elephantiasis in
the bazaars and bloating the revenues. Swarms of uncivil
servants [sic] with resonant but non-productive function are
being piled on a quaking agricultural base. The dance of
the gnats in the beams of the setting sun. Our servants have
been advised by Kenyatta and Co to steal everything and

hand it over to the junta so that they can buy ships to transport the Africans to Russia, Land of Hope and Glory – and so on and so on.

I had a short trip to the ground nut scheme a year or so ago. My hat off to the Labour Party for the first big imaginative attempt to open up Africa. Unfortunately they tried to rush it and it became overloaded and encrusted with bureaucrats but there are some good men there . . . It is a pity that they did not ask me to help from the first in some unpaid capacity as one who has been dealing with this class of land with big machinery for 20 years. I could have saved them millions and got better results . . . It will be a thousand pities if the scheme fails. The areas in question are typical of 999 per thousand parts of Africa (East). The whole future of British Tropical Africa depends upon what (if anything) of mundane use this class of environment can produce. If it fails Africa can be written off as a substantial contributory to the Common Weal. IT IS CERTAINLY WORTH MILLIONS OF INFLATIONARY MONEY TO FIND OUT . . . Well enough of this balderdash – my love to you and let me have your news when you can spare a moment.[26]

Amidst its more truculent opinions this letter shows that however upset Grogan was about Gertrude's death it had not robbed him of his grasp of what was going on around him. It was true that Kenyatta had returned from his fifteen-year study trip to Britain in 1946 to take the lead of the recently-formed Kenya African Union. It was equally the case that African unrest was increasing by the month, and Grogan's persistent warnings of trouble ahead were being ignored in the corridors of power; that the civil service was multiplying at an alarming rate; that the groundnut scheme in Tanganyika failed on a grand scale; and that the 'gnats' *were* 'dancing in the beams of the setting sun' – though few recognized that it was setting. But in spite of everything Grogan was indeed preparing to 'kick old Ma Africa a final one on the panties'.

TWENTY-FIVE

The Elephant with a Big Hoof

PAROCHIALISM (on the part of the settlers) and complacency (on the part of the Kenya government) ruled supreme in Kenya in the post-war years. On the face of it, everything *was* going swimmingly. Exports increased from £5m in 1945 to £25m in 1952, and European immigration increased so rapidly during Attlee's Labour government that by 1948 there were over 10,000 Europeans in Nairobi alone. Cavendish-Bentinck, who succeeded Lord Francis Scott as the settlers' official spokesman, even talked as though Kenya's future could still be that of so-called 'White Dominion' and the *African World* proclaimed that historians would view 1952 as 'the beginning of a new era'. But as the first black African – Eliud Matthu – took a seat on the governor's Executive Council, it was to prove not quite the sort of era the journal's editor had in mind.

Beyond the colonial outpost that was Kenya, the political sands were shifting fast. America was controlling the purse-strings of a bankrupt Britain; India gained its independence; and the imperialism of both the Labour government and liberal Conservatives was unrecognizable to most settlers. Closer to Kenya, there were riots in the Gold Coast in 1948 which led to an immediate concession of substantial political rights to the African population, and in Kenya itself political activity – and violence – among the black population grew by the month. Control over law and order in Nairobi was lost as early as 1947. The increasing prevalence of unrest was at least recognized by the more astute District Officers, but when they warned the government about it they were ignored. One settler encapsulated this situation by remarking that 'those at the top were lamentably hard to wake'.[1]

By 1951 there were many who sensed that Grogan's warnings of six years earlier – namely that 'terrible trouble' lay ahead – should not have been so readily dismissed. In the newspapers, and the bars and clubs of Nairobi, it was increasingly said that he had been 'much misunderstood'; and as it became more and more obvious that an emergency of some sort was brewing it was to 'Kenya's Churchill' that the settlers turned. On 4 July he was invited to address what turned out to be the largest meeting of Europeans ever held in the colony at the Command Theatre in Nairobi. From the moment he rose to his feet, Grogan held his audience spellbound and left it with some forthright, if paternalistic, advice:

> Our approach to the African should be kindly and benign. For myself I am 100% pro-African. I have had fifty-five years of experience of him. I have employed him by the tens of thousand. I have been involved in the most indescribable messes with him at times, and at the last resort the old African never let me down ... Please do anything you can to adopt a friendly attitude towards the African. Give him every opportunity to participate here, there and everywhere.

Grogan stopped short of advocating anything more than a 'limited' African participation in government, but his words were intended to be genuinely conciliatory. Kenya's 'man for an emergency' was back, and in June 1952 he was prevailed upon by the European community to stand once again for Legco. As he took his seat for Nairobi West he was also, in an event of great symbolic significance, elected President of the newly formed Pioneers Society.

In the first half of 1952 field administrators (and the European elected members of Legco, now led by the moderate Michael Blundell) reiterated that the militant wing of the Kenya African Union was on the rampage and requested the enforcement of emergency powers. Again the government ignored them. In June, Sir Philip Mitchell retired as governor and – at a crucial juncture – the Colonial Office left Kenya leaderless for three months. 'Then,' wrote settler John Lipscomb, 'Mau Mau boiled up and the bottom fell out of our world.'[2] By the time Sir Evelyn Baring arrived as Mitchell's replacement he felt that he had no option but to declare a State of Emergency, arrest Kenyatta and the entire leadership of the KAU, and put them on trial.

By the end of the year the first British troops were arriving from the Middle East to deal with the crisis.

The visible manifestations of Mau Mau shocked Europeans and all but participating Africans to the core. Anti-European, anti-Christian oaths involving horrific sexual rituals were sworn by the rebels, and the barbarity of their attacks – mostly directed at fellow Africans – almost defied description. Lipscomb observed the aftermath of one such attack and was told of 'women [who] have seen their children sliced to pieces before their eyes, pregnant ones ripped open with knives; old men, women and children barricaded in huts and burnt to death, recruits made to eat decaying human flesh'.[3] The only way that most Europeans could rationalize what they were witnessing was to attribute it to a mass hysteria that had overtaken the Kikuyu tribe, some sort of ghastly medical condition which had to be 'cured'.

Diagnosing the 'disease' did not make its causes any easier to pin down. The origins of Mau Mau are still hotly disputed, not least because they were many and varied. In Nairobi a shortage of jobs and housing and a high level of politicization among the black population were key elements; in the White Highlands and the Kikuyu reserve land was an important issue, as was the disaffection of the young both with colonial authority and with the traditional authority of the chiefs. Poor wages, an astronomical rise in the price of maize meal, and the unfulfilled aspirations of former servicemen also contributed to the dissatisfaction. What is certain is that the have-nots and the young were leading participants; that the uprising was not nationalistic in the European sense of the word, being largely confined to the Kikuyu tribe; that it was not particularly co-ordinated; and that Kenyatta was not directly its instigator. His refusal to denounce Mau Mau publicly in any way that could be construed as genuine was attributable less to his support for the rebels than to his own, understandable, fear of them.

Grogan's sympathy for the aspirations of the African population in general did not extend to the Mau Mau guerrillas. He accused them of being atavistic – 'just like a lot of the people in my country in the west of Ireland still are'[4] – and called for them to be declared guilty of treason. When asked how he would stop the rebellion in its tracks he replied that 100 guerrillas should be rounded up, driven to the

Northern Frontier District, and the majority hanged. Those spared could then walk the hundreds of miles back through the desert to the Kikuyu Reserve 'to spread the joyous tidings'[5] of what fellow transgressors could expect. For this suggestion he was immediately sentenced to death by the Mau Mau leaders.

Such petulance aside, in these early days of the Emergency Grogan frequently made suggestions which were rejected in Legco as the ramblings of a fractious old man, but were subsequently regarded as inspired. He was, for example, categoric in his belief that it was a grave mistake for the authorities to have imprisoned Jomo Kenyatta. Fellow politicians and friend Sir Charles Markham recalls Grogan's logic:

> [his attitude] was that Kenyatta had started the rebellion so he should stop it. But he got no support from the [European] elected members, or anybody, and I got a letter from Mervyn Hill who was editor of the *Kenya Weekly News* saying 'has Grogan gone mad?'. Grogan said, 'Well many thousands of people will die, many thousands. I'm right and they're wrong.' Which he was.[6]

Two years later, following one of the most brilliant, conciliatory and carefully worded speeches of Grogan's long political career, his fellow-Irishman (and frequent critic), the progressive Shirley Victor Cooke, expressed the regrets of the majority in Legco at not having listened to Grogan before:

> There are a lot of petty, mean-minded people in this country, 'dressed in a little brief of authority', as the poet says, who are inclined today to underestimate and undervalue the political importance of my honourable friend for Nairobi West. But today, Sir, the old lion has roared again with a real lion's voice [Cries of Hear! Hear!]; and yet beneath it all, Sir, there was a small voice of deep sympathy and deep appreciation, not only of the African people, but of the Kikuyu people. Very few people, I think, realize how much my honourable friend has done for the Africans of this country . . . If he had been [listened to] two years ago,

> I think the trouble would have been all over . . . the whole
> House is to blame that we didn't give him sufficient support
> in those days.[7]

Grogan was even asked at one point if he might be prepared to lead
the country, but wickedly replied that 'nobody has ever led Kenya.
We are much too individualistic a country. I have pushed occasionally.
I am a humble old owl who sits on the fence and hoots occasionally
and acts as a sort of book of reference to unrecorded history.'[8]

As a 'book of reference to unrecorded history', and a still mischiev-
ous one at that, Grogan's opinions were sought by almost every official
visitor to the colony during the Emergency. When two Labour MPs,
Fenner Brockway and Leslie Hale, arrived on a fact-finding mission
they were invited to lunch with Grogan at Torr's – and expected the
worst from the man they regarded as 'the veteran die-hard among the
European settlers . . . the central citadel of our critics'. But Grogan
completely disarmed them. Brockway wrote:

> The Colonel is certainly a character; he has been called an
> ancient monument; he is a very lively monument. I had
> expected a serious discussion about Kenya, but that was
> apparently the last thing in our host's mind. He was content
> to tell stories [which] was just as well, because the Colonel
> had many journalists as his guests and it is anyone's guess
> what might have happened.[9]

In December 1954 Grogan's eightieth birthday was celebrated in
Legislative Council. By now his eyesight was not too good and his
hearing had become increasingly selective. When it had first started
to deteriorate he took to using an ear trumpet in the chamber but
now he needed a hearing aid, which he made a great fuss about turning
off when anyone to whom he didn't want to listen rose to speak. All
things considered, however, he was in remarkably good shape. He was
still fully mobile, his back was ramrod straight and his voice still
strong. Glowing tributes were paid to him by speaker after speaker.
Cavendish-Bentinck said that he 'had had a career of which anybody
had a right to be proud . . . as one who had always tried to create
something where previously there was nothing in various parts of

Africa'. His good friend Humphrey Slade declared that 'Kenya owes more to Colonel Grogan than is yet realised', and added that he combined a 'relentless attack on enemies and hostile conditions with an equally relentless love of little children. His spirit and enterprise, his wisdom and humanity, not least his ever-present humour and his burning love of the colony are woven into the stuff of other men's lives.'

On behalf of the African members of Legislative Council Eliud Mathu affectionately likened Grogan to 'an elephant with a big hoof . . . everywhere he moves he leaves an impression that is always to the benefit of his country . . . Colonel Grogan,' he added, 'will leave a tremendous heritage for the future of all races in Kenya.' Sheikh Mackawi also thanked Grogan for 'always championing the Arab cause in Kenya'. Even C. B. Madan, speaking for the Indian members, declared that 'whether one agrees or disagrees with his views you cannot help admiring him . . . he will be regarded as one of the builders of history in East Africa'.

Grogan was visibly moved when he rose to his feet to express his 'profound gratitude for this great compliment'. He said that he hoped that Africans looked upon him as a fellow African, that had he been an Indian he would have pursued constitutional rights in exactly the manner that they had done, and that despite his constant criticisms he had nothing but admiration for the civil service. 'Many times I have been a nuisance in this Assembly,' he admitted, 'but the slings and arrows of my criticisms have never been barbed or pointed with venom.'[10]

In a wide-ranging interview with the *East African Standard* Grogan was more jocular than in the formal surroundings of Legco. He told the interviewer that 'being eighty isn't much different to being eighteen, except that one does not get quite so angry with people so easily. It is rather like sitting in the gallery spitting orange pips on the heads of people in the stalls.' He reiterated that he thought Mau Mau was a tragedy for Kenyans, black and white, but when pressed on what he thought the future held he simply replied that 'some poor man will touch the wrong button and poop off the whole world'. The secret of his longevity he attributed to 'smoking very heavily, eating and drinking very little, and taking nothing in life too seriously' – although he added that the doctor had ordered him to cut down on his ten cigars a day which had left him 'clinging to his pipe',[11] and when asked what he would like to be remembered for, he modestly replied that he didn't think he was worth remembering – or that he would be. To close friends, however, he confided that he feared that he might only be remembered for 'the bad things about me, like being in jail'.[12]

Over a drink in Muthaiga Club one friend pointed out to Grogan that Churchill, now always referred to by Grogan as 'the greatest living master of the Elizabethan tongue',[13] had also just celebrated his eightieth birthday. 'Yes, 1874 – a vintage year. Done well that boy,' was Grogan's chuckled reply.

It took Britain four years to suppress the Mau Mau uprising (although the worst was over in half that time). Neither the military nor the settlers shrank from fighting fire with fire, and some of their methods provoked as much controversy back in Britain as the oaths and barbarity of the 25,000 Mau Mau fighters. But all in all it was a very one-sided conflict, prolonged only by the logistical difficulties of clearing the forests of guerrillas and rounding up some 85,000 Kikuyu men – fully one third of the adult male population – and placing them in detention camps. Screening suspects was an extremely complicated business: Mau Mau was as much, if not more, of a civil war as an uprising against the colonial authorities. The general state of unrest created perfect conditions for old scores to be settled and for other tribes to vent age-old grievances against the Kikuyu. The question of loyalties was a complex one, the more so as over 25,000 Africans joined the Administration's Home Guard, determined to play their part in ending the chaos.

Just as Grogan had warned 'many thousands of people' were casualties of the conflict. The European population suffered remarkably little: cattle were killed and crops burned, but there were few determined attempts to sabotage roads, railways and dams; and just thirty-two deaths among the settler population could be attributed directly to Mau Mau. This 'escape', of course, only became evident with the benefit of hindsight: although Operation Anvil in April 1954, aimed at 'clearing up' Nairobi, greatly reduced the danger to blacks and whites alike in the capital, on isolated farms outside the capital the fear of attack was constant and debilitating. Compared to the small number of white casualties, however, some 14,000 Africans died, mostly as a result of internecine strife.

By the time Grogan finally retired from Legislative Council in 1956 the political map was changing fast in Kenya and all over colonial Africa. The first African had been admitted to the Council of Ministers, so for the first time the country had a multi-racial government of sorts. The 1955 East Africa Royal Commission also called for an end to the de facto colour bar, the opening up of land ownership in the White Highlands, and increased training for Africans and their greater participation in the civil service. Grogan declared that he was 'all for bringing in the African as fast as useful', but he regarded the inclusion of Indians in the highest echelons of government as 'a shocking betrayal of the African'.[14]

Grogan did not, of course, anticipate black majority rule in the *near* future any more than the ultra-conservative or the ultra-liberal among the European population. He also persisted in condemning the Kikuyu for carrying out 'the most profitable rebellion ever known: it cost them 10,000 men and very little money, for which they were seeing immense benefits in the rehabilitation of their land',[15] and in his final speech to Legco he denounced African activists' pursuit of 'this will-o'-the-wisp called democracy'[16] as likely to bring untold suffering to the continent. But, as ever, Grogan's stance was more complex than a selective appraisal of his public pronouncements indicated. He lunched on a number of occasions at Torr's with the trades union leader, Tom Mboya (thereby causing considerable consternation to Nairobi's chattering classes), and he pronounced his guest, and new friend, to be 'a very remarkable young African'.[17] He also appeared regularly at conciliatory meetings, playing host in 1956 at one for which the guest speaker was C. M. G. Argwings-Kodhek, President of the Nairobi African Congress. In his speech Argwings-Kodhek declared that Africans had been 'well served' by Britain, and Grogan, in reply, expressed his sympathy for 'up-and-coming Africans' and pressed his fellow Europeans to welcome 'these symbols of the new Africa'[18] into their homes. Most controversial of all, as far as more reactionary whites were concerned, Grogan also wrote that 'of the Africans of my time only one will live in history – Jomo Kenyatta. Anyone who can view these matters objectively and has read Jomo's writings must have ... a measure of sympathy for one who undoubtedly is a great African patriot as seen from the African angle'. In the same article, published in 1956, he rounded on the Colonial Office for having caused all the trouble through its policy of 'non-rule', and delivered a thunderous ultimatum to Whitehall: 'RULE OR GET OUT.'[19]

Grogan's pronouncements earned him considerable, though qualified, respect among emerging African nationalists. Twenty years later even the prominent former Mau Mau detainee, Achieng Oneko, declared that he had 'admired Colonel Grogan for his stand for the British people', and added emphatically 'I think he was a good man.'[20]

In the spring of 1956 Richard Meinertzhagen paid his first visit to the colony since World War I and spent much of it with his 'dear old friend' Grogan. 'I am devoted to Grogan,' Meinertzhagen wrote in his diary, 'he is a wise old man ... most of the time he was reminiscing about Cecil Rhodes, Charles Eliot and various governors he had known. He also told us about his walk from Cape to Cairo. Though physically aged, his brain is crystal clear.'[21] About the same time Grogan declared in a letter to his friend Oliver that he thought it unlikely that he would ever see England again as he was 'trying to clear up as against the Nunc Dimittis' and again confessed that he had felt himself to be 'much of a lost soul' since Gertrude's death.[22]

As part of the 'clear up' he finally sold his beloved Torr's Hotel to the Ottoman Bank for £250,000, but the impression of a man winding down or even mellowing in his old age was certainly not one recognized by his employees on his estates at Taveta, which went from strength to strength. To them he was still the same old Grogan. He kept an eagle eye on everything that was going on, and the sight of the dust thrown up by the approach of his twelve cylinder Lincoln Zephyr usually made his managers' hearts sink. Emerging from the car wearing his enormous topee, and brandishing a cigar, he would either interfere with whatever was going on, or issue impossible instructions, or pull a shovel from the car and set to work alongside them. The most frequently heard instruction was 'Clear! Clear!' After more than fifty years of clearing bush in Kenya Grogan was still as obsessed with taming the environment as the day he had arrived.

Development on the estates reached a peak in the mid 1950s. By then the Taveta township boasted six or seven shops including Lalji's (with the petrol pump outside), an African butchery and Singh's saw mill, and anything up to sixty vehicles would pass through each day. Grogan's Castle was the real seat of power. Successive District Officers made specific entries in their diaries recording when Grogan was 'in residence', and all of them recognized that 'the fact is that 25 years ago these estates were all thick bush. The capital investment has been very great. Development is continuing on a large scale, with admirable vision and faith and labour conditions for the 2700 employees are outstanding.'[23] At much the same time the great Nimrod, J. A. Hunter, the game ranger at nearby Makindu, wrote nostalgically that 'there were many young men like Colonel Grogan in the England of fifty years ago. Today I fear they are a vanishing breed. The world is poorer for their passing.'[24]

By 1955 there was a total of 12,000 acres under sisal on Taveta, and 8,000 acres on Ziwani, producing an annual harvest of over 2,500 tons. Also on Ziwani 250 acres of the irrigated area were used for Grogan's famous citrus orchards, and a further 750 acres for maize. The experiments with cattle succeeded, thanks to the virtual eradication of tsetse fly through extensive bush-clearing, and a hardy strain of long-eared goat from Pakistan was introduced. Among the locals, the most popular initiative was Grogan's decision to donate £10,000 and thirty acres of Eldoro, south-west of Taveta town, for the construction of an African Trades School. This was built by the Holy Ghost Fathers: Grogan had concluded during the trek from Cape to Cairo, and still believed over half a century later, that the Catholic orders made the best and most practical missionaries. The colourful

Father Witte (for whose cigars Grogan had a great weakness) began the project in 1952, and he was succeeded in 1955 by the Irish Father Whelan. Courses were offered in carpentry, surveying, brickwork and other useful skills, and they proved so successful that in 1958 Grogan leased another 65 acres to the Fathers with the sole stipulation that it was to be used 'for the betterment and advancement of Africans in the locality'.

Despite all the change wrought by yet more irrigation work, and an unrelenting campaign by Mrs Towers, life at Grogan's Castle altered little and the interior of the huge building atop the hill remained distinctly Spartan. One of the abiding memories of anyone who visited at this time is of Grogan's half a dozen beloved Pekinese dogs. They seemed to many to be an eccentric choice of pet but Grogan, as ever, had an explanation: they stood lower than the level at which tsetse flies flew and were therefore perfectly adapted for conditions at Taveta. For hours on end he would chatter away to them, often to the exclusion of conversation with visitors, and claimed that no one had ever loved him as much except Gertrude. He completely ignored the fact that the dogs were not house-trained, and when they relieved themselves on a cushion he would simply turn it over and carry on with whatever he was doing. Grogan adored being at Girigan: he loved planning his next project; he delighted in taking his grandchildren into the tower to survey what game was out on the plains below; and to anyone who broached the question of what he would do when he became infirm he replied that he would die there, in the wide open spaces at the foot of the 'great white mountain'.

During 1958, however, a number of factors began to conspire to deny him his wish. The first was that both his partners, Maurice Egerton and Sir John Ramsden, died and somehow their share of the estates had to be realized in cash as neither had a son to continue with their businesses. The second was that Grogan, although described in one interview as a 'hardy and ageless pioneer',[25] was eighty-four that year and starting to alarm both his advisers and family by showing absolutely no signs of wanting to retire. Indeed, at Nairobi's agricultural show that year he, unbeknownst to anyone, placed an order for two new pieces of gigantic earth-moving equipment costing tens of thousands of pounds. It became clear to his advisers and Dorothy, the only daughter who sat on the boards of Grogan's companies, that if anything were to be left in the pot for his family something had to be done – or he would go on spending to his dying day.

Changes in the political climate also started to accelerate at a rate that no one could have envisaged just a few years earlier. Emboldened by the grant of full independence to the Gold Coast, considered by Britain to be a colonial showplace, in 1957 African leaders boycotted constitutional talks and demanded more seats in Legislative Council. Tom Mboya, for one, began to realize that all the cards were in African hands: the local government was dependent on African soldiers to police the continuing, though greatly diminished, unrest; the economy was dependent on stable labour relations in order to maintain its impressive growth rate of 6 per cent per annum and the colony's ability to service loans from the British Treasury; and he knew, with even greater certainty after the Suez Crisis, that there was absolutely no chance of Britain sending imperial troops to rescue Kenya for the second time in a decade. As the situation grew more tense European politics fragmented: there were those who embraced change, and those who accused Britain of abandoning the settlers to an uncertain fate. Such then was the background against which Grogan's holding company, East Africa Ventures, was broken up – a process over which Grogan had less and less control as time went on and the conduct of which remains a contentious issue among his descendants. In 1959 Taveta was the first of the estates to go: in August that year the DO at Taveta reported that it was 'in the process of being sold to a Greek concern',[26] the Criticos family.

Taveta was the first estate to be sold for the simple reason that it had the largest acreage under sisal of the three estates and so produced the most cash. The disposal of Jipe and Ziwani took a little longer. In 1960 both were reported in the District Officer's Monthly Intelligence Reports to be being run on a 'care and maintenance' basis only. That year the Criticos family sold Taveta to an Indian-owned company called New Era Estates, and in 1961 that company proceeded to buy Jipe and Ziwani as well. The closing-down sale was finally complete.

Although the Grogan family trusts and Grogan's deceased partners were reputed to have received approximately £1m for the three estates (which is what Grogan claimed they had cost to develop), and although he publicly declared that 'only a fool' wouldn't have sold the estates given the political climate, privately he was very angry and upset about the manner in which he was ousted from his kingdom. Money had never meant anything to him, except as a means to finance his developments. But leaving the estates in what seemed to him an indecent hurry greatly wounded his pride – the more so as the Castle was where he had always thought he would die. As late as August 1961, in a last ditch attempt to frustrate the sale of Jipe by his long-suffering and scrupulous advisers he again offered the estate to the government: a letter from the African member of Legco for the Taveta constituency to the DC at Teita states that

> due to the hardship facing some Africans in Tanganyika the proprietor, being in sympathy with the situation, agrees to let those living on the Tanganyika side of Lake Jipe as fishermen settle on Jipe Estate; [he is also] prepared to donate the Castle to the Taveta and Teita people as an agricultural college and to add more land in order to satisfy the needs of such a college which can cater for the whole district or even province. This is an act of great faith by the proprietor.[27]

The timing of this 'act of great faith' on Grogan's part illustrates that events were now quite out of his control: when he made his offer, the Jipe estate was already in the hands of its new owners.

It was a sad end to Grogan's reign at Taveta. The new owners found everything in the Castle just as he had left it: the beds were even made up, as if he somehow expected to return. Since then no one has ever made the Castle their home. It still stands as a monument, though now dilapidated, to an era when a man driven by development fever turned a desert into productive agricultural land.

In 1972 all the estates were again purchased by the Criticos family (who subsequently sold Ziwani to the Kenyatta family). There are still large compounds of machinery bought by Grogan in the 1950s, which are used for spares, on Taveta and Ziwani; his Rushton and Hornsby diesel engines still power the sisal factories; the irrigation schemes that he developed are still the lifeblood of the area; and many thousands of people still rely on the estates for their livelihood. It is a legacy of which Grogan would have been proud. In 1998 the then owner of Jipe and Taveta recently remarked that 'Grogan has not been given full credit for what he achieved down at Taveta. What is our dream [for these estates] was his reality in the 1930s. He should get more credit for his amazing development.'[28]

By the time the sale of the estates was complete, and the money distributed between Grogan's children (legitimate and illegitimate) and nine grandchildren either as capital or trusts, his world had become unrecognizable. In 1959 the last Mau Mau detainees were released, the security situation in Kikuyu areas worsened again, and constitutional reform reached a standstill. Kenya was far from being the only hot-spot in the Empire and by the autumn, when the Conservatives won the General Election in Britain, Harold Macmillan decided that a new approach to colonial policy in Africa was called for. With that in mind he chose the forty-six-year-old Ian Macleod as his new Colonial Secretary. Macmillan's victory was lauded by Europeans in Kenya, because they didn't believe that a Conservative government would 'abandon' them. They were wrong. Macmillan was a man who, when Resident Minister in the Mediterranean seventeen years earlier, had investigated the possibility of buying the European settlers out. Furthermore, the shameful legacy of the Suez Crisis, Britain's inability to continue to finance its Empire in Africa, the scandalous murder of detainees by their jailors at the Mau Mau detention centre at Hola earlier in the year – all these events, and much else besides, decided Macmillan and Macleod that the timetable for Kenyan independence should be greatly accelerated. Few in the colony guessed how accelerated, let alone what form of independence Macmillan had in mind.

The result of the 1960 Lancaster House Conference, to which all parties from Kenya were hastily summoned, left the settlers in a catatonic state of shock: Macleod brokered a deal which was intended as the first step towards handing majority rule to the Africans in the not-too-distant future. A date was set for elections the following year on the basis of a modified common roll, thereby guaranteeing them – first of all – a majority in Legco. Grogan was livid. It was not that he was unable to contemplate that black majority rule was inevitable. Indeed he had tacitly acknowledged as much as early as the 1930s, was all for incorporating Africans in government 'as fast as was useful', and envisaged an eventual handover of power as the ultimate achievement of colonial rule. Rather it was the feebleness with which Britain was abandoning its Empire that he objected to. 'Who', he wrote, 'could have dreamt that one of Rhodes's escort would live to see the day when the proud and mighty England which he loved faded in the world picture to a nation of no particular consideration . . . Lord, Lord the pity of it.'[29]

Grogan also considered that Macmillan and Macleod's 'sell-out' was a monstrous betrayal of Britain's responsibilities to the African people (as opposed to their leaders). He referred to the Conservative duo as 'those rather ignorant, cynical practitioners of professional politics',[30] disliked the 'overwhelming self-esteem'[31] of Macleod in particular, and dreaded that he 'might even find myself doing my mandoline stuff in the celestial choir sitting between Harold Macmillan and Ian Macleod . . . In such a case,' he asked rhetorically, 'could one get one's entry permit rescinded?'[32] Above all he was paternalistically concerned that 'foisting the Westminster pattern of Parliamentary Government' on Africa was likely to lead to 'the elimination of all individual freedom and a reversion to the murder, massacre, arson which are already suppurating over the whole width of the Continent'.[33]

During the momentous events which followed the Lancaster House Conference Grogan, having left the Castle at Girigan, lived with Camilla Towers in a modest house in Muthaiga that had belonged to his sister Dorothy and Wilfrid Hunter until they separated in the 1950s.[34] Grogan made no modifications to the house except the essential one: he built a concrete bunker in the garden, which housed a varied collection of books, magazines and maps. He virtually lived in this bunker, while Camilla Towers occupied the house – but he was far from reclusive. Muthaiga Club, where Grogan was usually to be found at lunch and dinner, was only a short stroll away; Gertrude's Garden, whose young patients Grogan dropped in on daily, was at the end of the road; and he continued to carry out 'official' duties like presenting the annual Grogan History Prize at the Duke of York School (where there was also a Grogan House). However betrayed he felt by the conduct of the British government, he never lost his sense of humour. He still adored attending Muthaiga Club's Christmas staff cabaret, and did not need his eyes and ears to be in perfect working order to be able to guffaw at the Africans' impersonations of Indian *duka-wallahs* or over-pompous settlers. He could also see comedy in his increasing decrepitude and that of many of his friends: when an elderly general entered the dining room at Muthaiga Club with a stick, accompanied by his wife with two sticks, Grogan casually remarked to his lunch guests, the Taylors, that he'd always thought it odd that the Club was renowned for being 'some sort of Moulin Rouge'.

In the elections that followed the Lancaster House Conference many of Grogan's worst fears were confirmed. The Kenya African National Union won the most seats, but refused to form a government unless Kenyatta was released from detention. When the British government acceded to this demand the tentative timetable for independence drawn up the previous year was blown away. A putative ten years (or more) was suddenly reduced to two, and on 12 December 1963, Grogan's eighty-ninth birthday, the reins of government passed from Britain to an African government led by Kenyatta.

The transfer of power was remarkably peaceful, and Kenyan nationalism soon proved to be of the most conservative variety. Hatchets were buried on both sides. In front of all his cabinet ministers Kenyatta graciously told Grogan's friend Humphrey Slade, whom he had asked to stay on as Speaker of his new Parliament, that 'whatever we may feel or say about the European settlers in colonial times, it's entirely thanks to them that Kenya is so far ahead of her neighbours and will stay so',[35] and he went to great lengths to reassure the European farming community in particular. A comprehensive programme of land reform and redistribution was completed with remarkably little acrimony, and was paid for by the British government.

For the Europeans there was a straightforward choice of whether to embrace life in the new Kenya – or to make for pastures new. Of the 61,000 whites resident in the colony in 1959, 20,000 had left by 1965 – the vast majority of them urban-dwellers and relative newcomers to Africa. As far as the 125,000-strong Asian community was concerned, Kenyatta issued them with an ultimatum in 1967: he gave them a choice of taking out Kenyan citizenship as a sign of their loyalty and commitment to the new Kenya, or leaving. So great was the exodus that Whitehall abruptly removed their automatic right to British citizenship, an action which Enoch Powell among others slammed as a 'moral disgrace'.

It was ironic that in many ways Kenyatta had grasped the nettles that the Colonial Office had always effectively refused to touch. A lasting settlement of the land question had been effected, the Indian Question was 'solved', and 'trusteeship' over the indigenous population had become a matter for Africans themselves to handle. Grogan recognized as much and though he publicly (and mischievously) declared himself ready to 'watch the folly' after independence, in private he continued to admit to harbouring a not inconsiderable admiration for Kenyatta – 'that great African patriot as seen from the African angle'. And when asked if *he* might leave Kenya, Grogan emphatically replied that he had no intention of abandoning the country that had been his home for over half a century.

When dictating his memoirs in 1963 Grogan reflected that 'no solitude is more terrible than old age deprived of the loved ones of one's lifetime', and wished that he could be subjected to 'the application of that kindly method now used in farewell to beloved and too aged dogs'.[36] His sight had become so poor that he had to fly to Johannesburg for treatment, his hearing was seriously impaired, and a mild heart attack in 1960 had left him dependent on pills of various sorts which he called his 'devil dodgers'. While Grogan was recovering from that heart attack Camilla Towers, an ardent Catholic, had even brought a priest to hear his confession. Grogan swiftly despatched the man, telling him that he had no intention of divulging eighty-five years of 'interesting sins'.

But the longer Grogan cheated death the fewer became his pleasures, even though he remained wholly lucid. He 'goo-gooed' for hours on end to his Pekinese, continued to visit Muthaiga Club and Gertrude's Garden, took a certain delight in outliving Churchill, and was pleased to have seen his family right. In a letter to his daughter Cynthia, whom he had not seen for over a decade until she came to Kenya for the wedding of one of his granddaughters in 1962, he wrote in a still firm hand:

> I was so happy at seeing you again after all these long years; and I was so glad when Jean [Cynthia's daughter] decided to stay on a bit. It was lovely having her around and I was very sorry when she departed. She has grown into a very attractive young woman and full of common sense . . . It is a great comfort to me to know that I have made you all sure of a roof and bread-and-butter as long as the £1 has any reasonable buying power! I am always glad to get news of the family.

The letter ended 'best love to you all – Daddy'.[37] This is a rather touching signature: Grogan is not 'your father' or, worse still, *pater*, but 'Daddy'. It harks back to a time, when his daughters were little, when they still thought Grogan was 'the best father in the world'.

In 1966 Grogan was also visited by Joyce, whom he had not seen for decades, and was proud to say that 'she radiated goodness, just like her mother'. But by then his eyesight was so bad that he could not even read, and he lived in increasing isolation. This was not entirely of his own volition: Camilla Towers became increasingly protective – and possessive – of her elderly charge, and as Grogan was wholly dependent on her he had to toe the line for the first time in his life. What's more, Towers could be fierce, and some visitors to the house were surprised to find that Grogan, Kenya's 'Grand Old Man', appeared to be actually frightened of her. At some point she told Grogan that everyone at Muthaiga thought he was a nuisance, so he stopped visiting the club, and 'appointments' had to be booked through her to see him, so the number of callers soon dwindled. Various members of the family, while conceding that Towers looked after Grogan admirably (it was, after all, not exactly a glamorous job cutting the toenails of a pair of feet that had trekked from Cape to

Cairo almost seven decades earlier) increasingly suspected her of trying to turn him against them.

In early January 1967 Grogan's last Pekinese was put down, causing Grogan considerable distress. Then, just weeks later, he disappeared without a word to Dorothy, who lived nearby in Limuru, or to Jane, who lived on the coast. When the former arrived at his house for her weekly visit the furniture was all in place, and nothing seemed to have been removed, but it was clear that Grogan and Camilla Towers were no longer in residence. After making some investigations Dorothy was alarmed to find that her father had left the country, or as she put it, that he had been 'kidnapped' by Towers.

On 1 February, Grogan resurfaced in Cape Town. South Africa was one of the few places outside Kenya where, despite his great age, he had not been forgotten, and where the handful of surviving old men who had participated in the Scramble for Africa *and* witnessed Britain's scramble out of Africa were still held in great esteem. The *Cape Times* reported that

> a contemporary of Cecil Rhodes and the explorer Henry
> M Stanley flew into Cape Town yesterday. Col. ES Grogan,
> a spry 92, walked off the aircraft . . . aided by an arm from
> Mrs Camilla Towers, his granddaughter . . . [He] has a
> grizzled Jan Smuts beard and the bearing of a man 30 years
> his junior . . . Friends indicated that he might settle in Cape
> Town.[38]

It has never been clear why Grogan flew to Cape Town. Quite possibly he had very little say in the matter: Camilla Towers was in charge of his life and she not only had many friends in Cape Town but knew that medical facilities were better than in Kenya. The *Cape Times*'s assertion that 'friends indicated that he *might* settle in Cape Town' does admittedly point to another possibility: that Grogan was paying, or *thought* he was paying, a short visit only and would be returning to Kenya. This would account for his not having breathed a word to anyone about his departure. But he never did return, and the events of his last months showed that there were reasons for this in addition to failing health.

Grogan's granddaughter, Jean Crawford, was working as a nurse in Cape Town when he arrived and was soon caught up in what he described as 'this nasty business'. He advised her that no matter how fond of him she was it was better 'not to get involved'. It did not take Jean long to discover what 'the nasty business' was. A handful of friends of Grogan's from the pre-war days in Kenya, including Lady Moore and barrister Walter Shapley, lived in Cape Town and among them the word was circulating that Grogan was being hounded by Dorothy and Jane, and that they had 'taken all his money but were still intent on wringing every last penny from him'. It is certainly true that Dorothy told friends that she was half-minded to remove her father from Towers's clutches by legal action but money cannot have been a motive: all the family – and Towers – knew that everything in the Grogan coffers had been distributed and Grogan himself had an annuity from a trust (amounting to a handsome £4,000 per annum).

As the only member of the family on the spot Jean's position was an unenviable one. On the couple of occasions she managed to see her grandfather in the block of service flats in Rondebosch where he was living, he hugged her and was obviously pleased to see her, but seemed confused and apprehensive. Towers, on the other hand, made it clear that she was not welcome and tried a variety of means to prohibit her visits. As Jean left her grandfather for the last time, Towers – who because of Jean's presence in Cape Town now styled herself Grogan's 'adopted daughter' or 'housekeeper' as opposed to his 'granddaughter' – said 'There you are, Grogs, the last one of your family deserting you.'

Grogan had two strokes during the Cape's winter months, and was also suffering from prostate cancer. He spent much of the time in the Monastery Hospital in Seapoint, but was in his flat in Rondebosch when he died on 16 August. Jean heard the news from a friend the following morning and only just had time to rush to the funeral at St Michael's Church, Roouwkoop. There were no friends of Grogan's there, so hastily had the funeral been organized by Towers; just a few parishioners and Towers, wearing a white fur coat and dark glasses and moaning, 'My darling, darling Grogs – what am I going to do without you?'[39] She had the final say in Grogan's life: the service was held according to Catholic rites which implies that she had succeeded in converting Grogan that winter, although it is most unlikely that this involved a considered and profound decision on his part. Afterwards the priest tore a strip off the unfortunate Jean, telling her how terrible it was that her family had treated Grogan so badly and how kind and considerate Mrs Towers had been. Right to the bitter end, it seems that Grogan divided those around him 'like the hairs on a man's head' – as the Wataveta chiefs used to say of him.

He was buried by the Revd Petersen in the Maitland Cemetery. The grave, which was paid for by Camilla Towers, faced west and had a magnificent view of Table Mountain – the sight of which heralded the start of his African adventures fully seventy-one years earlier. He would no doubt have appreciated the fact that in the next plot lay a young adventurer by the name of Cecil Oggier, who had died while climbing on the mountain in 1917. The boy's gravestone reads 'a short sunny life well spent'.

Grogan died unnoticed, except by the newspapers in South Africa and Kenya: even his decades-old allies at *The Times* failed to mark his passing. His gravestone, bearing the inscription, 'In Loving Memory Of Lt. Col. Ewart Scott Grogan DSO', is a simple but solid one. If anyone other than young Jean had been present at his interment who both knew and cared about the Grogan of yore, they might perhaps have added the words that he himself once penned in the introduction to a book of children's stories: 'But the agony and sweat of the work done, the England of today can never know, though the England of tomorrow shall, the men who dared to stand clear and crisp above the trivial vapours of the age; and the unborn shall reap where the Silent Ones have sown.'

NOTES

ABBREVIATIONS

MON	Grogan, E. S., *Musings of a Nonagenarian*
CtoC	Grogan, E. S. and Sharp, A. H., *From The Cape to Cairo*
'Sixty Years'	Grogan, E. S., 'Sixty Years In East And Central Africa' in *Rhodesia and East Africa* (ed. F. S. Joelson)
EAS	*East African Standard*
Leader	*The Leader of British East Africa*
RH	Denotes private collection lodged at Rhodes House, Oxford
CO	Colonial Office files, lodged at the Public Record Office, London
FO	Foreign Office files, lodged at the Public Record Office, London
KNA	Files lodged in the Kenya National Archives Followed by a departmental designation:
LO or LND	Land Office
MOH	Ministry of Health
FOR	Forestry Department
AG	Attorney General
PC	Provincial Commissioner
DC	District Commissioner
DO	District Officer
Legco	Minutes Minutes and Proceedings of the Kenya Legislative Council 1921–56

CHAPTER 1

1 *CtoC*, pp. 300–301.
2 It has not been possible to prove otherwise, or even to establish Nathaniel Grogan's provenance. Cornelius's friends mostly seem to have believed that he never married and therefore had no heir. Even if the only piece of evidence to the contrary – a mention in *Walker's Hibernian Magazine* in July 1786 of marriage to Rebecca Frost, his housekeeper – is true there is no mention of Nathaniel, Ewart's great-grandfather, or any other son in Cornelius's Will (see Barrett's *The Reluctant Rebel, passim,* acknowledging the research of Nicholas Furlong). The only alternative hypothesis for a

close link between Ewart's family and the Johnstown Grogans rests on the fact that the Grogan who first obtained Johnstown – John Grogan of Antrim – married twice. The eldest son of his second marriage was Nicholas (coincidentally the same name as Ewart's grandfather), who inherited the Ardcandrisk estate, Johnstown having passed to a half-brother. Nicholas died in 1758, aged sixty-four, and could conceivably have fathered Nathaniel. Unfortunately no record survives of the names of his children, and if Nathaniel was one of them he inherited little or nothing.

3 *Staffordshire Sentinel*, 27 January 1910.
4 Walter Grogan family papers.
5 Ibid.
6 This partnership remained in business until September 1958, by which time its offices were in Charles Street, Mayfair. *The Times*, 7 August 1958.
7 Grogan would later publicly declare that it was 'to my dying shame' that he had been named after Gladstone, whom he regarded as 'one of the most detestable and maleficent figures in English history'. Legco Minutes, 4 January 1937.
8 Quentin Grogan, unpublished memoirs, and Diana Wasbrough, his daughter.
9 Quentin Grogan, ibid.
10 *MON*, pp. 3–4.
11 Ibid., p. 4.
12 Ibid., p. 9.
13 Ibid., p. 18.
14 Many years later Ewart met Rider Haggard at an Authors' Club luncheon at which the two men were guests of honour and he 'accused', or rather thanked, him for inspiring him to 'seek romance in Africa'. Ibid., p. 226.
15 Another contemporary of Grogan's at Winchester was clansman Edward Grogan, who succeeded to his (loyalist) family's baronetcy in 1891 and later became an Irish MP.

16 Hedworth Herbert shared this inheritance because, of his elder brothers, William had fled to Canada and was therefore excluded from the reckoning, James had died in infancy, and Henry was almost certainly dead as he is not mentioned anywhere in the Will. Thirty-seven year old Walter was still alive, but had already been 'seen right' with a row of houses in Tulse Hill which he sold in 1918–19 for almost £8,000 (Walter Grogan family papers). Walter may also have already been given a share in Grogan & Boyd, for whom he carried out work in his capacity as a moderately successful building contractor. That he remained closely involved with the firm is certain and his son, Harold, worked there until 1912.

CHAPTER 2

1 *MON*, p. 22.
2 Whymper's four companions perished in the descent, though one of their guides survived.
3 Alpine Club records list his ascents in his first two seasons as follows: 1892 – Gramont, Dent de Jaman, Dent de Morcles, Petite Dent de Morcles (twice, the second time without guides), Diablerets, Grand Moeuveran; 1893 – Petite Dent de Morcles, Diablerets, Dent Jaune/Cime de l'Est, shoulder of Matterhorn (twice, the second time from Zermatt direct).
4 Gray, Arthur, and Brittain, Frederick, *History of Jesus College*, p. 187.
5 *MON*, p. 27.
6 Grogan's accredited ascents and traverses in 1894 were as follows: Tête à Pierre Grépot, in the Grand Moeuveran north-west of Sion; Matterhorn, Weisshorn, Riffelhorn, Rothorn, Obergabelhorn, Dom, and Dent Blanche, all in the Zermatt

area; Petite Aiguille de Charmoz, Aiguille de Blaitière, Aiguille de Charmoz, Grand and Petit Dru, and Grépon, all in the Chamonix area.

7 *MON*, p. 31.

8 Sir Arthur Fairfax Charles Coyndon Luxmoore (1876–1944), England rugby international, Lord Justice of Appeal (1938–44) and Privy Councillor (1938).

9 *MON*, pp. 32–3.

10 Quentin Grogan, unpublished memoirs.

11 *MON*, p. 37.

12 Jesus College Cambridge Society Report 1968, p. 32.

13 Grogan's accredited ascents in 1895 were as follows: Rimpfischhorn, Monte Rosa, Dent d'Herens and Riffelhorn (four times).

14 Author's correspondence with the Honourable Society of the Middle Temple. Grogan's premature departure from Cambridge proved no hindrance to a legal career as a degree was not a requirement for being called to the Bar.

CHAPTER 3

1 *MON*, p. 51.

2 Ibid., p. 42.

3 Ibid., p. 47; Henry du Pré Labouchère, Liberal MP for Northampton, was an ardent anti-imperialist and one of Rhodes's very few persistent critics; his journal *Truth* was his mouthpiece.

4 So called after the June 1840 meeting of the 'Society for the Extinction of the Slave Trade and for the Civilization of Africa' at Exeter Hall in London.

5 Pakenham, Thomas, *The Scramble For Africa*, p. xxv.

6 Ibid., p. 495. The French called the Scramble the *course de clocher* (steeplechase).

7 *CtoC*, p. 15.

8 *MON*, p. 44.

9 Selous, Frederick, *Sunshine and Storm in Rhodesia*, p. 90.

10 *MON*, p. 44.

11 Ibid., p. 45.

12 Sir Robert Coryndon was to spend a number of years in the employ of Rhodes's British South Africa company before joining the Colonial Office. Sir John Norton-Griffiths became an engineer of great repute and the architect of the 'Underground War' which culminated in the blowing up by his 'claykickers' of Messines Ridge in 1916 in an attempt to 'straighten' the Ypres salient. The blast was heard by Lloyd George in Downing Street.

13 'Sixty Years', the pay for troopers was in fact 5/- a day plus 2/6 for forage, compared with 1/3 a day for a private in the British army.

14 *MON*, p. 51.

15 Ibid., pp. 52–3.

16 It was not until 1902 that Sir Ronald Ross was awarded the Nobel Prize for his discovery of the part played by the *anopheles* mosquito in the life cycle of 'the fever', as malaria was commonly referred to. Grogan's contemporaries had no knowledge of how the disease was contracted, although Livingstone had discovered that quinine was an antidote of sorts. Similarly, it was only in 1903 that a medical commission led by Sir David Bruce concluded that the cause of sleeping sickness was a trypanosome carried by the tsetse fly.

17 *MON*, p. 56.

18 Thomas, Anthony, *Rhodes: The Race for Africa*, p. 338.

19 *MON*, pp. 63–4.

20 Ibid., p. 64.

21 'Sixty Years', p. 55.

22 *MON*, p. 67.

23 Foran, Robert, *A Cuckoo in Kenya*, pp. 36–7.

24 Ibid.

CHAPTER 4

1 *MON*, p. 72.
2 Ibid., pp. 77–8.
3 Ibid., p. 82.
4 Ibid., p. 84.
5 Grogan's exact definition of a 'Johnnie' was as follows: 'one could see [them] strolling down Piccadilly ... swapping drinks with one another in their respective clubs ... Mostly they consisted of the landed gentry, elder sons who had squandered their portions and younger sons who rather than join the services or the church preferred to seek fame and fortune in the wide open spaces ... Almost unconsciously they were building the greatest Empire in history. They were of the same precursors as P. G. Wodehouse's "Drones". They were the "By Jove's" before the "whats"'. (Ibid., p. 59).
6 James Watt (1834–79) was related to the eponymous inventor of the steam engine and emigrated to New Zealand as a young man. He settled briefly in Auckland before moving to Napier where he established a merchanting and station agent's business which imported supplies from Auckland by sea and shipped out the Hawke's Bay wool clip. In 1873 he bought the 9,500-acre Longlands station and, in partnership with a man named Farmer, soon became one of the Hawke's Bay's largest sheep ranchers. Watt was also an enthusiast of the turf, establishing a racing stud at Waiperera, and became the first president of the Auckland Racing Club. He ran his business empire from his house on the hill at Napier.
7 James Coleman (1833–1928) was one of fifteen children of John Coleman, a farmer and miller from Norwich, and had emigrated to New Zealand on the sailing ship Mataoka in 1859. He started out by managing the Te Aute College Estate before leasing the Longlands station in 1866. There he remained until 1873 when he sold out to James Watt and Robert Farmer and joined Alex McHardy in the purchase of the 23,000-acre Blackhead station. This partnership was dissolved in 1878, when McHardy paid Coleman £71,500 for his share, the equivalent of £3 million in today's money. The legacy of Coleman and McHardy's five-year venture was the well-known C & M wool brand. Biographical details on James Watt and James Coleman are drawn from Macgregor, Miriam, *Early Stations of Hawke's Bay*, Mrs Gertrude Chapman (Eddie Watt's niece) and Adrian Coleman.
8 *MON*, p. 87.
9 See Wymer, Norman, *The Man From the Cape*, and Farrant, Leda, *The Legendary Grogan*, pp. 19–20.
10 To this day the Coleman Shield for rifle shooting is contested annually.
11 *MON*, p. 87.
12 Ibid., p. 89.
13 Ibid., p. 93.
14 Ibid., p. 91.
15 Ibid., p. 92.
16 Ibid., p. 94.
17 Ibid., p. 95.
18 Ibid., p. 94.
19 *The World's Work: A History of Our Time*, vol. I, 1900–1901, p. 369. Even in Walter Huston's classic 1936 film *Rhodes of Africa* – 'the drama of a man who set out singlehanded to unite a continent' – Jameson's actions were still being portrayed as his own initiative designed to force the 'cautious' Rhodes's hand.
20 *MON*, p. 96.
21 Ibid., p. 100.

CHAPTER 5

1 *MON*, p. 101.

2 First Baron Lugard (1858–1945), created 1928; Pakenham wrote of him that 'no other proconsul would put such a powerful moral stamp on the character of European rule in Africa'. Op. cit., p. 413. He was the embodiment of Rider Haggard's character Allan Quatermain. A soldier by training, he had worked for the African Lakes Corporation in their efforts to stop slaving and the Imperial British East Africa Company which attempted to run Uganda between 1888 and 1894, when the territory became a British Protectorate. The story of his pacification of the warring factions there, and his subsequent battle to ensure that the British government did not abandon Uganda, is told in Margery Perham's *Lugard: The Years Of Adventure*.

3 *CtoC*, p. 3; DOA was the Deutsch Ost Afrika Cie: it was many years before a British shipping company would start a service to East Africa despite the nation's burgeoning interests there.

4 Ibid., p. 5.

5 Ibid., p. 7.

6 Ibid., p. 12.

7 Ibid., p. 44.

8 Ibid., p. 15.

9 Ibid., pp. 21–2.

10 A sandflea originally 'imported' to Africa from Brazil; gangrene is the most dangerous complication of infection.

11 *CtoC*, p. 42.

12 Ibid., p. 44.

13 Ibid., p. 57.

14 Ibid., p. 59.

15 Ibid., p. 56.

16 Ibid., p. 58.

17 Ibid., p. 57.

18 Ibid., pp. 77–8.

19 Ibid., p. 59.

20 Ibid., p. 61.

21 Ibid., p. 308.

22 Ibid., p. 64.

23 Ibid., p. 65.

24 The specimen, although now not considered a distinct species but a sub-species of *Redunca arundium* (reedbuck) is still in the collection of the Natural History Museum.

25 *CtoC*, p. 76.

26 Joseph Conrad's *Heart of Darkness*, in which the horrific conditions in the Belgian Congo were first alluded to, was published three months before Grogan arrived in M'towa. Adam Hochschild's *King Leopold's Ghost* (Houghton Mifflin Company, 1998) is the definitive account of what amounted to genocide.

27 *CtoC*, p. 91.

28 Ibid., p. 92.

29 Ibid., p. 59.

30 Ibid., p. 101. Grogan added: 'Fortunately for other countries he is our uncontested monopoly.'

31 Ibid., p. 96.

32 Ibid.

CHAPTER 6

1 *CtoC*, p. 103.

2 Ibid., p. 115.

3 Ibid., p. 109.

4 Ibid., p. 105.

5 Ibid., p. 110.

6 Ibid., p. 106.

7 Ibid., p. 110; *pombe* is an alcoholic drink usually made from millet.

8 This does not appear to have been disputed in subsequent years and was still acknowledged in Weinthal, Leo (ed.), *The Story of the Cape to Cairo Railway and River Route*, published in 1925 (see vol. I, p. 279). I have only found one reference that could conceivably place the statement in question: there may have been an Englishman, Mr J. E. S. Moore, in Count von Götzen's expedition.

9 *CtoC*, p. 114.
10 *Geographical Journal*, vol. xvi, no. 2, August 1900, p. 169.
11 Ibid., p. 168.
12 *CtoC*, p. 114.
13 Ibid., p. 115.
14 Letter of Sharp's to the RGS from Toro, Uganda, dated 30 August 1899. Published in *Geographical Journal*, vol. xv, January–June 1900, p. 280.
15 *CtoC*, p. 119.
16 Ibid., p. 116.
17 Ibid., p. 117.
18 Ibid., p. 118.
19 Ibid., p. 121.
20 Ibid., p. 118.
21 Ibid., p. 127.
22 Ibid., p. 122.
23 Ibid.
24 Ibid., p. 123.
25 Ibid., p. 133.
26 *Geographical Journal*, vol. xvi, no. 2, August 1900, pp. 175–6.
27 *CtoC*, p. 137.
28 Ibid., p. 143.
29 Grogan, E. S., 'The Nile as I Saw It', in Goldmann, C. S. (ed.), *The Empire and the Country*, p. 811.
30 *CtoC*, p. 144.
31 Ibid., p. 141.
32 Ibid., p. 146.
33 *Geographical Journal*, vol. xvi, no. 2, August 1900, p. 173.
34 *CtoC*, p. 150.
35 Ibid., pp. 152–3.
36 Ibid., p. 154.
37 Ibid., p. 157.
38 Ibid., p. 169.
39 Ibid.
40 Ibid., p. 171.
41 Ibid., p. 180.
42 The Kazinga channel which connects Lake Albert Edward and Lake Ruisamba was confirmed by Dr A. F. R. Wollaston's expedition of 1905 to be twenty miles long.
43 *CtoC*, p. 181.
44 Emin Pasha, a German naturalist whose real name was Dr Eduard Schnitzer, was one of Gordon's lieutenants who held out at the southern end of Sudan's south-western province of Equatoria for over three years after Gordon's defeat at Khartoum. He was somewhat reluctant to be rescued by Stanley as his position did not become parlous until some months after Stanley's arrival. If anything Emin 'rescued' Stanley whose expedition had been decimated during its 2,000-mile trek to Lake Albert from the Atlantic Ocean. This relief expedition was at the time the most expensive ever mounted, costing some £30,000 and involving a caravan of 800 men. Stanley recounted the journey in his book *In Darkest Africa*, published in 1890.
45 *MON*, p. 118.
46 *Geographical Journal*, vol. xvi, no. 2, August 1900, p. 177.
47 *CtoC*, p. 200.
48 Ibid., p. 204.
49 Ibid., pp. 209–10.
50 Ibid., p. 222.
51 Ibid., p. 224.
52 Ibid., pp. 222–3.
53 Ibid., p. 223.
54 Ibid., pp. 227–8. Grogan's findings were further grist to the mill for the 'Red Rubber' campaign of Edmund 'Bulldog' Morel (of the Congo Reform Association) and Roger 'Tiger' Casement (the British Consul in the Congo for eleven years) which was seeking to prove the horrendous extent of atrocities committed by the Belgians in the Congo.
55 Grogan, E. S., 'The Nile as I Saw It', in Goldmann, C. S., op. cit., p. 814.

CHAPTER 7

1 Grogan, E. S., 'The Nile as I Saw It', in Goldmann, C. S., op. cit., p. 813.

2 *CtoC*, p. 232.
3 Ibid., p. 233.
4 Pocock, Roger (ed.), *The Frontiersman's Pocket-Book*, pp. 396–7.
5 *CtoC*, p. 236.
6 Ibid., p. 237.
7 Ibid., p. 241.
8 Ibid., p. 245.
9 Ibid., p. 250.
10 Ibid., p. 253.
11 Ibid., p. 255.
12 Ibid., p. 256.
13 Ibid., p. 257.
14 Ibid.
15 Ibid.
16 Ibid., p. 259.
17 Ibid.
18 Ibid., p. 261.
19 Literally 'the Mountain River'.
20 *CtoC*, p. 262.
21 Ibid., p. 266.
22 Ibid., p. 268.
23 As recently as September 1899 Shambeh had still been occupied by Lieutenant A. de Quengo de Tonquédoc, Sous Officier Salpin and thirty Senegalese *tirailleurs*. Their mission had been related to, but independent of, the Marchand lunge at Fashoda, and they had marched 1,100 miles from West Africa to take their objective. By Christmas 1899 the small force was ordered by the French government to evacuate Shambeh and proceed home, thus ending the last French presence on the Nile.
24 *Sudd* is Arabic for 'barrier' and refers to the flat swamp area of southern Sudan which covers many tens of thousands of miles liable to blockage by papyrus, elephant grass, water hyacinth and weed; it boasts, among other hazards, sixty-three recorded species of mosquito.
25 *CtoC*, p. 268.
26 Grogan, E. S., 'The Nile as I Saw It', in Goldmann, C. S., op. cit., p. 815.
27 The Dinka who had survived Dervish rule were huddled as close to the river as possible. The Hon. Sidney Peel, in his article 'British Rule in the Sudan', estimated that out of a population of eight million in the Sudan some six million had perished under Dervish rule, during which time agriculture in many areas came to a standstill and the only trade in the further provinces, including Dinkaland, was in slaves. (See Goldmann, C. S., op. cit.)
28 *CtoC*, p. 281.
29 Ibid., p. 278.
30 Ibid., p. 276.
31 Ibid., p. 277.
32 Ibid., p. 276.
33 Ibid., p. 303.
34 *MON*, p. 127.
35 *CtoC*, p. 286.
36 Ibid., p. 289.
37 Ibid., p. 290.
38 Ibid.
39 Literally 'Giraffe River'.
40 *CtoC*, p. 296.
41 Ibid., p. 299.
42 Ibid., p. 300.
43 Ibid., p. 305.
44 Ibid., p. 303.
45 *MON*, p. 130.
46 *CtoC*, p. 303.
47 Ibid., p. 268.
48 'Sixty Years', p. 55.
49 *CtoC*, p. 65.
50 *MON*, pp. 131–2.
51 The Norwegian professional runner Mensen Ernst was probably the first European seriously to consider a north–south traverse of the African continent. Known throughout Europe as a very impressive 'performer', in 1832 he ran from Paris to Moscow in fourteen days, stayed for a week's sightseeing, and then ran back. In 1842 he set out for Cairo to run to the source of the White Nile before carrying on to Cape Town. He was found dead under a tree (on 22 January 1843) at Syene, just 315 miles north of Cairo.

CHAPTER 8

1 Blumenfeld later became editor of the *Daily Express* (1904–32) and chairman of the London Express Newspaper Company (1915–48).

2 While these three men all shared the same goal – that of a South African Dominion, in which the Boer and British territories were united under the British flag – they were not always hand-in-glove. Milner and Chamberlain both distrusted Rhodes, but could not ignore him. Milner and Rhodes were more conspicuously hawkish than Chamberlain, who had already narrowly escaped being pitched into political oblivion in the aftermath of the Jameson Raid and therefore decided to let Milner set the pace. But when the conflict began Salisbury always referred to the war as 'Joe's war'.

3 *Pall Mall Gazette*, 31 March 1900.

4 *MON*, p. 138.

5 Ibid., p. 133.

6 Ibid., p. 133; his 'ribbon' was the Matabele War campaign medal.

7 Wolseley had led the Gordon relief expedition in 1885.

8 Enteric fever accounted for over 10,000 British casualties during the war – compared with 6,000 deaths in combat.

9 Originally the Bengal Europeans from 1652–1756, thenceforth the Kerry regiment until incorporation into the Royal Munster Fusiliers in 1881. The regiment was disbanded on 31 July 1922.

10 *MON*, p. 134.

11 The Royal Geographical Society did not move into Lowther Lodge, its existing premises, until 1913.

12 *Geographical Journal*, vol. xvi, no. 2, August 1900, p. 164.

13 The ubiquitous Labouchère, Britain's 'liberal conscience' took issue with Grogan over these

incidents, but was silenced when Grogan asked him what he would have done in the same situation.

14 *Geographical Journal*, vol. xvi, no. 1, July 1900: address to RGS by the President on 21 May 1900. There was, unusually in the history of African exploration, no disputing Grogan's claim to completion of the first ever south–north traverse of the continent. The feat was immediately recognized in, among other works of reference, the *Encyclopaedia Britannica* where it has remained ever since.

15 *Geographical Journal*, vol. xvi, no. 2, August 1900, pp. 183–4.

16 *The Chanticlere*, Summer Term 1900.

17 *MON*, p. 138.

18 Ibid.

19 Ibid.

20 The sole surviving evidence of Grogan's reports for the FO and CO is a map. FO 925/442.

21 *MON*, p. 143.

22 'Sixty Years', p. 55.

23 Dorothy Slater family papers, Ponsonby to Grogan, 17 October 1900.

24 Rhodes hung the flag in Groote Schurr, his Cape Town home, which became one of the residences of South African premiers.

25 Dorothy Slater family papers, Jourdan to Grogan, 17 September 1900.

26 *MON*, p. 135.

27 Quentin Grogan, unpublished memoirs.

28 *MON*, p. 138.

29 Crawford family papers. The full text of a commendation from Viscount Castlerosse reads as follows: 'I have much pleasure in stating that Captain Grogan, an officer in my battalion, is a very capable officer & I feel sure wd. do credit to any post he may be appointed to – I shall always be very ready to answer questions

concerning him – as I have a very high opinion of him.'

30 Crawford family papers.

31 *MON*, p. 139.

32 Harcourt was a former Leader of the Commons, briefly leader of the Liberal party in 1898, and an ardent opponent of aggressive imperial expansion of the type that Rhodes advocated; he was also, as mentioned earlier, a member of the Select Committee which investigated the Jameson Raid in 1897. Only he and Labouchère could really claim to have 'pushed' Chamberlain, the Colonial Office and Rhodes in that investigation.

33 Grogan was, of course, no longer an undergraduate and was not on a vacation but it is unlikely that in their discussions in the summer of 1900 Rhodes was bothered by the minutiae of Grogan's curriculum vitae. Rhodes never did see 'the spray of the water over the carriages' as the railway crossed the Zambesi; the bridge was completed in 1906, four years after his death.

34 *CtoC*, pp. vii–viii. Original letter in Crawford family papers.

35 *Alpine Club Journal*, vol. xx, February 1900–1901.

36 Grogan, Maggie, *Parodies and Other Poems*, p. 60.

CHAPTER 9

1 Estimates of the magnitude of the dowry seem to have varied between £50,000 (*c.* £2.5m in today's money) and £200,000 (*c.* £10m). Considering what is known about James Watt's wealth, and taking into account that he had four children, it is likely that the figure was at the lower end of this scale.

2 *New York Times*, 11 November 1900, p. 16; the Grogans arrived the previous day.

3 *MON*, p. 146.

4 Ibid., p. 144.

5 Ibid., p. 145.

6 'Sixty Years', p. 56.

7 Grogan, E. S., 'Kenya: The Logic Of Facts', *National Review*, April 1923, p. 243.

8 *MON*, p. 144.

9 *National Geographic*, vol. xi, April 1900.

10 *The World's Work: A History Of Our Time*, vol. I, November 1900–April 1901.

11 *MON*, pp. 141–2.

12 See Lockhart, J. G. and Wodehouse, the Hon. C. M., *Rhodes*, p. 453.

13 *MON*, p. 147.

14 Ibid., p. 148.

15 Francis ('Frank') Baden-Powell, an artist, was Robert Baden-Powell's brother. According to Tim Jeal's biography *Baden-Powell*, marrying 'a rich New Zealand girl' enabled Frank to move from a state of being 'virtually penniless' into 'one of the finest houses in Kensington'; it also enabled him to put £300 per annum towards his mother's living costs. The significance of this information is that Grogan, although by no means a pauper, also experienced a considerable upturn in his financial fortunes through marriage into the Watt family.

16 Quentin Grogan, unpublished memoirs.

17 *MON*, p. 156.

18 See Jourdan, Phillip, *Cecil Rhodes – His Private Life by His Secretary*, p. 7.

19 *The World's Work: A History Of Our Time*, vol. I, November 1900–April 1901.

20 *MON*, pp. 158–9.

21 Grogan, E. S., '*Ons Jan* is Eighty Today', *EAS*, 24 May 1950.

22 Pakenham, Thomas, *The Boer War*, p. xvii.

23 Quentin Grogan, unpublished memoirs. Grogan's insistence that almost all his siblings join him may

have had something to do with the
fact that 'Uncle' Walter, their
guardian, had by now married again
and it was not a match of which
Grogan approved. He considered
Walter's new wife to be
'preposterous'; worse still, she was a
Parnell. Jermyn Boyd, the senior
partner in the family firm of Grogan
& Boyd, was instead appointed as
guardian to Hilda.

24 *MON*, p. 162.
25 Ibid., p. 160.
26 *The World's Work: A History Of Our
    Time*, vol. I, November 1900–April
    1901.
27 *MON*, p. 164.
28 Ibid., p. 166.
29 Lingham Trading and Timber Co.
    Ltd, was established in 1893. With
    one career already behind him as the
    'Cattle King' of Ontario, Lingham
    was astonishingly successful in
    meeting the demand for timber in
    the Transvaal generated by the
    mining boom of 1894 and
    subsequent years. Although he had
    yards in Pretoria and Johannesburg
    the company's principal centre of
    operations was a 500-acre site at
    Delagoa Bay, known as Port
    Matolla, which was linked to
    Lourenço Marques's railhead by a
    six-mile private railway built for him
    by Lawley. Port Matolla comprised a
    vast saw-mill, a flour mill, over
    100,000 square feet of cold storage,
    workshops, warehouses and offices.
    In addition to timber the company
    was the largest importer of cement
    to South Africa and it also imported
    some 15,000 head of cattle each
    year. Goods were loaded from, and
    unloaded to, a sixty-foot concrete
    pier. By 1905 over 100,000 tons of
    exports and imports were being
    handled annually. The significance
    to Grogan of Lingham's successful
    business formula will become
    clear.

30 *MON*, p. 167.
31 *African Standard*, 14 May 1904.

CHAPTER 10

1 Cranworth, Lord, *Kenya Chronicles*,
   pp. 16–17.
2 *MON*, p. 169.
3 Joseph Chamberlain and Lord
   Hartington had led the imperialist
   Liberal Unionists out of the main
   Liberal Party in 1886 over the issue
   of Home Rule for Ireland. Following
   this coalition with Salisbury's
   Conservatives the terms
   'Conservative', 'Tory' and 'Unionist'
   became to some extent
   interchangeable.
4 See Coupland, Sir Reginald, *East
   Africa and Its Invaders, passim*.
5 Miller, Charles, *The Lunatic Express*,
   p. 243.
6 Grogan, E. S., introduction to
   Newland, V. and Tarlton, L.,
   Farming and Planting in BEA, p. viii.
7 *CtoC*, p. 198.
8 Eliot, Sir Charles, *The East African
   Protectorate*, p. 59.
9 *The Times*, 2 December 1892.
10 *MON*, p. 172.
11 Ibid., p. 173.
12 Hindlip, Lord, *British East Africa:
    Past, Present and Future*, p. 38.
13 Grogan in Newland, V. and Tarlton,
    L., op. cit., p. vii.
14 *MON*, p. 174.
15 Hardy, Ronald, *The Iron Snake*,
    p. 242, quoting a missionary from
    the Sagala mission station.
16 *MON*, p. 175.
17 They were standing by the river
    crossing at the meeting point of
    today's Kijabe and Kirinyaga Streets.
18 The original twenty-five-year lease
    for this property was dated
    September 1903. When Grogan
    purchased the land by negotiating
    with Cross it transpired that the
    beneficial owner (to whom the

consideration was paid) was, in fact, a Mr Clarence Wilson (se KNA/ MOH/1/1533). A replacement lease, extending the tenure to 99 years from 1/9/1903 was issued in 1914 for 16.136 acres. See East African Protectorate Blue Books and KNA/ AG/22/289.

19 The lease for this land was granted in 1910, and was relinquished the following year for a new lease covering an enlarged area of 113.652 acres. The land was further subdivided (and marginally enlarged) in 1916 into two areas of 38.62 acres and 75.83 acres. See East African Protectorate Blue Books. This tract of land to the west of today's Chiromo Road is still marked on city maps as 'Groganville' and is part of the University of Nairobi's campus.

20 Eliot, Sir Charles, op. cit., p. 73.

21 Meinertzhagen, Colonel Richard, *Kenya Diary*, entry for 23 May 1904.

22 Eliot, Sir Charles, op. cit., p. 88.

23 This offer was first made in a letter to Eliot dated 2 June 1904, FO 2/837.

24 CO 519/1.

25 CO 533/12.

26 The Indian rupee was the currency in BEA, at a rate of 15 rupees to the pound sterling.

27 'Sixty Years', p. 57.

CHAPTER 11

1 Miller, Charles, *Lunatic Express*, p. 411.

2 *African Standard*, 25 June 1904.

3 'Sixty Years', p. 57.

4 FO 2/835.

5 *The Times*, 27 August 1904.

6 Ibid.

7 Crawford family papers, Blakiston to Grogan, 23 October 1904; Sir Valentine Chirol was head of *The Times*'s foreign department from 1896 to 1912.

8 'Sixty Years', p. 57.

9 Cd. 2099 (1904), *Correspondence relating to the resignation of Sir Charles Eliot, and to the Concession to the East Africa Syndicate.*

10 FO 2/835, Eliot to Lansdowne, 11 April 1904.

11 Eliot took up the position of Vice-Chancellor of Sheffield University for seven years and then became Principal of the University of Hong Kong. Not until 1919 did he return to diplomacy, having been given the important post of Ambassador to Japan. He retired in 1926.

12 'Sixty Years', p. 58.

13 FO 2/835, Eliot to Lansdowne, 11 April 1904.

14 Crawford family papers, Eliot to Grogan, 3 April 1907.

15 Hobley, Charles, *From Chartered Company to Crown Colony*, p. 127.

16 CO 533/54, Grogan to Antrobus, 25 May 1908.

17 Quentin Grogan, unpublished memoirs.

18 CO 533/1, Stewart to Lansdowne, 16 March 1905.

19 The lease on the second 64,000 acres was signed on 16 March 1905.

20 CO 533/1, Stewart to Lansdowne, 16 March 1905.

21 CO 533/1, Grogan and Lingham proposal to Stewart, 8 January 1905.

22 *CtoC*, p. 319.

23 Quentin Grogan, unpublished memoirs.

24 See *Journal of the African Society*, vol. xiii, October 1904, p. 246: 'In succession to Mr. Grogan and Monsieur Lionel Décle he [Gibbons] carried out the scheme of a journey from the Cape to Cairo which at one time was the ambition of every would-be African explorer.' Major Gibbons's book about his traverse of Africa, *Africa from South to North through Marotseland*, was published in 1904.

25 I am grateful for correspondence from Dr Bob Weisbord (18 February 1998) on this matter. Elspeth Huxley, who perpetuated this myth in *White Man's Country*, and Wilbusch both confirmed to him that the notion of a settler conspiracy was in fact untrue. When Dr Weisbord interviewed Grogan in 1964 he gained further confirmation that Grogan's part in the affair was 'completely peripheral' and that he 'did not accompany the Commission'.

26 CO 533/1, Ellis to Read, 16 March 1905.

27 CO 533/1, Stewart to Lansdowne, 16 March 1905.

28 CO 533/10, Grogan to Lyttelton, 11 August 1905.

29 The Uasin Gishu plateau is about 4,000 square miles in extent; as already described if Grogan were to obtain 32,000 acres per mile of railway built that equated to a grant of 2,500 square miles.

30 CO 533/10, Lyttelton to Grogan, 26 August 1905.

31 Grogan had declared himself in favour of this system of government of African colonies in his 'Native Questions' chapter in *From The Cape To Cairo*. Regarded at the time as somewhat 'progressive', the merits and mechanics of this system were to become widely publicized by Goldie's protégé, Lugard, in his book *The Dual Mandate* (published in 1922). Lugard first arrived in Goldie's Nigeria in 1897, fresh from making his name in Uganda. By then Goldie's system of indirect rule had been established for many years, and it was not one which Lugard initially supported. He not only became a convert, but in time was credited with its instigation, a process in which he was greatly assisted after his death by his biographer, Margery Perham. When

Grogan first approached Goldie about his Uasin Gishu railway scheme the first signs of a falling-out between Goldie and Lugard, caused by this misappropriation of credit were already discernible.

32 Goldie, Sir George, speech to the Royal Colonial Institute reported in *The Times*, 16 January 1901, reproduced in Muffett, D. J. M., *Empire Builder Extraordinary: Sir George Goldie*, p. 179.

33 Goldie, letter to *The Times*, 22 December 1901, reproduced in Muffett, op. cit., p. 180.

34 CO 533/10, Goldie to Lyttelton, 29 September 1905.

35 *The Times*, 25 April 1905.

36 Crawford family papers, Grogan's doctor, S. King Farlow, to Churchill, 9 April 1907.

CHAPTER 12

1 Cranworth, Lord, *A Colony in the Making*, pp. 84–92 *passim*.

2 Cranworth, Lord, *Kenya Chronicles*, p. 36.

3 Ibid., p. 37.

4 CO 533/54, Grogan to Antrobus, 25 May 1908.

5 CO 533/14, R. U. Moffat's report for the Principal Medical Officer.

6 *EAS*, 24 March 1906 (the *African Standard* had become the *East African Standard* in 1905).

7 Crawford family papers, Baden-Powell to Grogan, 19 November 1905. Baden-Powell was so taken with the country that he eventually settled there.

8 See McLynn, Frank, *Hearts of Darkness*, p. 187. He adds that 'the intellectually impressive, like Livingstone, Burton and Stanley, despised the pursuit. The intellectually deficient, like Speke and Baker, revelled in it.'

9 *EAS*, 21 April 1906.

10 Meinertzhagen, Colonel Richard, *Kenya Diary*, p. 265. Meinertzhagen was the leading figure in the so-called 'Nandi Field Force' and had himself killed the Nandi *laibon* (spiritual leader). For this he was subjected to three Courts of Inquiry and was cleared of wrongdoing. But his commanding officer felt that his reputation for fair dealing and honesty had been compromised, and Meinertzhagen left the Protectorate in mid-1906. Meinertzhagen had been uneasy from the outset about his orders as he had a considerable liking for the Nandi, and felt that the Reserve to which the British administration was intent on transferring them was too small for them. 'This', he declared, 'is a very short-sighted policy and must lead to grievances; after all, it is African land, not ours to dispose of', p. 266.

11 Ibid., p. 292.

12 *MON*, p. 185.

13 CO 533/54; Grogan to Antrobus, 25 May 1908.

14 CO 533/25, Herbert Read memo, 2 November 1906. The smallest land grant that had at this stage been formally offered to Grogan – and rejected – was 6,400 acres per mile of railroad, which amounts to ten square miles. This memo suggests the possibility that there were those in the CO who considered that even this was too generous and favoured an offer of one tenth the size (640 acres at a value of 1*d.* per acre).

15 *EAS*, 4 August 1906.

16 CO 533/25. To put this latest offer in perspective, and indeed his earlier more 'outrageous' one, 'homestead' grants to the settlers in the Protectorate were usually 640 acres; 'pastoral' leases were 5,000–10,000 acres; and any land application over 10,000 acres, which only the Protectorate's 'big men' could afford, was considered sufficiently exceptional to require referral to the Secretary of State. The scale of Grogan's proposed enterprise was therefore colossal.

17 CO 533/25.

18 *MON*, p. 188.

19 Leys, Norman, *Kenya*, p. 155. Leys worked as a government doctor in the Protectorate until Bowring had him 'removed' in 1913, leaving him nursing a sense of personal grievance. The cause of his removal was his active opposition to, and condemnation of, the government's plan to move the Masai tribe from the Rift Valley. He was subsequently instrumental in securing legal counsel for the Masai to challenge the move in the courts. In 1924 Leys's book *Kenya* was published, heavily criticizing the way the colony was run.

20 'Sixty Years', p. 58.

21 Cranworth, Lord, *Kenya Chronicles*, pp. 25–6.

22 *MON*, p. 177.

23 T. L. Hately in the *East African Annual*, vol. ii, 1931–2, p. 123.

24 *EAS*, 21 April 1906. It was later disputed, usually by men who were trying to take the credit themselves, that Grogan *was* the first to introduce trout to the country. A plethora of contemporary records, however, such as this newspaper report, make it quite clear to whom the credit should be attributed. By 1913 Grogan's trout project had been passed into the hands of the Trout Acclimatization Society, run by a man called Buckland. When it was unable to raise the funds to pay for a further shipment of 150,000 ova from Howietoun Fisheries Grogan came to the rescue; he paid two thirds of the amount on the condition that the remaining third was raised by subscription, which it was. (See CO 533/19.)

25 *The Times*, 25 April 1905.

26 Jackson, Sir Frederick, *Early Days in East Africa*, p. 384.

27 See CO 519/1, minute of 4 August.

28 Huxley, Elspeth, *White Man's Country*, vol. i, p. 96.

29 Crawford family papers, Delamere to Grogan (undated, *c.* 1907–1908), asking Grogan's permission that his brother-in-law, Wilfrid Hunter, be appointed the company secretary of 'our Nakuro Township business'. Their scheme for the creation of a 'superior suburban area with a civic centre' (*MON*, pp. 184–5) in the hills surrounding Nairobi was put forward by a company they named 'The Upper Nairobi Township Company'.

30 *MON*, pp. 184–5.

31 This complicated case was reported in the *East Africa Standard* on 4 May 1906 after the court had found against Grant on all counts.

32 The Shariff and Jaffer families had been established on the coast for almost fifty years; their extensive business interests included everything from a land agency to a postage stamp dealership.

33 See Playne, Somerset, *East Africa (British)*; by 1908 the farm under the management of F. S. Clarke had 2,500 sheep, including twenty-two merino rams and thirty-five merino ewes imported from Australia; it also had a number of Shorthorn bulls imported from New Zealand.

34 Cranworth, Lord, 'When I Look Back', in Joelson, F. S. (ed.), *Rhodesia and East Africa*.

35 In fact neither absenteeism nor dummying were illegal, but they were greatly frowned upon by the authorities. They could only do anything to try to curtail them, in the absence of appropriate legislation, during a first application to the Crown for newly available land. Thereafter, once someone had been granted land, they could sell it on to a third party who could legally purchase as many holdings as he wanted in the secondary market.

36 Jackson, Frederick, op. cit., pp. 383–6 *passim*. Jackson, Grogan's fellow alumnus of Jesus College, was reputed to be the model for Captain Good in Rider Haggard's *King Solomon's Mines*.

37 *MON*, p. 184.

38 The first official mouthpiece for the settlers was the Planters' and Farmers' Association, formed in 1903 with all of twenty-three members and Delamere as President; this was subsequently renamed the Colonists' Association. Delamere resigned the presidency in January 1906. Grogan's only opponent in the 1907 election was a barrister by the name of Burn.

CHAPTER 13

1 Churchill, Winston, *My African Journey*, p. 14.

2 CO 533/4, Colonists' Association AGM, 19 July 1905.

3 *EAS*, 23 November 1907.

4 *MON*, p. 304.

5 Dinesen, Isak, *Out of Africa*, p. 213.

6 *MON*, p. 185.

7 *The World's Work: A History of Our Time*, vol. i, 1900–1901, p. 369.

8 Cranworth, Lord, *A Colony in the Making*, p. 218.

9 In addition to being a cunning and evasive wingless insect which lives in larders, cupboards and old files, the Silver Fish was also the highest award of the Girl Guides Association – a fact of which Grogan (a member of the central committee of the Legion of Frontiersmen) would certainly have been cognizant.

10 Jackson, Frederick, op. cit., p. 377.

11 *The Times*, 28 December 1907.

12 *Report of the Kenya Land Commission*

(1934), Grogan's evidence, p. 3048.

13 *CtoC*, p. 308.

14 See Buchan, John, *The African Colony*, p. 53.

15 See minutes of the Colonial Economic Development Committee, 1920, p. 62.

16 Cd. 2164 (1904), *Report of the Uganda Railway Committee*, p. 13.

17 Naipaul, Shiva, *North of South*, p. 109.

18 Ibid., p. 118.

19 See Hollingsworth, L. W., *The Asians of East Africa*, p. 144.

20 *The Times*, 28 December 1907.

21 *Report of the Kenya Land Commission (1934)*, Grogan's evidence, p. 3046.

22 *CtoC*, p. 366.

23 Based on a similar system in operation in the Transvaal this Ordinance was intended to lay down the rules for the employment of African 'squatter' labour. It provided for the hire by European settlers of African labour on annual contracts in exchange for the right to cultivate one acre of land of their own on the settlers' farms, thus creating a type of feudal tenancy agreement. Labourers had to work for a minimum of three months a year and payment was set at Rs.3 per month – which equated to their annual hut tax payment.

24 The Pass laws were framed with the intention of deterring African labourers from deserting, breaking their contracts or avoiding paying tax.

25 Cd. 4117 (1908), *Correspondence relating to the Tenure of Land in the East African Protectorate*, p. 4.

26 Sorrenson, M. P. K., *Origins of European Settlement in Kenya*, p. 146; author's italics; alienated land was land that had been appropriated by the Crown.

27 CO 533/54.

28 Cranworth, Lord, *Kenya Chronicles*, p. 8.

29 CO 533/5, Hobley memo dated 11 November 1905.

30 Hobley, C. W., op. cit., p. 13.

31 In 1907 the administration's annual budget, although double its level three years earlier, was still less than £900,000.

32 CO 533/5, undated memo, end 1905.

33 Jackson, in a revealing moment of amnesia, subsequently claimed however that he had 'nothing whatsoever to do with the negotiations that led [the Masai move], or with the move itself' (Jackson, p. 330).

34 Hobley, C. W., op. cit., p. 141.

35 *MON*, p. 185.

36 CO 537/28.

37 FO 2/870.

38 CO 537/28.

CHAPTER 14

1 Hobley, C. W., op. cit., p. 141.

2 David (later Sir David) Hutchins was accorded a full two pages in Grogan's memoirs. His eccentricities were legion: not only did he have a strange penchant for jumping over hedges, but his wife told Grogan that her husband's odd gait was due to his having amputated his little toes in order to fit into a new pair of boots which he found too small. Grogan's over-riding opinion of Hutchins was that he was a 'very likeable old rascal [who] tried to bilk me out of my concession and failed'. *MON*, pp. 198–200.

3 CO 533/28.

4 *Staffordshire Sentinel*, 27 January 1910.

5 The subsequent judgement of Acting Commissioner Frederick Jackson. All quotations relating to the 'Nairobi Incident' are drawn from Cd. 3562 (1907) (*Correspondence relating to the flogging of natives by certain Europeans*

at Nairobi) except where otherwise indicated.

6 CO 533/28, memo of Ellis to Read, 9 April 1907.

7 Foran, W. Robert, op. cit. p. 288.

8 CO 533/11, Colonists' Association AGM, January 1906.

9 *EAS*, 16 March 1907.

10 Foran, W. Robert, op. cit., p. 288.

11 Ibid., p. 289.

12 CO 533/28, opinions expressed by Hobley and Ainsworth respectively.

13 CO 533/28, memo of Ellis to Read, 9 April 1907.

14 There has always been considerable confusion about the location for the simple reason that the Court House was also generally known as the 'Town Hall'.

15 In his memoirs Grogan claimed that 'a senior police officer presided over the chastisement to see that it was conducted in strict accordance with police procedure' (E. S. Grogan, *MON*, p. 186). This was stretching the truth but the Colonial Office were to be severely embarrassed – and compromised – by Logan and Smith's inaction. Logan nevertheless went on to be Chief Justice of Northern Rhodesia and was knighted.

16 *MON*, pp. 186–7.

17 Ibid., p. 187.

18 *EAS*, 16 March 1907.

19 Crawford family papers; this remark was one of the hand-written notes in the margins of Grogan's personal copy of Cd. 3562. No evidence was ever offered by the Crown to substantiate its allegation that members of the crowd were armed.

20 *MON*, p. 187.

21 CO 533/28.

22 *EAS*, 20 April 1907.

23 Ibid.

24 CO 533/29.

25 *MON*, p. 188.

26 The convictions of Fichat, Low and Bowker were also 'revised' which

effectively meant that they too were quashed.

27 CO 533/28.

28 CO 533/30.

29 *The Times*, 26 December 1908.

30 CO 533/28.

31 Crawford family papers, Cockburn to Grogan, 29 September 1907.

32 Grogan attacked Churchill on this point in a letter to *The Times* (29 May 1907) with the words 'I spear this fleeting jest as it is so typical of the anaesthetics applied to our East Africa Administration by the home authorities.'

33 See Hansard, 11 April 1907. That Churchill knew as much about Grogan as Grogan knew about Churchill, given their prominent reputations and Grogan's business dealings with Moreton Frewen (Churchill's uncle), is indisputable. The record of a meeting in April 1907 between Churchill and the eminent doctor S. King Farlow at which the state of Grogan's health was discussed is just one item of supporting evidence (Crawford family papers).

34 Foran, W. Robert, op. cit., p. 290.

35 Cranworth, Lord, *Kenya Chronicles*, p. 26.

36 Crawford family papers, Delamere to Grogan, July 1907. Delamere added that 'you and I have both been in trouble lately. Let's put it behind us and settle down to pushing the true interests of the country ... your case has, in a way, a parallel in that of Jameson. Look what he has risen to. We can't afford to lose you'. Jameson, leader of the eponymous Raid on the Transvaal in 1896, had completed a spectacular political rehabilitation by becoming Prime Minister of Cape Colony.

37 *EAS*, 13 September 1907.

38 Ibid., 5 October 1907.

CHAPTER 15

1 *MON*, p. 190.
2 Hobley, C. W., op. cit., p. 136.
3 Churchill, Winston, op. cit., p. 15.
4 *The Times*, 17 March 1908.
5 The significant policy introductions of Asquith's first term, in which Churchill had a major hand, were: old age pensions (1908), the Development Act (1909), the labour exchanges (1909) and Lloyd George's National Insurance Bill (1911).
6 Crawford family papers, Chamberlain to Grogan, December 1907. Although Chamberlain had retired from active politics following his stroke almost two years earlier he was still a powerful man in Tory politics, the more so as the debate about Tariff Reform and Imperial Federation – his twin causes – remained high on the political agenda.
7 *MON* pp. 190–92.
8 Crawford family papers, Coleman to Grogan, 2 September 1908.
9 *MON*, pp. 265–6.
10 Grogan, E. S., *Economic Calculus*, pp. 161–2.
11 *MON*, p. 266.
12 In December 1908, just ahead of important final decisions on the terms of the Crown Lands Ordinance, Grogan treated the CO to a twenty-page lecture on land values (CO 533/54). The central thesis was that land in the Protectorate had no value until money was spent developing it. Grogan himself had spent a massive £25,000 in four years and his interest costs on that money exceeded his income by an unhealthy £600 per annum. He therefore argued for lenient leases for the settlers and cheaper prices, claiming with some justification that the Crown was the largest beneficiary of the land market

as it held a monopoly. This was the last shot at the CO in a campaign waged all summer by Grogan and Lord Hindlip, an assistant Whip in the House of Lords. The Bill, which broadly speaking acceded to the demands of the larger landowners in the Protectorate, was passed in 1909. It was subsequently redrafted in 1913 and a 'final version' became law in 1915.
13 Crawford family papers, a letter from Lady Delamere to Grogan states, 'it is very nice of you to have tried to reinstate him', undated.
14 Crawford family papers, Lady Delamere to Grogan, 23 June 1908.
15 Crawford family papers, letter from Lady Delamere to Grogan, undated.
16 Crawford family papers, letter from A. S. Bellington to Grogan, 3 May 1908.
17 Crawford family papers, Hobley to Grogan, 24 July 1908 and 10 June 1908; this scheme never came to fruition.
18 CO 533/32.
19 CO 533/47.

CHAPTER 16

1 1906 election result: Josiah Wedgwood (Liberal) – 5,155 seats, Sir Alfred Seale Haslam (Unionist) – 2,948 seats.
2 Wedgwood, Josiah C., *Memoirs of a Fighting Life*, p. 70; Grogan was in fact thirty-five.
3 Ibid., p. 70. Grogan's book mentioned by Wedgwood was in fact his *Economic Calculus*, which was a study of economic theory only peripherally concerned with the issue of protection. After the election however he published his election speeches in a pamphlet entitled *Tariff: The Workers' Charter*.
4 *MON*, p. 192.
5 *Staffordshire Sentinel*, 27 January

1910. This was why Grogan fought in the summer of 1910 to force the Colonial Office to publish Papers admitting that many of the allegations contained in its 1907 White Paper (Cd. 3562) were untrue. The CO had at the time of the incident said that it would do so if Grogan could prove that he was suffering as a result of these smears. Grogan thought that the election campaign was ample proof that he *was* suffering. In the House of Commons on 21 April 1910 Lord Balcarres, speaking on behalf of Alfred Lyttelton, the former Tory Colonial Secretary, stated that 'no official record has been issued of the fact that the conviction was quashed on appeal', and requested that as 'improper and defamatory use has been made of the official record of the conviction ... equal publicity [should be given] to the record of the quashing of the same appeal'. Colonel Seely, the Liberal Colonial Under-Secretary reiterated that the government would 'lay Papers in continuation of Cd. 3562 if it can be shown that Captain Grogan is suffering'. Despite the fact that this was obviously the case, no such Papers were ever laid. (See Hansard 21 April 1910.)

6 *Staffordshire Sentinel*, 27 January 1910.
7 Ibid., 26 November 1910.
8 *MON*, p. 195.
9 Women over thirty eventually received the vote in 1918, but it was not until 1928 that all adult women were granted the franchise.
10 *Staffordshire Sentinel*, 25 November 1910.
11 *MON*, p. 197.
12 *Staffordshire Sentinel*, 1 November 1913.
13 Crawford family papers, document of commendation, undated.
14 Wedgwood, Josiah C., op. cit., p. 70.

15 *MON*, p. 192.
16 *Staffordshire Sentinel*, 1 November 1913.
17 Ibid.
18 Cranworth, Lord, *Kenya Chronicles*, p. 61.
19 CO 533/63.
20 Cranworth, Lord, *Kenya Chronicles*, p. 66.
21 *Leader*, 12 November 1910.
22 As Sorrenson points out (op. cit., p. 154), and Grogan and Delamere knew from bitter experience, the settler economy had taken time to get established; its exports were minimal before World War One. The Blue Book for 1913–14 shows that total exports from Uganda and EAP were £1,482,876 of which African-grown cotton accounted for £410,833; African-produced hides £373,076 and goat skins £105,639. The highest earning European-grown product was coffee (£68,793).
23 *The Times*, 25 April 1905.
24 Crawford family papers, Coleman to Grogan, 2 September 1908.
25 *Leader*, 2 March 1912.
26 'Sixty Years', p. 58.
27 *Leader*, 7 September 1912.
28 Cranworth, Lord, *Kenya Chronicles*, p. 92.
29 RH/Mss.Afr.s.782, box 1, Huxley interview with Grogan, 1933.
30 Lloyd Papers (24/2), Lloyd to Grogan, 9 May 1913.
31 Lloyd Papers (24/3), Grogan to Lloyd, 8 November 1913.
32 Lloyd Papers (24/3), Grogan to Lloyd, 5 December 1912.
33 Lloyd Papers (24/3), Grogan to Lloyd, 15 February 1914.
34 Lloyd Papers (24/3), Grogan to Lloyd, 28 February 1914.
35 Grogan clearly owned the majority of Equator Saw Mills, but the odd surviving document shows that he had some interesting co-investors. Moreton Frewen and the Earl of

Warwick had invested as early as 1907; then, the following year, Frewen also persuaded his nephew, Churchill, to put some money behind Grogan. At the time – in the wake of the Nairobi Incident – Churchill was denouncing Grogan in Parliament with the words 'we must not let a few ruffians steal our beautiful and promising Protectorate away from us'. The 'ruffian' Grogan was, it seems, an acceptable investment. (See Crawford family papers and Hansard, 1908.)

36 KNA/MOH/1/1533 shows that Grogan threatened the government with legal action when they cast aspersions on what he had or hadn't done with the Cross Estate and the government retracted their allegations.

37 Crawford family papers, Coleman to Gertrude, 5 August 1908.

38 Muthaiga Country Club details from 'Titus' Oates Papers, RH/Micr.Afr.s.595 and *MON*, *passim*.

39 *Leader*, 18 July 1914.

CHAPTER 17

1 *MON*, p. 202.

2 The last entry in the immensely likeable Quentin Grogan's unpublished memoirs, which at times provide important insights into Ewart's character, relates to the battle at Longido. He married Irene Sanderson in 1915 and they had a single daughter, Diana.

3 Meinertzhagen, Col Richard, *Army Diary*, p. 84.

4 Ibid., p. 105.

5 Ibid., p. 89.

6 Ibid., p. 86.

7 *MON*, p. 202.

8 Meinertzhagen, Col Richard, *Army Diary*, p. 110.

9 Meinertzhagen, Col Richard, Unpublished Papers, vol. 16, p. 166;

he perceptively added, 'I should imagine he [Grogan] is a far-sighted businessman but rather speculative.'

10 *MON*, p. 209.

11 Jackson, Frederick, op. cit., p. 385.

12 *MON* p. 211.

13 The *Muansa*, with its two one-pound guns and brace of machine guns, was scuttled during an attack by the British steamers *Winifred* and *Kavirondo*. Its captain subsequently managed to refloat the vessel but its guns were no longer operational and the British were able to control Lake Victoria for the rest of the war.

14 Joelson, F. S., *The Tanganyika Territory*, p. 239.

15 *MON*, p. 212.

16 Meinertzhagen, Col Richard, *Army Diary*, p. 167.

17 *MON*, p. 213 and Wymer, op. cit., pp. 191–2.

18 *MON*, p. 213.

19 Ibid.

20 Ibid.

21 Meinertzhagen, Col Richard, *Army Diary*, p. 108 and Unpublished Papers, vol. 16, p. 66.

22 *MON*, p. 217.

23 Ibid., p. 227.

24 Just over a year later Malleson, after leading a disastrous assault on Salaita Hill to the east of Taveta, effectively deserted (according to Meinertzhagen) rather than attack the Latema–Reata line to the west of the town. He was therefore removed to another command in India, one of many of the 150-plus British generals who took the field during the East African conflict to depart in disgrace.

25 Meinertzhagen, Col Richard, *Army Diary*, p. 118.

26 *MON*, p. 235.

27 Meinertzhagen, Col Richard, *Army Diary*, p. 99.

28 *Leader*, 11 September 1914.

29 Meinertzhagen, Col Richard, *Army Diary*, pp. 151–2.

30 Ibid., p. 119.
31 *MON*, p. 209.
32 Meinertzhagen, Col Richard, Unpublished Papers, vol. 16, p. 177.
33 *MON*, p. 209.
34 In March 1916 the Protectorate became the first territory in the Empire to introduce conscription.
35 *MON*, p. 235.
36 Jackson, Frederick, op. cit., p. 383.
37 *MON*, p. 228.
38 Ibid., p. 215.
39 Grogan, E. S., '*Ons Jan* is Eighty Today', *EAS*, 24 May 1950.
40 *MON*, p. 235.
41 Ibid., p. 243.
42 Ibid., p. 241.
43 Ibid., p. 206.
44 Von Lettow-Vorbeck entered politics after the war and served for ten years in the Reichstag. In 1929 he was guest of honour at a dinner hosted by Smuts on Armistice Day; Grogan and Meinertzhagen were present and both later contributed to a relief fund for their old adversary when the German mark collapsed. In 1930, appalled by the rise of Nazism, von Lettow-Vorbeck resigned from the Reichstag; five years later he even refused Hitler's offer to be Ambassador to London, a snub which put him on the Nazi blacklist. By the end of World War II the Nazis had ruined him. Destitute, he survived on parcels of food and other necessities sent to him by Meinertzhagen and Smuts. By the early fifties his affairs resumed some semblance of normality and in 1953 he decided to visit Tanganyika, formerly German East Africa. On the dockside were numerous old men at work. He stopped and asked one of them if he knew any *Schutztruppe*. Many old men pressed forward telling him their long-forgotten tales of war. Suddenly one of them asked the unrecognized von Lettow-Vorbeck who he was. He told them, whereupon one old man threw himself on his knees and, in tears, hugged the general's knees. Von Lettow-Vorbeck died in 1964, aged ninety-four. That year the Bundestag finally paid his surviving *askaris* their back pay. Claimants were identified as genuine by being able to perform the German arms drill faultlessly. Not one aged claimant failed: not a single impostor had dared to masquerade as one of von Lettow's faithful élite.
45 *MON*, p. 239.
46 Ibid., p. 246.
47 Smuts, Jan, lecture to RGS, 28 January 1918, *Geographical Journal*, vol. li, no. 3.
48 *MON*, p. 202.
49 Mentioned in despatches 1 January 1918 (by Smuts) and 21 January 1918 (by van Deventer); DSO at the recommendation of Smuts, 8 February 1917. See *London Gazette*.
50 *MON*, p. 248.
51 Ibid., p. 249.
52 *Reveille*, September 1918.
53 *MON*, p. 250.
54 Ibid., p. 208.
55 *Reveille*, September 1918.
56 Author's correspondence with Mrs Gertrude Chapman through Mr Adrian Coleman, 9 June 1998 et seq. Mrs Chapman is the daughter of Gertrude's sister Helen, who married T. H. Lowry; she was born in 1902.
57 Mrs Doris Tate-Smith was born in 1890 and died in 1993. Her husband, Ronald, arrived in BEA as a draughtsman in the Public Works Department in 1907. A few years later he set up his own architects' practice in partnership with Mr H. E. Henderson. By the outbreak of war they were the premier practice in the country, and must have been well-known to Grogan: they not only designed Muthaiga Club, but also Sixth Avenue's

Nairobi House in which Grogan's business empire was headquartered. Ronald Tate-Smith died of malaria during the war, while serving with the East Africa Road Corps.

CHAPTER 18

1 *MON*, p. 252.
2 Ibid., p. 250.
3 'Sixty Years', pp. 56–9, *passim*.
4 Grogan, E. S., '*Ons Jan* is Eighty Today', *EAS*, 24 May 1950.
5 *MON*, p. 252.
6 Milner Papers, Mss. Eng. Hist. 704 (Bodleian), Grogan to Thornton at the CO, 5 June 1919.
7 Newland, V. and Tarlton, L., op. cit., p. viii.
8 *MON*, p. 257.
9 Lloyd Papers (24/3), Grogan to Lloyd, 5 May 1914.
10 CO 533/194.
11 Huxley, Elspeth, *White Man's Country*, vol. ii, p. 52.
12 *EAS*, 15 February 1919.
13 Letter from the Aborigine Protection Society, *Leader*, 12 July 1919.
14 *Hansard*, vol. 41, speech of Lord Emmott, 14 July 1920.
15 *EAS*, 15 February 1919.
16 *Economic Commission: Final Report*, Nairobi, 1919, *passim*.
17 CO 533/207, Sir Cecil Bottomley memo, 17 April 1919.
18 *The Times*, 19 July 1919.
19 The legal unit of value in Kenya was the sovereign or 'pound' (backed by gold) although the Indian silver rupee was for historical reasons the common coinage. In 1905 the rate of exchange had been fixed at 15 rupees to the pound (or 1s.4d. to the rupee) where it had remained ever since. During the war Britain left the gold standard and subsequently prohibited the importation of sovereigns into the Protectorate (and India) in response to a request from the South African government for assistance in controlling the illicit export of gold from South Africa. As the Protectorate's pound was no longer backed by gold, its rupee currency effectively became tied to the Indian rupee. The rupee then started to rise in value, both in East Africa and India, as currency traders bought silver in the absence of gold.
20 *MON*, p. 121.
21 CO 533/251, Grogan to Amery, 1 January 1920.
22 CO 535/251, Grogan to Amery, 8 January 1920.
23 It was Grogan's contention that the currency appreciation was only a temporary one, and that all the government had to do was publicly to reaffirm the old (legal) rate of exchange and allow the importation to East Africa either of sovereigns or, if that were impossible, of £1 Treasury notes. The latter, known as 'Bradburys', Grogan described as 'those little pieces of inscribed paper which ran about pretending to be golden sovereigns'. The effect, he argued, would be – according to Gresham's Law – that 'bad money' (i.e. a cheaper sterling-backed currency) would drive 'good money' (an overvalued rupee) out of circulation.
24 Letter reprinted in *EAS*, 19 June 1920.
25 See CO 323/1314/8.

CHAPTER 19

1 *Leader*, 10 January 1920.
2 Ibid., 29 December 1919.
3 *EAS*, 5 March 1920.
4 *Leader*, 21 February 1920.
5 Tannahill had arrived in the Protectorate in 1908 to take up a position as a land ranger in the Land Office. He had a great talent for

land law and surveying, and was instrumental in the drafting of the final version of the Crown Lands Ordinance 1915. He then left the government to go into partnership – at Grogan's instigation – with the latter's brother-in-law, Wilfrid Hunter. His specific remit was to advise Grogan on property matters; given Tannahill's links with the government, Grogan was continually being accused of being privy to inside information in his post-war property dealings. Tannahill, like Hunter, was also a leading figure in the very powerful Nairobi Chamber of Commerce.

6 *Leader*, 27 March 1920.
7 Cranworth, Lord, *Kenya Chronicles*, p. 68.
8 *Leader*, 18 June 1921.
9 Ibid., 29 October 1921.
10 Legco Minutes, 25 May 1922.
11 *EAS*, 23 April 1922.
12 *Leader*, 29 October 1921.
13 CO 533/280.
14 *National Review*, April 1923; E. S. Grogan, *Kenya: The Logic Of Facts*.
15 Speech by Winston Churchill, Secretary of State for the Colonies, to the Kenya and Uganda dinner (as reported in *African World*, vol. xix). Grogan did not attend the dinner but was officially represented by Gertrude and his eldest daughter, Dorothy.
16 Coryndon Papers, RH/Mss.Afr.s.633(3/1), Churchill to Coryndon, 6 September 1922.
17 Robert Coryndon had had a brilliant career as an administrator since he and Grogan had first met in the *laager* in Bulawayo in 1896. After serving briefly as Rhodes's private secretary after the Matabele War in 1897 he became – in succession – Resident Commissioner in Barotseland, Resident Commissioner in Swaziland, Chairman of the Southern Rhodesia Native Reserves Commission and Resident Commissioner in Basutoland. Then, from 1917 until he took up his appointment in Kenya, he was Governor and Commander-in-Chief of Uganda.
18 In addressing Grogan's one-time 'Big Noise', the Convention of Associations, just prior to his departure for London, Delamere affirmed the unswerving loyalty of Kenya's European population to the King but warned that 'if in consequence of the ill-considered advice of His Majesty's ministers his loyal subjects should be forced into action prejudicial to His Majesty's peace and abhorrent and ruinous to themselves, then the full responsibility for such a calamity must rest upon those advisers who in their ignorance of, or indifference to the true issues involved, shall have advised His Majesty to sanction a policy disastrous to the future of white settlement in colonization in Africa, and the welfare of millions of his African subjects and which this Convention believes to be calculated ultimately to endanger the integrity of the British Empire' (*EAS*, 3 March 1923). In addition to echoing the sentiments of the Ulstermen these words directly foreshadow those used by Ian Smith in declaring Rhodesia's Unilateral Independence from Britain four decades later.
19 Cmd. 1922 (1923) *Indians in Kenya*, *passim*.
20 *Leader*, 6 December 1919.
21 Uncatalogued item in Convention of Associations Papers, RH/Mss.Afr.s.594.
22 Coryndon Papers, RH/Mss.Afr.s.633(3/2).
23 Meinertzhagen, Col Richard, *Kenya Diary*, 18 March 1904.
24 *Leader*, 29 November 1913.

CHAPTER 20

1 Cranworth, Lord, *Kenya Chronicles*, p. 277.
2 *MON*, p. 269.
3 CO 533/194.
4 Milner Papers, Mss.Eng.Hist. 704 (Bodleian), Grogan to Milner, 21 November 1919.
5 CO 533/151.
6 CO 533/19.
7 McGregor Ross was nothing if not tenacious. He responded to his humiliation by trying to discredit Major Robertson, the government's chief railway engineer. In this he failed: the Colonial Office pronounced that his 'attacks are so obviously coloured by personal animus' (CO 533/280) that they were not worth taking seriously. McGregor Ross then attacked his fellow-official Bowring, Grogan and Delamere with such virulence when the 1922 Economic and Finance Committee, on which they all sat, expressed its support for the Nakuru route that Northey was forced to take action. Writing to Churchill the governor called McGregor Ross's diatribe 'uncalled for, unjust and deplorable', and added that 'insinuations of personal advantage are to my mind beneath contempt' (CO 533/280). Churchill concurred; and he forcefully quashed McGregor Ross's demand for a Public Inquiry into the workings of Major Robertson's domain, the Uganda Railway.
8 *MON*, p. 271.
9 Buchanan, Sir George, 'British East Africa: Wanted – A Policy!', p. 10.
10 Coryndon Papers, RH/ Mss.Afr.s.633(5/1), Dutton to Coryndon, 28 November 1921.
11 CO 533/27.
12 *The African World*, vol. xxiii, p. 64.
13 *MON*, p. 272.
14 Coryndon Papers, RH/

Mss.Afr.s.633(8/2), Coryndon to Secretary of State, 9 January 1923. The opinion of Mr Follett Holt, a renowned civil engineer and railway expert during his visit to Kenya in September 1922.
15 CO 533/292.
16 Coryndon Papers, RH/ Mss.Afr.s.633(8/2), Coryndon to Secretary of State, 9 January 1923.
17 Coryndon Papers, RH/ Mss.Afr.s.633(8/2), 17 October 1923.
18 CO 533/292.
19 Excluding the Magadi Soda Company's dedicated wharf, which was handling 80,000 tons of soda p.a., Mombasa's exports were 103,000 tons of which Mbaraki was handling 50,000 tons.
20 Grogan personally owned 14,747 of the 31,453 shares in the company; his Equator Saw Mills company, in which he held a majority of the equity, owned an additional 9,900 shares; and the third largest shareholder was C. S. Goldmann with 3,300 shares. Lord Howard de Walden held an interest in Mbaraki by dint of his being Grogan's partner in ESM. Once described by the *East African Standard* as 'The Richest Young Man In England' and 'that rather eccentric young nobleman who is not much known and avoids Society', the 8th Baron Howard de Walden's first business venture in the Protectorate was a (failed) attempt to establish a zebra stud farm by Lake Victoria as early as 1904. After that he largely left his East African affairs in the hands of factors. Grogan was first introduced to him by Coryndon in about 1920, and swiftly sold him a minority holding in ESM. Not only was Grogan immensely impressed by the fact that his Lordship's income had been estimated in 1904 to be in excess of £200,000 per annum, but he was also very fond of this fellow

maverick, whom he once described as 'a quaint fellow [who] sometimes successfully attempts to disguise the fact that he is a very intelligent and large-minded person' (Coryndon Papers, RH/Mss.Afr.s.633(1/4), Grogan to Coryndon, 21 March 1921). This observation, in Grogan's language, amounted to fulsome praise.

21 The most serious of these allegations was that Grogan was not authorized by his shareholders to sell Mbaraki to the government. This was incorrect, for the simple reason that Grogan was the majority shareholder both in KHW&E and Equator Saw Mills.

22 Coryndon Papers, RH/ Mss.Afr.s.633(8/2), Grogan to Coryndon, 1 February 1923.

23 Coryndon Papers, RH/ Mss.Afr.s.633(8/1), Grogan to Coryndon, 17 October 1923.

24 *MON*, p. 46.

25 CO 533/314.

26 CO 533/311.

27 See CO 533/324.

28 CO 533/329.

29 CO 533/325, Sir Cecil Bottomley memo, 10 December 1924.

30 Coryndon Papers, RH/ Mss.Afr.s.633(8/2), 2 October 1923.

31 CO 533/340.

32 Conclusion of the *Report Of The Port Commission Of Inquiry*, December 1925.

33 Legco Minutes, 11 August 1925.

34 The vengeful McGregor Ross's departure was not the end of his involvement in Kenyan affairs. In 1927 he published *Kenya From Within*, which earned him the lasting hatred of both settlers and government officials. Historians have tended to over-estimate the impact on the British public of his tome and Dr Norman Leys's *Kenya* (see note 19, chapter 12), published in 1924. The appeal of both was limited by the fact that they were clearly written by men nursing a personal grievance and were so riddled with factual errors that it was relatively easy for both colonists and officials to discredit them. As Michael Redley rightly points out in his outstanding thesis 'The Politics of a Predicament: The white community in Kenya 1918–22', Florence Riddell's *Kenya Mist*, published at much the same time, achieved far greater notoriety. Painting 'a picture of passion amongst white renegades from the conventions of British society', as Redley puts it, it sold some 375,000 copies (see p. 81, note 2).

CHAPTER 21

1 After Hilda had finished school at Eastbourne she studied music for four years in Karlsruhe and then at the London Academy of Music and became an accomplished violinist. Although both of her parents were Anglican, she converted to Catholicism during World War I and became a nun, taking the name Sister Mary Simeon. She had a long teaching career at the famous convent school of St Leonard's, Mayfield; although she left there in 1939 to serve elsewhere it was to Mayfield that she returned for her 'retirement'. She died in 1977. I am grateful to Sister Dominic Crauford for a wealth of biographical information about her friend's life.

2 *MON*, p. 307.

3 Ibid.

4 Ibid.

5 In 1918 Grogan had wanted Lloyd as a military governor and only switched his choice to Girouard when Lloyd made it clear he wanted to accept his posting to Bombay. By 1925 Grogan's hand was

strengthened by the fact that the Conservatives were back in power and Leo Amery, the Colonial Secretary, urged Lloyd to take the Kenya posting (while hinting that it might be the only offer he got). But Lloyd, however close his friendship with Grogan and shared belief in Federation, once again had set his sights on higher things, and refused. He was ennobled as 1st Baron Lloyd of Dolobran and made High Commissioner for Egypt.

6 KNA/LO/43/38/1/6, Grogan to Felling, 10 August 1926. Grogan's assets were listed as the 110-acre Swamp Estate; the Cross Estate (now just 11 acres following sales of portions of it); Equator Saw Mills' Nairobi headquarters in Sadler Street (today's Koinange Street); his forest concession with its four sawmills and his 50 per cent share in Kenya Creosoting. 'Are these *all* his assets?' reads a wary note written by an unnamed official in the margin of the letter.

7 Crawford family papers, Grogan to Hunter, 23 November 1916.

8 KNA/FOR/2/297, Nicholson Report, 2 February 1928.

9 Author's interview with Mrs Leslie James, 28 May 1998.

10 Huxley Papers, RH/Mss.Afr.s.2154, box 12, notebooks for *White Man's Country*.

11 Coryndon Papers, RH/ Mss.Afr.s.633(8/2), Grogan to Coryndon, 2 October 1923.

12 *The Times*, 7 August 1926.

13 Cranworth, Lord, *Kenya Chronicles*, p. 312.

14 Huxley, Elspeth, *White Man's Country*, vol. ii, p. 323.

15 CO 533/439/11.

16 Huxley, Elspeth, *Out In The Midday Sun*, p. 66.

17 Huxley Papers, RH/Mss.Afr.s.2154, box 12, notebooks for *White Man's Country*.

18 Huxley, Elspeth, *Out In The Midday Sun*, p. 66.

19 Cobbold, Lady Evelyn, *Kenya: The Land of Illusion*, p. 3. These words were written the same year that *White Man's Country* was published, during Lady Cobbold's first visit to Kenya.

20 The aim of Grogan's action was obviously to illustrate that Huxley's command of facts was not all that it was thought to be. In her book *Sorcerer's Apprentice*, published in 1948, a character makes the following observation: 'It is a curious commentary on human nature that Torr's, Nairobi's largest hotel, is Indian owned and most of the others belong to Indians or Jews.' Torr's was in fact still owned by the man who had built it – Grogan – and his response was to threaten a libel action. Chatto & Windus were forced to publish a full apology in *The Times* and insert *erratum* slips in the book; by its third reprint the error had been corrected. This intriguing episode is revealed in Cross, Robert and Perkin, Michael, *Elspeth Huxley – A Bibliography*.

21 Waugh, Evelyn, *Remote People*, p. 138; Waugh's observation was both right and wrong. The majority of farmers *were* busy on their farms; but equally they were – just as they had always been – only a small minority of the total European population. By 1931 this had almost reached 17,000 souls, of whom less than half were adult males. Only 2,522 listed their profession as 'farmer' whereas over 3,000 were in 'commerce and industry', and during the Grigg years the number of government officials and civil servants had swelled to 1,735. In other words, to Grogan's disgust, there were almost as many officials as farmers and both those sections of the community were outnumbered

by those in what might be termed
the 'service sector'.

22 Joyce Papers, RH/Mss.Afr.s.2157,
Grogan to Frank Joyce, 12
December 1938.

23 Legco Minutes, 22 September 1943.

24 Foran, W. Robert, op. cit., p. 116.

25 Grogan, E. S., *Kenya: The Settlers'
Case*.

26 'Sixty Years', p. 55.

27 *The Times*, 9 February 1920.

28 *Daily Express*, 28 February 1932.

29 *EAS*, 5 March 1932.

30 Cobbold, Lady Evelyn, op. cit.,
p. 13.

31 *EAS*, 27 February 1932.

32 *EAS*, 5 March 1932.

CHAPTER 22

1 Author's interview with Heini
Lustman, 2 April 1998.

2 Author's interview with Mickey
Migdoll, 25 March 1998.

3 Huxley, Elspeth, *Out In The Midday
Sun*, p. 47.

4 Lady Moore Papers, RH/
Mss.Brit.Emp.s.466, diary entry for
20 January 1929.

5 Lady Moore Papers, RH/
MSS.Brit.Emp.s.466, diary entry for
17 June 1929.

6 Farson, Negley, *Behind God's Back*,
pp. 234–7.

7 Lady Moore Papers, RH/
MSS.Brit.Emp.s.466, diary entry for
23 December 1929.

8 Grogan and his Indian friend
Shams-ud-Deen had surveyed the
area soon after the war and in 1922
proposed it to the Economic and
Finance Committee as an Indian
agricultural settlement area. So poor
did the land appear to the untrained
eye, and so numerous were the
rhinos in the vicinity, that the
scheme was rejected by
Shams-ud-Deen's fellow Indian
leaders.

9 The 1932 government hut count
showed a population in the Taveta
area of 1,128 men, 1,083 women and
1,156 children – a total of 3,367
souls.

10 Sources: KNA/DC Teita, KNA/DC
Voi and KNA/DO Taveta reports
1930–40; Margaret Layzell, 'Taveta
Past and Present', *East African
Annual*, 1937–8.

11 KNA/DC Teita (H. Elphinstone)
1/1: Annual Report 1935.

12 To put this figure in context it was
four times greater than the export
revenue of the gold mined in the
Kakamega gold rush in 1933 – its
peak year – which has often been
erroneously portrayed as having
saved the colony from bankruptcy.

13 That this was indeed the case can be
deduced from two subsequent
government-sponsored reports into
the timber industry. Neither
mention ESM by name which, as it
had been the market leader, is quite
sufficient evidence on its own that
ESM folded. It raises the question of
what happened to Grogan's
state-of-the-art mills. Some no doubt
remained moth-balled; others may
have been dismantled and the
equipment sold for whatever it
would fetch. Some, like the huge
flagship mill at Maji Mazuri, the
skeleton of which still stands today,
continued to operate on a
care-and-maintenance basis – but
not for Grogan. A paragraph in the
1937 Oliphant Report answers the
question of who took on their
ownership; it mentions the
formation of the East Africa Timber
Co-Operative Society 'which
included most of the mills of the
colony' (p. 22); equally significantly
it also stated that 'the Society has
acquired a sawmill and storage yard
in Nairobi, where drying conditions
are good'. As there were only two
significant timber yards in Nairobi –

ESM's in Sadler Street and that of the Uganda Railway (which remained in its possession) – the conclusion must be that the Society took over the running of the remaining mills as well. Paragraph 330 of the 1935 Report of the Economic Development Committee also supports this contention by stating that 'mills inside the Society cut some 70% of the [colony's] timber'.

13 Huxley, Elspeth, *Sorcerer's Apprentice*, p. 133.

CHAPTER 23

1 The author's grandfather, in his capacity as a partner of Jones & Brown and a long-standing friend of Grogan's, was approached twice by the latter in a single week towards the end of 1931. Grogan was seeking to borrow £25,000 from the bank.

2 Hunter family papers, Grogan to Wilfrid Hunter, 23 November 1916 and Wilfrid Hunter to Grogan, 26 November 1916.

3 As late as the 1930s female teachers were required to spend one year in every three 'resting', so grave were though to be the climatic risks to a European's health – especially a female European.

4 Author's interview with June Sutherland, 27 May 1998 and correspondence, 17 July 1998.

5 Author's interview with Diana Wasbrough, 30 April 1998.

6 Quentin and Irene predeceased Grogan, dying in South Africa within four months of each other in 1962.

7 Margaret Layzell, unpublished diary, 16 August 1936.

8 *EAS*, 21 August 1926, remark by R. Montgomery endorsed by the majority at 'the largest gathering ever known at the Mombasa Club'

to hear Grogan attack government profligacy on 20 August 1926.

9 *MON*, p. 274.

10 Legco Minutes, 19 April 1939.

11 Legco Minutes, 16 November 1937.

12 Grogan, E. S., 'Is Kenya Dropsical?', *EAS*, 16 October 1945.

13 Legco Minutes, 9 August 1937.

14 Although this was largely a titular recognition of Furse's rôle ever since the war, it gave this remarkable and secretive man the authority he needed to transform the calibre of officials employed by the Colonial Office. It was Furse's dramatic success, substantially based on a candidate's performance in interview, which by the time he retired in 1948 was credited with making the service an elite.

15 Among the main reasons cited by the Colonial Office and the Kenyan government for forbidding Africans to grow coffee was the assertion that they would harm the quality of the colony's coffee crop. The real fear, however, was that allowing Africans to grow coffee would not only give them greater economic power but also raise the cost of labour.

16 Legco Minutes, 14 April 1939.

17 *MON*, p. 303.

18 Legco Minutes, 20 April 1939.

19 *The Times*, 3 May 1934.

20 CO 323/1314/8.

CHAPTER 24

1 *MON*, p. 276.

2 *MON*, p. 281.

3 *MON*, p. 279.

4 CO 533/475/9.

5 CO 533/484/11.

6 Layzell, Major S. C., 'The Composting of Sisal Waste', *East African Agricultural Journal*, July 1937, p. 29.

7 'Kavirondo' was a term used to refer to the Luo, Luhya and other people

who came from the region around Lake Victoria.

8 Margaret Layzell, unpublished diaries, 6 June 1936.

9 Ibid., 11 February 1937 and 9 April 1937.

10 Sir John Ramsden had made a fortune from rubber estates in Malaya and had owned a large landholding – Marula – abutting the shores of Lake Naivasha since the early days of the Protectorate, where he was a neighbour of Grogan's Longonot Estate. Maurice Egerton had first met Grogan during the Matabele War when he and his father, Alan, had found themselves *laagered* in Bulawayo just when Grogan arrived with his wagon-load of ammunition. Egerton was Kenya's biggest owner of tea estates in the west of the country and had a large farm at Njoro which was managed for him by Sandy Wright, whose wife Doreen had borne Grogan's child in 1929. He shared with Grogan an enthusiasm for air travel, having been the fifth aviator in Britain to get his licence, indeed a love of travel in general; and he possessed an equally keen and knowledgeable interest in African traditions and customs. Like Grogan he was also unostentatious, living until after the war in a mud *rondavel* at Njoro, and was content in his own company.

11 Following the investment by Ramsden and Egerton the new Taveta Sisal Estates Company was capitalized at £130,000; Ziwani at £120,000; and Jipe, in which Grogan was the sole shareholder, at £70,500.

12 CO 533/536/5, Bednall to Roseway (Director of Finance at the War Office), 13 April 1944.

13 *EAS*, 6 July 1943.

14 Author's interview with Kit Taylor, 17 February 1998.

15 *EAS*, 7 July 1943.

16 *MON*, p. 288.

17 All extracts from E. S. Grogan's series of articles, 'Ruminations On Monetary Hysteria', *EAS*, October–December 1945. Grogan saw mass education as being crucial to countering the demographic consequences of colonial rule, of which he had stridently warned in his evidence to the 1934 Kenya Land Commission (p. 3044): 'Under our method of looking after these people, preventing them from fighting, and stopping them from dying etc., of course the numerical factor makes the whole thing a reductio ad absurdam. In another twenty-five years' time, most of the tribal natives, taking them as tribes, will be reduced to a condition bordering on destitution.' At the start of the 1950s the black African population of Kenya was 5 million. In 1960 it had increased by over 40 per cent to 7.2 million.

18 Grogan was often derided for his claim that sisal poles contained a strand that was stronger than steel, but was substantially correct. Bamboo used in the making of fishing rods, for example, has a tensile strength greater than mild steel. When the gaps between the poles were filled with a special Grogan-manufactured cement made from mixing ash with pozzolanic properties with lime produced by calcining kunkar from nearby Salaita hill, the floors and ceilings were sturdy enough to last over twenty years without any visible signs of dilapidation.

19 Grogan, E. S., *Kenya: The Settlers' Case*, p. 96.

20 Author's interview with Heini Lustman, 2 April 1998.

21 It was through this friendship that Grogan also became involved with the setting up of a camp near Arusha for Jewish refugees from Poland.

22 KNA/DC Teita 3/16/5.
23 CO 533/536/6, Surridge to Stanley, 26 March 1945.
24 Author's interview with Husseinbhai A. Hebatullah, 25 March 1998.
25 Fifty years on, thanks to the strenuous efforts of trustees, staff and donors, Gertrude's Garden is still the only specialist hospital for children in East and Central Africa. It handles over 4,000 outpatients per month, has eighty beds and carries out some hundred operations per month in its two operating theatres. It remains a non-profit making organization, and 'harambee beds' – where a child's treatment is funded by charitable donations – account for one third of admissions. At the hospital's Golden Jubilee celebrations in 1998 Dr Paul O. Chuke of the World Health Organisation declared that 'Gertrude's Garden Children's Hospital is indeed one of the acknowledged assets of Kenya'. Furthermore, the size of Grogan's bequest proved to be of enduring importance: the quantity of land donated was not only sufficient for the hospital to expand over the years but, by selling off the parcel on which 'the Gallows' still stands for residential development the trustees averted the financial collapse of the hospital in the late 1980s.
26 Hunter family papers: Grogan to Oliver, 31 August 1949. One curiosity about this letter is that it reveals one of Grogan's more curious foibles – that of pretending to be older than he really was: when he had his operation he was seventy-two, not seventy-five. Occasionally this backfired on him: when organizing a dinner party for his 'sixtieth' birthday in the 1930s his forthright sister Dorothy pointed out to him that he couldn't be sixty yet as that would mean that their parents had not been married when he was born. 'And *they*,' she added censoriously, 'had morals.'

CHAPTER 25

1 Lipscomb, John, *We Built A Country*, p. 127.
2 Ibid.
3 Ibid., p. 132.
4 My thanks to Peter Colmore for his tape of 1954 Radio Newsreel interviews.
5 Legco Minutes, 26 November 1952.
6 Author's interview with Sir Charles Markham, 23 March 1998.
7 Legco Minutes, 9 June 1955.
8 *EAS*, 2 May 1953.
9 Brockway, Fenner, *African Journeys*, p. 140.
10 Legco Minutes, 14 December 1954.
11 *EAS*, 13 December 1954.
12 Author's interview with Sir Charles Markham, 23 March 1998.
13 *EAS*, 7 April 1955.
14 Hunter family papers, Grogan to Oliver, 26 September 1955.
15 Powles Papers, RH/Mss.Afr.s.1121, remark of Grogan's at a lunch during 1955 with 'Buster' Powles, Lord Howard de Walden's manager, 30 September 1955.
16 Legco Minutes, 24 February 1956.
17 *Star of East Africa*, 22 April 1956.
18 *EAS*, 24 April 1956.
19 'Sixty Years', pp. 58–9.
20 *Daily Nation*, 3 November 1987.
21 Meinertzhagen, Richard, Unpublished Papers, vol. 66, pp. 3–4.
22 Hunter family papers, Grogan to Oliver, 26 September 1955.
23 KNA/DO Taveta 1/3/18.
24 Hunter, J. A. and Mannix, D., *African Bush Adventures*, p. 46.
25 *The Kenya Sisal Board Bulletin*, April 1957.
26 KNA/LND 17/1/26/2.

27 KNA/CA/10/21, D. Mwanyumba to D.C. Teita, 20 August 1961.

28 Author's interview with Basil Criticos, 19 January 1999.

29 *MON*, p. 64.

30 *EAS*, 21 April 1961.

31 *EAS*, 12 January 1961.

32 *MON*, p. 141.

33 *Kenya Weekly News*, 4 March 1960.

34 Of all Grogan's siblings Dorothy had stayed within his 'orbit' the longest, dying in Nairobi in 1961. She was the most like him, renowned for being outspoken: on one occasion, when a Secretary of Muthaiga Club (who was known to be having an affair) tried to stop her from bringing her dog into the club, her brusque riposte was that if he was allowed to bring his 'bitch' to the club then she could too.

35 Huxley Papers, RH/Mss.Afr.s.782, box 1, interview with Sir Humphrey Slade, 13 December 1982. Slade, a man of high principle and intellect, was one of the first whites to take out Kenyan citizenship and remained as Speaker of the House until his retirement in 1969, a service for which he was knighted.

36 *MON*, p. 21.

37 Hunter family papers, Grogan to Cynthia Crawford, 14 February 1962.

38 *Cape Times*, 2 February 1967.

39 Author's interviews with Jean Crawford, 9 May 1998 and 28 July 1998.

BIBLIOGRAPHY

Authors of publications marked with * are acknowledged with thanks as having provided particularly useful background material.

BOOKS

All titles were published in London unless otherwise indicated.

Baden-Powell, Col. R. S. S., *The Matabele Campaign*, Methuen & Co., 1900

Barrett, Eamonn, *The Reluctant Rebel*, privately published, 1998

Bealey, F., Blondel, J. and McCann, W., *Constituency Politics: A Study of Newcastle-under-Lyme*, Faber and Faber Ltd., 1965

Bennett, George, *Kenya: A Political History*, OUP, 1963

Best, Nicholas, *Happy Valley: The Story of the English in Kenya*, Secker & Warburg Ltd, 1979

Blundell, Sir Michael, *A Love Affair With The Sun*, Kenway Publications Ltd, Nairobi, 1994

Brockway, Fenner, *African Journeys*, Victor Gollancz Ltd, 1955

Buchan, John, *The African Colony*, William Blackwood and Sons, 1903

Cell, John W. (ed.), *By Kenya Possessed: The Correspondence of Norman Leys and J. H. Oldham, 1918–1926*, University of Chicago Press, 1976

Churchill, Winston S., *My African Journey*, Hodder & Stoughton, 1908

Cobbold, Lady Evelyn, *Kenya: Land Of Illusion*, John Murray, 1935

Coupland, Sir Reginald, *East Africa and Its Invaders*, Clarendon Press, 1938

Cranworth, Lord, *Kenya Chronicles*, Macmillan & Co. Ltd, 1939

Cranworth, Lord, *A Colony In The Making or Sport and Profit in British East Africa*, Macmillan & Co. Ltd, 1912

Cross, Robert and Perkin, Michael, *Elspeth Huxley – A Bibliography*, St Paul's Bibliographies, 1996

Curtis, Arnold (ed.), *They Made It Their Home: Stories of the Pioneers*, Evans Brothers Ltd, 1986

Davis, A. and Robertson, H. J., *Chronicles of Kenya*, Cecil Palmer, 1928

Dinesen, Isak, *Out of Africa*, Random House, 1938

Eliot, Sir Charles, *The East Africa Protectorate*, Frank Cass & Co. Ltd, 1905

Farrant, Leda, *The Legendary Grogan*, Hamish Hamilton Ltd, 1981

Farson, Negley, *Behind God's Back*, Victor Gollancz, 1940

Flint, John E., *Sir George Goldie And The Making of Nigeria*, OUP, 1960

Foran, W. Robert, *A Cuckoo In Kenya*, Hutchinson & Co. Ltd, 1936

Gilbert, Martin, *A History Of The Twentieth Century, Volume I*, HarperCollins*Publishers*, 1997

Gillett, Mary, *Index Of Many Of The Pioneers Of East Africa*, J. M. Considine, undated

Goldmann, C. S. (ed.), *The Empire and The Century*, John Murray, 1905

Gray, Arthur and Brittain, Frederick, *History of Jesus College*, Heinemann, 1979

Grigg, Sir Edward (Lord Altrincham), *Kenya's Opportunity*, Faber and Faber Ltd, 1955

Grogan, Maggie, *Parodies and Other Poems*, Digby, Long & Co., 1901

Hake, Andrew, *African Metropolis*, Sussex University Press, 1977

Harding, Col. Colin, *Frontier Patrols: A History of the British South Africa Police And Other Rhodesian Forces*, G. Bell & Sons, 1937

Hardy, Ronald, *The Iron Snake*, Collins, 1965

Harlow, Vincent, Chilver, E. M. with Smith, Alison (eds), *History Of East Africa, Volume II*, OUP, 1965

Hately, T. and Copley, H., *Angling in East Africa*, East Africa Ltd, 1933

Hays Hammond, John, *The Autobiography of John Hays Hammond*, Farrar & Rhinehart, New York, 1935

Headlam, Cecil (ed.), *The Milner Papers 1899–1905*, Cassell & Co. Ltd, 1933

Hemsing, Jan, *Old Nairobi and the New Stanley Hotel*, Church Raitt & Associates Ltd, 1974

Hindlip, Lord, *British East Africa: Past, Present and Future*, T. Fisher Unwin, 1905

Hobley, C. W., *From Chartered Company To Crown Colony*, Frank Cass & Co. Ltd, 1929

Hochschild, Adam, *King Leopold's Ghost*, Houghton Mifflin Company, 1998

Hollingsworth, L. W., *The Asians Of East Africa*, Macmillan & Co. Ltd, 1960

Hunter, J. A. and Mannix, D., *African Bush Adventures*, Hamish Hamilton Ltd, 1954

Bibliography

Huxley, Elspeth, *White Man's Country*, Chatto & Windus, 1935

Huxley, Elspeth, *Nine Faces of Kenya*, Collins Harvill, 1990

Huxley, Elspeth, *Settlers of Kenya*, Longmans, Green and Co. Ltd., 1948

Huxley, Elspeth, *Out In The Midday Sun*, Chatto & Windus, 1985

Huxley, Elspeth, *The Sorcerer's Apprentice*, Chatto & Windus, 1948

Jackson, Sir Frederick, *Early Days In East Africa*, Edward Arnold & Co., 1930

Jeal, Tim, *Baden-Powell*, Hutchinson, 1989

Joelson, F. S. (ed.), *Rhodesia and East Africa*, Rhodesia and East Africa, 1958

Joelson, F. S., *The Tanganyika Territory*, T. Fisher Unwin Ltd, 1920

Jourdan, Phillip, *Cecil Rhodes – His Private Life By His Secretary*, John Lane, 1911

*Kennedy, Dane, *Islands of White: Settler Society and Culture in Kenya and Southern Rhodesia, 1890–1939*, Duke University Press, 1987

Leys, Norman, *Kenya*, Hogarth Press, 1924

Lipscomb, J. F., *White Africans*, Faber and Faber Ltd, 1955

Lipscomb, J. F., *We Built A Country*, Faber and Faber Ltd, 1955

Lockhart, J. G. and Woodhouse, the Hon. C. M., *Rhodes*, Hodder and Stoughton, 1963

Macgregor, Miriam, *Early Stations of Hawke's Bay*, A. H. & A. W. Reed, 1970

Manchester, William, *The Last Lion: Winston Churchill 1874–1932*, Michael Joseph Ltd, 1983

McCance, Capt. S., *Royal Munster Fusiliers*, Gale and Polden, 1927

McLynn, Frank, *Hearts Of Darkness: The European Exploration Of Africa*, Carroll & Graf Publishers, Inc., New York, 1993

Meinertzhagen, Col. R., *Kenya Diary 1902–1906*, Oliver & Boyd, 1957

Meinertzhagen, Col. R., *Army Diary 1899–1926*, Oliver & Boyd, 1960

Miller, Charles, *The Lunatic Express*, Macdonald & Co. Ltd, 1971

Miller, Charles, *Battle For The Bundu*, Macdonald & Co. Ltd, 1974

Mosley, Paul, *The Settler Economies*, CUP, 1983

Muffett, D. J. M., *Empire Builder Extraordinary: Sir George Goldie*, Shearwater Press, 1978

Mungeam, G. H., *British Rule in Kenya 1895–1912*, Clarendon Press, 1966

Naipaul, Shiva, *North of South*, Penguin Books Ltd, 1980

Newland, V. and Tarlton, L. (eds and publ.), *Farming & Planting in BEA*, Nairobi, 1917

Nock, O. S., *Railways of Southern Africa*, A. & C. Black, 1971

Ochieng, W. R. (ed.), *A Modern History of Kenya 1895–1980*, Evans Brothers (Kenya) Ltd, 1989

Pakenham, Thomas, *The Boer War*, George Weidenfield & Nicolson Ltd, 1979

*Pakenham, Thomas, *The Scramble For Africa*, George Weidenfield and Nicolson Ltd, 1991

Pauling, George, *The Chronicles of a Contractor*, Constable & Co. Ltd, 1926

Playne, Somerset (ed. Holderness Gale, F.), *East Africa (British)*, Foreign and Colonial Compiling and Publishing Co., 1908–9

Plumer, Col. H., *An Irregular Corps in Matabeleland*, Kegan Paul, 1897

Pocock, Roger S., *The Frontiersman's Pocket-Book*, John Murray, 1909

Praagh, L. V. (ed.), *The Transvaal and its Mines*, Praagh & Lloyd, 1906

Ranger, Terence, *Revolt in Southern Rhodesia*, Heinemann, 1967

Robinson, R., Gallagher, J. and Denny, A., *Africa And The Victorians: The Official Mind Of Imperialism*, Macmillan & Co. Ltd, 1961

Rodwell, Edward, *Coast Causeries*, Heinemann (Nairobi) Ltd, 1972

Rosberg, C. G. and Nottingham, J., *The Myth of Mau Mau: Nationalism In Kenya*, Praeger, New York, 1966

Ross, William McGregor, *Kenya From Within: A Short Political History*, Allen and Unwin, 1927

Selous, Frederick Courtenay, *Sunshine and Storm in Rhodesia*, Rowland Ward, 1896

Selous, Frederick Courtenay, *Travel and Adventures in South Africa*, Rowland Ward, 1893

Shorten, John R., *The Johannesburg Saga*, Johannesburg Municipal Council, 1970

*Sorrenson, M. P. K., *Origins of European Settlement in Kenya*, OUP, 1968

Strage, Mark, *Cape to Cairo*, Jonathan Cape, 1973

*Thurston, Anne, *Guide To Archives And Manuscripts Relating To Kenya And East Africa In The United Kingdom*, Hans Zell Publishers, 1991

Tidrick, Kathryn, *Empire & The English Character*, I. B. Tauris & Co. Ltd, 1992

*Thomas, Antony, *Rhodes: The Race For Africa*, Penguin/BBC Books, 1996

Trzebinski, Errol, *The Kenya Pioneers*, Heinemann, 1985

Unsworth, Walter (ed.), *Encyclopedia of Mountaineering*, Hodder & Stoughton, 1992

Waugh, Evelyn, *Remote People*, Penguin Books Ltd, 1985

Waugh, Evelyn, *A Tourist In Africa*, Chapman & Hall Ltd, 1960
Wedgwood, Josiah C., *Memoirs Of A Fighting Life*, Hutchinson & Co.
    Ltd, 1940
Weinthal, Leo (ed.), *The Story of the Cape to Cairo Railway and River
    Route*, Pioneer Publishing Co., 1923
Weisbord, Dr Robert G., *African Zion*, Jewish Publication Society of
    America, 1968
Wymer, Norman, *The Man from the Cape*, Evans Brothers Ltd, 1959

SIGNIFICANT PUBLICATIONS BY EWART GROGAN

From The Cape To Cairo (with Arthur H. Sharp), Hurst & Blackett, 1900
From The Cape To Cairo (with Arthur H. Sharp), Hurst & Blackett, 1902
From The Cape To Cairo (with Arthur H. Sharp), Thomas Nelson and
    Sons Ltd, 1908
Tariff: The Workers' Charter, McCorquodale and Co. Ltd, 1910
Economic Calculus and its Application to Tariff, G. T. Bagguley, 1909
Musings of a Nonagenarian, unpublished, 1962
Animal Stories (unpublished, *c.* 1900)
'Sixty Years In East and Central Africa' in *Rhodesia and East Africa* (ed.
    F. S. Joelson), 1958
'The Nile As I Saw It' in *The Empire and The Century* (ed. C. S.
    Goldmann), 1905
Trusteeship!!!, East African Standard, 1935
Kenya: The Settlers Case, Round Table, vol. xxvi 1935–6
Ruminations On Monetary Hysteria, East African Standard, October–
    December 1945
'Kenya: The Logic Of Facts', *National Review*, April 1923

OFFICIAL PUBLICATIONS

London

i)   Hansard (The Parliamentary Debates: Official Report) 1906–30

ii) Foreign Office Archives (FO/2 series relating to Africa)
     Colonial Office Archives (CO/533 series relating to the East Africa
     Protectorate and, after 1920, to Kenya Colony)

iii) Parliamentary Command Papers

Cd. 2164 (1904), *Report of the Uganda Railway Committee*

Cd. 2099 (1904), *Correspondence relating to the resignation of Sir Charles Eliot, and to the Concession to the East Africa Syndicate*

Cd. 3562 (1907), *Correspondence relating to the flogging of natives by certain Europeans at Nairobi*

Cd. 4117 (1908), *Correspondence relating to the tenure of land*

Cd. 5193 (1910), *Report of the Committee on Emigration from India to the Crown Colonies and Protectorates* Part II (Minutes of Evidence) and Part III (Papers laid before the Committee)

Cmd. 1922 (1923), *Indians In Kenya* (The 'Devonshire White Paper')

Cmd. 2387 (1925), *Report Of The East Africa Commission*

Cmd. 2500 (1925), *Correspondence with the Government of Kenya relating to an exchange of land with Lord Delamere*

Cmd. 2629, *Correspondence with the Government of Kenya relating to Lord Delamere's acquisition of land in Kenya*

Cmd. 3234 (1928–9), *Report Of The Committee On Closer Union*

Cmd. 4556 (1934), *Report of the Kenya Land Commission*

iv) *Report On The Work Of The Commission Sent Out By The Zionist Organization To Examine The Territory Offered By His Majesty's Government For The Purposes Of A Jewish Settlement In British East Africa (1905)*

Report Of The Colonial Economic Development Committee (1920)

East Africa Protectorate/Kenya Colony

i) Minutes and Proceedings of the Legislative Council 1921–56

ii) East Africa Protectorate (subsequently Kenya Colony and Protectorate) Blue Books

iii) *Report of the Land Committee, 1905*

Report of the Land Settlement Commission, 1919

Kenya Census Reports, 1911, 1926, 1931

Economic Commission: Final Report, 1919

Report of the Economic and Financial Committee, 1922

Report of the Port Commission of Inquiry, 1925

Report of the Kenya Tariff Committee, 1929

Report of the Standing Timber Committee, 1931

Report Of The Economic Development Committee, 1935

The Oliphant Report: The Commercial Possibilities and Development of Forests in British East Africa, Major F. M. Oliphant, 1937

Bibliography

*The Chipp Report: The Possibilities of Development of Timber Production in
    Kenya*, Major W. Chipp, 1939
*Report of the Standing Finance Committee on the Taveta and Ziwani
    Irrigation Schemes*, 1946
The Bear Report: Geology of the Taveta Area, L. M. Bear, 1955

South Africa

South African Year Book 1903–4
Anglo-African Who's Who 1905

DISSERTATIONS

Cashmore, T. H. R., *Your Obedient Servants: Studies In District
    Administration In The East African Protectorate, 1895–1918* (PhD
    dissertation, Cambridge University, 1965)
*Redley, Michael, *The Politics Of A Predicament: The White Community In
    Kenya 1918–32* (PhD dissertation, Cambridge University, 1976)

ARCHIVAL SOURCES

i) RHODES HOUSE

Chandos, Lord (RH/Mss.Brit.Emp.s.525)
Convention of Associations (RH/Mss.Afr.s.594)
Coryndon, Sir Robert (RH/Mss.Afr.s.633)
Dutton, Eric (RH/Micr.Afr.s.587)
Grogan, Quentin (RH/Micr.Afr.s.605)
Huxley, Elspeth (RH/Mss.Afr.s.782 and 2154)
Joyce, Francis H. de Vere (RH/Mss.Afr.s.2157)
McMillan, Sir William Northrup (RH/Micr.Afr.s.641)
Meinertzhagen, Col. Richard (restricted collection)
Moore, Lady (RH/Mss.Brit.Emp.s.466)
Nestor, T. R. L. (RH/Mss.Afr.s.1086)
Oates. C. O. (Titus) *Muthaiga Country Club – A History* (RH/
    Micr.Afr.s.595)
Powles, S. H. (RH/Mss.Afr.s.1121)
Ross, William McGregor (RH/Mss.Afr.s.1178)

ii) THE BODLEIAN LIBRARY

Milner Papers (Ms.Eng.Hist.c.704)

iii) CHURCHILL ARCHIVES CENTRE, CAMBRIDGE

Churchill Papers
Lloyd Papers

iv) GROGAN FAMILY COLLECTIONS

Walter Grogan family papers
Crawford family papers
Hunter family papers
Dorothy Slater family papers

v) ROYAL COMMONWEALTH SOCIETY COLLECTION, CAMBRIDGE
UNIVERSITY LIBRARY

Buchanan, Sir George, *British East Africa: Wanted – A Policy!*, 1921
Fothergill, Pauline, *Zionism, Colonialism and Jewish Nationalism* (Library
Notes for RCS: no. 287, Oct. 1988, and no. 290, April 1989)
The Matson Papers
Ofcansky, Thomas P., *A Bio-Bibliography of E. S. Grogan*, originally
published in *History in Africa*, vol. 10 (1983), pp. 239–245.
Arnold Paice Papers

vi) MISCELLANEOUS

Layzell, Margaret, unpublished diary
Mumm, A. L., *Alpine Club Register 1896–1901*
Rutherfoord, E. D., *Sisal in Kenya*

INDEX

Index